LATIN AMERICAN
PROSPECTS
FOR THE 1980s

LATIN AMERICAN PROSPECTS FOR THE 1980s

Equity, Democratization, and Development

edited by
Archibald R. M. Ritter
and David H. Pollock

PRAEGER

PRAEGER SPECIAL STUDIES • PRAEGER SCIENTIFIC

Library of Congress Cataloging in Publication Data

Main entry under title:

Latin American prospects for the 1980s.

  1. Latin America—Economic conditions—1945-
—Addresses, essays, lectures. 2. Latin America—
Politics and government—1948-   —Addresses, essays,
lectures. 3. Political participation—Latin America—
Addresses, essays, lectures. 4. Latin America—Social
conditions—1945-   —Addresses, essays, lectures.
I. Ritter, Archibald R. M. II. Pollock, David H.
HC125.L353   1983   338.98   82-18039
ISBN 0-03-061363-9

Published in 1983 by Praeger Publishers
CBS Educational and Professional Publishing
A Division of CBS, Inc.
521 Fifth Avenue, New York, New York 10175 U.S.A.

3456789   052   987654321

Printed in the United States of America

PREFACE

This book is based upon the proceedings of a conference held at Carleton University in Ottawa during November 1980, under the combined auspices of the Normal Paterson School of International Affairs, the Canadian Association for Latin American and Caribbean Studies, and the Ontario Cooperative Program for Latin American and Caribbean Studies.

The conference was the second of its kind organized by the School of International Affairs. The first had been convened ten years earlier, in November 1970, under the theme of "Latin America During the 1970s: What Kinds of Revolution?" As events subsequently unfolded, that title was most prescient: The 1970s was indeed a decade of widespread ferment throughout the Latin American region.[1] By the word "revolution" we do not restrict ourselves to the narrow concept of violent military upheaval aimed overtly or covertly at the overthrow of governments. Rather, as the book emanating from the 1970 conference noted in its opening chapter,[2] "revolutionary change" was used in a much broader sense, encompassing agricultural, industrial, and technological revolutions, as well as a host of other fundamental structural transformations with far-reaching socioeconomic and political ramifications. Indeed, if there was any one salient characteristic emerging from the decade of the 1970s—and therefore from the earlier Carleton conference that sought to foretell the realities forthcoming from that era—it was precisely the fact that the winds of revolutionary transformation blew so widely and fiercely throughout the length and breadth of the hemisphere. The book that was published after the 1970 conference, under the same joint authorship as is this present publication, therefore provides a unique retrospect as it reveals the revolutionary themes uppermost in the minds of participants at the turn of the prior decade, and how those participants felt such themes would unfold during the ensuing ten years.

The second conference, entitled "Latin American Prospects for the 1980s: What Kinds of Development? Reformation, Transformation, or Deformation?," was organized on the belief that Canada's growing interests in Latin America merited fully as much attention by academic bodies as by individuals and institutions in the public and private sectors. There has been an expanding current focus by Canada on issues pertaining to

Latin America—intensified dramatically by recent events in
Central America, the Caribbean, and the South Atlantic—and
hence it was considered particularly appropriate for the School
of International Affairs to organize a follow-up conference with
approximately the same basic theme and substantive emphasis
as had been the case ten years earlier. The results were to
speak for themselves: More than 400 persons were in attendance,
a figure approximately double the total that had been registered
for the first conference.

A substantial number of papers were presented during the
1980 conference. Regretfully, space limitations have enabled
the editors to publish only a portion of that number in this book;
so many of the remaining papers were interesting and insightful.
Nonetheless, it is our belief that the papers here will provide a
representative sample of the overall conference coverage, and
that they will serve as useful a function for students of Latin
American development during the 1980s as had been the case
for the initial conference proceedings published almost exactly
a decade earlier.

As the countries of the Latin American region proceed into
the 1980s, the closely interrelated issues of distributional equity,
on the one hand, and democratization, on the other, will unquestionably be of central concern and importance. Unfortunately,
during the past two decades, Latin America's development process
has been characterized by growing inequities in income distribution, and by the continued existence of severe poverty in many
countries, despite reasonably high economic-growth rates for
the region viewed in aggregative terms. Simultaneously, the
movement toward political democratization—which seemed to be
evolving, albeit fitfully, during the latter years of the 1970s—
now appears to have been quite vulnerable and prone to sudden
and substantial reverses.

Although this book focuses fundamentally upon the possibilities of improving distributional equity in the region and of
moving toward more genuine participatory democracy generally,
it was not intended to provide a comprehensive survey of the
region from these dual viewpoints. The part on democratization,
for example, does not include analyses of certain countries that
do possess democratically functioning institutions (inter alia,
the Commonwealth Caribbean, Venezuela, Colombia, Mexico, and
Costa Rica), or of other longstanding military regimes (e.g.,
Paraguay and Bolivia). A high degree of selectivity on this
important issue was unavoidable, largely due to space and related
editorial constraints. Similarly, treatment of the equity issue
was, of necessity, also limited to certain key analytical and policy
elements.

It will be seen that the book is highly pluralistic in terms
of the visions of the future that were generated by the analyses
of the different authors. Some are reasonably confident of
improvements in regard to the particular issues falling within
their respective areas of specialization. Others are less confident
or are frankly pessimistic. It is encouraging, for example, that
Claudio Orrego was optimistic, albeit cautiously, arguing as he
did that there had developed a "massive moral conscience . . .
with a solid organizational base and active international solidarity"
to defend human rights more securely. On the other hand,
there are mixed reactions concerning the potential for authentic
democratization. Jorge Nef concludes that democratization by
any name is a "hallucination" in South and Central America
generally, and in Chile specifically. Liisa North, in her discussions concerning Ecuador and Peru, also writes in a pessimistic
vein, emphasizing the probable continuing exclusion of the
marginalized populations of those countries and the overall
fragility of current political systems. She speculates on the
emerging coalitions of interests in those countries that are similar
to the ones in Nicaragua. Arch Ritter argues that, at the level
of the National Assembly, Cuba's political system could not be
considered authentically democratic and that change in the future
would be unlikely unless the monopoly position of the Communist
Party were to be broken. Concerning Brazil, however, Maria H.
Moreira Alves is somewhat optimistic that, in the absence of
renewed state coercion, the gradual "corrosion from below" will
eventually change Brazil's authoritarian structures and social-
control mechanisms, and permit a peaceful transition toward a
civil government. On the bases of these and other related analyses, however, one could not predict genuine democratization or
military withdrawal as being either imminent or pervasive in Latin
America. More of the same would appear to be the basic prog-
nostication.

The outlook on the issue of equity is also mixed and not
overly encouraging. David Pollock makes a powerful case for
greater emphasis on equity in national policy making and argues
that this will be the central development issue during the 1980s.
Albert Berry, conversely, in his attempt to forecast income
distribution, concludes cautiously that only a slight improvement
can be expected, i.e., through a reduction in labor surpluses
in some cases and through narrower income differentials between
skilled and unskilled laborers in the other. The aid program
offered by Trinidad and Tobago to certain neighboring countries
constitutes an interesting income-redistribution arrangement,
although, as Basil Ince makes clear, one that is uniquely geared

to the complex political and economic realities of the Caribbean countries concerned. Enrique Iglesias casts his net more widely, probing the extent to which the analyses and recommendations of the Brandt Report—and hence of northern countries generally— are or are not relevant to Latin America's basic economic- and social-development constraints. Viewed overall, the general tone of the chapters on equity suggests a continuation of recent discouraging trends, although perhaps with some hopeful prospects by the end of the 1980s.

Whereas the 1960s might be viewed, in retrospect, as a "boom decade" for Latin America, and much of the 1970s as a decade of transition, it would appear from these essays, as well as from the conference deliberations generally, that the 1980s will be remembered as a decade of uncertainty and malaise. This book, in microcosm, mirrors such a pattern of thought, not only as regards the technical aspects of economic growth and modernization but also the deeper social and humanitarian aspects of equity and democratization. There are, unquestionably, severe fundamental weaknesses characterizing the model for internal development currently existing in many countries of the Latin American region. This model, far too often, is not merely rooted in social inequities; it is based upon and perpetuates such inequities. What can be done in the light of this disturbing reality? The book has not set for itself the goal of providing answers; rather, it has concentrated its primary focus upon posing topical and relevant questions as an essential first step. Nonetheless, it does highlight the primordial need to effect structural internal transformation as well as to urge international cooperation for development. For far too long the emphasis has been heavily geared to the latter alone. The new priority should be to link both policy lines: i.e., greater support from abroad for those in Latin America who are ready, willing, and able to undertake reforms that view growth as a means to the dual ends of equity and democratization. There should be no illusions about either side of the equation: They will not be easily attained. The North has become increasingly inward-looking, obsessed with its own stagflation problems and, in some cases, with ideologies geared to the "magic of the market" as solutions to such problems. Latin America in turn is resentful of the rigidities of the North: rigidities that do not seem to vary whether the North is booming without inflation (pre-1973) or retrogressing with it (post-1973). But a central issue concerning Latin America's prospects during the 1980s does not, as stated above, impinge directly upon the North-South dialogue. Instead, there is a new and fundamental policy orientation that has yet to be fully understood abroad: namely, a stubborn resistance to those structural internal transformations that can change the inequitable and authoritarian regimes currently characterizing many countries of the region.

In the proceedings of the 1970 conference, the editors stated, "As Latinists—both within the region and outside of it— look back over the postwar era and seek to set out some milestones that could serve as guideposts to the 1970s, perhaps this volume can help to facilitate that process." The current editors hope that this book, looking into the 1980s, will be of utility in that important and continuing process.

NOTES

1. In this Preface, as throughout the book itself, the phrase "Latin America" is understood to encompass South America, Central America, Mexico, and the Caribbean.
2. David H. Pollock and Arch R. M. Ritter, eds., Latin American Prospects for the 1970's: What Kinds of Revolution? (New York: Praeger, 1973), pp. 3-7.

CONTENTS

PART I
INTRODUCTION

1

A LATIN AMERICAN STRATEGY
TO THE YEAR 2000
David H. Pollock

INTRODUCTION

This chapter will range widely over time, space, and subject matter as it seeks to cover three main points.

The first will present, as one colleague called it, "the
germ of a beginning" of my own and very personal definition
of development. The second will trace out, in broad strokes,
a few of the principal socioeconomic trends characterizing Latin
American development during the postwar period 1950-80. Third,
and flowing largely from the latter, the chapter will conclude
by presenting some tentative judgments concerning the design
of a Latin American strategy running into the 1980s, and even
to the end of this century.

All this signifies, in consequence, that I will seek to cover
trends and issues encompassing some 30 Latin American countries
during 50 years. If, therefore, in attempting such a widely
ranging tour d'horizon, I exceed the reader's tolerance, please
be patient. It is my hope that, at the end of the journey, some
of Latin America's basic strategy issues will come more sharply
into focus even if other aspects of Latin America's economic and
social panorama become a bit blurred by the rush of our voyage.

TOWARD A PARTIAL DEFINITION OF DEVELOPMENT

Since I am focusing on developmental trends and strategies,
it is only fitting that I should begin by trying to define what I
mean by the word "development." That deceptively simple little

word, however, conjures up a real Pandora's box since development is such an elusive, complex, and troublesome concept. As you have read about development in the past, have you not wondered what others mean by that word? Interestingly, there is no universally accepted definition of development. True, there have been any number of partial approaches toward it, but no one has yet evolved a clear and comprehensive definition that is acceptable to all, or even to a majority of developmental theoreticians, let alone practitioners. To guide myself during some 30 years of work in hemispheric and international development issues, therefore, I prepared, long ago, a brief definition for my own private use. It is a very personal definition indeed, as you will see. But it has provided me with some kind of conceptual framework, albeit partial, as I sought to assess past trends, on the one hand, and put forth some judgments about the future, on the other. To think clearly about the ever-changing world of development is difficult enough in the short run. To do so without some kind of longer-term conceptual overview is even harder. I hope, therefore, that the reader will find mine of some interest and utility.

My definition consists of four pairs of words: words each person must enlarge, transform, delete, or otherwise adapt to suit his or her personal objectives and priorities. I shall present the four sets of words in descending order of quantifiability. W^2 at their respective qualitative priorities should be will undoubtedly vary as between readers, for reasons that will become obvious as we proceed.

The first two words are "economic growth," measured in terms of increases in real GNP. Throughout the post-World War II era, many international organizations and individuals concerned with development had long equated development with economic growth. If a country's real GNP was increasing rapidly, and especially if this was occurring in per capita terms, it was typically stated that such a country was undergoing rapid development. In the recent past, a number of arguments have been put forward by writers, especially those from developing countries, to counter this single-variable definition of development: to dethrone growth, as it were. In my opinion, these writers have marshaled some very powerful arguments to bolster their case. Nevertheless, at this particular historical juncture, with the decade of the 1980s just beginning to unfold, it appears that, while growth may have been partially dethroned, it has not yet been banished from the kingdom. In any event, I list "economic growth" first in my definition since, for so many individuals and agencies concerned with development, economic growth is

still put forth as the sole proxy for development. The principal
reason for this is undoubtedly the fact that an expanded supply
of goods and services should be a central precondition for satis-
fying minimum levels of basic human needs. Another reason
derives from the fact that economic growth is quite easy to
quantify. After all, GNP statistical data, despite their methodological shortcomings, are now accessible throughout almost all
the developing world. "Relevancy" and "quantifiability" thus
combine to explain why I have listed economic growth as a major
element in my definition of development. But what weight—what
qualitative priority—should be given to those two words? That
is a value judgment that each of us must decide as we pursue
our own different developmental tasks in different regions of
the world. For my part, I certainly accept the reality that
growth is an important component in any overview definition of
development. On the other hand I by no means equate growth
and development as being one and the same thing.

My second two words are "distributional equity." By
equity I mean a lesser degree of skewness—an enhanced degree
of symmetry—in the manner by which the fruits of increased
growth are diffused throughout all income strata within any
given developing country. It is one thing for a country's economic pie to grow. But if the same few large mouths consume
steadily larger bites of the expanding pie while the large number
of smaller mouths obtain inadequate portions, of what avail is
the expansion? Clearly, then, equity in the distribution of
growth must provide a second variable in any overall developmental equation. As for ease of quantifiability, equity is harder
to measure than growth. True, steps have been taken over time
to ameliorate the problem of measuring distributional equity:
for instance, through the use of gini coefficients in determining
the degree of skewness in income distribution; by new statistical
approaches to measuring the unemployment equivalent of underemployment; and by more comprehensive and accurate approaches
for measuring basic human needs. Nonetheless, the fact remains
that equity is harder to measure, in a quantifiably precise manner,
than growth. As to its qualitative importance—its rank order
of priority within any organic definition of development—again,
each of us must evolve our own personal priorities. In my mind,
it rates very highly, indeed—as high as growth, if not higher.

My third set of words is "participation/vulnerability."
These words are harder to conceptualize, and to measure, than
is growth or equity. Nonetheless, they are of enormous importance to any definition of development in a dual context: one
with internal and the other with international connotations.

Whenever decisions made by one group of persons integrally affect the economic and social destinies of another group, then the decision makers should be directly accountable to those whose destinies are being integrally affected. This is certainly true where political and human rights are involved and it should be equally true where the production and consumption of goods and services are involved. If the market is left completely alone to determine what is produced, why, and for whom, that process might be highly efficient from the viewpoint of resource utilization, but the market is not renowned for its long-term social-welfare horizon. In consequence, the state has been playing an increasing role in determining what should be produced and consumed. However, when national planners make such fundamental decisions, they in turn should be accountable to the individuals affected by their decisions. And exactly the same analogy should apply at the international level: i.e., all nations should participate in the process of international decision making whenever the decisions taken affect them. To me it is both unwise as well as unjust to envisage an international development system where one or a few large nations—or international organizations—can take global decisions affecting a large number of other nations, unless the latter participate directly and with appropriate weight in the decision-making process. Thus the two words "participation/vulnerability" represent the reverse sides of the same coin: to the extent that participation in decision making increases, to that same extent, countries and individuals will become less vulnerable to those making the decisions. Sensitivity to external shock (dependencia) increases as participation in external decision making falls. Hence, incorporation of the words "participation/vulnerability" into any future definition of development would be essential in overcoming the longstanding trauma of external vulnerability.

My fourth and last pair of words are "transcendental values." I use those two words because I cannot think of any others that would briefly and readily encapsulate the definitional concept I have in mind. Let us assume that a country's economic pie increases. Let us assume further that there is a heightened degree of equity in the way the fruits of that economic pie are distributed. Let us, finally, assume that decisions affecting production and consumption of the economic pie—internationally and nationally—involve the full participation of all affected parties. Is that the end of the matter? Does man live by GNP alone? Perhaps the latter has been the prevailing line of thought throughout the postwar period since policy makers have focused so intently, during the short run, on the issue of expanding incomes for the masses, particularly those below the poverty line. Despite the importance of such short-run objectives, however, we should also be asking ourselves other, more uplisting, questions. Should we not take advantage of our longer-term vision and ask what kind of person Latin America may wish to evolve by the end of this century? What are the transcendental values— cultural, ethical, artistic, religious, and moral—that extend beyond the current workings of the purely economic and social systems? How do we appeal to youth, who so often seek nourishment in dreams, as well as in bread? What, in short, should be the new face of the Latin American society in the future, and what human values should lie behind that new countenance? These concepts are obviously the hardest of all, in my four-point definition, to quantify. Indeed, to some they may even appear irrelevant and illusory: out of place in the search for solutions to the other, more pressing and pragmatic, issues facing us from now to the year 2000. For reasons of space, therefore, I will confine myself here to only the first three sets of words: "economic growth," "distributional equity," and "participation/vulnerability." However, despite the conceptual and quantifiable difficulties surrounding the words "transcendental values," I did not want to exclude the latter from my efforts at coming to grips with some kind of a definition of development.

ON LOOKING BACK: SOME PRINCIPAL TRENDS DURING 1950-80

If we look back over Latin America's major economic and social trends during the last 30 years, which ones stand out, in synthesis, as primus inter pares? To my way of thinking, and with due apologies to George Orwell, although all developmental trends are equal, some are unquestionably more equal than others. And three—relating specifically to the three definitional points that I outlined earlier—appear to me to have been the most equal of all: namely, Latin America's persistent search for substantial rates of economic growth throughout the postwar years; a constantly changing set of external-sector strategies designed to enable Latin America to participate more effectively in (that is to say, become less vulnerable to) a rapidly changing international economic order; and the declining social-welfare content of Latin America's national development planning. I will therefore begin this section by looking at this basic trinity—of internal growth, external vulnerability, and social welfare—in

order to see how each one evolved during three quite different
time periods between 1950 and 1980.[1]

1950-64: The Period of Import-Substitution Industrialization

The first such period would encompass the approximately
15 years between 1950 and 1964. I say "approximately" because,
of course, the terminal years are not as precise as I am setting
them out to be; clearly I could be off by some years on either
side. But that is not the issue. What is important is the fact
that this period of roughly 15 years represented an epoch when
Latin America's initial postwar efforts at evolving a cohesive
approach to accelerated growth ran headlong into a disturbing
reality: namely, that the international economy existing at that
time was not functioning effectively as a Latin American motor
for growth. On the contrary, two important balance-of-payments
problems served to significantly reduce the extent by which the
external sector could directly stimulate internal growth. One
was that, at the end of World War II, Latin America's structure
of production was still heavily geared to only a handful of primary
products that together accounted for over 95 percent of the
region's exports. At that postwar juncture, moreover, international demand for such primary products was relatively weak,
especially for agricultural foodstuffs and for beverages that,
in those days, comprised the bulk of Latin America's total exports. What was the consequence of all this? For most of those
initial 15 years, Latin America's export quantum grew only
slowly and the terms of trade moved against the region, such
that Latin America's overall external purchasing power rose by
only some 2 percent per annum in real terms over the entire
decade and a half. Additionally, a second important balance-of-
payments constraint—this time on capital account—was equally
in evidence throughout the period since financial inflows were
very modest. True, there was a brief period of expanded official-
development-assistance (ODA) inflows during the early years of
the Alliance for Progress. But this did not last very long, for
reasons that are now well known. As for private capital, the
large transnational bankers—remembering Latin America's debt-
default record of the 1930s, and noting the sluggish growth rates
for the region's primary-product exports—were not yet ready
to assign a high credit rating to the area. The net result was
that Latin America found it difficult to maintain its overall import
coefficient during this period. On the contrary, that import

coefficient fell, from some 17 percent in 1948-52 to only some
10 percent during 1962-66. What strategy, then, could Latin
American governments follow to stimulate their internal economic
growth when external commercial and financial flows were both
relatively stagnant? The answer became progressively clearer
to policy makers of that era: that they should obtain, from
domestic resources, those capital goods and intermediate products
that were needed for internal economic growth, but that they
could not afford to import, because of the deficiencies in commodity exports, and the inadequate private and public financial
inflows, as just mentioned.

Thus we see the origin of Latin America's import-substitution
industrialization (ISI) policy of the first 15 postwar years.

Note parenthetically that this ISI policy did not arise, in
the first instance, from some abstract ideological concept. Today
there are those who criticize the ISI strategy as having resulted
from some doctrinaire anti-Northern or anti-free-market bias.
This is a facile criticism that, in my opinion, is quite incorrect.
The ISI strategy was forced upon Latin America—not by ideology,
but by a new reality. And the new reality was that the postwar
external bottleneck did not enable the region to pay for those
capital goods and other imports that were essential for higher
levels of investment and higher rates of growth. For very practical reasons, therefore, Latin America embarked upon a vast
continentwide experiment in ISI involving capital goods and
intermediate products—in some cases, at the national level; in
others, through the creation of new subregional and regional
economic-integration schemes; and in many cases, at all three
levels. I am not suggesting that the ISI strategy was free of
impediments. On the contrary. But despite the difficulties
implicit in that strategy, it nonetheless helped fulfill a major
policy objective of the region: namely, to maintain internal
economic growth despite a relatively stagnant external sector.
And Latin America did in fact succeed quite well in this objective.
Viewing the period 1950-64 as a whole, Latin America was able
to record an overall growth in GNP of approximately 5 percent
per annum in real terms.

Gradually, however, it became evident that, as the Latin
American economies became more complex and increasingly
sophisticated, they would require larger quantities and different
types of capital goods than could be produced at home. Thus,
beginning in the mid-1960s and gathering momentum by the end
of that decade, Latin America began to put into effect its second
major postwar strategy: a strategy designed to link internal-
growth prospects more directly with the international economic
environment. This second phase was to span the decade 1965-74.

1965-74: An Outward-Looking Strategy
of Internationalization

This second postwar phase was very different from the
preceding 15 years in terms of the impact of the external sector
upon Latin America's internal growth. The Organization for
Economic Cooperation and Development (OECD) countries of
North America, Western Europe, and Japan had been recording
substantial rates of growth in GNP and trade during the 1950s
and early 1960s, but they all began to pick up a particularly
strong head of steam thereafter. Thus, for the decade beginning
in the mid-1960s and ending with the first oil shock of 1973-74,
virtually all the OECD countries were growing very rapidly and
in tandem, thereby contributing to the highest and most sustained
combined rates of real growth—in both GNP and foreign trade—
ever recorded in their history.

Those industrialized market economies were in the midst of
an unparalleled boom—a boom that in turn was transmitted to
Latin America through two main conduits. One was an accelerated
demand shown by OECD countries for Latin American exports,
including both primary products and manufactured goods. The
second followed from the first: As Latin America's expanded
export earnings strengthened its international creditworthiness,
there was a correspondingly increased flow of capital to Latin
America from the OECD countries, especially from private transnational banks in the latter countries. In short, a completely
new economic scenario had begun to unfold—new insofar as the
nexus between national and international trends was concerned.
Primary-product exports from Latin America (which had been
relatively stagnant during most of 1950-64) now entered an era
of "commodity bonanza," as both their quantum and prices
strengthened significantly. Moreover, manufactured goods
(which had begun to benefit from domestic economies of scale
during the previous period of import-substitution industrialization) now began to enter, with increasing dynamism, into the
total Latin American export stream.

Clearly the basic trends sketched out here so broadly
differed significantly by countries. Nonetheless, as clearly
shown in the ECLA studies cited earlier, there is no question
that, for the Latin American region as viewed overall, the decade
ending in 1974 was characterized by an unprecedented external
bonanza. Virtually all the macroeconomic indicators had changed
in a dramatically buoyant way. Export quantum rose significantly
and continuously. The terms of trade reversed their prior deteriorating tendency and began to move substantially in Latin

America's favor. Capital inflows rose sharply, especially in the form of new private loans. As a consequence of all these factors, Latin America's overall export purchasing power grew at an average rate of over 7 percent per year during 1965-74—more than triple the annual rate recorded during the previous 15-year period. And the region's import coefficient reversed its prior downtrend, rising from 10 percent in 1962-66 to 16 percent during 1973-75. Saying the same thing in a different way, Latin America's imports had grown by only 0.4 percent for each 1 percent increase in its GNP during 1950-64. During 1965-74, conversely, Latin America's imports grew by 1.4 percent for each 1 percent increase in its GNP. Thus we find Latin America inserting itself more and more integrally into a booming global economy in three main ways during this period: namely, by obtaining greater access to private financial inflows; by an increasingly outward-looking industrialization process that now caused manufactured goods to account for over 15 percent of total exports; and by a strengthening in the purchasing power of most primary products and hence of the regional terms of trade. There had been a major turnaround in the region's external strategy, and this in turn was reflected by a rapidly expanding rate of internal GNP growth that exceeded 7 percent per annum in real terms—a rate higher than had ever before been achieved in its recorded history. By the mid-1970s, the annual increments in Latin America's GNP, investment, and industrial output were exceeding the total of each of those variables in the early 1950s. Each year, a completely "new" Latin America—in terms of economic resources—was being added to the region in comparison with the situation existing at the beginning of the post-World War II period. In macro dimensions, Latin America had grown to an economic space that was roughly analogous to that of Western Europe two decades earlier. In the euphoria of the moment, it seemed to Latin America that its longstanding problem of vulnerabilidad had disappeared: that the external constraint was now but an unhappy memory of the past.

However, this euphoria melted rapidly in the cold hard light of the third and most recent postwar period, when still another major change in strategy was to characterize Latin American efforts to adjust domestic GNP trends within an ever-changing international economic environment.

1975-80: A Period of Debt-Lead Growth

During this third postwar period, still another major turn-
about was to characterize Latin America's domestic linkages with
the external economic environment. What were the central realities of this recent half-decade period? One new and fundamental
parameter entailed the impact of the oil shocks of 1973-74 and
1979-80. I am not suggesting that the oil-price increases were
the only factors responsible for the adverse global economy of
1975-80, although unquestionably they must be placed at the
head of the list. But other serious problems were also resulting
from the fact that, during this same period, most of the OECD
countries had entered a dramatically new (to them) era of inflation and stagnation.

For Latin America, in any case, the bottom line was clear:
1975-80 represented a completely new ballgame, insofar as the
international economic panorama was concerned. The terms of
trade, which had been moving in Latin America's favor since
the mid-1960s, now began to reverse as Latin American traders
faced higher and higher prices for imports (of oil from OPEC,
and of capital goods from the OECD) on the one hand, and lower
prices for their commodity exports, on the other. Added to
these problems, moreover, was a resurgence of Northern protec-
tionism, which redounded adversely against the region's new
labor-intensive manufactured goods. Worse yet, as Latin
America's overall current-account deficit widened, it was by
that same degree that its capital-account requirements had to
expand pari-passu. Still seeking growth at any cost, Latin
America took the only short-term option available: It resorted
increasingly to a financially oriented growth strategy in the
face of a deteriorating global economy. The need for massive
increases in the recycling of petrodollars led Latin American
levels of private debt (and related debt-servicing obligations)
to soar to historically all-time highs. The final result was self-
evident: Growth was maintained, though at a lower level than
in 1950-64. Indeed, 1975-80 comprised the period of lowest
growth (averaging 4.7 percent per annum in real terms) for
Latin America during the entire 30 postwar years.

1950-80: The Three Postwar Decades, in Sum
(Growth and Vulnerability)

On looking back at Latin America over the entire postwar
period, therefore, we see a region that has followed three very
different kinds of strategies as it sought to link internal growth
with an ever-changing external sector. What general conclusions
might be drawn from all this? I should like to focus on two.

The first is that, if development is defined solely in terms
of economic growth, one would have to assign a high grade to
Latin America's postwar development performance. Thus, viewing
the period 1950-80 as a whole, we find that Latin America's GNP
recorded an average growth rate of over 5.5 percent per annum
in real terms. An extraordinary performance: the highest continental average in the world during those 30 years. In reflecting
upon this, let us try to visualize how Latin America viewed its
developmental objectives and priorities at the end of World War II.
At that time, the region consisted of 20 water-tight compartments—
each quite backward in terms of technological modernization,
and none of them connected integrally to the others by any
overarching or organic concept of development. To emulate
their rich U.S. neighbor to the north, in the sense of increasing
their access to goods and services—to foment GNP growth, in
short—was what Latin America sought. And growth was, as we
saw, what Latin America got. An extraordinary performance,
indeed, when we bear in mind the relatively backward economic
structure characterizing the region in 1950, and the fact that a
5.5 percent growth rate compounded annually over the ensuing
30 years meant a fivefold increase in total GNP by 1980. Today,
the Latin American NICs (newly industrializing countries) have
grown to the point where they have begun to mirror many of
the economic characteristics of Western Europe after adoption of
the Marshall Plan, when Western Europe was the third largest
economic area in the world. Thus, if the words "economic
growth" are viewed as a key component in a definition of "development," as noted earlier, Latin America certainly developed
in an astonishingly rapid manner during the postwar era.

Let us next reflect upon the criterion of "participation/
vulnerability" to which I also made reference earlier. All in all,
Latin America has demonstrated a considerable amount of agility
and maneuverability in maintaining growth despite major changes
in the global economic scenario. In the first period (1950-64),
Latin America deliberately insulated itself from a stagnant external sector through the strategy of ISI. Yet, despite such
insulation, it nonetheless maintained a 5 percent real growth
rate. During the second period (1965-74), when the external
motor for growth was booming so vigorously, Latin America
altered its strategy by virtually 180 degrees, in order to link
itself dynamically to that motor. By reversing from an essentially
inward-looking to an increasingly outward-looking strategy, it
recorded a decade of unparalleled increases in real GNP, averaging more than 7 percent per annum. During the third period
(1975-80), although the world economy was undergoing serious
problems of stagflation, Latin America again made a major adapta-

tion in strategy. It maintained growth, albeit at a lower level of 4.7 percent per annum, by deliberately incurring a very significant increase in its external debt. Thus, whereas Latin America could be rated highly on the single criterion of economic growth, the rating would have to be lower in terms of participation/ vulnerability. For a while, Latin America thought its longstanding external constraint had disappeared, only to find that it had reappeared with a vengeance. Latin America's dependencia— its relative ability to participate in global decision making—is still a very real problem, and one that will have to be seriously reassessed between today and the year 2000.

Equity: The Social Content of Latin America's Postwar Development

In the sense of an academic musing, if asked to assign a grade to Latin America's postwar economic performance, it might warrant an A in the narrow context of GNP growth per se. As for participation/vulnerability, that grade might fall to a B or C since, despite its agility and maneuverability, the region still faces very serious problems in its efforts to overcome the long-standing external constraint. As for equity, the grade would clearly have to fall far lower, for the reasons briefly listed below.

The postwar era has been characterized by great contradictions between Latin America's economic-growth performance, on the one hand, and the social-welfare content of that growth performance, on the other. The economic pie grew significantly, as we have seen. But the ways by which the fruits of that pie were distributed proved to be very unsatisfactory, at least for a significant number of peoples and countries. Again, different countries responded in very different ways to the criterion that I called, at the outset, the need for "distributional equity." But the fact remains that the problems of pobreza crítica remain at the very heart of Latin America's postwar developmental performance: problems of increased urban concentration, of growing unemployment, of unequal income distribution, and of inadequate attention paid to the satisfaction of basic human needs. It is necessary to speak bluntly on these matters if the lessons of 1950-80 are to guide us along more equitable and ethical, let alone effective, developmental trajectories to the year 2000.

Let us look at the essence of some of these social problems. During the last 30 years, there has been a large and persistent migration of manpower from farms to cities throughout Latin America—a migration that has led to an enormous and a still-

growing population agglomeration in Latin American urban centers. The nature of this phenomenon is not widely known outside
the region, but its dimensions are truly staggering. At the end
of World War II, for example, less than 40 percent of Latin
America's population lived in urban centers. Today the percentage is over 60 percent and by the year 2000 it is expected to be
around 80 percent. In 1950, only six cities in Latin America
exceeded 1 million persons in number. Today, there are almost
30 such cities. When I lived in Mexico City during the late 1950s,
its population totaled only 4 million. Today it is closer to 14
million, and by the year 2000, it is projected to be around 30
million. It is mind-boggling to think that, by the end of this
century, as many Latin Americans will live in cities as there
were Indians in all of India only a decade ago: more than half a
billion persons.

The problem of population bunchiness in urban centers is,
of course, further compounded by the accompanying problem of
unemployment. Although the growth rate of Latin America's
total population did slow down during 1950-80, and is expected
to slow down even more during 1980-2000, what is not widely
known is that the growth rate of the region's labor force is
accelerating. This apparent anomaly is due to two factors: the
increasing number of women who are entering the labor force,
on the one hand, and the youthful age profile of Latin America's
population, on the other. The fact remains, in any case, that
the search for employment—currently one of Latin America's
major socioeconomic imperatives—will be further heightened in
the future. Today, for example, according to ECLA, the number
of unemployed plus the underemployed equivalent of the unemployed total 25-30 percent of Latin America's labor force. Also
according to ECLA, an economic-growth rate of 7 percent would
only absorb the increment to the labor force but would not reduce
the 25-30 percent who are currently under- or unemployed.
Here in North America, unemployment rates of 6-8 percent are
very politically agitating. Imagine, then, the situation in Latin
America where one out of every four employable persons is either
without work or employed at such a low level of productivity
and remuneration as to be effectively unemployed. The process
of marginalization of persons in Latin America is thus deteriorating
instead of improving.

This unhappy picture is further dramatized by data on
income distribution. During the 1960s, and continuing with
relatively little change into the 1970s, the lowest 50 percent of
Latin America's population earned only one-seventh of the
region's GNP; the next 20 percent of the population also earned

only one-seventh; and the top 30 percent of the population obtained more than 70 percent of the regional product. The obvious and unsatisfactory consequence is that, today, over 40 percent of all Latin American families are estimated to live at or near the poverty line. They are unable to generate sufficient income from their labors to enable them to satisfy even a minimum level of basic human needs.

These are devastating statistics, but they underline the cruel paradox—the fundamental postwar contradiction—that I mentioned earlier. Despite Latin America's rapid economic growth, and its considerable dexterity in adjusting to an ever-changing global economy, the region has indeed been characterized by an ever-deteriorating scenario of domestic marginalization. More and more poor people have been jammed together in urban centers, are working far below their capacities, and typically earning such a miserable pittance that they barely maintain minimum standards of physical survival, let alone of human dignity.

But on this matter of distributional equity, the paradoxes so evident during the years 1950-80 cannot continue unabated to the year 2000. This is so for three separate, though clearly interrelated reasons. One is economic: Too large a percentage of the labor force is redundant, making only a minimal contribution to the growth of product. Another is social: The large and ever-growing masses of under- and unemployed workers serve to distort still further an already highly skewed pattern of income distribution. And still another is political: The laborers who were marginal on the farms have become even more marginalized in the urban slums. There, as an analogy, they resemble an ever-growing mass of political dynamite, packed tighter and tighter together in what is currently an inert mass, but one which could, so very easily, be ignited by a political spark into a vast conflagration. The recent flash points in Central America and the Caribbean make us pause, in this context.

ON LOOKING AHEAD: SOME LINES OF STRATEGY
TO THE YEAR 2000

So much for the last 30 years. What about the next 20 years? I wanted to give these background data first because, in my judgment, the same three variables I have been concentrating on—economic growth, participation/vulnerability, and distributional equity—will remain the three variables to be given prime consideration in designing a new strategy for the region through the 1980s and 1990s, and to the end of the century.

Growth and Vulnerability Revisited

Let us begin with the external sector: What elements of strategy should Latin America put forward on the international side that could help maintain a buoyant global economic system and yet insulate the region from external shock? Here we might think along two main lines. One would be to focus upon the traditional policies of building international cooperation for development that were, for example, contained in the Brandt Report. The other would be to look for other, more controversial ideas, such as those encompassing the so-called relinking strategy. Let us examine growth and external vulnerability within this dual framework.

As regards growth, I do not think that Latin America will change, for many years to come, its longstanding emphasis upon a high-growth strategy. In the North there has been some attention recently to a slow-growth philosophy. This may have emerged by design (to minimize the adverse environmental impact of high-pollutant industries) or by default (as a psychological resignation to the stagflation that has characterized so many Northern countries in the 1970s). Be that as it may, however, in Latin America high growth is still considered essential, primarily because four out of every ten persons barely eke out an existence at destitution levels, and because the unemployment equivalent is still some 25 percent of the labor force. It is one thing to want high growth, however, but another thing to achieve it. And achieving a high-growth strategy during 1980-2000 will not be easy. According to ECLA, a real GNP growth rate of 7 percent per annum will merely absorb new increments to the labor force, and 8 percent will be needed to make significant inroads into the existing levels of unemployment. The domestic savings and investment efforts required to generate future growth rates of between 7 percent and 8 percent per annum will be Herculean, especially if we remember that Latin America grew by only 4.7 percent during 1975-80. Nonetheless, whatever the difficulties may be, I am convinced that Latin America will persist in its efforts to maintain high-growth strategy because of the need to defuse the serious socioeconomic and political tensions evidencing themselves throughout the region. In short, the two words "economic growth" will continue to have as high a priority in a Latin American strategy to the year 2000 as was the case during 1950-80.

What of the next two words in my definition, namely, "participation/vulnerability"? There is much talk these days about global economic interdependence. The Brandt Report focused explicitly upon that concept. Many in the North believe sincerely that the South will be able to attain high rates of growth

through a new type of "global compact": that changes in Northern
policies involving trade, finance, energy, and technology can
be merged into a harmonious package that would enable the South
to regain, and then maintain, its earlier dynamic trajectory. I
very much hope this proves to be feasible, and I realize that
there are good intentions shown by many Northern governments,
toward such ends. But who can tell? The short-term outlook
is certainly bleak. And recent governments in the United States,
Japan, Germany, and the United Kingdom, among others, cannot
leave one overly optimistic on this score. Governments of the
North were not very receptive to policies of international cooperation for development during the 1960s and early 1970s, when
their economic indicators were all very buoyant. So how can
one be sanguine today, when stagflation abounds? Global interdependence and policies of internationalization are laudable, and
I applaud them. But in many parts of Latin America, I detect a
clear desire to seek new forms of insulation against external
shock—in short, to reduce their external vulnerability through
a deliberate policy of "selective relinking." This will not come
as a great surprise to Canadian audiences who have heard
secretaries of state speak of the need for a "third option," and
whose prime minister cautioned publicly against "sleeping with
an elephant when the slightest twitch of the beast can throw
you out of bed." No one today will deny that it would be risky
for Latin America to link itself tightly with a locomotive that is
not only slowing down, but is simultaneously exuding great
clouds of inflationary steam. For such reasons, therefore,
Latin America is beginning to consider new South-South alternatives that could foster a greater degree of collective self-
reliance. New forms of import substitution appear to be in the
offing, not just at the national, regional, and subregional levels,
but also with other third-world nations, including OPEC. If
this does take place, however, a cautionary note for the North
is in order. One of the reasons why the North did not contract
more than it did during the 1970s was precisely because of the
economic buoyancy of many developing countries—certainly
including Latin America—during that decade. I do not suggest
that Latin America should try and insulate itself, in an autarchical
manner, from an increasingly interdependent global economy.
But as we view the 1980s and years beyond, there are many
disturbing indications that the North will continue to be inflationary, contractive, and protectionist. Hence relinking, albeit
gradually and selectively, seems destined to become an increasingly likely strategy option for Latin America. Not for ideological
reasons—as in the early case of ISI—but because reality may force

it upon the region. I stress this point because I feel a cautionary
note should be sounded to those in the North who ignore this
possibility, and to those in the South who magnify it.

It is my firm belief that Latin America, like many other
middle-income developing countries, will be thinking increasingly
of having a new South-South orientation to the year 2000. Not
an effort to withdraw into a "new solitude" but, rather, to seek
external dynamism increasingly from the South rather than solely
from the North, where for so long it had sought such buoyancy.
In this sense, Latin America's strategy to the year 2000 as regards participation/vulnerability will, I believe, change significantly from the North-South strategy so characteristic of 1950-80
to a new South-South orientation.

Distributional Equity: The Supreme Challenge

Growth and vulnerability will clearly pose formidable obstacles to any Latin American strategy during the coming 20
years. But in my view, they will pale into insignificance—both
in terms of complexity and of priority—compared with the problem
of ensuring a greater degree of equity in the internal diffusion
of the fruits of growth. Here lies Latin America's supreme
challenge to the year 2000. How to face that challenge? Again,
the answer must be sought along two separate lines: one fundamentally economic in nature, and the other essentially political.

The economic approach would follow, in essence, the following sequence of policies. A high and sustained level of economic
growth would be sought. To such ends, great dexterity would
be required for Latin America to respond appropriately to a
changing global economy—a dexterity that will require both a
North-South axis and, as I have suggested, increasingly a
South-South axis. Assuming growth does increase, a clearly
defined set of fiscal and other, more directly interventionist
policies would then have to be taken by the state in order to
channel—deliberately and preferentially—part of the region's
incremental growth away from investment for conspicuous consumption by the upper strata and toward investment for social
consumption by the lower strata.

These are general statements, to be sure, but their policy
intent is clear. To leave distribution solely or even mainly to
the spontaneous play of market forces and to the trickle-down
thesis has long been, and continues to be, suspect insofar as
issues of equity are concerned. The market was not designed
to have, nor does it pretend to have, a long-term social horizon.
The latter must originate from enlightened actions by the state—
enlightened in the sense that distribution is, in the final analysis,
an ethical issue.

Thus it is my thesis that, whereas strategies of growth and vulnerability are essentially technical in their design and implementation, strategies affecting equity are fundamentally ethical in their substance. If I am correct in this judgment, my point is that a deep struggle is at play within Latin America. This is a struggle that will continue for decades within the very soul of Latin America—a struggle between developmental technocrats who believe sincerely (though, I am convinced, misguidedly) in the thesis of "grow now, divide later," and developmental ethicians who rest their case on the social content of national development plans.

This struggle is being waged with increasing intensity throughout Latin America, not merely on intellectual grounds but also politically, through the play of power forces. There are some who believe that equity can be ensured, during the next 20 years, through an incrementalist approach: That is to say, if rapid growth can be attained, then the application of new fiscal and other policies affecting the surplus can eliminate the highly skewed manner by which the growth has typically been diffused. But there are others who do not believe this at all; who believe the regressive patterns of the past can never be changed through incrementalist strategies. From their point of view, true equity can be achieved only through fundamental structural transformations—transformations so fundamental that they will require deep political spasms. This theory of crisis may well be correct. I am not yet sure it is so. And I personally recoil from its human implications. But certainly it exists, and is spreading. For distributional equity is bound to become primus inter pares among the three concepts of the developmental definition I put forward at the outset. The central question, to repeat, is whether it will be effected through an economic strategy of rapid growth cum incrementalism, or by a political strategy of violent paroxysm.

SUMMARY AND CONCLUSION: A PERSONAL CREDO

First I put forward, in very embryonic and personal form, an attempt at defining development. Then I traced some of the principal socioeconomic trends characterizing Latin America, at the macro level, during the past 30 years. In linking these, it was my judgment that Latin America had been quite successful in terms of what I defined as participation/vulnerability; but not successful at all—indeed lagging far behind—in what I described as the concept of distributional equity.

Looking toward the year 2000, I then made some value
judgments about these same three definitional variables. One
was that economic growth would continue to have as much, if
not more, importance in a future Latin America strategy as in
the past. The second was that participation/vulnerability would
probably change considerably, from the heavy North-South
orientation of the past to an increased emphasis upon South-
South cooperation in the future. I warned of the costs as well
as the benefits of this potential shift. My third judgment concerned the issue of distributional equity. To ensure a more
symmetrical distribution of the fruits of growth should not be
difficult from a strictly technical point of view, and could undoubtedly be done through incrementalist measures. But the
latter would be fiercely resisted by the upper strata, and anyhow the lower strata have probably passed, by now, the limits
of their political patience. If this is so, then powerful political
spasms will surely characterize many regions within Latin America
during the 1980s and beyond. A somber panorama, but one that
can by no means be ruled out.

Is it true that "plus ça change, plus ça reste lc même cliuse?"
Not necessarily so, at least as regards a Latin America strategy
to the year 2000. Things may remain more or less the same in
terms of growth-oriented policies. They will undoubtedly change
considerably as regards vulnerability. But I believe they will
change enormously when it comes to equity. The latter will be
the bellweather of developmental viability, as the region moves
to the dawn of the twenty-first century. Equity must be attained.
It will be attained. For it is, at bottom, a moral force that nothing
can withstand.

NOTE

1. For a more statistically precise and disaggregated
presentation of the three time periods I have selected (namely,
1950-64, 1965-74 and 1975-80), see the following UN Economic
Commission for Latin America (ECLA) documents: E/CEPAL/1025,
June 1977, pp. 26-32; E/CEPAL/1106, November 1²79, pp. 7-11;
and E/CEPAL/G.1150, February 1980, pp. 34-37.

2

THE BRANDT REPORT AND LATIN AMERICAN
DEVELOPMENT IN THE 1980s
Enrique V. Iglesias

RELEVANCE OF THE BRANDT REPORT

This chapter seeks to evaluate the relevance of the Brandt
Report, with special emphasis on its implications for Latin American development in the 1980s. The Independent Commission on
International Development Issues, popularly known as the Brandt
Commission, consisted of 18 senior statesmen and politicians from
developed and developing countries. It began its work in 1978
and delivered its final report in February 1980. Its three main
themes were inter alia the increasing economic interdependency
of nations; that North-South linkages are based substantially
on outdated policies and organizational arrangements requiring
substantial modifications; and that there are no automatic sources
of development finance, an institutional gap that needs to be
filled.

The value of the report, in my opinion, is eminently political.
The fact that a group of prominent individuals from the North
were able to work together with other such prominent individuals
from the South, and were able to come to an agreement on the
need to introduce structural changes in international relations
between both parts of the system, represents in itself a political
fact of the greatest importance. The value of the report, therefore, should be measured not so much by the greater or lesser
originality of its substantive approaches (which anyhow have
been analyzed from so many angles and with such intensity in
recent years), but by its ability to promote an effective mobilization of political will around the search for a solution to these
problems, especially in the industrialized countries, which are

the ones that ultimately have the most influential role in this dialogue, because they are the only ones whose decisions can make certain changes possible. The importance of this effort, therefore, will have to be measured especially by the impact it has on the political scene.

Moreover, if we try to evaluate the report without taking into account the political difficulties surrounding the North-South dialogue, and without keeping in mind a realistic appreciation of the magnitude of the political efforts needed to overcome them, our conclusions on the report could be influenced by the developing countries' expectations of finally reaching profound and definitive solutions to the serious problems affecting their relations with the industrialized countries. From a point of view that excludes consideration of the feasibility margins surrounding the negotiations, the proposals in the report could be seen as very limited, although there are some who consider them excessive. I believe that this would be a simplistic view of the document. Its reading should be inspired by a clear understanding of the present climate of international negotiations—a climate that is certainly not very hopeful. The report has made a very valid contribution in presenting a vigorous argument in favor of the need to sit down at a negotiating table and find subjects of common interest, no matter how difficult it may be, in order to pave the way toward the rebuilding of the international economic order.

A second merit of the report is its ability to express the magnitude of the crisis presently being faced by both developed and developing countries. Since more than a decade has passed since its first disquieting symptoms appeared, initial doubts as to whether the contemporary international crisis is of a cyclical or a structural character should have been dispelled, and we should clearly recognize its secular and multifaceted nature. Undoubtedly, the characteristics, duration, and dimensions of the current crisis are very different from those of other crises that have affected the world since World War II but that never had the depth or complexity of the situation being faced today.

In the 1970s the prolonged cycle of economic expansion of the industrialized countries after the war may have come to a definitive end, along with the idea of unlimited progress and the uncritical confidence in the value of growth per se that were fostered by that expansive cycle in the industrial centers. Since the beginning of the past decade, the industrial societies have entered a prolonged period of stagflation and economic imbalances, in the midst of a generalized debate on the very foundations of the extraordinary period of prosperity that preceded the crisis;

indeed, the crisis is reflected in the discussion of the limits of growth, the questioning of certain materialistic values, and the search for a better quality of life. It will be even more disturbing to many that the causes of this phenomenon are to be found not only in the end of an era of artificially cheap and abundant supplies of oil, on which the previous period was based, but in certain structural features of industrialized societies. These explain the persistent fall in the productivity of their economies and the decreasing profitability of their enterprises, which are due to the profound change in public and consumer preferences, set against a background of tense competition between stagnation and technological change, both among the various sectors in the advanced economies and among the various economies themselves.

We should not be surprised, then, that great confusion reigns today. This confusion encompasses not only the functioning of these economies, but also the alternative technologies among which they must choose in the future, their political evolution, and their changing values. I believe that the international community has never before been so devoid of technological alternatives or so perplexed in the face of the available options, and this in a world in which these problems are intertwined and are becoming more complex, due to the growing interdependence among the various national societies. Today it is often impossible to tackle a specific problem without affecting the environment, the evolution of the great urban conglomerates, the possibility of rationally using resources that are part of humanity's common heritage, or simply the quality of life and peace in the world.

In this state of affairs, the Brandt Report takes a very suitable approach in that it gives due weight to the seriousness of these global problems.

SOME BACKGROUND DETAILS

The Brandt Report is certainly not the last or the only word. During the past few years, various efforts have been made toward the same goal: to promote structural changes in international relations and, through these changes, to attempt to establish a new international economic order.

During this time, to be fair to ourselves, the UN system has made a series of efforts since the 1960s, when the UN Conference on Trade and Development (UNCTAD) was set up. UNCTAD was perhaps the first attempt to globalize analysis and negotiations in the field of international economic relations.

It also had the merit of initiating a world dialogue on this subject that still continues.

The energy crisis of 1973 presented a new challenge to the ability of the UN machinery to find an answer. Among the responses made by the system were the two special sessions of the General Assembly held in 1974 and 1975, respectively, to examine these problems; at these sessions, the Declaration and Program of Action on the Establishment of a New International Economic Order were adopted. Later, the General Assembly endorsed the Charter of Economic Rights and Duties of States. These documents served as antecedents for the subsequent Paris dialogue, in which a representative number of governments met in that city between 1975 and 1977, seeking agreements aimed at resolving these problems—unfortunately, with scant success.

But not all the initiatives originated in the UN system or were inspired by actions taken by oil-exporting countries. Another type of response came from private circles, which, in both the North and South, became increasingly interested in the problem of international economic relations and began to seek deeper solutions. These trends were inspired by the progressive or structural thinking that, as I have said, has followers and similar positions in both industrialized and developing countries. Some of these groups met under the auspices of the Dag Hammarskjold Foundation and expressed their opinions in the report entitled "What Now?". Others were led by the Nobel Prize winner in economics, Jan Tinbergen, and presented their conclusions in a report entitled "Restructuring the International Economic Order." The common denominator of these contributions lies in their more structural and, therefore, more advanced proposals: the ideas, for example, of indexing raw-materials prices; establishing an international levy to finance the process of transferring resources; organizing a world institute to promote the process of technology transfer; establishing a central monetary authority for the whole world; or organizing a joint administration for the management of the common assets of humanity. Whatever the degree of feasibility of these proposals, they have the merit of representing a level of cooperation and consensus among intellectuals of various parts of the world who are genuinely interested in improving North-South relations. The Brandt Report reveals the influence of some of these positions.

Of course, there have been much more radical trends than those already mentioned. Socioeconomic thought in recent years has seen, for example, the rise of the center-periphery scheme of analysis, the appearance of the theory of dependence, and, more recently, the advocacy of an unlinking or a radical dis-

association of North and South.   According to this last point of
view, the only alternative for dealing with the international
economic crisis, in a world in which the great industrial powers
have not shown the clear-sightedness and generosity needed
to introduce the structural changes required by the system,
would be to limit the relations between developing and industrialized countries and strengthen the ties of cooperation within the
South.

  We can thus see how the international community has responded to these problems and presented alternatives that are
more bureaucratic or private, more realistic or more utopian,
and more conservative or more progressive, according to the
circumstances surrounding them, the groups who originate
them, and the goals they pursue.   This plurality of responses
or alternatives contains, in my opinion, a great richness, and
it has helped to encourage the world dialogue.   However, all
these positions have some dangers, and I would like to point
out some of them.   One is the danger of falling into a sort of
technological obsession, in the search for solutions.   There is
a risk of being seduced by purely technological assumptions,
of forgetting that the improvement of North-South relations is
basically a great political challenge.   What the international
community needs today is to have a broad political vision,
followed by a vigorous attitude of political courage, without
denying, obviously, the need to provide solutions that have
appropriate technological content.   In this respect, I believe
that the Brandt Report's message, encouraging the search for
mutual areas of interest that would put the negotiations on a
firmer basis, is realistic and could be fruitful.   But this strategy
should not lead us to ignore the importance of ethical values
and policy decisions in the conduct of these relations.   Another
type of obsession into which we could fall is the desire to perfect
diagnostic studies to the maximum and to include all kinds of
subjects in our lists of demands, without taking into account
the limitations imposed by everyday reality.   This is a familiar
phenomenon at the national level.   The interests and problems
of societies have become so complex that their protest movements
tend to be increasingly global, including a large number of
demands and seeking immediate structural reforms.   This
approach poses the problem of the feasibility of such demands.
It also presents the problem of whether these demands can be
adapted to changing realities.   The very globality of the diagnostic study and demands means that both are falling out of
step with economic realities, resulting in a growing disjunction
between the program of negotiations for the developing countries

and the relevance and appropriateness of the questions that should, at any given time, be the object of such negotiations. We are faced with very profound changes, both in national and in regional and international realities.

Unity and Diversity

These changes are accompanied by a growing differentiation between the attitudes of the various groups of countries. This differentiation makes it more difficult to identify the common denominators on which the third-world countries could base a common position in international forums.

The distinction between North and South—or between center and periphery—is becoming increasingly inadequate for explaining the realities of the different categories of countries. These categories have been multiplying due to the emergence of new realities, and this growing differentiation between various groups of countries, due to their diverse realities, is challenging traditional assumptions that grouped them into the neat categories of center and periphery. Also being challenged are the systems developed by the United Nations for classifying countries into broad, homogeneous categories based on a few generalizations. In today's world, it is increasingly difficult to understand a reality that has become full of nuance and change in the light of these generalizations.

In this sense, Latin America has strong elements in common with the rest of the third world. But this fact should not lead us to ignore its own characteristic features, derived from its peculiar traditions and structures, and also the level of development reached by these countries in the past decades. The same differential elements are found within this region, where countries with an impressive industrial potential, enabling their manufactured goods to achieve deep penetration into international markets, coexist with other countries that may still be characterized as primary-export economies. We need to know how to recognize these differences; and to distinguish common interests, which link all the countries of the region, from those which are specific to certain groups among them, as a necessary condition for formulating a common negotiating position that will also be flexible enough to adapt to the changing realities of the international scene.

The Crisis in the Industrialized Countries

The more uncertain and changing the transitional period in which the industrialized countries find themselves today, the

more this unity of action will be necessary. Here I would like
to point out some of the features of this transition or crisis.

Above all, we must remember that we are talking about
countries with well-rooted democratic structures, where the role
of popular opinion, parliaments, and consensus is important.
The main aspects of this crisis are seized by public opinion,
which then uses them as a basis for making demands and protests.
Everyone emphasizes the decline in productivity, the stagnation
of production, the increase in unemployment, and the inflationary
pressures affecting these societies. Everyone also points out
the perverse and previously unknown connection between inflation and unemployment—a spurious phenomenon in economic history.

At the bottom of this debate lies a crisis in confidence that
is perhaps the central factor in the overall crisis. The capitalist
world has lost some of what had been the permanent basis for
its development: the confidence in progress. This is what is
influencing the low levels of productivity, rates of investment,
and rhythm of technological innovation, which were traditionally
the catalysts for development in these countries.

This crisis in confidence in the industrialized countries
may come from an inadequate capacity to respond on the part
of their political systems. But we must remember that the
magnitude and complexity of the problems pressuring these
societies drastically reduces the respective governments' ability
to negotiate and maneuver. We thus observe an understandable
inability of the industrial societies to impose lasting solutions
and to introduce structural changes, because of the multiplicity
of contradictory interests in play and the delicate balance of
power that prevails. It is not surprising that this same inability
manifests itself in the search for solutions at the international
level.

The Newly Industrializing Countries

Among the new realities of the contemporary international
scene is the emergence of a group of countries called newly
industrializing countries, or NICs. This is a rather vague
category. We know, in general, which ones they are and what
characterizes them, but it is difficult to define them precisely.
These are countries that have profoundly transformed their
strengths and productive structures, thereby reaching levels
of production and of diversification of their economies that would
have been unimaginable a few years ago. These are countries,
moreover, that have experienced unprecedented advances in
their ability to export nontraditional products to world markets,

integrating themselves very closely with the world economy and
becoming important trade partners of the large industrial countries.

This evolution has not been the result of chance. These
countries have improved the management of their economic policy
in order to enter the external cycle more effectively, especially
in the realm of international capitalism. They have carried out
a true revolution in foreign trade, fully participating in world
trade flows. They have also become important recipients of the
financial surpluses derived from oil. Similarly, they have started
to attract multinational corporations. In general, they have
begun to establish new forms of association with Northern interests: new industrial groups or exporters associated with groups
connected with industrialized countries. They are thus immersed
in an accelerated process of internationalization of their economic
interests.

These countries are indeed beginning to count in world
dynamics. They are no longer only isolated or eccentric cases
on the international scene, but have decisive weight in world
trade, finance, investment, and technology. They form a part
of the dynamic mechanism of the international economic system.

On the other side of this phenomenon, we must recognize
that these countries have had a rather passive attitude to their
form of insertion in world trade and an international strategy
that has been flexible but not very well defined. Thus, at the
level of the international dialogue, there is a rather uneasy feeling as regards the interests and attitudes displayed by these
countries in their bilateral or collective relations with the rest
of the world. The fact is, however, that these countries, on
the one hand, have important relative weight within the third
world and, on the other hand, are playing an increasingly
active role at the international economic level.

Repercussions of the Energy Crisis

Another basic factor in contemporary reality is the energy
crisis and its consequences for different groups of countries.
It put an end to a whole era in which the predominant style of
development was based on an abundant and cheap supply of oil.
Secondly, it brought out the third-world's ability to work together
when, as happened in the case of OPEC, it discovers a trump
negotiating card. Finally, the energy crisis emphasized the
interdependence between the industrial and developing countries,
changing previous perceptions that saw the phenomenon of dependence as a one-way relationship.

The energy crisis perhaps contributed, more than any other factor in contemporary life, to putting an end to dependence as a unilateral relationship in which the developing countries, on one side, and the developed countries, on the other, took on homogeneous, foreseeable, and stereotypical roles. Since then, we can better appreciate that center-periphery relations are complex and penetrated by many power circuits involving such vital elements as energy, natural resources, food, technology, and, of course, finance. These circuits have changed the balance of powers, making it much more complex, and have led to an international scene composed of many roles and actors who interact in ways which are not always compatible with our traditional perceptions.

International Financial Permissiveness

The world economy today is characterized by an extraordinary degree of international financial permissiveness: a phenomenon unknown in world capitalism during the past decades—at least since the collapse of the international capital markets that occurred in the crisis at the end of the 1920s.

The fact is that in the past decade, there has been an unprecedented accumulation of financial surpluses, basically originating in the surpluses of the oil-exporting countries, which have flowed rapidly toward the private banks and capital markets of the industrialized countries. The latter institutions have begun to play a central role in the process of recycling or redistributing these surpluses and maintaining the financial balance between the oil-exporting countries, the industrialized countries, and the oil-importing developing countries. This process has caused the resurgence of international financial markets. In turn, this resurgence has made certain developing countries, which previously did not qualify for access to these markets, into attractive customers. This is what has happened with some Latin American countries that have become important clients of private banks and international financial markets; and that have found external debt to be a palliative that can be resorted to, rather than more orthodox adjustment policies, in fighting international recession and thus avoiding a major slump in their own economies. In 1979, $24 billion flowed into Latin America: a sum worth comparing with the ideas put forward in the era of the Alliance for Progress, when President Kennedy proposed an aid plan for Latin America based on the transfer of $1 billion annually.

It must be emphasized, however, that this vast process of transferring foreign resources, through private banks and international financial markets, has some anaesthetic effects. On the one hand, these effects are positive since they enable countries to finance the transition. For that reason, it is very important that access to these markets should continue to be open and that Latin American countries should continue to be included in these financial flows. But on the other hand, this abundance of financial resources often also has the effect of postponing the implementation of certain adjustment measures that must be faced sooner or later. At all events, I believe that the new forms and extent of Latin American participation in international financial trends are a new fact of great significance that has changed some of the basic features of the external economic relations of the countries of the region.

Transnational Corporations

Another element in the changing international reality is the new set of actors who have taken on leading roles in this scene. The appearance of the transnational corporations on the international scene has been repeatedly analyzed. We are accustomed to examining North-South relations between governments. But we should not forget that transnational corporations have their own strategies. Who could be unaware, for example, that the position of the oil corporations is crucial to the solution of the energy problem and that the decisions taken by these corporations will have a very strong influence on the solution to this problem? How could we ignore, moreover, the appearance of new actors such as the group of countries belonging to OPEC?

The emergence of these new actors contributes significantly to the transformation of the scenario with which we must work. The North now is different. The South has changed. The dynamic circuits connecting the two segments of the system have changed. And the actors who take part in this relationship are different. We must make a very great effort to update the analytical schemes and data needed to identify the true parameters of the dialogue and the negotiation.

THE POSITIONS INVOLVED IN THE DIALOGUE

As a result of the transformation of these parameters, the attitudes of the various groups of countries that participate in the dialogue have changed. If we ask the United States or the European countries what they expect from the international dialogue, they will surely answer that the fundamental variable at this moment is the challenge of facing the energy transition.

If we ask the same question of a Latin American country, in
spite of the importance of the energy question, we will probably
be told of the crucial importance of the need to introduce a
measure of order and stability into the process of external financing. Some Latin American countries, and many countries of
Asia and Africa, would emphasize food security. It is not easy,
therefore, to find a unanimous response. This is because
various groups of countries find themselves in situations very
different from one another. Hence it is useful to try to identify
the fundamental positions of the various groups of countries.

What are the attitudes prevailing today in the developed
countries? During the past few years, the concern with the
East-West conflict has tended to displace concern for North-
South relations. We have entered a stage that seems to presage
a new cold war. Somehow the North-South topic has been set
aside in the minds of the industrialized countries. At the same
time, these countries undoubtedly give priority to their bilateral
relationships, a trend that can be clearly seen when we observe
the attempts to arrive at bilateral agreements on oil or when we
examine the financial agreements between the central banks of
certain countries. There is a crisis in multilateralism, as conceived by the United Nations in the past three decades, and
there is instead a predominance of bilateralism. At the same
time, as I have pointed out, the developed countries are giving
high priority to the energy dialogue, a factor that is creating
increasing difficulties with the third world, and that tends to
distort or break down the agenda of North-South relationships,
converting energy to a central element of negotiation. Of course,
quite apart from the preceding considerations, there is another
central element in the North's attitude, an attitude that appeared
clearly in the last summit conference in Venice: the idea that,
first, matters should be settled within the North and that only
then, if there is time, should the problems with the South be
dealt with. This approach considers that the various groups
of problems should be tackled in stages, beginning with "taking
care of things at home," and postponing the solution to the
problems of the poorer neighbors in the South. This is a somewhat dangerous attitude, because the interdependence among
the various questions and countries tends to cause problems
and tensions to accumulate, and it could easily result in threats
to the orderly functioning of the international economy and even
to world peace.

Another dangerous attitude is that of those groups of
countries that have chosen to remain apart from the North-South
dialogue, such as the socialist countries, which believe that they

owe no historical debt to the developing countries and that therefore their commitments to them are basically ideological or nominal.

Another equally dangerous attitude that has developed among countries of the North is the tendency to postulate a radical differentiation within the South, as a way of organizing the dialogue separately with each of the groups into which developing countries are divided, and to postulate a different treatment for each one of these groups. This strategy of the industrialized countries tends to divide the third world, and it should not be confused with the genuine need to recognize the differences existing between the countries making up the latter category, so as to better articulate their interests, without weakening their essential solidarity.

Let us now briefly examine some of the positions taken by the countries of the South.

First, I would say that there exist two extreme tendencies that are equally dangerous. The first is a tendency toward an excessively global approach, in which everything must be negotiated at the same time. This is a dangerous trend because it is unrealistic, especially in view of the difficulties of the present international situation. The other tendency is the temptation to act alone: to prefer to conduct bilateral relations with the industrialized countries, instead of entering into a commitment to multilateral dialogues. This attitude prevails in many of the newly industrializing countries to which I referred earlier. It is understandable if we consider their better ability to maneuver in the international context and, above all, their higher eligibility as important clients in the international financial markets. These two extreme tendencies, in my opinion, are not constructive, and both ignore important elements in present reality. The first trend ignores the need to adopt a selective or priority strategy to tackle the different problems involved in a complex situation, over different time spans, and between different groups of countries. The second ignores the power of solidarity and the need to participate in a united manner in collective negotiations.

Even in the OPEC countries themselves, there are dissimilar attitudes. Within this organization, there is a group of countries that is apparently postulating the need to establish an important negotiating alliance with the countries of the South, while others are giving priority to their bilateral contacts with other countries of the world. These are the realities and attitudes of the international situation in which we have to live. They are changing realities, and there are new problems. We should not forget to emphasize a fundamental option that is always present in these negotiations, but that is undoubtedly not exclusive: the option between policies of those who favor a strategy based on confrontation and those who prefer to maintain negotiations and dialogue. As I said, these two strategies, in certain stages and faced with certain problems, may be complementary. I must, however, express my belief that, whatever strategy is adopted, the most important point, from the perspective of the international economy and world peace, is to maintain the dialogue.

Latin America's Position

In this dialogue, it is unfortunate that Latin America has not maintained the capacity for initiative that it showed in the 1960s. In the past few years, it has lost ground to other regions of the developing world, which have used the international forums with more aggressiveness, vigor, and political power. In Latin America there has been a certain attitude of withdrawal that, in my opinion, must be reversed.

This attitude is expressed, first, in the adoption of a defensive strategy in the region's external economic relations that is unsuitable for taking advantage of the opportunities that—along with undeniable dangers—present themselves in an international economy in full transition. Secondly, there has been a certain lack of creativity at the level of both institutions and policies, which has frustrated the region's possibility of presenting the international community, as it had done in the past, with alternatives for revitalizing the North-South dialogue. Finally, this attitude is shown in the growing difficulties that seem to confront the Latin American countries in finding joint positions in the face of the great tasks that must be undertaken, both in the area of reciprocal relationships and in that of ties with the world economy.

This passive attitude has a great influence on the present stagnation of North-South relations. Because of their rapid process of transformation and their active presence on the world economic scene, the newly industrializing countries should play a very important role in this dialogue. However, up to now, they have not distinguished themselves by seeking or defending common positions within the group of developing countries, and they seem to have avoided becoming firmly committed to the success or failure of these negotiations. We believe that the results of the negotiations will depend largely on whether these countries commit themselves politically to this dialogue

and assume more active positions. For this reason, we should
keep in mind that a large part of Latin America belongs to this
category of countries and therefore is facing these same responsibilities.

WHAT NOW?

The central theme of these reflections revolves around
what should be done in the face of the period of stagnation
through which the North-South negotiations are now passing.
In trying to think of some guidelines for action, I have come
up with five ideas I would like to propose here. These ideas,
in general, are related to the need to adopt a new negotiating
attitude as a necessary condition for reactivating the dialogue
between the two groups of countries.

The first of these guidelines refers to the need for the
third-world countries—and especially the newly industrializing
countries—to make intelligent use of their bargaining power in
conducting their external economic relations. In these countries
there is a very significant potential market, an appreciable
degree of financial solvency, and an ample reserve of natural
resources—particularly energy resources—all of which constitute
elements of the greatest importance for the contemporary world
economy. The rational and concerted use of these elements
would enable these countries to organize their bargaining power
better in order to realize their hope of basing their relations
with the North on the identification of common interests. These
areas of common interest can only be discovered through sustained
negotiations, and will not immediately leap to the eye as a kind
of preestablished harmony of interests, since clearly such harmony
does not characterize the asymmetrical relationships that have
traditionally linked the countries of the North and South. The
result of any negotiations depends upon the power that each of
the parties involved is able to exercise. The developing countries thus need to organize their bargaining power, taking into
account their own economic and political interests, but also
having a clear understanding of the interests and needs of the
developed countries. This ability to concert action and interests,
which is still weak in the third world, is the first condition for
sitting down effectively at the bargaining table.

The second idea is related to the need to bring a greater
degree of realism to the bargaining table. This means that the
agenda for the negotiations should be ruled by the principle
of selectivity, whereby the countries participating in this exercise

must seek realistic goals and propose topics that can be negotiated
in the current situation, leaving the search for more ambitious
goals and negotiations on a broader number of topics for later
stages in the negotiation process. This is where the emergency
program proposed for the short term by the Brandt Report is
valuable. In other words, we will not go far as long as the
developing countries insist on bringing to the negotiation table
a comprehensive list of all the problems in their relationships
with the industrialized countries and on negotiating all of them
at the same time. Some crucial problems must be selected that
are important within the temporary context of the negotiations,
and around which it is feasible to mobilize the different political
wills. An all-embracing approach, which seeks to negotiate
everything at the same time, amounts to condemning, in advance,
any effort at international negotiations to irrelevance or defeat.
These considerations have not always been well understood,
since they imply overcoming a certain bureaucratic ritualism
into which the international dialogue has fallen, and which tends
to formulate broad agendas and ambitious negotiation programs.
I think that, in spite of appearances, this strategy plays into
the hands of those who are not interested in the progress of this
dialogue and tends to favor the status quo or, simply, inaction.

The third guideline I would like to propose is the need to
set about internal negotiations within the developing countries
themselves. There is a latent crisis in the solidarity of the
third world, for the growing differences among the countries
sometimes make the search for joint positions difficult. We must
not allow these differences to be used, consciously or uncon-
sciously, by the countries of the North to divide the developing
countries or to handicap some of them. But we should not ignore
them either, since such a smug attitude can only favor the
elaboration of negotiation program based on such broad common
denominators that they either lead to nothing or encourage
silence among those countries who do not see their interests
specifically reflected in the programs. Consequently, to identify
this diversity of interests and place third-world solidarity on a
new and more realistic basis, we must open up a dialogue among
the developing countries themselves. And this dialogue should
begin by seeking a strategy for promoting cooperation among
third-world countries, in order to go on to formulate a strategy
aimed at the outside world. In any case, I do not believe that
the existence of a certain number of differences within the third
world is bad in itself. On the contrary, the recognition of this
diversity will make the common position of the developing countries more solid. The important thing is that, once these differ-

ences are recognized, areas of common interest should be identified, priorities defined, and working or tactical alliances sought
to support the particular interest of specific groups of countries.
This would help to maintain the unity of the third world in the
North-South dialogue, in spite of the inevitable diversity of
interests that, whether for historical or circumstantial reasons,
exists among the various groups of countries making it up.

A fourth line of action is the strengthening of Latin American
regional cooperation. Latin America will never have the ability
to develop joint action with regard to the rest of the world if it
does not have the ability to strengthen and vitalize cooperation
among its own countries. For many years, we have been discussing the success or advantages of specific instruments of
integration and cooperation that have become obsolete over time
or have been left behind by reality. What is important is not
the form these instruments assumed at a particular time, but
rather the pursuit of the objectives that were sought through
them: that is to say, the strengthening of economic complementar-
ity among the Latin American countries. From this perspective,
it is important to know how to adapt these instruments or forge
new tools to reach these objectives. It is also important to
recognize that the bases that were taken into account in establishing the first instruments of integration in Latin America still
exist and have even been extended. Latin America has a large
regional market to defend and use in its internal economic relations
and in its relations with the rest of the world. In periods of
serious international economic upheavals, experience shows that
the internal market is one of the great defenses available to the
region and a factor of stability in the face of the impact of a
world in turmoil. We at the ECLA began by defending the importance of the internal market as a means of stimulating the
industrialization of our countries. Later, we argued for the
opening up of national economies to the regional market, as a
means of overcoming the limitations of national markets, and still
later, we investigated the possibilities of entering international
markets under better conditions and advocated policies to promote
exports. The experience accumulated in these various stages,
which in their turn responded to the characteristics of the
external context in each period, leads us today to emphasize
the need to combine in various ways—according to the respective
realities—the national, regional, and international markets,
depending on the size, structure, and orientation of each national
economy. It is unrealistic to aim at exaggerated self-sufficiency,
which would clash with the reality of the increasingly interdependent world in which we live, and we do not believe, either,

in the advantages of an indiscriminate opening up to the world economy. I think that Latin America should do all it can to defend its internal market—its regional market—not only as a requirement for ensuring the efficiency of its productive systems, but as a necessary condition for increasing its ability to defend itself against a changing international economic situation. To that end, it must move toward new frontiers of regional economic cooperation that take into account the new realities created by the profound economic transformation being experienced by our countries, as well as their different political evolution. To such ends, it will be necessary to renew the thinking, procedures, and institutions related to the promotion of this process.

A fifth and final idea is related to the need to impart a new political impulse to the North-South dialogue at the appropriate forums. Ultimately, these forums must be fully representative and, for that reason, the United Nations will be called upon to play an irreplaceable role. But the idea of calling together a group of heads of state who represent a significant spectrum of countries and who are in a position to make a political commitment toward the reactivation of North-South negotiations seems to be a very positive one.

Final Observations

We are living in a period of profound changes in the international scene. For the Latin American countries, these changes present both great risks and great opportunities. If our countries want to respond adequately to both, they cannot remain solely dependent on market forces: They must develop some form of deliberate international action.

The changes occurring in the international scene tend to modify the traditional forms of insertion of Latin America in the world economy. The shaping of these new forms of international insertion cannot, however, be simply left to market forces. The countries of the region must be able to achieve an active insertion that allows them to find the most advantageous forms of participation in an international economy in transition, while, at the same time, strengthening their safeguards or defenses against the turmoil of an uncertain and changing external cycle.

In this context, the Latin American countries must resume their former role of protagonist in the international economic negotiations. They should not be caught up in the debate between those seeking dialogue and those desiring to promote confrontation, a dilemma which is rapidly becoming sterile. A strategy of confrontation could become irrelevant and discredited if it failed to produce substantive results as fully and promptly as expected, and there is the additional risk that this could cause division in the third world if there were countries or groups of countries that were prepared to come to an agreement with the North in certain areas and that therefore abandoned the official strategy of confrontation. In this sense, I have already pointed out that maintaining the dialogue is the only way to advance toward an improvement in North-South relations. But a purely bureaucratic dialogue could lead us to fall into ritualistic rhetoric, with consequent frustration of the expectations placed in these negotiations, and even destroy the institutional machinery through which this dialogue has been carried on up to now.

We must know precisely what new forms the dependency relationship of the developing countries has taken in an increasingly interrelated world, the margins of maneuver available to these countries, and the risks and opportunities they face as a result of the growing internationalization of their economies. Only a thorough knowledge of these parameters will enable us to carry forward intelligent negotiations with the developed countries, according to realistic goals and stages, but without renouncing the great objectives and, above all, the ethical values involved in this dialogue.

3

LATIN AMERICA:
A HUMAN RIGHTS PERSPECTIVE
FOR THE 1980s
Claudio Orrego Vicuña

The panorama of human rights in Latin America appears
very different, at the beginning of the 1980s, from how it did
at the start of the 1970s. After a tragic decade, one can now
nourish some hope for the future.

The violation of human rights is a painful historical reality
of the continent. Nevertheless, the past ten years seem particularly inauspicious in comparison to high standards of the past.
The phenomena of random terrorism and state terrorism reached
Dantesque dimensions. Systematic torture, arrest and disappear-
ance, kidnapping, people's prisons, assassination as a habitual
method of politics, and many other horrors completely changed
the civic features of the continent.

It is enough just to list the countries involved to comprehend the dimensions of the problem. In the southern cone,
Argentina, Brazil, Chile, and Uruguay could be counted, for
many consecutive years, among the most serious violators of
human rights in the world. Bolivia has recently joined them,
and one must also add the chronic case of Paraguay's violation
of human rights. In Central America, we saw the genocide
committed against the Nicaraguan people by Somoza. El Salvador
is living a bloodbath, whether it be in the name of revolution or
reaction. Guatemala has suffered successive waves of massive
political violence. And to the inhuman tradition of the Duvaliers

---

This chapter was translated by Howard Wallack of the
School of International Affairs, Carleton University.

in the Caribbean has been added the consolidation of a totalitarian political regime in Cuba.

It was during the 1970s that a virtual ideology of violence had taken form, inspired as much from the left as from the right. Whether it be from a revolutionary focus or a doctrine of national security, this ideology has established violence and political crime in a manner hitherto unknown.

It is, however, this same situation that provokes a reaction equally without precedent. The theme of human rights has converted itself into a subject of political concern and transcends the exclusive limits of morality. In every nation important organizations are growing in their defense. Violations are denounced and fought against. The churches are taking a decisive and militant role on the issue. The Carter administration made human rights a critical variable in international affairs. The academic community includes the subject among its concerns, publishing prolific works on it in every language. The region received a Nobel Peace Prize; in a particularly critical area, it is a symbol of solidarity and of respect for the defense of human dignity.

At the end of the decade of the 1970s, the subject of human rights was not a marginal one in Latin America. It formed part of the agenda at all levels of civic life. It surpassed its earlier historical limits as a matter for the clergy and individuals of extraordinary spiritual sensitivity. And, to some degree, experience is converting human rights into a significant ingredient of the intellectual, academic, and political life of Latin America.

What lessons of the past can enlighten the next decade? We will suggest a few.

THE POLITICAL STERILITY OF VIOLENCE

A careful analysis of the effects of political violence in Latin America must lead to a thorough questioning of its purported utility. Facts lead to the conclusion that whoever has taken recourse to violence has ended in the most noted failures.

One part of the ideological aura that has adorned violence and terrorism is their condition as rapid and efficient mechanisms to annul political conflict. It is the last resort for the impatient and desperate individuals who seek, by its use, the shortcut to dialogue, persuasion, and electoral victory at the polls. It is a handbook of simple application and easy acquisition, to which has been added an aura of romantic idealism.

But what has happened in practice? Seen from the standpoint of the left, it has not been the midwife of the revolution;

seen from the right, it has not been the foundation for a stable
and legitimate political order. And from the point of view of the
center, it is the beginning and end of a historical disaster that
has demolished democracy and erased any possibility of harmonious
coexistence.

We begin with the left, which, with great idealism, devoted
itself to the belief that the experience of the Sierra Maestra had
discovered the secret road to a new historical era. But everywhere it only reaped ruin, leaving in its wake the lives of tens
of thousands of revolutionary youth. A generation was sacrificed
in the name of an illusion. The Argentine Ejército Revolucionario
del Pueblo (ERP), which was attempting to arm a rural core,
was decimated early, and the action culminated with the Monto-
neros in urban warfare that dragged Peronism to its disintegration and the entire country to an internal bloodbath. The
Uruguayan Tupamaros were also wiped out, and, in their downfall, confronted an old democracy and one of the most solid and
advanced social states on the continent. The Chilean Miristas,
marching to the chant of "votes no, guns yes," through the
streets of democratic Chile, met a mass of guns that had replaced
votes in a massacre unprecedented in the history of their nation.
The Foquista attempt in Bolivia achieved the miracle of establishing dictatorships in that country; that attempt is today invoked
as an excuse to deny its people a right to democracy. Due to
cultural incompatibility, the rural guerrilla movement in Peru
was unable to establish roots among the people in whose name
it was launched. In Brazil another generation was wiped out
by a military dictatorship that moved toward a new institutionality
very different from the inevitable one suggested by Marighela
in the "Mini-Manual of the Urban Guerrilla." In El Salvador and
Guatemala, it is only with idealistic candor that one dares to
think of these two nations as being closer to revolution than to
a Pinochetazo. Once again, we are deluded into confusing the
exception with the rule.

Briefly, the only two successful armed experiences achieved
in Latin America by the left have been products more of an
opponent's errors than of their own merit. Both were cut from
the same mole: Batista and Somoza were both principal actors
who antagonized their people beyond resistance and lit the fuse
of a generalized civil insurrection. In Cuba and Nicaragua, it
was the middle classes, radicalized by the repression and corruption, who tipped the loyal balance. In both cases, it was the
inability of the dictators to generate even minimal legitimacy to
maintain their power that forced them to flee; in neither case
was it due to a lack of military strength or to the imminence of

an armed victory by the guerrillas. For this reason, each of
these triumphant revolutions has lead, through a dogmatic interpretation of reality, to an idealistic generalization with dramatic
results.

If we look toward the right, we must conclude that empirical
proof is less abundant because the majority of applied political
formulas are still being applied. The regimes born under the
doctrine of national security are still in power. Despite this
dearth of empirical proof, we can look at tendencies and examine
some signs of the past.

Perhaps the only case of an institutional military, or
bureaucratic-authoritarian, regime that completed its full cycle
was that of the Ongania-Levingston-Lanusse triad in Argentina.
In perspective, this regime appears moderately repressive, but,
nonetheless, the sequel to this legacy is not at all encouraging:
massive terrorism and political instability that were the fruits
of an indestructible myth immune even to force; and the necessity
of a new intervention that sunk the country into a domestic
bloodbath and international dishonor. What is yet more serious
is that it left Argentina much further than it had earlier been
from achieving the base of a legitimate and stable political order.

Looking at Argentina, Chile, and Uruguay, it is difficult
to find any signs that the military regimes there are ready to
mobilize conducive and solid political processes. In Chile it is
even more improbable than in the other two, given the personalist
connotation that General Pinochet has imposed on all purported
maneuvers for normalization. The systematic recourse to violence
and repression, far from facilitating a new consensus, polarizes
society, radicalizes groups, and compels a spiraling of increased
repression that erases all liberalization. In other words, the
violation of human rights does not permit the creation of stable
political orders; rather, it adds proof to the sterility of violence.

If there exists little available proof, there are surprisingly
illuminating analogies to Latin America that exist on other con-
tinents. The massive repression that led to the political defeat
of the French in Algeria; the consensual crisis that the Vietnam
war unleashed in the United States, obligating that nation to a
retreat that represented a military victory for the Viet Cong;
the inability of the dictatorship of Greek colonels to survive;
and the complete erasure of the Franco and Salazar dictatorships—
these are all examples of the futility of violence to generate
stable political orders. The similarities highlighted by these
cases are not in the least bit surprising when one examines the
dictatorships of the right in Latin America.

Although briefly mentioned earlier, the most expressive case remains that of Somoza in Nicaragua. As a dynastic dictator with enormous economic and military power in both the country and the region, he saw it all collapse in a few months, as a result of an agitated response to the violence he himself deployed. Prior to the assassination of Pedro Joaquin Chamorro, the opposition remained divided and the Sandinista guerrillas were distant. Afterward, it was as if a trickle of gunpowder had converted Nicaragua into a bonfire in a matter of weeks, taking the dictator from his people and from the international community; at this point, the maintenance of the National Guard served him little. After more than 40 years of power, the exercise of systematic violence did not enable the Somozas to build a stable political order. Can there be any clearer demonstration of the political sterility of violence?

One optimistic contrast is the experience of Romulo Betancourt in Venezuela during the 1960s. It was the only instance in which the challenge of violence was confronted while a regime simultaneously built the foundation of a stable political order, thus demonstrating the possibility of defending an existing legal system without the violation of human rights. It clearly demonstrated to the common man of Venezuelan society that terrorism was a human rights violation to be rejected, but not through the use of equivalent means.

THE DEVELOPMENT OF WORLDWIDE AWARENESS OF HUMAN RIGHTS

An awareness of the importance of human rights is not a localized phenomenon in Latin America. In the last decade, there has been a generalized trend in the Western world to establish it as a substantive issue of public opinion in countries that can act and react to violations. Without social, moral, political, or economic power capable of maintaining it, the fight for human rights cannot extend beyond mere verbalism. It is thanks to the awakening of awareness in Western Europe, Canada, the United States, and the democratic states south of the Rio Grande that the issue has been able to gain importance.

After World War II, human rights became a fundamental element of legitimacy in the new international order. In light of the Holocaust and the tragedy of the armed conflict, the human conscience demanded a set of principles with which to guarantee that such a tragic event could never recur. Though one may question the sincerity of the powers that signed the

Universal Declaration of Human Rights of the United Nations, there can be no doubt that the spiritual mood of the times left little option for decisive opposition to it. To oppose enthusiastic acknowledgment of human rights would have been tantamount to admitting the futility and sterility of the sacrifice suffered by so many nations in their battle against Nazism and fascism.

A more active mobilization was nevertheless necessary. Needed were feelings of solidarity with any suffering human beings worldwide; an ability to organize and make humanitarianism a dynamic and efficient force; necessary influence to make moral indignation a sufficient force to dissuade torturers, tyrants, and assassins; and sufficient power to infuse fear and respect into the violators of human rights.

In this regard, the decade of the 1970s was a happy one. There was a constant development and strengthening of nongovernmental, humanitarian organizations. There was a constant consolidation of international solidarity among political parties, unions, religious groups, and cultural organizations. But, above all else, it was a time when the prophets of human rights violations made their passionate eruption before the public, denouncing to the entire world the horrors that were secretly hidden in vast sectors of society. It was Solzhenitsyn and Sa.harov who led the Soviet dissidents, the signatories to the Charter of 77 in Prague; and it was the intellectuals of Europe who acknowledged, supported, and multiplied their accusations. It was Helder Camara in Brazil and Raul Silva Henriquez in Chile who were symbols of broad movements, along with Adolfo Perez Esquivel in Argentina, Monsignor Romero in El Salvador, and Chamorro in Nicaragua. It was President Carter in the United States who put all the resources of a superpower at the service of a humanitarian cause. It was the incessant sermons of Pope Paul VI, defining peace as the respect of human rights; and the pilgrimages of Pope John Paul II throughout the world, carrying with him this new ideal. It was the Helsinki Accords and the ratification, in San José, Costa Rica, of the American Human Rights Pact. It was Amnesty International, the International Commission of Jurists, and the Human Rights Commissions of the United Nations, the European Community, and the Americas, respectively, that began to function with new power, resources, and influence. In sum, a very good decade indeed.

We can see that the development of a world moral conscience is not a fleeting phenomenon. A strong network of solidarity and influence has grown as a response to antihumanitarian forces and now extends throughout the world. This network is constantly attuned to the events in every nation of Europe, Africa,

Asia, and the Americas. More and more individuals of good faith and strong spirit devote their time, resources, and lives to the cause of human rights. There is no reason to discourage continued progress.

In Latin America, it is especially possible to embrace a more realistic hope due to the increasingly militant and mobilizing role of religious groups, most notably the Catholic church. In the post-Vatican II Council era, one can hardly sustain the Marxist vulgarism that "religion is the opiate of the people." On the contrary, it has been converted into a mobilizing force for personal and collective consciousness that could scarcely have been envisioned in the past.

In Argentina, Bolivia, Brazil, Chile, El Salvador, Honduras, Nicaragua, Paraguay, and Uruguay, the Catholic church has made the defense of human rights a special part of its vocation. There are few documents that exhibit as much clarity on the issue as the statement of the Latin American Episcopal Conference in Puebla. It was ratified by Pope John Paul II in Mexico, by the Organization of American States, and in Brazil. The list of martyrs expands daily. The decision to confront repressive regimes is increasingly decisive and clear. The will to protect the persecuted, the exploited, the suffering, and the defenseless has reached inspirational limits.

In review, no one can guarantee the desire to which respect for human rights will grow in Latin America during the 1980s. One can, however, be certain that the battle in their defense will be increasingly decisive and influential. There is no reason to entertain a relapse into the past. Likewise, the cost of violations of human dignity will be much higher for their perpetrators. The more immediate political effects may vary—for example, a policy change by the U.S. government—but it is doubtful that the more profound consequences will change. In particular, those sectors and institutions, both within and outside Latin America, that have dedicated themselves to the defense of human rights will always be able to mobilize consciences and groups with differing degrees of power and influence in each society. Since that moment when the issue of human rights began to first receive serious consideration on the part of governments, international governmental and nongovernmental organizations, pressure groups, the mass media, political parties, and other representative forces of society, it has been difficult to conceive of a reversal of this tendency. It may suffer the advances and aggravations common to all conflict, but it will hardly return to a no-man's-land where violations can be committed with impunity.

THE PERFECTION OF LEGAL MECHANISMS

At the beginning of the 1970s, the Latin American states could be roughly divided into two categories: those unconcerned with the ratification of the San José Pact on Human Rights because they considered it as something superfluous to their own traditions; and those overly concerned with blockage of its ratification due to the full awareness that they were already violating it systematically. Thus one can explain the fact that a significant number of democratic governments, all signatories to the treaty, have not yet ratified it, while the dictatorships, whether they be of longstanding tradition or recent appearance, do not have the least urgency about seeing it in full force. The experience of the tragic decade was necessary so that the pact could finally be put into effect in 1978 under the sustained diplomatic pressure of the Carter administration and of a handful of democratic governments, such as those of Venezuela, Colombia, and Costa Rica. Unfortunately, in cases such as those of Chile and Uruguay, the indolence of democratic majorities has inhibited ratification such that it becomes an integral part of the internal legislation of those states.

We presume that this lesson will be duly learned in the future. The democratic governments of the region have developed an aggressive capacity for solidarity with the values of political democracy and for the respect of human rights. The examples of Ecuador, Peru, Nicaragua, and Bolivia bear witness to this new concern. Institutionally, the Inter-American Human Rights Commission has garnered solid prestige in diverse sectors of the continent due to its seriousness, valor, and rigorous avoidance of any double standard in the judgment of national realities.

What is lacking is a function of the Inter-American Court of Human Rights that would adjudicate and overcome the continental pessimism of the moral fortitude and impartiality of law tribunals. Nonetheless, few doubt that it would constitute a new element in the treatment of human rights issues and a step beyond the traditional claims of sovereignty made by governments in order to violate the fundamental dignity of its constituents without having external interference.

There has been progressive application of the concept, both in public opinion and international jurisprudence, that all signatory states to the Universal Declaration of Human Rights are formally obliged to respect the rights recognized therein. Therefore, one cannot accept violations as part of the discretionary and private domain in which each government manages its domestic affairs. To the degree that this thesis continues to gain legal, political, and moral acceptance, the defense of human rights will become easier and more fruitful.

Part of the lesson learned rests in understanding the permanent attention due the issue of human rights, rather than having a mere reaction whenever excesses manifest themselves. It is the moral duty of humanity to create the legal bodies, institutions, and organizations that constitute a framework for the dispute of potential violations. It is a matter of anticipating episodes of barbarism and creating barriers to block their occurrence before they can develop.

In the last analysis, the respect for human rights should be an integral part of all democratic education and all humanistic training. Its values and principles should be inculcated into all citizens as an integral element in their moral and cognitive preparation to confront life. Human rights should be as elemental for peaceful civic harmony as the respect for traffic regulations is for the principles of urban social life. Experience has shown that even the most solid democracies may have weak moments in which human rights are dramatically violated.

The international network of solidarity that defends human rights must engage itself in a permanent preventive campaign devoted to the creation of the legal framework in which all states are obligated by the international community to respect the fundamental rights of citizens. The world of tomorrow is too threatened to foresake caution and moderate pessimism to prevent the cruel and frequent repetition of surprise against which we are defenseless and respond much too slowly.

It is useful to adopt a classification and hierarchy of primary and secondary human rights. We must distinguish between those rights that depend upon the simple exercise of human will and those that involve structural limitations and rigidity; between those that correspond to the area of crime and human cruelty and those that stem from a relation to social injustice and underdevelopment.

It is not unusual to hear rhetoric to justify political assassination, torture, deportation, and the suppression of all social, political, and cultural liberties in the name of "development" and a more promising future. This logic is nothing more than another chapter of human abjection proffered by individuals at the altar of ideology and provisional power. Whether it be from the left or the right, because one hears both melodies, the issue of human rights cannot be reduced to that of underdevelopment. A poor peasant is not, and will never be, the same as one who has been shot or physically and psychologically destroyed by torture or in a concentration camp. They are both different magnitudes of a serious problem, but in the former case, the elimination of human suffering depends on simple human will, while the latter depends on complex mechanisms, the solution of which is, at best, technically ambiguous and controversial.

Underdevelopment and poverty adversely affect human rights and the full development of human potential. Yet they are at different levels than is the violation of the right to life, to freedom of conscience, and to more fundamental personal liberties. The subject undoubtedly has its theoretical complexity, but it has none whatsoever for those who have personally lived the tragedy of terrorism from above or terrorism from below. Nor can it have any for the realistic observer, despite the distinctions one may care to make between one case or another in defense of each's intellectual sophistication. Every individual pushed to the situation's limits can recognize the difference between the two phenomena. In Latin America we have witnessed the proof of this affirmation.

Neither can one accept, in light of historical experience, the "social" revolution as a synonym for the respect for human rights. The more than 60 years of socialism in the world, and the more than 20 in Latin America, disallow maintenance of such a gratuitous assertion. Rather, they facilitate a different conviction, especially in reference to recent episodes of the socialist world.

Human rights exist in the realm of concrete proof, and not in that of theoretical abstractions, especially when these are rather dogmatic. No power can be free of suspicion; more so if it exists in the name of future utopias that demonstrate a greater propensity to sacrifice human beings to the deities of power. All powers must be controlled in their temptation to establish absolute power. It is difficult to believe that the human rights movement hasn't learned this lesson well. The danger is no more distant each time a dictator falls. On the contrary, one must take advantage of democratic times to limit the potential power of future dictators as drastically as possible. Recent history in Latin America dispels the extremism and pessimism of such a proposition: We have already seen the impossible!

HUMAN RIGHTS: ARE THEY THE FOUNDATION
OF A NEW MINIMUM CONSENSUS?

Recent Latin American experience augurs a new continental hope: the possibility of building a minimum common denominator for political consensus that is able to transcend utopias and dogmatism, and that is based upon a foundation of human rights that crosscuts all ideological, partisan, denominational, cultural, and social lines. Everything must begin from this minimum.

Even when violations of human rights may be cited in terms of winners and losers within a single society, at the continental level, all the groups in the hemisphere know firsthand what losses these violations truly mean. In the Southern Cone, it is the left that has excessively suffered, while the center has been less intensely, yet sufficiently, affected for lessons to have been learned. And it is those on the right in Cuba, and, in terms of certain basic civil liberties, those in Peru during the early years of the military revolution there, who know what these violations represent.

Events in each country condition the attitudes of all groups within that society. But the world is no longer so parochial that experiences are not shared. It is logical that if a rightist is upset by Castroism, a leftist will equally concern himself with the rise of Pinochetism and Videlism. Until now it has been quite amusing to see the right deliriously militarist in Argentina, Chile, and Uruguay, yet profoundly antimilitarist in Peru and Panama; to see how the left can revile Solzhenitsyn and be captivated by Helder Camara while the right does just the opposite. However, this represents a definitive contradiction only to the extent that one side or the other invokes the same principles in defense of similar situations; they differ only in reference to geography and the political militancy of proponents.

A world that is not entirely insane would seek a rational solution to this misunderstanding. As the Chilean poet Nicanor Parra graciously would say, "The left and right united together will never meet defeat." In the field of human rights, this seems self-evident. What meaning can worldwide solidarities have for the defense of human rights if each individual cause seeks to resolve only its own humanitarian aims? What is the use of condemnation when the majority of the condemned in turn condemn others and fail to recognize their own infractions? Who is served when the double standard discourages the defenders of human rights and comforts the violators, permitting the latter to circumscribe their own errors with those of the former?

If we add here the failure of violence to establish stable political orders, human rights becomes the threshold of a new Latin American harmony. We find ourselves in an age in which even the most active minds reexamine all myths and dogmatism: the ideas of the French philosophers; Eurocommunism; the challenge of dissidents to the incommensurable powers of Eastern

Europe; a liberalism in the United States that has rejected the affectation of the cold war; and the moderate Social Democratic and Christian Democratic currents in Latin America that can maintain the limit of a possible democratic consensus. All of these factors begin with certain basic presumptions: that the occurrences of the past are without pardon or justification whatsoever; that the world needs innovative solutions; and that the past should not only not repeat itself, but must be contained by the shadow of past tragedy.

How can we not agree that crime, torture, terrorism, kidnapping, and all forms of violence against humanity must be eradicated in Latin America? Is not all advantage nothing more than a fleeting success to be interrupted at any moment by infamy? How can we not agree that we all lose as long as secret police forces replace parliamentarians or machine guns exercise the role of the ballot box? How can we not comprehend that any victory is relative and momentary, that what I now gain by blood is later lost by a comrade down the line?

The new Sandinist government in Nicaragua, to the extent that one can judge from the outside, has been an example of moderation and solidarity for the rest of Latin America. Any excess against human rights would have served as the indispensable justification for greater repression by dictators on the right. Any temptation toward Cuban-style reprisal would have been a tragedy for all democracies of the continent, despite the fact that such action would have been much more justified after the genocide committed by Somoza than under the reign of Castro. In the aftermath of Nicaragua, how can respect for human rights not be considered the minimum common denominator for any political experiment, and especially those spawned by most dramatic and tense circumstances?

It would be naivete to think of eradicating passion in a day. But it is not ingenuous to also consider the possibility of a broad coalition whose union would extend from the left to the right, from disbelievers to Christians to Marxists, and transcend social class. In Argentina, Brazil, Chile, and Uruguay, glimpses of such a potential coalition can be seen. It is more visible in Venezuela, Colombia, Costa Rica, Ecuador, and, now, Peru. Many are those who have profited from the lessons of the last decade and who, whatever their position on the political-ideological spectrum, have reexamined the causes of this continental tragedy. The achievement of this wide coalition that could foster a minimum consensus remains the greatest challenge to our societies for the future human rights movement.

THE NEW ROLE OF THE MILITARY

The lack of knowledge exhibited by Latin American society in regard to its own military is truly surprising. This could be explained, but not justified, in those countries with civil and democratic traditions where the armed forces were relegated to an institutional ghetto for decades. Yet it is hardly explicable in those countries in which the military has a long history of political intervention.

The truth is that the military avalanche of the 1970s caught everyone equally by surprise. The doctrine of national security, which took years of study and elaboration, was unknown in political and intellectual circles. No one suspected the use of counterinsurgency tactics in which officials were so carefully trained. The operative ability of a modern professional army was unknown even to those who had introduced concepts of war, strategy, and military logic into politics. Thus, no one knew the true extent of the thought, training, and capabilities of the professional military in a world of high technology and military organization. Despite historical influence in politics, the military was indeed still an unknown commodity.

We may each have a greater or lesser sympathy for the military profession, but no one can discount its existence; it must be recognized. If we do not wish to see the military as a force for the occupation of its own people, nor as immense factories for the violation of human rights, we must be ready to define an institutional role for the armed forces that is compatible with democracy and humanism.

This is an urgent challenge that is being met much too slowly. The human rights movement must accept this challenge as its own: Its work rests not only in the denunciation of present violations but in the prevention of future infractions. As long as close relations exist between the Latin American military and the Pentagon, this challenge also demands the thought and action of human rights groups in the United States. As long as military ideology remains incompatible with the fundamental dignity of man and the military continues to have a significant political role, meeting this challenge is impossible.

These reflections conclude on an optimistic note for human rights in Latin America during the 1980s. We cannot discard the possibility of gross violations in the future, but a massive moral conscience has developed, with a solid organizational base and active international solidarity. The defense of human rights is much stronger and more agile than it has ever been and thus serves to dissuade violators.

In the issue of human rights, Latin America can find a forceful starting point from which to build peaceful and civil coexistence, while controlling the pressures specific to socio-economic development. The defense of human dignity, too, is a forceful starting point for the construction of a new international order and serves as a basic inspiration for worldwide solidarity.

PART II
EQUITY AND DEVELOPMENT

4
PREDICTING INCOME DISTRIBUTION
IN LATIN AMERICA
DURING THE 1980s
Albert Berry

INTRODUCTION

Few topics are as important to the future of Latin America
as the evolution of its income distribution. With a history of
considerable political instability and with a notorious reputation
for extreme income inequality, the region could hardly look
forward to a tranquil decade were there not some signs of
greater economic justice in the making. While the relationship
between income inequality and sociopolitical turmoil is not a
simple one, there can be no doubt that inequality has played a
significant causal role in the recent Nicaraguan and Salvadorean
tragedies and in many earlier conflicts. And, of course, regardless of its political implications, inequality is particularly sad in
a continent whose average income levels are well above subsistence. In these "middle-income" developing countries, in most
of which the average per capita income in 1978 fell in the range
of U.S. $700 to $1,500,[1] serious poverty would not exist in
the absence of high levels of income inequality.[2] In Brazil, for
example, as of 1974-75, the top 10 percent of families had perhaps
52 percent of total income while the bottom 40 percent had only
about 8.5 percent, implying a differential of about twenty-five-
fold in favour of the former group.[3] Millions of persons will
continue to suffer avoidable malnutrition and deprivation if
income distribution does not improve. As of the 1970s, to further
cloud the picture, it was widely believed that inequality was
worsening in a number of Latin countries.

To assess the likelihood that the 1980s may witness an
improvement, it is necessary to identify the major determinants

of a country's income distribution. One possible classification distinguishes the distribution of productive assets (physical capital and land) and skills (human capital); the (pure) labour share of income;[4] government tax, transfer, and expenditure policies. In the early stages of a country's economic development, the major income-producing asset is land; later, physical capital and human capital become important, so access to capital and to education become important determinants of income distribution. In general, the higher the share of national income that accrues to pure labour (as defined above)—the part which is not a payment for a person's special skills or for the services of land or capital—the more equal will be the distribution of income. When an unskilled worker can earn an income not far below the average for the economy, the pure labour share is high, and the distribution of income is relatively equitable. Finally, the distribution of disposable income depends on the size and progressivity of the public-sector taxes, transfers, and expenditures.

In the early stages of development, the fiscal process tends to have rather little impact on income distribution, mainly due to the low tax burden.[5] At the same time, the pure labour share often goes down as the unskilled workers' wages remain constant or nearly so, while per capita income climbs. Under these conditions, distribution will tend to worsen unless the distribution of human and physical capital becomes more equal over time. Eventually, if the development process is successful, unskilled labour becomes scarce and its relative income rises, providing some grounds for optimism about trends in income distribution during the later stages of development. In fact, this event has been argued to be pivotal in income-distribution improvements witnessed in a number of developed and developing countries. We turn now to a brief review of the evidence underlying such optimism as exists with respect to distributional trends in the later stages of development.

THE OPTIMISTIC HYPOTHESIS: LABOUR SCARCITY AND DISTRIBUTIONAL IMPROVEMENTS

As early as the 1950s, Kuznets suggested that the process of development tended to be characterized by a worsening of income distribution followed by an improvement.[6] He contended that this pattern had characterized the evolution of many now-developed countries.[7] Subsequently, the pattern of income distribution across countries was observed to be consistent with this hypothesis in the sense that inequality tended to be highest in middle-income developing countries and lower both in poor countries and in developed countries,[8] the pattern illustrated in Figure 4.1. While, as the figure indicates, there is considerable variability of inequality among countries at a given income level, it is striking that at most, one of the developed countries, which we may, for present purposes, define as those with per capita income above U.S. $3,500 in 1978 or U.S. $1,500 in 1965, has a level of inequality nearly as bad as such typical (in this respect) Latin countries as Brazil, Mexico, Colombia, and Peru.[9]

Neither the overtime nor the cross-sectional evidence just cited constitutes proof that improvements in distribution are just around the corner in Latin America's middle-income developing countries, but such evidence obviously lends interest to the hypothesis. The cross-section evidence suggests that the income range involving the highest level of inequality is about U.S. $800-1,200 in 1978.[10] Meanwhile, the main countries whose incomes still fall in this range (or did not too long ago),[11] and

FIGURE 4.1. Country Scattergram: Per Capita GDP (1965) and the Gini Coefficient

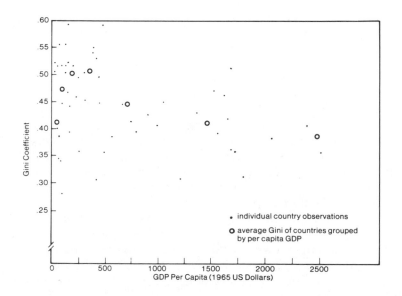

Source: F. Paukert, "Income Distribution at Different Levels of Development," International Labour Review, CVIII, Nos. 2-3, August-September 1973.

where there is reasonably persuasive evidence of recent improvements in the distribution of income are Japan and Taiwan. The
former case is more clear-cut; the improvement in distribution
seems to date from about 1960.[12] Since that time, real wages of
lower-income groups have risen rapidly and virtually all wage
differentials—by age, education, and occupation, for example—
have narrowed.[13] In Taiwan the improvement, coinciding with
a tightening of the labour market, dates from the late 1960s and
is less well established since income-distribution data are available for only a few years after the turning point was reached.[14]
There is no doubt, though, that real wages of realtively low-
skilled workers rose sharply after about 1968.

A major hypothesis used to explain and predict the improvement in income distribution subsequent to an earlier worsening
(and elaborated in detail for the cases of Japan and Taiwan)
involves the transition from a labour-surplus situation to one
of labour scarcity. Under labour surplus, the wage rate of
persons with few skills stays low and perhaps constant,[15] so
that the income of these people declines relative to the average.
When this labour becomes scarce, its wage rises, perhaps rapidly
(as in Japan). While many other factors might affect distribution
positively as a country develops, this one perhaps offers more
hope because of its being a result of market forces,[16] rather
than government policy. Most of the major government policies
one might expect to have beneficial effects on income distribution
are not potent enough to make a big impact. The histories of
Mexico and Bolivia belie the hope that significant land redistribution would be adequate by itself to generate a reasonably equitable distribution.[17] Other types of assets are even harder to
redistribute significantly. As mentioned earlier, it is unlikely
that fiscal policies will have a large effect. The presence of
unions and minimum-wage legislation falls in the same category.
A redistribution of educational opportunities (discussed below)
would have greater potential but is also politically difficult. A
judicious combination of these policies could have a major effect,
but the combination of political constraints (since the policies
would, in the main, work against the interests of the more powerful groups) and the rather sophisticated understanding needed
to design the policies will make it highly unlikely that governments of nonsocialist countries will take the steps needed to
bring about an equitable distribution in an essentially labour-
surplus economy.

The interpretation of the Japanese and Taiwanese cases is
complicated a little by the fact that each country had a thorough
land reform leading to an egalitarian agrarian structure. The

impacts of this change and of the arrival of labour scarcity are no doubt somewhat intermingled. Nevertheless, since the land reforms preceded the onset of labour shortage by a decade or more in each case, it seems unlikely that any lagged effects of agrarian reform on income-distribution trends could account directly for much of the post-labour-scarcity improvements.

IS THE END OF EXTREME INEQUALITY NEAR IN THE LATIN COUNTRIES?

Unqualified acceptance of the "worsening-then-bettering" hypothesis would lead one to be optimistic about coming trends in Latin America since countries like Mexico, Brazil, Venezuela, Uruguay, Chile, and Argentina have all reached the income range at which distribution should begin to improve. While many factors could play a role in such an improvement, the above discussion suggests that rising wages of unskilled workers and a tendency toward a more equal distribution of human capital are two of the more obvious possibilities. We now turn to a consideration of the likelihood that they will play this role in the near future in Latin America.

The data on overall income distribution in the Latin American countries point to no emerging tendency toward decreasing inequality, as of the early 1970s.[18] The most thorough study for Brazil, by Pfefferman and Webb, indicates that there was probably some worsening between 1960 and the mid-1970s,[19] though there is no evidence that this was occurring in the early 1970s and indeed some improvement probably occurred. In Colombia, where the data are less satisfactory, the level of inequality appears to have fluctuated over the decades, with no clear long-run trend. Over 1965-75, wage data suggest a decline in the relative position of the lower-income groups and, therefore, an overall worsening of distribution.[20] One factor in the probable worsening was the accelerating inflation of these years; so it remains to be seen whether, when the inflation ceased to accelerate in the later 1970s, distribution returned to its earlier level. Peru's distribution appeared to worsen somewhat over the earlier period 1950-66,[21] but no more recent detailed study has been undertaken. Comparable in-depth studies have not yet been undertaken for some of the other interesting cases, like Mexico[22] and Venezuela, but the weak evidence available leaves one with the general impression that the typical pattern involves fluctuations with no significant trends. As of the early 1970s, then, there was little to be optimistic about in the observable distributional trends in Latin America.

Latin America as a region has never been viewed as being one of labour surplus in the same sense as are the densely populated Asian countries. Nevertheless, the difference is more quantitative than qualitative, and there is no doubt that most Latin countries have had a relative abundance of unskilled labour, even if they do not fit all the characteristics of the Lewis labour-surplus model. The relevance of the labour-surplus model is suggested by the lack of a trend in various unskilled wage rates in countries like Brazil and Colombia. Pfefferman and Webb report that rural wages in Sao Paulo state indeed showed no trend between the late 1940s and the early 1970s;[23] rural wage data for Brazil as a whole do not go back far but are consistent with the Sao Paulo trends in recent years, as are unskilled-construction wages. In Colombia the agricultural and construction real wages showed little or no trend (though considerable fluctuation) from the mid-1930s to the early 1970s. In Mexico, although no systematic agricultural wage series are available, the loose evidence from income surveys and real minimum wages suggests little or no increase prior to sometime in the 1960s, possibly even decreases.

In each of these three countries, however, recent trends have been more positive. A dramatic turnaround occurred in Brazil, where between 1968 and 1977 the casual rural wage rate rose by 56 percent; in Sao Paulo state, it doubled over 1970-77. Although economic stagnation could lead to a falling back, the fact that such a dramatic increase could occur over a five- to ten-year period—time enough for considerable labour-supply response to occur were there still a large labour surplus—suggests that the surplus is turning into a scarcity and that a renewed growth in demand for labour would lead to a continued increase in these wages.

The picture in Colombia is similar, though the increase in the agricultural wage is less certain and probably smaller. After no more than a modest increase over a period of three decades prior to 1970,[24] there appears to have been an increase of 25-50 percent since 1969.[25] For unskilled construction workers, the pattern is somewhat similar, though with more fluctuations prior to 1970.[26] In any case, after a decline in real wages during the early 1970s—a decline common to all major groups of workers, it appears—this wage (for the four largest cities) rebounded to reach, in June 1980, a level 12 percent above the 1971 figure.[27] Over this period (1971 to June 1980), the wage differential between unskilled workers (ayudantes) and maestros decreased by over 10 percent, while the semiskilled workers' wages grew at a rate between those of the other two.[28]

Low-income wage earners are, of course, only one of the poor groups in Latin countries. The other (larger) one consists of small farmers. While their income level reflects the labour-supply situation less directly than does that of wage earners, it is not unrelated to it. Evidence from Brazil, Mexico, and Peru indicates that this group has achieved some income increases over the last few decades; in the former two cases, probably somewhere in the neighbourhood of 2 percent per year—significant but considerably less than the economy-wide increase in income per capita over the corresponding years.[29] In the case of Brazil, it appears that the income trends for this group have been similar to those for wage earners, and that rapid gains were made in the early 1970s.

The evidence on wages and on small-farmer incomes illustrates the fact that some of the benefits of growth have accrued to the lower-income groups in most or perhaps all Latin countries, but often the incomes of people toward the upper end of the distribution have risen faster. A change in this pattern could come from a narrowing of the income differentials across people with different levels of physical or human capital, or from a decrease in the inequality of distribution of these forms of capital. A rising unskilled wage rate, which could be due mainly to an increase in demand or a decrease in the relative supply of unskilled labour, is one source of narrowing income differentials. An increase in the relative supply of persons with higher skill and educational levels helps to decrease the relative supply of unskilled workers. The next section reviews some evidence on such changes and on the evolution of certain income differentials.

EVOLUTION OF THE EDUCATIONAL COMPOSITION
OF THE LABOUR FORCE IN LATIN AMERICA
AND OF INCOME DIFFERENTIALS

In all or virtually all countries, there is an increase in the average educational level of the labour force over time and, almost as certainly, an increase in some sort of average skill level. These trends contribute to total output growth. Whether human capital tends to become better or more poorly distributed as time goes on is much less clear.

A good indicator of the distribution of human capital is the distribution of education since, especially in urban areas, education is a major determinant of income levels. As of the late 1960s, the human-capital share of national income in Colombia was about one-third.[30] The income inequalities that result from a given composition of education and skills in the labour force depend also on the income differentials by education and skill level, so trends in these differentials are also very important. Data on recent trends in the educational composition of the labour force are available for most countries, whereas the skill composition is not. Income differentials over time, by level of education, are available in only a few cases.

The last two or three decades have seen very fast growth in the levels of education attained by school-age children in Latin America, as elsewhere in the developing world. Table 4.1 provides a rough indication of the speed and nature of this process. Note that the figures cannot be compared across countries since the same age groups were used as the denominators in all countries, even though the length of primary and secondary school varies across countries. Despite this and other deficiencies in the figures, they give an adequate picture of the direction of change within most of the countries. The expansion of primary school, likely to improve the distribution of human capital, has, as expected, been a good deal slower than that of secondary and higher education, which are likely to have the opposite effect. The heavy priority given to these levels in countries where primary is still not universal constitutes a source of continuing income inequality for the future.

For an assessment of the implications of educational trends for income distribution, we turn to individual country cases. In Brazil rough figures are available on income differentials by level of education, permitting illustrative experiments.[31] Over the period 1960-76, it seems probable that some decrease occurred.[32] Pfefferman's and Webb's revision of Langoni's estimates of income increases, by level of education, between the 1960 and 1970 population censuses (reproduced with one adjustment in Table 4.2) indicates no systematic relation between educational level and income increase, though the gains for persons with no education are the smallest.[33] The 1960-72 comparison suggests a narrowing of differentials, except that between no education and primary and possibly that between no education and junior high.[34] Though comparable data were not presented in the 1976 household survey,[35] Pfefferman and Webb note that over 1970-76, there was no widening of occupational differentials, though some had occurred in the 1960s, and suggest that this implies a falling premium by education levels, at least for the college level, for which there was evidence of occupational downgrading.[36]

No simple calculation can sort out the effects of educational expansion on income distribution. But it is of interest to measure

TABLE 4.1. Children Enrolled in School as a Percentage of the Relevant Age Group, 1960 and 1977, Latin American Countries

Country	Primary School		Secondary School		Higher Education	
	1960	1977	1960	1977	1960	1977
Honduras	67	89	8	13	1	6
Bolivia	64	80	12	26	4	10
El Salvador	80	77	13	22	1	8
Peru	83	110	15	52	4	16
Colombia	77	103	12	39	2	9
Ecuador	83	101	12	44	3	28
Guatemala	45	65	7	16	2	5
Mexico	80	116	11	39	3	10
Chile	109	117	24	50	4	13
Costa Rica	96	111	21	44	5	18
Brazil	95	90	11	24	2	12
Uruguay	111	95	37	60	8	13
Argentina	98	110	23	41	11	29
Venezuela	100	104	21	38	4	21

<u>Source</u>: World Bank, <u>World Development Report 1980</u> (Washington, D.C., 1980), pp. 154-55.

TABLE 4.2. Brazil: Income Increases by Level of Education, 1960-72, and Relative Incomes by Level of Education, 1960

Level of Education	Percent of Labour Force 1960	Percent of Labour Force 1972	Percent of Income, 1960-70[b]	Percent Increase, 1960-72	Relative Income, 1960[d]
None	42.5	32.0[c]	7	35	0.53
Primary	49.1	49.6[c]	19	62	1.00
Junior high	3.6	9.8	26	55	1.81
Senior high	3.4	5.6	11	43	2.93
College	1.3	3.1	27(22-34)[a]	41(35-48)[a]	6.51

[a]Range within which the figure in question is expected to lie.

[b]Based on a revision of calculations by C. Langoni, Distribucao (Rio de Janeiro: Editora Expressao e Cultura, 1973).

[c]Adjusted from the figures presented by the authors in an attempt to make the data conceptually consistent with those of 1960. The 1970 figure for "none" was 36.0 percent.

[d]Base is primary = 1; family helpers are excluded.

Source: Columns 2-5 are from G. Pfefferman and R. Webb, The Distribution of Income in Brazil, World Bank Staff Working Paper #356 (Washington, D.C., 1979), p. 41, except as noted. Column 6 is calculated from data in the same source.

the association of income inequality with educational inequality at different points in time; trends in this association would tell us something about the distributional effects of educational expansion were the effects of educational level on personal income unrelated to effects of other determinants (native skills, physical capital, etc.), were the composition of labour demand to remain unchanged over time, and were we to forget the cost side. If we assign to each individual, in both 1960 and 1972, the average income for persons at his/her educational level, the resulting level of (education-associated) inequality is reflected in Gini coefficients of .308 in 1960 and .351 in 1972.[37]

Were one to project the 1960-72 changes in educational composition of the labour force to 1985, say, and assume the same relative incomes as in 1972, the education-related inequality would correspond to a Gini coefficient of .399, representing a rapid increase in income inequality.38 Were income increases for each educational group to be those we used for the period 1960-72, this Gini coefficient would be .373. Evidently, an increase in the inequality associated with different levels of education would occur unless the incomes of persons without education and with primary education rose faster than in the case just considered, where the differentials closed only moderately between the primary and the higher levels, and where the income of persons without education grew less rapidly than the overall average. A more rapid narrowing might, of course, be predicted if the system were reaching a sort of unskilled labour-scarcity situation, as suggested by the agricultural-wage movements of the early 1970s. For example, if instead of the income gains for 1960-72 shown in column 2 of Table 4.3, those of column 3 were to prevail, then the level of inequality associated with education differences would in 1985 be reflected in a Gini coefficient of .327, i.e., about the same as that for 1972. The figures of column 3 for the low-education groups are not implausible in the light of the rapid growth of agricultural wages in the early 1970s, but they do nevertheless reflect a rapid narrowing of differentials and probably an optimistic prediction. While changes in the educational composition of the labour force and in income differentials could thus at least cease to be a factor pushing toward greater inequality, it is evident that a rapid increase in the wages of persons with little education is not a sufficient condition for an improvement in distribution since the

TABLE 4.3. Brazil: Observed Income Increase for 1960-72, by Level of Education, and Assumed Increase for 1972-85

Education	Observed Increase, 1960-72	Assumed Increase, 1972-85
None	45%	100%
Primary	65	80
Junior high	55	55
Senior high	43	43
College	41	29

Source: For column 2, the data of Table 4.2, adjusted. Column 3 is presented as an optimistic assumption.

educational levels of the top quintiles of the income distribution
are rising rapidly.

It must be reemphasized that these calculations do not
measure the effects of educational expansion on income distribution, but simply indicate the degree of association of income
inequality with educational inequality at different points in time.
Nor do they take into account the possible distributional benefits
of other phenomena that might occur at the stage of development
of a country like Brazil, e.g., an increase in the labour share,
and a more progressive tax, transfer, and expenditure system.
Nevertheless, educational level does appear to be a quite important determinant of distribution (however defined), so other
factors would probably have to be quite positive for a substantial
improvement to occur.

The experience of Colombia, where the role of education
as a determinant of income distribution has also received a good
deal of study, is in many respects similar. The education composition of the labour force in 1971 (see Table 4.4) was rather
similar to that of Brazil in 1972, but characterized by less inequality; a slightly smaller share had a college education (2.7
percent versus 3.1 percent), while many fewer had no education
(19.6 percent versus about 32 percent). The income differentials by level of education are also probably a little less extreme
than in Brazil.[39] The available evidence, though less complete
than for Brazil, suggests a narrowing of income differentials,
by level of education, over the decade from the mid-1960s to
the mid-1970s, possibly a sharp one. In Bogota the ratio of
earnings of university-trained males to those of males with no
education fell from 11.5 in 1963-66 (Selowsky's study) to 6.57
in 1977 (Mohan's study).[40] The ratios are not monotonically
declining for all pairs of educational levels, but there is a general
pattern of narrowing between the two years. Since, however,
it results entirely from the presence of the high 1963-66 differentials from Selowsky's study, corroboration from other sources
would be very desirable.[41]

If we perform the same experiment as for Brazil, we find
that with the income differentials just cited for 1973 and the
1971 educational composition of the labour force, the amount of
education-related inequality is measured by a Gini coefficient
of .305. With the same income differentials, the 1978 educational
composition would imply an education-related Gini of .35. If the
relative income (base: no education) had moved to 1.5 for primary
education, 3.2 for secondary, and 9.0 for university, then the
education-related Gini would have been .311, i.e., about the
same as in 1971. Since some of the evidence suggests a faster

TABLE 4.4. Educational Composition of the Labour Force, Colombia, Selected Years, and Income Differentials, 1973

Education	1951	1964	1970	1971	1973	1978	Relative Income 1973
None	41.03%	26.37%	18.41%	19.63%	16.78%	16.30%	.621
Primary	49.74	60.60	59.14	59.58	55.61	54.91	1.00
Secondary*	8.33	11.64	19.56	18.13	23.34	24.04	2.38
Higher	0.90	1.39	2.89	2.66	4.27	4.75	7.03
Total							1.515

*Includes "other," which is relatively small, and "normal." In the 1964 census, "other" and secondary other than bachillerato (i.e., technical, etc.) were lumped together with "no education." On the basis of the occupational breakdown of persons with no education or "other, including non-bachillerato secondary," we estimated 130,000 fell in the latter category. This would constitute a participation rate of 45.6 percent for this group, perhaps not implausibly high, given their presumed youth.

Source: The 1951 figures are from Departamento Administrativo Nacional de Estadísticas (DANE), Censo de Población de Colombia: Resumen (Bogota, n.d.), pp. 132-33. The 1964 figures are from DANE, XIII Censo Nacional de Población: Resumen General (Bogota: Imprenta Nacional de Colombia, 1967), p. 115. Since in this source "other" levels were not distinguished from persons without education, we had to make the adjustment described above. The 1970 figures were calculated by the author on the basis of data presented in DANE, Boletín Mensual de Estadística #237, p. 81. The 1971 figures are an average across samples taken in March-April and November-December of that year and are from DANE's Encuesta Nacional de Hogares, Etapas 3,4,y 5, Fuerza de Trabajo (Bogota: DANE, 1976), p. 68 and p. 386. They refer only to employed persons, as do the other sources except the 1964 census, which includes the unemployed, 4.9 percent of the labour force. The 1973 data are based on figures presented in Gary S. Fields and T. Paul Schultz, "Sources of Income Variation in Colombia: Personal and Regional Effects," Yale Economic Growth Center Discussion Paper #262 (New Haven), p. 10, which correspond to a 4 percent sample of the 1973 population census.

narrowing than this over the period 1963-66 to 1977,[42] it is
possible that the combined effects of changing educational composition of the labour force and narrowing differentials had a
positive effect on income distribution. But the evidence is still
scattered and ambiguous, so no firm conclusion can be reached
at this point. Were both effects to continue through 1990 at
about the same intensity as just assumed for 1971-78, the
education-related Gini would remain roughly unchanged.[43] A
very marked narrowing of differentials would have to occur for
the coefficient to fall by, say, .03 or .04.[44]

POSSIBLE RELEVANCE OF THE ASIAN
SUCCESS STORIES?

Judging by their past, one cannot be too optimistic that
the Latin countries will use fiscal tools as a major redistributive
device in the 1980s. Equally unlikely is a sophisticated battery
of policies of various types whose overall redistributive impact
is significant, even though no single item has a large effect.[45]
One is pushed toward the conclusion that the major source of
distributional improvements is more likely to lie in market forces
than in public policy. The labour-surplus model suggests a
possible improvement when the economy reaches the stage of
labour scarcity, and some evidence (especially agricultural-wage
trends) in Brazil and Colombia indicates that they may be entering this stage. Were the labour force reasonably homogeneous,
this factor might be expected to have a clear positive effect on
distribution. But the rapid buildup of human capital via education, and its tendency to become less equally distributed over
time in countries like these, would be countervailing forces
unless income differentials by educational level narrowed substantially. In both Brazil and Colombia the evidence does suggest
such a narrowing, but occurring only about fast enough to prevent the degree of income inequality associated with the inequality
of education and hence to remain roughly constant. Since education is such an important correlate of income differences across
earners, one possibly important area of public policy involves
the government's role in determining the distribution of education
and the education-related income differentials. Generous funding
for public education at the primary levels, in the rural areas,
instead of at the university level, for example, could be important, as could maintenance of reasonably equal access to the
higher levels for children from low-income families. Public
policy may affect the income premium for higher levels of educa-

tion by legislating educational requirements for certain jobs, by
setting the government-pay structure itself, and in a variety of
other ways. Once again the prospect is certainly not for dramatic
policy changes. As a result, the significant distributional improvement to which the arrival of labour scarcity might contribute
is unlikely to be achieved.

Before reaching this somewhat pessimistic judgment, it is
useful to study the educational evolution of Japan and Taiwan,
two countries that achieved distributional improvements after
the end of the labour-surplus stage was reached. Both have
relatively egalitarian educational structures, and a rapid rise
in educational achievement in each case has been associated with
their rapid economic growth.[46] In 1977 Taiwan, with a per capita
income similar to that of Brazil, had the same enrollment in higher
education (12 percent of the relevant age group) but ranked far
higher in secondary (76 percent versus 24 percent) and had
complete primary schooling (see Table 4.5). Compared to typical
enrollment ratios, those of Japan, Taiwan, and Korea (included
for further comparison) stand strikingly high at the secondary
level, but only about normal at the higher level. In 1977 their
primary coverage was virtually complete,[47] and in 1960 it was
well above predicted (i.e., typical) levels. The most striking
difference with Colombia and Brazil in 1977 is the lower ratio
of higher-to-secondary enrollment, given the income levels;
Colombia was at the predicted level and Brazil far above it. The
evolution of educational structure in Brazil over 1960-77 was
toward a quite atypical amount of higher education relative to
the other two levels; the three Asian countries were atypical
in the other direction both in 1960 and in 1977.

The more equitable distribution of recent education flows
in the three Asian countries is paralleled by a more equal distribution of the stock of education in the labour force only in
the case of Japan (see Table 4.6). There, as of 1950, for
example, when about 5 percent of the labour force had a junior
college or university education, less than 3 percent had no
education[48] (as contrasted with 16 percent in Colombia in 1978).
Interestingly, the low share of workers with higher education,
relative to those at the other levels, was not manifested in large
income differentials by level of education—rather, the opposite.
In 1954, for males over 25, the relative wage of those with
university education, vis-à-vis those with primary, was only
1.7; by 1969 it had fallen to 1.4.[49] In both Taiwan and Korea
the educational structure of the labour force has been similar
to that in Brazil and more unequal than that in Colombia. The
Taiwan and Korean cases are striking in that the educational-

TABLE 4.5. School-Enrollment Ratios for Selected Latin American and Asian Countries

| Country | Per Capita Income, 1978 (U.S. $) | | Enrollment Ratios | | | | | | | |
| | 1960 | 1978 | Primary | | Secondary | | Higher | | Higher/Secondary | |
			1960	1977	1960	1977	1960	1977	1960	1977
Korea—actual	349	1,160	94	111	27	88	5	11	.19	.13
predicted			65	98	15.2	39.4	2.8	10.4	.18	.26
Taiwan—actual	443	1,400	95	100	33	76	4	12	.12	.16
predicted			70	98	15.8	41	3.2	11.6	.20	.28
Japan—actual	1,948	7,280	103	100	74	93	10	29	.14	.31
predicted			93	100	35.6	81.6	8.8	31.4	.25	.38
Colombia—actual	500	850	77	103	12	39	2	9	.17	.23
predicted			73	98	16.1	34	3.4	8.3	.21	.24
Brazil—actual	664	1,570	95	90	11	24	2	12	.18	.50
predicted			81	98	17	42.2	4	12.2	.24	.29

Source and Methodology: Data are from World Bank, World Development Report, 1980, Tables 1 and 23. Predicted values are based on the typical enrollment ratios for a country's income level, which are based on a simple linear interpolation made between the average income-enrollment combinations characterizing the three broad groups of nonsocialist countries into which the World Bank divides countries in the cited source. The points made in the text are quite robust vis-à-vis the precise way in which one estimates these predicted enrollment ratios.

TABLE 4.6. Educational Composition of the Labour Force,
Selected Years: Korea, Taiwan, Japan, Brazil, and Colombia

Country/Year	None	Primary	Secondary	Higher
Korea—1960	45.5%	39.4%	13.4%	2.4%
Colombia—1951	41.0	49.7	8.3	0.9
Brazil—1960	42.5	49.1	7.0	1.3
Brazil—1972	32.0	49.6	15.4	3.1
Colombia—1964	26.4	60.6	11.6	1.4
Taiwan—1965	26.0	54.3	16.5	3.1
Korea—1970	23.8	43.7	26.5	6.2
Colombia—1978	16.3	54.9	24.0	4.8
Taiwan—1975	15.9	47.9	30.1	6.1
Korea—1975	18.0	44.2	31.5	6.3
Japan—1950	2.9	26.9	65.6	4.6
—1970	0.4	8.6	80.4	10.6

Source: Data for Brazil and Colombia are from Tables 4.2
and 4.4, respectively. For Korea, 1960 and 1970, Parvez Hasan
and D. C. Rao, Korea: Policy Issues for Long-Term Development,
Report of a World Bank Mission (Baltimore, Johns Hopkins University Press, 1979), pp. 1545. For 1975, data are estimated on
the basis of D. Snodgrass et al., Education and the Modernization
of the Republic of Korea 1945-75, Korea Development Institute,
Working Paper No. 7806, p. 131. Data for Japan, from Patrick
and Rosovsky, Asia's New Giant (Washington, D.C.: The Brookings Institution, 1976), p. 115; for Taiwan, Walter Galenson,
"The Labour Force, Wages, and Living Standards," in Walter
Galenson (ed.), Economic Growth and Structural Change in
Taiwan, p. 396.

stock (Table 4.6) and educational-flow (Table 4.5) figures could
only be consistent if the ratio of university to secondary enroll-
ments had fallen over time—i.e., if an unusual equalization of
educational opportunity had occurred.[50]
    In Taiwan as of 1966, the earnings gap was far larger than
in Japan—workers with university training in Taiwan averaged
4.2 times as much as workers with primary[51]—but still nothing
like the Brazilian and Colombian figures, both above 6.5 times
higher. Data for 1976 from a different source indicate a much

lower differential of only 1.73; even if the two sets of data are somewhat noncomparable, the suggestion is that of a clear decline in differentials,[52] especially between junior high school and primary. In Korea the higher-to-primary earnings ratio was estimated at only 2.65 in the early 1960s.[53] Regardless of its subsequent trend, this suggests the same stark contrast with the Latin countries under discussion.

The comparison of Latin countries with these Asian success stories is exploratory, and only with more refined analysis and inclusion of other countries could the differences be meaningfully interpreted. Of particular interest is the fact that the distribution of the stock of capital based on education, once as unequal in Korea and Taiwan as in Brazil or Colombia, became more equal or became less equal at a surprisingly slow rate,[54] compared to the Latin countries, where higher education has grown considerably faster than secondary. Was this fact a source of the superior income-distribution trends in these countries relative to Latin America, was it in part a result of independent impulses toward more equal distribution (e.g., the land reforms), and how hard is it to replicate? Can the distribution of new educational capital be markedly affected, for example, by changing the structure of public subsidies to education? Do the smaller income differentials by education in Korea and Taiwan, for a similar educational composition of the labour force and income levels, as in Brazil, for example, reflect differences in economic structure, or do they imply important credentialist or noneconomic components of the wide differentials observed in countries like Brazil?

A sharp increase in the labour share of national income, if it resulted from the coming of labour scarcity, would be an additional force for equality, but its probable extent is not clear. In Japan, where the end of labour surplus is usually dated at around 1960,[55] there was an increase in the labour share, following a decline in the 1950s, but it was not permanent. The share fell from 78.9 percent in 1952-54 to a postwar low of 72.1 percent in 1960-62, then rose to 75.4 percent in 1964-66, but was back down to 71.9 percent in 1968-70.[56] In Taiwan, the labour share appears to have risen since 1950, but two available sources of data, the national accounts and the household surveys, provide conflicting evidence on the extent of increase just after the onset of labour scarcity in the late 1960s. According to the former source, the increase was from 61.2 percent in 1952 to 65.9 percent in 1968 and only on up to 67.0 percent during the 1968-72 period, just after labour scarcity arose,[57] while the latter showed a small increase of 61.8 to 63.1 percent from 1964 to 1968, but a sharp one, to 68.1 percent, by 1972.[58] Probably the latter source is the more reliable. In Korea, where the period of dramatic growth began in the mid 1969s, the real agricultural wage shot up in the late 1960s, reaching nearly 60 percent above its 1968 level in 1973, before slipping the next year.[59] As in Japan, there was an increase in the labour share, from 31.2 percent in 1963 to a peak of 39.0 percent in 1970-71, before it dropped to 36.8 percent in 1974.[60]

CONCLUSION

Perhaps the only two plausible hopes for a marked improvement in the income distribution of Latin American countries in a reasonable period (e.g., 10-20 years) are a tightening of the unskilled-labour market and a better distribution of human capital based on education. There are grounds for optimism on the former count but it is hard to see how, by itself, it could substantially reduce inequality of labour income;[61] with existing trends in the educational composition of the labour force, it would have to be accompanied by a general and substantial narrowing of education-income differentials,[62] and/or an increase in the labour share of income. The experiences of Japan, Taiwan, and Korea suggest that some increase in the labour share can be expected as labour surplus ends, but it is not clear whether it would typically be big enough to affect overall income distribution much.

As the possible source of distributional improvements most directly affected by public policy, an equalizing of educational opportunity could clearly be important, as could a rapid narrowing of income differentials by education. Since the combined effect of changing educational composition of the labour force and changing differentials seems to have been to increase inequality in Brazil and perhaps in Colombia, an alteration of past trends would have to occur. The likelihood of continued narrowing of differentials is high, and if strong enough, this phenomenon could produce a considerable improvement in distribution; but pending a better understanding of the determinants of income differentials, such a prediction would be on the optimistic side. The most likely event, as Latin countries reach the present income range of Brazil, Uruguay, etc., is a moderate improvement in the trend of inequality (probably negative in some countries at present), but seldom a strong enough shift in that trend as to imply important absolute inequality reduction.

NOTES

1. National currency values are converted to U.S. dollars at the official exchange rate. The average income of Latin America as a whole was around U.S. $1,400 in 1978.
2. This is as distinct from very poor countries where even a quite equal distribution of income would leave many people in poverty.
3. Guy Pfefferman and Richard Webb, The Distribution of Income in Brazil, World Bank Staff Working Paper #356 (Washington, D.C., 1979), p. 10.
4. That is, that share of income that can be thought of as accruing to the very basic skills a labour force has with very little education or on-the-job training. It is estimated by attributing to all workers the income of those with few skills and comparing the figure with total national income.
5. Morrisson has reviewed evidence on the effects of fiscal activities in several developing countries, concluding that the median reduction in the Gini coefficient is around 0.03. Christian Morrisson, "Les Consequences Sur La Redistribution De Choix Publics, Selon le Developpement Des Economies," in Karl W. Roskamp (ed.), Public Choice and Public Finance, Proceedings of the 34th Congress of the IIPT, Hamburg, 1978.

In the case of Colombia, Berry and Soligo, reviewing primary studies of fiscal incidence, conclude that the tax side of the budget probably lowers the Gini coefficient by .02 to .03 and the combined effects of both sides of the budget by .03 to .05. A. Berry and R. Soligo, "The Distribution of Income in Colombia: An Overview," in A. Berry and R. Soligo, Economic Policy and Income Distribution in Colombia (Boulder, Colo.: Westview Press, 1980), p. 24 and p. 28).

With respect to the tax side, and referring to Latin America as a whole, Bird and De Wulf observe:

> Probably few will disagree with the proposition that
> taxation in most Latin American countries appears to
> have done little to correct this initial inequality,
> both because of its relatively light burden in total
> in most countries, and, more specifically, because of
> the apparent regressive or proportional nature of its
> incidence. We, too, do not disagree with what we
> take to be the major message of this line of argument—
> that taxes have done and can do little to correct the
> distribution of incomes generated by the combination
> of imperfect markets and myriad interventionist policies

that characterizes most Latin American countries. But we think the argument is both too optimistic in assuming that we know or can know what the burden of taxes is and, perhaps, although of this we are less certain, too pessimistic in ignoring the potential distributional effect of certain kinds of taxes in reducing the income, wealth and power of the rich.

Richard Bird and Luc De Wulf, "Tax Incidence and Income Distribution in Latin America: A Critical Review of Empirical Studies," IMF Staff Papers, Vol. 20 (Washington, D.C.: International Monetary Fund, 1973).

6. S. Kuznets, "Economic Growth and Income Inequality," American Economic Review, Vol. 45, No. 1, March 1955.

7. S. Kuznets, "Quantitative Aspects of the Growth of Nations: VIII, Distribution of Income by Size," Economic Development and Cultural Change, Vol. 11, No. 2, 1963.

8. See, for example, F. Paukert, "Income Distribution at Different Levels of Development: A Survey of Evidence," International Labour Review, CVIII, Nos. 2-3, August-September 1973.

9. For rough data on income distribution by country, see World Bank, World Development Report 1980 (Washington, D.C., 1980), Table 24. The possible exception to this rule is France, but the Gini coefficient used by Paukert (.50) is too high judging by more recent evidence.

10. A rough estimate based on the calculations in M. Ahluwalia, "Inequality, Poverty, and Development," Journal of Development Economics, 1976, No. 3, p. 311. Ahluwalia estimates, with two different sets of countries, the "turning point" for the income share of the bottom 60 percent, 40 percent, and 20 percent, finding the turning point to be higher for the poorer groups selected. Our concern here would be with the bottom 40 percent or the bottom 20 percent. The figure U.S. $800-1,200 is very approximate since Ahluwalia's regressions (and other studies) refer to early periods and the regressions might turn out somewhat differently now.

11. And excepting the oil countries like Libya, Saudi Arabia, and Kuwait, with their unusual economic structure.

12. Toshiyuki Mizoguchi, "The Distribution of Household Income in Post War Japan," in Income Distribution, Employment, and Economic Development in Southeast and East Asia, papers and proceedings of the seminar sponsored jointly by the Japan Economic Research Council and the Council for Asian Manpower Studies, Vol. II, 1975, p. 473. There was an improvement just

after the war due to destruction of physical capital and other war-related factors, and a mild worsening in the late 1950s. The improvement which seems related to the stage of development is the one beginning around 1960.

13. Hugh Patrick and Henry Rosovsky (eds.), Asia's New Giant: How the Japanese Economy Works (Washington, D.C.: The Brookings Institution, 1976), p. 35.

14. A detailed discussion of the Taiwanese case is presented in John C. H. Fei, Gustav Ranis, and Shirley W. Y. Kuo, Growth with Equity: The Taiwan Case (New York: Oxford University Press, 1979).

15. See, for example, John C. H. Fei and Gustav Ranis, "The Theory of Economic Development," American Economic Review, Vol. I, No. 4, September 1961.

16. The government does of course affect how the market works, and the fostering of capital-intensive technologies or pronatalist policies, for example, would delay the arrival of labour scarcity.

17. In both countries, a significant amount of land was redistributed to a significant number of families, but both still suffer a very unequal distribution of income.

18. Because of lags in the availability of data needed for the analysis of income-distribution trends, it is not yet possible to say much of interest about the late 1970s.

19. Pfefferman and Webb, The Distribution, p. 10. Weaknesses and noncomparability of the data corresponding to different points in time make it impossible to be sure that distribution worsened, as the authors amply demonstrate.

20. Albert Berry and Ronald Soligo (eds.), Economic Policy and Income Distribution in Colombia, pp. 15-16.

21. Richard Webb, "Government Policy and the Distribution of Income in Peru, 1963-1973," in Abraham Lowenthal (ed.), The Peruvian Experiment, Continuity and Change under Military Rule (Princeton: Princeton University Press, 1975).

22. Joel Bergsman's recent study, Income Distribution and Poverty in Mexico, World Bank Staff Working Paper #395, June 1980, suggests some worsening since 1950 but the Mexican data are particularly problematic.

23. Pfefferman and Webb, The Distribution.

24. A. Berry, "Rural Poverty in Twentieth Century Colombia," Journal of Inter-American Studies and World Affairs, Vol. 20, No. 4, November 1978, p. 364.

25. The evidence is somewhat ambiguous since what would normally be the main source, wage data compiled by the Departamento Administrativo Nacional de Estadísticas (DANE), as reported

from the various municipalities, was interrupted between 1970 and 1976, and it is not clear yet whether the new series is fully consistent with the old one. If it is, the increase in the "mean" wage for 1969-80 was about 48 percent, or 3.9 percent per year. Between 1976 and the first semester of 1980, there was an increase of 24.5 percent based on the presumably consistent series beginning in 1976. The Colombian Social Security Institute (ICSS) also provides wage data for persons covered; without adjustments, these indicate an increase in the median agricultural wage of 14 percent for 1969-78. But coverage almost doubled over these years, and it seems certain that the average wage of the newly covered workers was below that of those covered earlier. If this differential were 20 percent and everyone's wage rose by the same percent, the increase would be 26 percent. In using this source, however, one would also have to allow for possible differences in the trends of covered and noncovered workers, on which we have no good information.

26. See A. Berry, "Changing Income Distribution Under Development: Colombia," Review of Income and Wealth, Income and Wealth Series 20, No. 3, September 1974, p. 294.

27. Calculations are by the author on the basis of data presented in DANE, Boletin Mensual de Estadistica, various issues.

28. Calculations are taken by the author from DANE, Boletin, #341, and Boletin #348, for the four largest cities.

29. See A. Berry, "Agrarian Structure, Rural Labour Markets and Trends in Rural Incomes in Latin America" (Paper presented at the International Economics Association meetings, Mexico City, August 1980).

30. Berry, "Changing Income Distribution," p. 312.

31. Pfefferman and Webb, The Distribution, p. 41, present income data by level of education for 1960, 1970, and 1972. The data refer to all income (not just that from work). There was serious underreporting of income in the sources, plus a number of other difficulties discussed in detail by these authors.

32. This is a surprising conclusion in the light of the rather general conclusion that the opposite was the case during the 1960s: e.g., Carlos Langoni, Distribuçao da Renda E Desenvolvimiento Economico do Brasil (Rio de Janeiro: Editora Expressao e Cultura, 1973). Pfefferman and Webb identify a variety of methodological errors that led to an exaggerated view of any widening that may have occurred in the 1960s.

33. Some upward bias is present in the estimated gains for other categories, since the average years of school presumably tend to rise within each category, leading to a greater increase

for a broad category like college than would emerge for the typical year of college, e.g., for year 2.

34. Because of a change of definition of the categories
"no education" and "primary" between the 1970 and 1972 sources,
the 1960-72 income growth for both categories is probably downward biased (Pfefferman and Webb, The Distribution, p. 44).
Allowing for this, and for the upward bias noted above for all
other levels relative to the no-education group, leaves the impression that the percent-income gains were generally negatively
related to level of schooling, except that the no-education group's
income grew less than that of persons with primary and, possibly
(though not likely), than that of persons with junior high. The
figures are subject to many reservations, of course, and at best
create a probability as to what really happened. Cash incomes
were better reported in 1972 (Pfefferman and Webb, The Distribution, p. 45), which could create a bias either way. And
the implications of the inclusion of nonlabour income and a
general underreporting of total income by 40-45 percent are
not at all clear.

35. Fundacao Instituto Brasileiro de Geografia e Estadistica
(IBGE), Pesquisa Nacional Por Amostra De Domicilios—1976, Vol.
1, Tomo 8 (Rio de Janeiro: IBGE, 1978).

36. Pfefferman and Webb, The Distribution, p. 45. More
college-educated persons were beginning to be found in lower-
income occupations than before.

37. For the benchmark calculation in 1972, we assume,
between 1960 and 1972, a growth of income, for persons with
no education, of 45 percent and, for persons with primary, of
65 percent, both probably conservative in the light of the biases
present in the figures of Table 4.2, as discussed in notes 33
and 34. But plausibly higher figures for these two categories
would not reverse the conclusion that the educational structure
of the labour force was pushing the distribution of income toward
inequality. The figures understate the amount of inequality
associated with education, since the educational categories are
very broad, so some covariance within these broad categories
is missed; and no account is taken of the variance of income
that occurs with educational quality.

38. Such a projection is necessarily arbitrary in many of
its elements. We have assumed the following 1986 distribution
of the labour force by level of education: none, 17 percent;
primary, 43.1 percent; junior high, 20.9 percent; senior high,
10.6 percent; college, 8.4 percent.

39. These two countries appear rather typical of Latin
America in this regard. Psacharopoulos reports income ratios,

between persons with higher education and those with no education, of 10.46 for Mexico and 7.41 for Chile. (George Psacharopoulos, Returns to Education (San Francisco: Jossey-Bass, 1973), p. 185.

The 1973 population-census data indicate ratios of 11.3 and 3.83 between persons with higher and secondary education, respectively, and those with none. The corresponding ratios in Brazil as of 1970 were 15.6 and 6.14, though in 1972, with the persons in the bottom category being illiterates rather than those with no education, and thus a smaller and presumably lower-income group, the ratios were 12.9 and 5.87; with no education as the bottom category, both ratios would presumably have been less, so it is not entirely clear that the income differentials are less in Colombia, although it seems likely. These ratios are, in any case, very sensitive to the sex and age composition of the labour force and to adequacy of income reporting for such groups as domestic servants. Analysis of trends in the ratios is even more problematic.

40. These and several intervening studies are discussed in F. Bourguignon, "The Role of Education in the Urban Labor-Market During the Process of Development: The Case of Colombia," Document No. 27, Laboratoire d'Economique Politique, Ecole Normale Superieure, 1979, p. 6.

41. Other data on income differentials by education exist but seldom for comparable groups at two points in time. Between a 1967 Centro de Estudios sobre Desarrollo Económico (CEDE) survey (eight cities) and a 1975 DANE survey in seven cities, the differentials for males and females together narrowed sharply. The 1967 differentials for males were far below those for males and females together, but above those for males and females together in 1975. The relevant indices were as follows:

Level of Education	1967		1975
	Both Sexes	Males	Both Sexes
None	1.00	1.00	1.00
Primary	2.44	1.57	1.39
Secondary	4.91	2.86	2.69
University	13.65	7.87	6.77

The 1967 figures are open to some questions since the source (International Labour Office, Towards Full Employment [Geneva: ILO, 1979], p. 373) does not indicate the methodology—e.g., whether they were calculated as a weighed or an unweighted average of the data for the eight cities in the CEDE survey on which they were based. The 1975 figure has, surprisingly, lower differentials than for Bogota alone. The former is based on the data presented in F. Bourguignon, "Pobreza y Dualismo en el Sector Urbano de las Economias en Desarrollo: El caso de Colombia," Desarrollo y Sociedad, No. 1, January 1979, p. 54. Although further work will be required to demonstrate conclusively that a narrowing has occurred, the evidence presently available makes this likely.

42. See Bourguignon, "The Role of Education," p. 6.

43. With an educational composition of 10.6 percent with none, 46.9 percent with primary, 34.2 percent with secondary, and 8.3 percent with university, and differentials, relative to no education, of 1.4 for primary, 2.9 for secondary, and 7.5 for university, the education-related Gini coefficient would be .318. These figures represent a somewhat slower narrowing of differentials than do those for the 1971-78 period.

44. If the differentials vis-à-vis no education were: primary, 1.3; secondary, 2.5; and university 5.5, the resulting Gini would be .272. This is not impossible but is unlikely. The higher/primary ratio would then be 4.23, still of course far above the ratio observed in developed countries—the average across the United Kingdom, the United States, Canada, the Netherlands, and Norway, as of the 1960s, was 2.36 (Psacharopoulos, Returns to Education, p. 185). It would also be above the 1973 Sri Lanka figure (3.43), and above the ratios observed in such other Asian countries as Taiwan, Korea, and the Philippines. The narrowing of differentials would be of comparable magnitude to that which occurred in Sri Lanka in 1963-72, according to data reported in Peter Richards, Education and Income Distribution in Asia: A Preliminary Analysis, ILO, World Employment Programme Research Working Paper (Geneva, 1977), p. 34.

45. It seems possible that a varied but consistent and well-executed set of policies might reduce inequality significantly without triggering enough political opposition to be brought down. But this is an unlikely scenario in most countries.

46. Although the trend in income distribution is not so clear, Korea may be added to this group in that it is a country with a relatively low level of inequality together with rapid growth.

47. The figures are not precise for this level; those above 100 percent reflect some combination of extensive repeating, overreporting of enrollment, and underestimation of the size of the relevant age group.

48. See Edward F. Denison and William K. Chung, "Economic Growth and its Sources," in Hugh Patrick and Henry Rosovsky, Asia's New Giant: How the Japanese Economy Works (Washington, D.C.: The Brookings Institution, 1976), p. 110.

49. T. Watanabe, "Improvement of Labour Quality and Economic Growth: Japan's Postwar Experience," Economic Development and Cultural Change, Vol. 21, No. 1, October 1972, p. 39.

50. In Korea secondary enrollment had, by 1975, risen to 3.63 times its 1960 level while tertiary enrollment had risen to only 2.94 times its 1960 level; this was a reversal of the trend during the 1960s. See Parvez Hasan and D. C. Rao, Korea: Policy Issues for Long-Term Development (Baltimore: Johns Hopkins University Press, 1979), p. 151.

51. Fei, Ranis, and Kuo, Growth with Equity, p. 134.

52. W. Galenson, "The Labour Force," pp. 417-18. His source was Economic Planning Council, "Taiwan Regional Manpower Utilization Survey Report," Table 4.1. Fei et al. used the 1966 Report on The Survey of Family Income and Expenditure of the Directorate General of Budget, Accounting and Statistics.

53. Datum cited in Psacharopoulos, Returns to Education, p. 185.

54. It depends on how that stock is defined.

55. The most detailed work has been that of Ryoshin Minami, "Further Considerations on the Turning Point in the Japanese Economy: Parts I and II," Hitotsubashi Journal of Economics, Vol. 10, No. 2, February 1970, and Vol. 11, No. 2, June 1970.

56. Edward F. Denison and William K. Chung, "Economic Growth and its Sources," in Patrick and Rosovsky, Asia's New Giant, p. 85.

57. And we assume about 55 percent of agricultural income should be attributed to labour, based on figures presented for 1953-56 by S. C. Hsieh and T. H. Lee, "Agricultural Development and its Contributions to Economic Growth in Taiwan," Economic Digest Series, No. 17 (Taipei), 1966.

58. The category "property income" presumably includes imputed labour income of nonagricultural workers, so these labour-share figures are all somewhat underestimated. We draw them from Fei, Ranis, and Kuo, Growth with Equity, p. 97.

59. Hasan and Rao, Korea, p. 510.

60. Ibid., p. 511. In this case some of the increase may be illusory, due to an increase in the share of the labour force working for pay.

61. Unskilled workers or low-skilled workers, in general, have either no education or a primary level. Labour scarcity as conceived in the labour-surplus model would imply an increase in the relative incomes of these two groups, especially the former, vis-à-vis more educated groups. But it would have no direct implications for that substantial share of inequality associated with income differentials among skilled workers with little educa-

tion, clerical workers (usually with secondary education), and groups with higher education.

62. The data deficiencies of the above analysis must be borne in mind. For some countries, the earnings data do not exclude capital incomes (although in many cases, these are seriously underreported), nor do they sort out the effects of factors other than education.

5
SOCIAL INEQUALITY AND
THE DEMOGRAPHIC TRANSITION
Alan B. Simmons

The 20 republics that constitute Latin America vary widely
in their current demographic profiles and trends in population
growth and distribution.[1] This variation reflects fundamental
differences in the social, economic, and technological changes
in each country. The patterns of population growth and distribution are interrelated with economic growth and inequalities
in the distribution of income. Some of the linkages between
population, social-economic organization, and technological change
are relatively well understood; many others are conjectural or
just beginning to be clarified. Research in Latin America over
the past decade has led to some new insights in this field. These
have implications for the revision of general theoretical models
of economic development and population change.

The purpose of this chapter is to propose a framework for
understanding changing mortality, fertility, population growth,
and urbanization patterns in Latin America, with particular
emphasis on the relationship between these demographic changes
and patterns of economic growth and inequality. The first part
of the chapter summarizes a classical model for understanding
social-economic and population interrelationships, outlines some
major criticisms of it, and advances several modifications for the
model that may make it more relevant to contemporary Latin
America. The second part describes recent population trends
in Latin America and their relationship to the hypotheses proposed previously. The final section discusses some overall
implications of the findings for models of social-economic and
demographic change in the third world.

THE CLASSICAL TRANSITION MODEL

The following is a brief presentation of a rather rich and evolving body of hypotheses that has served as the major theoretical model for research on social-economic and demographic interactions over the past 40 years. My purpose is merely to outline the basic elements of the model, prior to criticizing it and suggesting reformulations that may make it more relevant to contemporary Latin America. We may refer to the following basic version, devoid of elaboration, as the classical demographic-transition model.[2]

The classical model is composed of a small set of variables; several hypotheses specifying relationships between these variables, including their sequential pattern over time; and a number of overall systemic outcomes. Let us consider each of these components in turn:

The variables are mortality, fertility, population growth, urbanization (migration), and socioeconomic development (sometimes called modernization). The linkages are multiple and are best understood in terms of the following five sequential historical stages or transitions they produce:

1. Pretransition: This is a stationary point prior to the initiation of change. Socioeconomic modernization is low (pre-industrial period), mortality fluctuates at high levels (due to epidemics and famines), while fertility is also high, and population growth is slow.

2. Early transition: Socioeconomic development (broad improvements in nutrition, the quality of the habitat, etc.) brings about a fall in mortality and results in population growth in a society which is predominately rural.

3. Midtransition: Rapid population growth in rural areas, combined with agricultural mechanization, encourages outmigration to cities (urbanization), and this reinforces socioeconomic development by shifting the labor force to more productive industrial jobs.

4. Late transition: Urbanization and continuing economic modernization bring about a decline in fertility.

5. Posttransition: Fertility falls to very low levels, such that the population stops growing (and may even decline in size).

The overall outcomes, at the end of the stage sequence, are low fertility, low mortality, high urbanization, and a high level of economic development, all of which were mutually determined or interlinked in the five stages of population change.

The classical model is clearly a population-change theory, and only in a minor way takes into account the determinants of economic growth. The major determinants of economic growth (capital accumulation, technological innovation, etc.) are not explicitly considered in the model. The impact which economic growth has on the population, in contrast, is the major focus. The extent to which population growth may, at a certain point, reinforce other determinants of economic growth can nevertheless be considered an important element of the theory.[3]

The classical model corresponds broadly to the historical experience of a number (but not all) of the currently industrialized nations, such as those in Western Europe. It is, then, partially a descriptive device: a summary of population trends and their links to the economy in an earlier period of development. For example, Figure 5.1 shows some historical trends for variables in the model in the Swedish case.

FIGURE 5.1. The Demographic Transition in Sweden

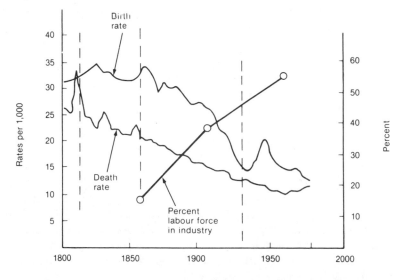

Sources: Birth and death rates are from Dorothy S. Thomas, Social and Economic Aspects of Swedish Population Movements, 1750-1933. (N.Y.: MacMillan, 1941) and United Nations Demographic Yearbook, 1954 and 1959. Labor force in industry figures are extrapolated from estimates given by Simon Kuznets, Modern Economic Growth (New Haven: Yale University Press, 1966) Table 3.2.

THE MODEL AND LATIN AMERICA: SOME DISPARITIES

In separate studies of mortality, fertility, urbanization, and economic development in Latin America, specific features of the classical transition model have been examined and found wanting. The initial investigations, undertaken in the early 1960s, noted so many problems with the model that some observers felt it to be culturally specific to industrially advanced nations at an earlier period in time, and not applicable to contemporary Latin America.[4] Subsequently, in the late 1960s and the 1970s a number of research findings came to light (particularly a long-awaited, but hitherto nonoccurring onset of fertility declines) that tempered this outright rejection, but that did not discount major problems still in need of rectification.[5] As yet, the criticisms have not been incorporated into an overall restatement of the model and its premises. Rather, they are expressed in terms of independent, specific points as follows:

1. The model incorrectly specifies the determinants of mortality decline in contemporary developing nations. Mortality decline in Latin America, as in other contemporary developing regions, came about largely through public health intervention that, since the 1930s, has been independent of social-economic development.[6] Some rather poor nations have experienced significant declines in mortality levels—the pattern of decline depends more on the spread and quality of public health programs than it does on economic growth and rising living standards.

2. The model is imprecise about the timing and rate of fertility declines. Populations have been growing rapidly in rural areas of Latin America since the 1930s, when death rates fell, but by 1960 there was little evidence of fertility decline except in a few atypical nations (Argentina, Uruguay, and Cuba) where fertility had already been low for many years.[7] Subsequent to 1960, fertility has begun to decline quickly in some countries but not in others, and gross measures of economic development and rates of population growth alone provide modest predictors of the rate of decline.[8]

3. The model implies close, reinforcing links between urbanization and industrialization; yet to many observers, urbanization in some Latin American nations appeared to be taking place without industrialization, in the sense that cities grew quickly even in countries where industrial growth and employment levels were low.[9]

4. The economic outcomes and their feedback into the demographic process seemed to be inadequately specified in the classical model. The model implies that population growth is favorable to industrialization, presumably because it expands the internal market and provides a large industrial labor force. However, income distributions in Latin America are highly distorted to favor the rich. As a result, internal demand for products is heavily determined by the spending patterns of the wealthy, and not by increasing numbers of low-income consumers. Similarly, a labor-surplus situation and low wages in urban areas do not necessarily benefit industries in the contemporary setting, because they are capital intensive, not labor intensive.

The problems listed challenge the major internal linkages of the model. As Kuhn has observed,[10] scientific paradigms that do not conform to empirical evidence are frequently tinkered with in minor ways, and if this does not help, they are supplanted by models that rest on a new set of assumptions. The following comments call into question several basic assumptions of the classical transition model.

The classical model was developed from a historical reconstruction of past events in industrially developed countries whose economic progress depended primarily on internally generated social, economic, and technological innovation. The retrospective view of these earlier events was rather vague on the specific social, economic, and technological changes that accompanied each stage in the transition. This vagueness resulted not only from incomplete historical research, but also from the fact that social-economic and technological changes that occurred in the European countries were closely intertwined and mutually reinforcing over a long period of time. Thus, those who first formulated the theory found it adequate to speak of "development" or "modernization" broadly, in a way that implied a variety of undifferentiated improvements in medical, industrial, and agricultural technologies and their application. The major thrust of contemporary research bearing on the transition model has been to distinguish more carefully between the specific social-economic and technological variables and to determine the separate demographic consequences of each. This has generated rather specific theories of mortality, fertility, and migration; and may explain the absence of integrative efforts to bring this complex body of theory together in a new transition model.

Lack of attention to specific features of technological and socioeconomic innovation in the classical model had another important consequence. The model did not speak to issues of development strategy and technological choice, nor to political-economic considerations that determine them. These issues, which seemed remote to those who developed the original model, are central to the understanding of third-world development today, given, especially, the role of imported technology (be it medical, agricultural, or industrial) in both contemporary patterns of development and their population consequences.

From the above we may conclude that attempts to reformulate classical demographic-transition theory for application to a contemporary developing region such as Latin America must, as a minimum, add three elements. Firstly, the model must elucidate major features of the political economy of the region that have determined development strategies and technological choices bearing on population variables. Secondly, the model should identify the social-economic consequences through which these development strategies and technological choices influence population variables. Finally, the model should clearly identify the demographic consequences of specific social-economic changes. Insofar as the demographic consequences feed back into the social-economic changes at various stages, these circular linkages should be spelled out. The following section is a preliminary attempt to test the possibility of meeting these three criteria and advancing hypotheses for a modified transition theory.

A LATIN AMERICAN MODEL

In order to update the demographic-transition theory for present-day Latin America, we begin by postulating several major features of the political economy of the region that are relevant for understanding population changes.

From colonial times to the present, the region has been characterized by wide social-class inequalities in the distribution of income and political influence. These differences, prior to the emergence of strong industrial and urban commercial interests in the twentieth century, were principally evident in unequal land distribution. As few as 10 percent of all owners controlled up to 80 percent of agricultural lands. And class differences in mortality have always been high.

Further, with the exception of Cuba and brief or partial socialist development strategies implemented elsewhere, Latin American nations have strongly endorsed capitalist free-enterprise development strategies. This has had a significant impact on patterns of technological choice in both agriculture and industry

and on the urbanization process, especially since World War II.
There are important national differences in the timing and nature
of social and technological change (Argentina, Uruguay, southern
Brazil, and Chile had early industrial growth), but broadly
speaking, there have been two periods for the region as a whole:
Prior to the 1930s, the economic transformation of Latin America
was largely gradual, based on exports of primary products (often
at prices which fluctuated widely over the short term). There
were few sudden or rapid changes brought about by the importation of modern technology. Then, from the 1930s to the present
time, technological imports for modernization of agriculture and
industry were encouraged under various import-substitution
and export-oriented policies. The policy tools were government-
supported credit for technical improvements, protective tariffs
for national industrial products, and international borrowing to
overcome shortages in funds for purchasing and importing technology and intermediate industrial goods. There are wide variations in the specific policies and in the details of their success
and impact, but they tended to have two significant overall
effects: They reinforced the expansion of large-scale commercial
agriculture (in virtually all countries), and they encouraged
large-scale modern manufacturing capable of competing in international markets (this occurred in the more developed nations
primarily). These shifts in social-economic organization have
reduced the demand for labor in agriculture, expanded urban
commercial employment, and accelerated the shift from household-
organized production to wage labor in both rural and urban areas.

The preceding economic policies were implemented by governments in which the political power and interests of capitalists
and landowners were very dominant. The tendency for the
policies to support further land concentration (expanding large
commercial farms) and large-scale industry (owned by the
wealthy) is consistent with continuing high levels of income
inequality. The introduction of modern machinery in agriculture
and industry implies a higher return (on investment) to the
owners of such machinery and a lower share to labor in wages).

Also beginning in the 1930s, public health technology has
been widely diffused through the region. However, this technology was not particularly expensive. Its diffusion was primarily
at the instigation of international agencies and a small number
of national health officials, and has therefore been largely independent of the financial and institutional constraints on the
importation of other kinds of technology. It has had a rapid
and continuing effect on reducing death from communicable dis-
eases, but has not had (and probably cannot have) an effect on

mortality stemming from poverty, poor nutrition, and inadequate habitats.

Quite clearly, these assertions are phrased in an oversimplified fashion and deserve further discussion and qualification that are beyond the scope of this chapter. For our present purposes, these assertions are merely taken as general premises upon which to construct a revised demographic-transition model.

The assumptions allow one to derive a revised model that retains some basic features of the classical version but that significantly modifies other elements. The major features of the revised model are: the variables in the model are now expanded to include specific kinds of technology (agricultural, industrial, and health), income distribution, and the shift to salaried work, in addition to the demographic and economic-growth variables of the classical model; and the linkages between variables at each stage of the transition model are now more specific and hence somewhat more complex. The principal revisions are as follows:

1. The mortality effects of overall economic growth and those of health technology are separated in the revised model. Both are relevant, but at different time periods. Economic growth reduces mortality prior to the introduction of modern health technology, and once modern health technology has run its course, social-economic factors may again become important.

2. Urbanization comes about as a result of rural population growth, increasing land concentration, agricultural mechanization, and the rapid growth of low-income urban commercial and service employment. Since all these factors have been in operation in Latin America, one would expect to find high and rapidly increasing levels of urbanization, even in nations which have low levels of labor force in industry.

3. The factors determining fertility decline are still not fully detailed in this revised model, but the shift away from household-centered production to wage labor in both rural and urban areas may be a key underlying factor explaining the decline. The hypothesis is one of a number that are currently being debated in the field of population and development.[11]

4. The economic consequences of population growth are much less pronounced in the revised model than in the classical one, but insofar as population growth has had any economic effects, these would appear to have been of three kinds: Firstly, they have possibly had a small positive impact on the size of internal markets. Secondly, a labor-surplus situation undoubtedly kept wages down in construction, transportation, and domestic

service, all of which may have indirectly supported modern economic enterprise. Finally, and perhaps most clearly, the surplus-labor situation has reinforced wide inequalities in income distribution, although it is not the fundamental cause of them.

The sequences and their timing in the revised model follow the overall pattern of the classical one. Death rates fall and population growth takes place first. Rapid growth in urban areas follows. Significant urbanization takes place prior to fertility declines and the slowing of population growth. However, the timing of all these events is faster; the transition stages are short in duration, and each demographic change, once it starts, is very rapid.

The overall outcomes also follow the logic of the classical model but are different in degree. Progress through the stages of the transition is accompanied by economic development (rising income per capita), but this is far less central to the revised model than are specific features of technology and social-economic organization. As a result, the overall transition, at least to the late stage, may take place at relatively low levels of industrial growth and low-to-moderate levels of economic development. Economic inequalities are a salient feature of the model. They are, however, not necessary components. They emerge from the way in which the political economy operates. Mortality and fertility reduction would be even faster and reach overall lower levels if gross class-income differences did not exist.

It is not possible to adequately investigate the preceding hypotheses in a short, conceptually oriented chapter. The next section therefore is restricted to providing some general empirical information on Latin American population trends, in an effort to determine whether the general thrust of the revised model is supported.

AN EMPIRICAL FIT

Transition Stages

Progress of societies through the demographic-transition stages is logically dependent, first and foremost, on the relationship between changing mortality patterns and changing fertility patterns. Population growth is a derived variable, depending on the mortality/fertility interrelationship. Analysis of the hypothesized relationships of technological and social-economic change to the mortality and fertility patterns can be carried out in a second, later step.

Mortality for the 20 countries of the region is measured here by life expectancy at birth (e_0), derived from recent national life tables. This measure has the advantage of being independent of age structure and, hence, less prone to influence that comes about through changing fertility in countries where infant deaths are a major component of current mortality. A fertility measure (such as the gross reproduction rate) that is also independent of age structure would be preferred, but as adequate recent data for constructing such rates are not universally available in the region, the following analysis utilizes the crude birth rate (CBR)—annual births per 1,000 inhabitants.

Figure 5.2 shows, for each of the 20 Latin American republics, the intersection points between life expectancy and fertility

FIGURE 5.2. Relationship between Birth Rates and Life-Expectancy Levels for Latin America, 1960-65 and 1970-75

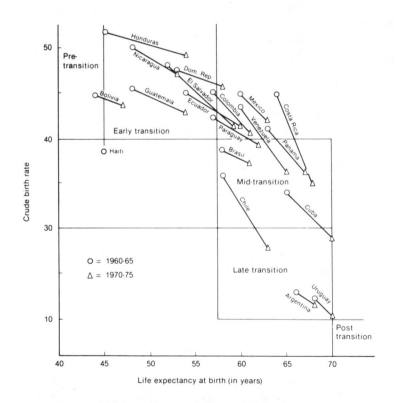

Source: United Nations, World Population Trends and Policies: Volume 1, Population Trends (N.Y.: U.N., 1979) Tables 74 and 75.

FIGURE 5.3. Relationship between Birth Rates and Life-Expectancy Levels for Latin America, 1970-75 and 1977

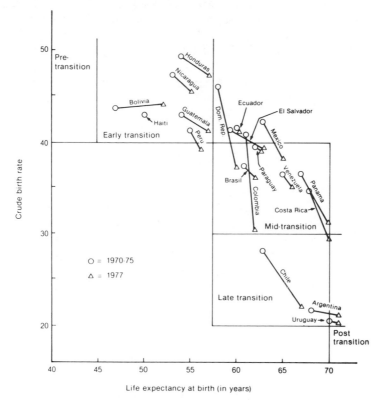

Life expectancy at birth (in years)

Sources: Data for 1970-75 from United Nations, World Population Trends and Policies: Volume 1, Population Trends. (N.Y.:
U.N., 1979) Tables 74 and 75. Data for 1977 from World Bank,
World Development Report (New York: Oxford University Press,
1979) Annex Table 18.

at two points in time: 1960-65 and 1970-75. The figure also
shows five distinct areas corresponding to the hypothetical
transition stages. The cutoff points used to define these five
areas in the figure were based predominately on criteria logically
consistent with the revised transition model.[12]

The results of Figure 5.2 indicate that by 1970-74, no
country in Latin America remained in the pretransition phase.
That is to say, by then, life expectancies were greater than
45 years in all countries of the region. Nine countries may be
classified in the early-transition phase, characterized by low

but rapidly increasing life expectancy and high, gradually declining fertility. Seven countries, including the three most
populous ones in the region (Brazil, Mexico, and Colombia)
were either in the midtransition category or on their way to it
from the previous phase. With the exception of Brazil, these
countries were all distinguished by having fertility declines that
were as high or higher than their mortality declines. Four
countries fell in the late-transition phase. Two of these (Chile
and Cuba) arrived at the phase only recently and still had relatively high levels of fertility. In 1970-74 there were no Latin
American nations in the posttransition phase, although both
Argentina and Uruguay seemed poised to enter it, and Cuba had
mortality levels at the border line for inclusion (but much higher
fertility).

More recent data on mortality and fertility are not reliably
or systematically available for all Latin American nations; hence
Figure 5.3, showing trends from 1970-75 to 1977 (and based on
World Bank estimates for the latter year), should be regarded
with caution. They suggest, however, a continuation of the
processes evident in Figure 5.2. Only five countries seem to
be in the pretransition phase by 1977. There were then eight
countries in the midtransition stage, and four of these showed
remarkable drops in fertility, with little corresponding fall in
mortality in this most recent period.[13] Ecuador, lying stationary
between the early stages and midstages, seems difficult to classify.
The fertility decline may be increasing in Brazil, but it was still
small, and the country remains an exception to general trends.
Paraguay, which had previously experienced a very rapid decline
in both fertility and mortality over the 1960-65 to 1970-75 period,
also seems to have changed little.

Table 5.1 provides a summary of the fertility and mortality
levels and trends for the countries classified at each stage in
the transition model. It also shows population-growth rates,
urbanization levels and trends, and two indicators of social-
economic organization (percent of workers in industry and GNP
per capita) for nations classified at each stage. The data show
that levels and temporal trends for each of these variables follow
the expected sequence: very rapid mortality declines at intermediate levels of development; high population growth in the
early- and midtransition stages, slow growth in the late-transition
phase; and extremely fast urbanization at low levels of labor
force in industry in the early-transition phase. Several countries
that experienced a very rapid fertility decline in this period
and that had continuing declines in 1970-75 to 1977, such as
the Dominican Republic, Colombia, Panama, and Chile, have

TABLE 5.1. Summary of Latin American Demographic-Transition Stages as of 1970-75

Data Item	Transition Stages		
	Early	Middle	Late
Number of countries	9[a]	7[b]	4[c]
Life expectancy, 1970-75	54.4	63.9	67.8
Percent change since 1960-65	+10.5	+7.6	+3.0
Crude birth rate, 1970-75	43.4	37.9	24.8
Percent change since 1960-64	-5.5	-10.8	-13.1
Annual population growth rate, 1970-75	2.90	2.93	1.54
Percent change in growth rate since 1960-65	+4.4	-6.0	-14.7
Proportion that was urban, 1970-75	40.2	57.0	76.3
Percent increase in proportion urban since 1960-65	+32.3	+21.2	+10.8
GNP per capita in 1970 (in 1960 $)	259	496	681
Percent increase since 1960	+24.6	+25.9	+23.8
Proportion of labor force in the industrial sector, 1977	17	23	30
Percent change since 1960	+20.3	+26.8	0.0

[a]Includes Bolivia, Ecuador, the Dominican Republic, El Salvador, Haiti, Honduras, Guatemala, Nicaragua, and Peru.

[b]Brazil, Colombia, Costa Rica, Mexico, Panama, Paraguay, and Venezuela.

[c]Argentina, Chile, Cuba, and Uruguay.

Note: All figures in items 2 through 7 are based on un-weighted means for the nations in each category.

Sources: Population statistics are from World Population Trends and Policies, 1977 Monitory Report, Volume 1 (New York: United Nations, 1979). Tables 74 and 75. Economic statistics are from World Development Report, 1979 (Washington, D.C.: World Bank, 1979); economic data exclude Cuba.

overall levels of GNP per capita averaging only about half of those in Uruguay and Argentina.

Mortality

Arriaga and Davis have presented rather convincing evidence on the lack of association between mortality declines and economic development in Latin America since the 1930s.[14] Prior to this date, national mortality declines in every decade were a linear function of each nation's previous mortality levels, which in turn were good proxies for national levels of income per capita. From the 1930s up to the 1960s, when their analysis ends, this was no longer the case, presumably due to the impact of modern health technology and its lack of association with levels of development. Have the nutritional levels, quality of habitat, and other variables linked to economic development lost their influence on mortality, or has their effect simply been hidden during the period in which modern health technology was introduced? The following evidence suggests the latter may be the case.

Figure 5.4 shows that between 1960 and 1970, there were significant improvements in length of life in early all Latin American nations, including the very poorest. In conformity with the Arriaga and Davis findings for the period 1930 to 1960, the mortality changes over this more recent decade were not correlated with levels of GNP per capita at the beginning of the period.[15] This provides further confirmation that life-expectancy improvements are unrelated to levels of development. However, the data in Figure 5.4 also emphasize the fact that the overall positive cross-sectional correlation between length of life and GNP per capita has not changed. At the beginning and at the end of the 1960s, the poorer nations in the region had substantially lower levels of life expectancy. What happened in this period was that the overall association between GNP per capita and mortality shifted upward but retained its same shape. This accounts for both the lack of correlation between mortality declines and the level of GNP per capita in this period, and the continuing relationship between mortality levels and GNP per capita.

Since modern health technology has been undergoing a process of diffusion for approximately 40 years in Latin America, it is at least reasonable to ask whether its effects are diminishing as a result of its having achieved virtually all it can accomplish. Table 5.2 shows that the rate at which mortality is declining in Latin America is substantially slower than it was in the 1940s and 1950s, when modern health technology was first widely

FIGURE 5.4. Relationship between Life Expectancy and GNP per Capita for Latin American Nations, 1960-65 and 1970-75

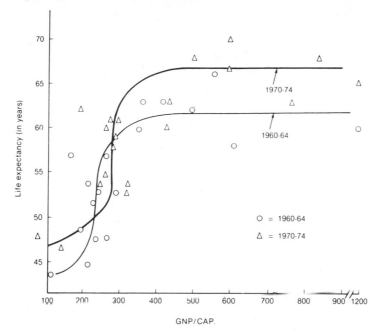

Sources: Life expectancy data from United Nations, World Population Trends and Policies: Volume 1, Population Trends. (N.Y.: U.N., 1979) Table 75. GNP/Capita from World Bank, World Development Report (New York, Oxford University Press, 1979) Annex Table 1.

introduced. In the 1940s, for example, life expectancy in Latin America increased, on the average, by 2.21 percent per year, while in the period 1970-75, it increased by only .61 percent per year. This slower extension of life expectancy does not appear to be a result of the fact that life expectancy is now high and naturally resistant to further increases. As Figure 5.5 indicates, when Europe had similar levels of life expectancy, its rates of improvement in longevity were much higher. The contrast between Latin America and Southern Europe in Figure 5.5 is particularly instructive. Both regions benefited from imports of health technology and from more rapid declines in death rates than had occurred in Western Europe. Whereas Southern Europe continued to enjoy a rapid increase in life expectancy, even when life expectancy at birth had reached 64 years, Latin America has been experiencing only moderate increases ever since life expectancy there reached 58 years.

TABLE 5.2. Life Expectancy: Levels and Annual Increments
in Latin America, 1890 to 1975

Period	Life Expectancy (years)	Annual Years Added	Annual Percent Change
1890-1900	27.2	.11	.42
1900-10	28.9	.17	.63
1910-20	31.1	.22	.76
1920-30	33.6	.25	.80
1930-40	38.0	.44	1.31
1940-50	46.4	.84	2.21
1950-60	55.8	.94	2.03
1955-60	55.3	.60	
1960-65	57.7	.48[a]	.86[a]
1965-70	59.5	.36	.62
1970-75	61.4	.38	.63

[a]These figures are calculated using the Arriaga-Davis estimate of life expectancy for 1960 and the UN estimate for the
period 1960-65.

Sources: Data for 1890 to 1960 are estimates for the end of
each period. See E. Arriaga and K. Davis, "The pattern of
mortality change in Latin America," Demography 6:3 (August
1969) 223-42.

Data for 1955 to 1975 are from UN compilations. See World
Population Trends and Policies, 1977 Monitorying Report, vol. 1,
Population Trends (New York: United Nations, 1980), Table 74.
Estimates are for the average in the period shown.

Research on the social-economic determinants of mortality
in Latin America is at an early stage. The few detailed studies
that exist on this topic suggest that malnutrition and poor-quality
habitat associated with poverty continue to exert a strong influence on mortality in the region. Carvalho and Wood have noted
large social-class differences in mortality in Brazil.[16] These
class differences may actually increase in metropolitan cities
such as Sao Paulo, although the reasons for this can only be
conjectured. Gwatkin has reviewed existing studies on mortality
in the world and noted that infant-mortality rates appear to be

FIGURE 5.5. Annual Increments in Life Expectancy at Each Level of Life Expectancy, Latin America, Southern and Eastern Europe, and Western Europe

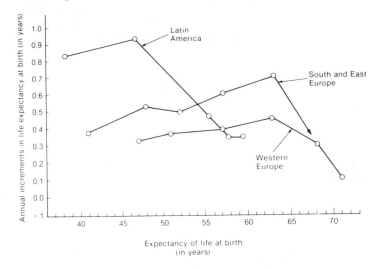

Sources: D. R. Gwatkin, The End of an Era: A Review of Literature and Data Concerning Third World Mortality Trends (New York: Overseas Development Council, 1981); World Population Trends and Policies, vol. 1 (New York: United Nations, 1980), Table 75.

stagnant or even climbing in a number of Latin American nations.[17] He notes further that adult mortality is very low in the region and that national differences in overall longevity are now highly dependent on infant mortality. Detailed epidemiological studies of high infant-death rates suggest that they have a double causation: Poor nutrition levels weaken body resistance to infection; and poor habitat conditions increase the risk of infection. Vaccination programs cannot reduce this source of mortality; potable water and improved sanitation will certainly help reduce it; but the overall problem probably can only be solved by a combination of measures that include improved nutrition and habitat, such as might come about through a better distribution of income.

Urbanization

In the revised transition model, rural-urban migration comes about through a combination of factors. Rapid rural-population growth, increased land concentration, and the mechanization of agriculture provide "push" factors, while the growth of commercial activity and of service jobs in the city provides a "pull" factor. These specific social-economic and technological changes, it is argued, provide a better explanation of rural-urban migration than do the basic determinants suggested in the classical transition model, namely, economic development and percent of labor force in industry.

There is considerable existing research that supports the revised model on this point. T. P. Schultz has carried out a regression analysis on net-migration rates for municipios (small political administrative units) in Colombia and notes that income/wage differences between regions are important in determining migration rates; but a number of other factors seem to contribute as well, including availability of schooling and of health services and rate of population growth.[18] R. P. Shaw has shown, for several Latin American nations, that changes in land tenure and high rural-population growth together were important variables explaining the number of people leaving an area.[19] P. Peek has summarized a number of features of rural-development policy and elite class interests that served in part to reinforce land-consolidation patterns.[20]

The net results of these multiple causes have been extremely slow population-growth rates in rural areas, and extremely fast growth of cities and towns. In some countries, such as Colombia, the rural population seems to have stabilized at a constant size. For the Latin American region as a whole, we may note that rural-population growth has been only about 20 percent of urban growth in the 1970-75 period (see Table 5.3). Latin America is more than two times more urbanized than other developing regions of the world.

The extremely high rates of urbanization in Latin America are often viewed as a puzzle by those who have examined the issue. The initial assumption is that these rates reflect the higher level of economic development, including industrial development, in Latin America as compared with Asia and Africa. However, this explanation is not adequate. Nations with equivalent levels of industrial development elsewhere in the world are less urbanized than are nations in Latin America.[21] Also, nations with similar levels of economic development elsewhere in the world have lower levels of urbanization. Figure 5.6 shows, for example, the results of a regression analysis carried out on the relationship between GNP per capita and percent of population that is urban, for nations in various regions of the world. As the results indicate, a Latin American nation with a GNP per

TABLE 5.3. Urban- and Rural-Population Growth, Latin American and Developing Regions of the World, 1950 to 1980

Item	1950-60	1960-70	1970-75	1975-80*
Percent that was urban at the start of each period				
Latin America	41.18	49.45	57.37	61.21
All developing regions	16.71	21.85	25.2	28.03
Average annual population-growth rates				
Latin America				
Urban population	4.57	4.21	4.01	3.86
Rural population	1.23	1.02	.82	.83
All developing regions				
Urban population	4.86	3.94	3.95	4.06
Rural population	1.36	1.75	1.69	1.65

*Population-growth rates over the 1975-80 period are based on projections for 1980.
Source: Patterns of Urban and Rural Population Growth, United Nations, Department of Economic and Social Affairs, Population Studies, No. 68. (ST/ESA/SER.A/80) (New York: United Nations, 1980), Tables 5, 7, and 8.

FIGURE 5.6. Relationship between Percent That Is Urban and GNP per Capita

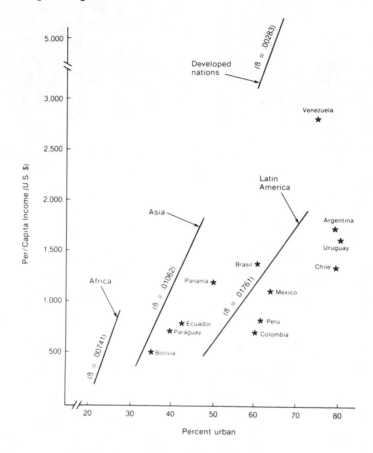

Sources: GNP per capita is taken from United Nations, Statistical Yearbook, 1977 (New York, 1977), pp. 742-50; percent living in urban areas, from United Nations, Demographic Yearbook, 1977, pp. 65-181. The figures refer to most recent data available, generally from the mid-1970s.

capita of about U.S. $1,000 in 1970 would be 60 percent urban; an Asian country with a similar GNP per capita would be less than 40 percent urban. These differences undoubtedly arise in part from historically conditioned patterns (indigenous urbanization prior to Spanish conquest; urban settlement during the colonial period), but they are also consistent with predictions from the revised transition model.

Fertility

At first glance, the results of recent studies on national fertility levels seem to clarify the variables that are important as determinants. At closer scrutiny, however, the results are disappointing. Findings from S. Beaver's analysis of national fertility levels in Latin America around 1970 are worth citing because they are recent, based on a careful and detailed choice of causal variables, and emerge from a multivariate model. [22]

Beaver was able to explain about 64 percent of the variance in an age-standardized natural-fertility measure of a linear-regression model utilizing, as predictors, GNP per capita, urbanization level, secondary-school enrollment levels, death rates, and four other modernization variables. The high level of prediction comes about because of the very wide range of national development levels in Latin America (from Argentina and Uruguay to Bolivia and Haiti) and the strong positive correlation between overall development and low fertility. However, these regression results are not very helpful in predicting, say in 1960, which countries were going to experience fertility declines. Those countries that actually experienced such declines after 1960 did so when many of their economic-modernization indicators were at much lower levels than were to be found among countries (such as Argentina) that had reduced their fertility earlier under different socioeconomic circumstances.

A more challenging and relevant research question is: What variables predict the rate of national fertility change and the timing of the onset of such change? Beaver also applied his model to this question. By lagging a number of his predictor variables and by controlling initial fertility levels in the regression analysis itself, he was able to explain only 18 percent of the variance in fertility change (the significant predictor variable was GNP per capita).

The weak research findings to date suggest the need for modifications in theory and analytic method. This task of testing new hypotheses is beyond the scope of this chapter, but it should be noted that the Latin American transition model developed earlier in the chapter has implications for future research in this area: It points to the need for new variables, possibly associated with mortality decline, which may be more relevant for understanding fertility changes. The shift from domestic production to salaried work in particular is noted. Equally important, the model suggests a modification in analytic techniques. Linear-regression models, even when the variables are transformed to minimize nonlinear relationships, may not be appropriate, since many of the empirical associations under consideration are more like those which occur in some chemical reactions. For example, heat is applied until a "critical point" is reached, and then a sudden rapid transformation takes place; after the transformation is complete, more heat has no effect. The problem is to find the variables that provide the necessary conditions for the reaction, and to determine their relationships at the moment that the reaction starts.

DISCUSSION

Major differences and similarities between the classical or Western-industrialized-nation's demographic transition and the developing-country's demographic transition, such as we find in Latin America, have been noted for at least a decade. The principal distinguishing features of the Latin American transition include the lack of association between mortality decline and socioeconomic development; the more rapid fall in mortality; higher overall population growth during the early and midtransition phases; rapid urban growth at low levels of industrial employment; and the unpredictable timing and precipitous nature of fertility decline, once it begins. In common with the classical transition, the Latin American model seems to follow the same broad sequence of stages: First, mortality declines and population grows quickly; then urbanization takes place; and, finally, fertility declines. In the classical model, these sequences are perceived as necessary and derived from internal linkages. In Latin America the linkages seem more complex and the sequences seem to depend much more on the historical timing of technological inputs entering from outside. Some of the variable linkages within the classical model still seem relevant for developing countries (e.g., population growth in rural areas pushes rural-urban migration), while others (e.g., socioeconomic development as the major determinant of mortality change) require considerable modification.

The many distinct characteristics of Latin America and other population trends pose a theoretical challenge. Should the classical transition model be updated or should it simply be discarded? The case for discarding the model could point to the historical and cultural specificity of demographic changes, and indicate that the sequential parallels in demographic stages between Europe and Latin America are perhaps coincidental, since the changes came about through quite different mechanisms in each case. The argument for retaining and modifying the model rests on the idea that the model includes an integrated body of useful hypotheses but excludes a specification of historical and cultural circumstances that will influence how the model operates. Since the original formulations of the model did not indicate the basic assumptions about what kind of society the model was best suited to, these assumptions must be brought to light and the theory modified to take into account different social settings.

This chapter advances a number of plausible demographic assumptions relevant for Latin America. It also argues that a number of hypotheses derived from these are not original, but are ones that have been selected from research on particular population topics, and were not previously integrated into the transition model. Finally, it presents some new empirical information bearing on our interpretation of the new model. The assumptions include historically specific features of the political economy of Latin America (its class structure and choice of development strategies) and of the international context (the kinds of economic and health technology available, and some of the conditions of technology transfer to developing countries). These assumptions, while simply stated, lead to greater attention, in the Latin American transition model, to the specific features of technological choice and of related social-economic organization that determine the timing, speed, and sequence of demographic changes. The linkage from technological choice and development strategies to relevant population outcomes was most clearly supported for mortality change and urbanization, and would also seem likely for fertility decline, though the precise mechanisms influencing the latter still need further clarification.

The findings presented in this chapter are encouraging with respect to the Latin American transition model. An important question going beyond the chapter is the relationship of the Latin American model to population changes taking place in Asia and Africa. Must each region have its own model based on a unique set of assumptions? Perhaps so, but many of the processes of economic dependence, technological change, capitalist development strategy in agriculture, and social-economic organization that one finds in an advanced stage in Latin America are taking place elsewhere. The Latin American model thus may have broader relevance.

NOTES

1. The 20 are the Spanish- and Portuguese-speaking countries of Central America, South America, and the Caribbean, and Haiti.

2. For a review of the demographic transition as both a descriptive framework and a theoretical paradigm, see Steven Beaver, Demographic Transition Theory Reinterpreted: An Application to Recent Nationality Trends in Latin America (Lexington, Mass.: D. C. Heath, 1975), chaps. 1 and 2. Beaver's discussion focuses more narrowly on the social and economic determinants of mortality, fertility, and population growth. In the present essay, an effort is made to incorporate these population-growth issues into a broader model of economic development in which migration, urbanization, and the changing sectoral composition of the labor force are also considered. This broader framework follows the approach found in S. Kuznets, Modern Economic Growth (New Haven: Yale University Press, 1966), chaps. 1 and 2.

3. This is a much debated point in the literature. A. Coal and E. M. Hoover (Population Growth and Economic Development in Low Income Countries: A Case Study in Indian Prospects [Princeton: Princeton University Press, 1958]) argue that rapid population growth increases dependency ratios and decreases savings, such that economic growth is slowed. A. Hirchman (Strategy of Economic Development [New Haven: Yale University Press, 1958]) has argued that rapid population growth can, in some cases, expand markets and consumer demand as well as increase economies of scale, resulting in increased economic growth. In other cases, population growth may have little effect on these variables. At the other extreme are those such as Julien Simon, who argues that rapid population growth nearly always favors economic growth. See J. Simon, "Resources, Population, Environment: An Oversupply of False, Bad News," Science 28:23 (June 1980):1431-37.

4. Arriaga and Davis were particularly critical of the hypothesis that mortality declines accompany economic development. See E. Arriaga and K. Davis, "The Pattern of Mortality Decline in Latin America," Demography, 6:3 (August 1969):223-42. Schultz wondered when the long-expected fertility decline in countries other than Argentina, Chile, Uruguay, and Cuba would begin, and noted that existing theoretical models predict that such a decline should eventually take place, but did not precisely specify the conditions or when. See T. Paul Schultz, "Demographic Conditions of Economic Development in Latin America," in Charles T. Nisbet (ed.), Latin America: Problems in Economic Development (New York: The Free Press, 1969).

5. See D. Kirk, "A New Demographic Transition?," in Rapid Population Growth: Consequences and Policy Implications, vol. 2, (Baltimore: Johns Hopkins Press, 1974). See also, F. W.

Oechsli and D. Kirk, "Modernization and the Demographic Transition in Latin America and the Caribbean," Economic Development and Cultural Change 23:3 (April 1975):391-419.

6. Arriaga and Davis, op. cit.

7. Schultz, op. cit.

8. Beaver, op. cit.

9. In international comparisons, Latin American countries have high levels of urbanization relative to levels of industrial employment. For details on this, see A. Simmons and C. Vlassoff, "Industrialization and Urbanization in Colombia," in Peter Peek and Guy Standing (eds.), State Policies and Migration (London: Croom Helm, 1982), pp. 207-50.

10. T. S. Kuhn, The Structure of Scientific Revolution (Chicago: University of Chicago Press, 1962).

11. See the various relevant hypotheses proposed in J. C. Caldwell, "A Theory of Fertility: From High Plateau to Destabilization," Population and Development Review 4:4 (December 1978): 553-77, for example.

12. In order to produce a matrix in which five transition stages could be separated, life expectancy and CBR were each subdivided into four segments (i.e., three cutoff points for each variable). The choice of cutoff points was based primarily on criteria logically consistent with the demographic-transition model. For example, a life expectancy of less than 45 years is typically found only in preindustrial societies without the benefits of modern medicine. Life expectancies over 70 years are found today only in a few very medically advanced, highly industrialized nations. Between the two extremes, the third cutoff point, for life expectancy, of 57.5 was chosen because it is after this point that fertility in Latin America seems to fall most quickly. On the fertility variables, pretransition birth rates are typically more than 40 per 1,000; and modern industrial nations have had for some time rates of less than 20 per 1,000; the third point chosen lies just halfway between these extremes.

13. The four countries were the Dominican Republic, Colombia, Mexico, and Panama.

14. Arriaga and Davis, op. cit.

15. Gwatkin, op. cit.

16. J. A. de Carvalho and C. Wood, "Income Distribution, and Rural-Urban Residence in Brazil," Population and Development Review 4:3 (September 1978):405-20.

17. D. R. Gwatkin, The End of an Era: A Review of Literature and Data Concerning Third World Mortality Trends (New York: Overseas Development Council, 1981).

18.   T. Paul Schultz, "Rural-Urban Migration in Colombia," The Review of Economics and Statistics 53 (May 1971):157-63.

19.   R. Paul Shaw, Land Tenure and the Rural Exodus in Chile, Colombia, Costa Rica and Peru (Gainesville: The University Presses of Florida, 1976).

20.   P. Peek, "The Political Economy of Rural Emigration in Latin America," (Geneva: International Labor Office, World Employment Programme, 1979), mimeographed.

21.   Simmons and Vlassoff, in op. cit.

22.   Beaver, op. cit.

6

COPING WITH OIL WEALTH:
THE CASE OF TRINIDAD/TOBAGO
AND THE COMMONWEALTH CARIBBEAN
Basil A. Ince

INTRODUCTION

A phenomenon of the contemporary international system is
the shift from the East-West confrontation of the cold-war period
to the new struggle between the North and South, with the latter
insisting on the emergence of an international economic order
that might better balance the economic inequities between both
areas of the globe. To this end, they have pressed for a transfer
of resources totaling 0.7 percent of the GNP from Northern
countries and for commodity agreements, among other things,
to help minimize the economic inequalities. Simultaneously, the
Southern countries also advocate self-reliance at both the national
and international levels. The latter dimension has emerged in
South-South relationships. The most evident case of this sort
of relationship is the case of the Arab countries that have created
programmes to assist the less fortunate Arab states and some of
the other developing countries. This South-South interaction
has manifested itself not only in the Arab world but also in the
Caribbean, where Mexico and Venezuela, rich with oil money,
especially since the soaring prices of that commodity in the post-
1973-74 period, have designed programmes to assist other Caribbean countries. In the English-speaking subregion of the
Caribbean, now often referred to as the Commonwealth Caribbean,

---

The author wishes to thank Ana Romero for the invaluable
assistance offered in bringing this phase of this research project
to a conclusion.

111

Trinidad/Tobago, one of the more developed countries (MDCs) of the subregion (the others are Jamaica, Guyana, and Barbados), has benefited from the hike in oil prices, although it is not a member of OPEC. This country has attempted to assist not only the less developed countries (LDCs) but also the MDCs of the region that have been adversely affected by the energy crisis. This essay focuses on this case study in the English-speaking subregion of the Caribbean and on Trinidad/Tobago's assistance to fellow Caribbean Community and Common Market (CARICOM) members; on the domestic and external factors that influenced and continue to influence its assumption of the role of aid donor and the mechanisms through which this assistance is extended.

THE REGIONAL SCENE AND TRINIDAD/TOBAGO'S ROLE IN THE SUBREGION

With the signing of the Treaty of Chaguaramas on July 4, 1973, by the prime ministers of Barbados, Guyana, Jamaica, and Trinidad/Tobago, the Caribbean Free Trade Association (CARIFTA) was upgraded to the Caribbean Community and Common Market. These four states, by virtue of their "superior economic capabilities," were regarded as being relatively "better off" than their fellow CARICOM members, which, for purposes of classification, were labeled the less developed countries of this regional grouping. These four MDCs have traditionally been regarded as constituting the pivot of integration efforts. Not only were they expected to play key roles in making the West Indies Federation viable, but even after its collapse in 1962, the LDCs regarded them as likely to participate in small-scale regional integration schemes. In the same vein, it was from within the ranks of the MDCs that efforts materialized to make a reality of the idea of integrating the Anglophone Caribbean in an economic grouping—CARIFTA.

In 1965, an agreement for the establishment of a Caribbean Free Trade Association had been signed by the three English-speaking islands, of which two were MDCs—Barbados and Guyana. We mention the key roles played by the MDCs at different times and on different occasions because, as a result of their past involvement in schemes for engendering regional integration, there have developed certain role expectations that help to explain the position and actions of Trinidad/Tobago in the wake of the energy crisis.

The initial impact of the drastic increase in the price of petroleum introduced new economic problems and exacerbated

TABLE 6.1. MDCs: Balance of Trade, 1972-76 (U.S. $ million)

Country	1972	1973	1974	1975	1976
Barbados	-43	-52	-47	-39	-66
Guyana	-4	-51	13	-2	-114
Jamaica	-100	-142	-49	-208	-193
Trinidad/Tobago	-89	70	500	551	499

Source: ECLA Economic Survey of Latin America, issues for 1973-77.

old ones in all CARICOM states. Among the MDCs, Trinidad/ Tobago was the only one in a position to even contemplate assuming a key role in plans to help the integration movement through what was to be the start of a severe economic crisis. It was the only member that registered large surpluses on its current account and balance of trade, as well as significant increases in international reserves. Tables 6.1-6.3 illustrate the position of this MDC in comparison with its MDC counterparts, with respect to its current account, balance of trade, and international reserves, immediately before and after the start of the energy crisis.

Recession in the industrialized nations, imported inflation, and declines in foreign-exchange reserves all interacted to adversely affect both the oil-importing MDCs and the LDCs of

TABLE 6.2. MDCs: Balance on Current Account, 1972-76 (U.S. $ million)

Country	1972	1973	1974	1975	1976
Barbados	-44	-53	-48	-41	-58
Guyana	-14	-64	-8	-21	-136
Jamaica	-190	-240	-83	-288	-307
Trinidad/Tobago	-155	-19	280	313	223

Source: ECLA Economic Survey of Latin America, issues for 1973-77.

TABLE 6.3. MDCs: Variation in Net International Reserves, 1972-76 (U.S. $ million)

Country	1972	1973	1974	1975	1976
Barbados	-5.1	-8.9	-0.8	18.2	-18.5
Guyana	10	-26	46	50	-104
Jamaica	-25	-30	70	-74	-261
Trinidad/Tobago	-13	-7	333	509	261

Source: ECLA Economic Survey of Latin America, issues for 1973-77.

CARICOM. Influences from both the domestic and regional environments motivated Trinidad/Tobago's policymakers to undertake activity conducive to the assumption of the role of regional aid donor.

FACTORS MOTIVATING ITS ROLE AS AID DONOR

The sources of Trinidad/Tobago's national role conception constitute the philosophical foundations of the country's predisposition to play a key role in assisting its non-oil-producing CARICOM counterparts that were hit hard by the fourfold increase in the price of petroleum. K. J. Holsti noted:

> High-level policy makers divulge at least some of
> the sources of national role conceptions. They
> define their government's on-going tasks and func-
> tions in the international system within regions and,
> in so doing, occasionally they point out why their
> country should fulfil these roles.[1]

Of the 14 national roles identified by Holsti, there are two which could be meaningfully applied to the case of Trinidad/ Tobago for an examination of the rationale behind the country's initiatives in the subregion. These are the roles of regional leader and regional collaborator. It may be stated that, prior to the oil boom, the country's leadership demonstrated a willingness to play a significant part in efforts to promote closer relations among Commonwealth Caribbean territories. At that time, the role it seemed prepared and able to assume was that of regional collaborator. However, after the deluge of petrodollars, Trinidad/Tobago, the wealthiest CARICOM member, was well poised to assume the role of regional leader.

According to Holsti, "economic needs; sense of 'belonging' to a region; common politico-ideological cultural traditions with other states; and geographic location" constitute the main sources of the conception of the role of regional collaborator. There is evidence that the geographic reality of being situated in the Caribbean Sea; the shared cultural and societal characteristics; the common historical experience of slavery, indentureship, and prolonged British colonialism; and the economic need to attempt to challenge the extreme dependence on the metropole were the main factors that motivated this state's interest and involvement in promoting intra-Commonwealth Caribbean relations. As we shall see, this history of involvement in integration schemes formed the basis of present-day convictions that the state has a responsibility to assist its regional neighbours, which, in turn, expect this MDC to fulfill this role. For instance, in 1959, the government of Trinidad/Tobago, in a document entitled "The Economics of Nationhood," supported its argument on the value of a West Indian Federation by emphasizing that "the economic integration of the Area is an indispensable condition for its economic development."[2] When the impact of the energy crisis took its toll on the oil-importing CARICOM members, Trinidad/ Tobago's prime minister's words were consistent with those quoted in "The Economics of Nationhood." He believed that Trinidad/Tobago had a role to play in helping member states hit by the energy crisis since "Caribbean integration can be lubricated by Trinidad's petroleum resources."[3]

This feeling of an affinity with CARICOM member states with which Trinidad/Tobago shares political, economic, and cultural similarities, merged with its newly acquired financial resources, placed it in the position to play the role of regional economic leader. The affinity Trinidad/Tobago feels with its neighbours is somewhat similar to that felt by the oil-rich Arab states in regard to its less fortunate neighbours. It was this affinity that helped to explain the creation of the Abu Dhabi Fund for Arab Economic Development (ADF) and the Kuwait Fund. And it was this feeling of affinity with CARICOM members who share political, economic, and cultural similarities that formed a significant part of Trinidad/Tobago's rationalization of its initiatives in extending financial assistance to other members of the group. There existed a feeling of obligation, as the

Trinidad/Tobago prime minister stated in 1976 when his government approved a loan of TT$184 million. "There can be no improvement in the Caribbean," he declared, "when one of Trinidad/Tobago's best economic partners in the region has been in serious difficulty. . . . Trinidad/Tobago had that obligation not only to Jamaica, but to the entire Caribbean to avoid such a fatality."[4]

Public opinion within and without Trinidad/Tobago was another force that impelled the Trinidad/Tobago government to come to the assistance of its CARICOM partners. This opinion called on Trinidad/Tobago to "take the lead." For example, the Caribbean Task Force reasoned that "geographically, historically and politically, Trinidad/Tobago has been strategically placed for a crucial role in regional affairs."[5] Members of the business sector of the opposition United Labour Front, as well as independent senators, kept impressing upon the leadership that it was the duty of this MDC to help the debt-stricken members of the Caribbean community. Within the region, these calls have been echoed, with the belief that the very existence of the integration movement depended upon the aid-donor role assumed by its richest member.

The opinions and role expectations expressed by sources in Trinidad/Tobago and within the CARICOM subregion served to buttress the Trinidad/Tobago rationale that the state had to be at the forefront of efforts to relieve CARICOM oil importers of their onerous oil bills and balance-of-payments deficits.

Domestic Factors Influencing Trinidad/Tobago's
Initiatives as Donor

Economic developments in Trinidad/Tobago's domestic economy significantly influenced the state's interest and initiatives in the subregion. The revenue accruing from petroleum sales endowed the state with the financial capacity to embark on resource-intensive industrialization projects, which were, and still are, perceived as potential vehicles for vertically integrating domestic resources and sectoral economic activity. Plans were also formulated with a view to expanding the manufacturing sector and promoting agroindustry. The dream of establishing a steel project, which dates as far back as the 1960s, was destined to become a reality with the availability of financial resources for sustaining this capital-intensive activity. The emphasis is on steel, fertilizer, liquified natural gas, methanol, aluminum, cement, and other vital infrastructural development necessary

TABLE 6.4. Energy-Based Projects

Project	Total, 1974-76 (TT$)
Joint Venture Fertilizer Project (AMOCO)	13,589.71
Regional Aluminium Smelter	400,000.00
Petrochemical Complex	75,522.00
Iron and Steel Project	8,657,021.00
Tringen	97,115,347.80
Point Lisas Development	1,100,000.00
Point Lisas Power Station	28,474,832.68
Other	3,400,000.00
Total	139,236,323.19

Source: Government of Trinidad/Tobago, Accounting for the Petro-Dollar (Port of Spain: Government Printery, 1977).

for the efficient functioning of these projects. Up to the end of 1976, the government of Trinidad/Tobago had made outlays for the energy-based projects listed in Table 6.4.

Government's expenditure on these eight projects was TT$139.2 million up to 1976, and there is evidence that the long-range goal of securing regional markets to absorb some of the products of government's heavy and light industrial-processing activity constituted one of the bases of the country's policy of helping its neighbours. Fertilizers, asphalt, and petroleum products are the main commodities on which there is emphasis for securing significant regional absorption. Commenting on prospects for exports of fertilizer, one government source noted:

The fertiliser plant at Point Lisas was completed in March 1978, and is now at full production. The capacity of the plant is approximately 15,000 tons of mixed fertilisers per year. Local requirements are expected to be of the order of 8,000 tons, with the surplus being exported to the CARICOM region and external markets. [6]

It is not accidental that Trinidad/Tobago's aid policies contain provisions that would enhance the deployment of these products, by assisting buyers in the region. It was clearly stated:

> . . . the Government of Trinidad and Tobago has
> been examining the scope for increasing its aid to
> the region on the basis of the country's sales of oil,
> fertiliser and asphalt to the CARICOM market.[7]

In addition to the goal of finding regional outlets for oil,
asphalt, and fertilizer, there was also a concern with marketing
"good items and such other products as may be determined from
time to time."[8] This provision is defined broadly enough to
encompass a wide range of non-oil-based goods coming from the
manufacturing sector, in which output had grown by 44 percent
in real terms between 1972 and 1976. As activity and production
in the manufacturing sector began to expand, policymakers began
to think in terms of formulating economic policies that would be
advantageous to the search for assured markets. Within the
framework of the aid extended to CARICOM members, mechanisms
for promoting exports were built in, tying aid to commodity absorption in the regional market. Provision 3 of the Guidelines
of the Caribbean Aid Project specifies that: "Priority should be
given to commodities and trade from Trinidad/Tobago over all
third countries, subject to the provisions of the CARICOM
Treaty."[9] Similarly, Provision 12 of the guidelines states:
"Loans may also be made to establish a line of credit for Trinidad/
Tobago products and would be denominated only in Trinidad/
Tobago currency."[10] Trinidad/Tobago's industrialization drive
and the expanded activity in the manufacturing sector provided
the impetus for the conduct of a resource diplomacy whereby
petroleum, asphalt, and fertilizer could be marketed in the subregion, as well as serve as a basis for extending aid to neighbour-
ing states.

In addition to these factors, the massive accumulation of
government revenues after 1973 led to a concern about the amount
of liquidity in the monetary system. Official sources note:

> Total revenues, including receipts from the Unemploy-
> ment Levy, increased at the phenomenal annual average
> rate of 54 percent in the period 1973-1977 and the
> proportion of GDP captured by the revenue system
> rose from 19.3 per cent in 1973 to 38.4 per cent in
> 1977.[11]

Policies were formulated to control, as much as possible,
increases in the price of consumer items; to boost domestic output
and, hopefully, employment through government incentives and
subsidies; and to profitably invest, at home and abroad, some

of the surplus capital. Aspects of these safety-valve measures
included the buying of government securities to the tune of
TT$3 million, with the breakdown as follows:

Seller	TT$ Million
Grenada	1.85
Saint Lucia	0.05
Dominica	0.75
Saint Vincent	0.35

World Bank bonds for use in CARICOM countries were also pur-
chased for a total of TT$12 million, while direct balance-of-
payments support to the MDCs was also extended. Jamaica
received U.S. $112 million; Barbados, U.S. $10 million; and
Guyana, U.S. $20 million.[12] These are but a few examples of
the areas in the external environment to which surplus petrodollars have been directed as a result of the unprecedented
influx of revenue.[13]

The gaining of regional endorsement and, hopefully, the
ultimate institutionalization of Trinidad/Tobago's national airline
so that it would be the regional air carrier was another domestic
or, rather, national economic interest that was taken into consideration in the making of the government's plan to help its
neighbours. This issue of whether or not British West Indian
Airways (BWIA) should be established as the regional airline
has been a perennial source of controversy among members of
the English-speaking Caribbean. In the 1960s, one Trinidad/
Tobago government minister, commenting on this problem, stated:

> . . . all major points of dissatisfaction must be pushed
> aside in the interest of regional unity. I have no
> doubt that BWIA will be accepted as the Regional
> Airline in the not too distant future.[14]

The enhanced financial status of this state in the post-1973
period placed it in the position to conduct an aid programme
into which there would be built-in safeguards to rule out possible
competition that could keep its airline from attaining the long-
coveted status of regional air carrier in the long run. With
BWIA being the "airline with the energy," and with the Trinidad/
Tobago government in a financial position to cope with deficits
incurred by the airline, this objective of making BWIA the regional
airline has not been abandoned. The government has agreed to
give loans on condition that applicants do not utilize these funds

to either set up, expand, or subsidize operations of other national airlines that could compete with that of the donor. Provision 9 of the guidelines states: "Financial assistance to beneficiaries should be predicated on enhancing the role and expansion of the national airline, Trinidad and Tobago Airways Corporation (TTAC)."[15]

Yet another situation in the domestic setting that has influenced, in some way, the conditions under which this MDC has agreed to give financial aid to CARICOM member states was the demand among the local businessmen. With the severe economic crisis and the shortage of foreign exchange with which to pay for imports, CARICOM members found themselves in debt. Import restrictions were imposed by Jamaica and Guyana as emergency measures, and this contributed to tensions in the relations among these states and Trinidad/Tobago, where some 39 businesses were reportedly affected. Having assumed the role of aid donor, this MDC seized the opportunity to indirectly influence recipients to use loans received for clearing outstanding debts to its local exporters.

The foregoing illustrates that Trinidad/Tobago's aid policy is directly related to particular circumstances (e.g., the oil bonanza, rapid industrialization, and superior economic capabilities) and to changed needs (e.g., expanded market outlets and profitable deployment of surplus capital).

THE RATIONALE AND SCOPE OF TRINIDAD/TOBAGO'S ACTIVITY AS DONOR

The strong feeling of obligation on the basis of affinity is certainly one of the characteristics of the aid activity amongst third-world states. Whatever motivations may lead the industrialized nations of the world to offer financial assistance to the third world, the feeling of affinity is perhaps not a major motivating factor. Aid from these sources is aimed primarily at promoting and/or maintaining certain ideological postures and protecting the economic interests of the donor. One analyst, commenting on the political implications and rationale of North American aid policies, points out:

> . . . aid in support of more rapid economic development can contribute to reducing the risk of revolutionary disorder through easing at least some of the frustrations of poverty and improving opportunity for nonviolent evolutionary change.[16]

It is, however, difficult to state that the donors of aid to
hinterland economies do not have their own political and ideological
considerations. The truth is that political and societal conditions
in the recipient states do constitute vital considerations in the
formulation of lending policies of these emergent aid donors.
States, whether or not they are relatively new donors, tend to
give aid either to states that share their political/ideological
posture or to those states whose geostrategic position may be
vital to their politico-economic interests. For example, Kuwait
and other Arab oil producers give aid to Arab and non-Arab
nations for a variety of political reasons. One analyst noted:

> During the Pakistani-Indian war, it is reported that
> Libya offered its help to Pakistan. . . . States such
> as Algeria, Libya and Iraq have been known to
> support anti-imperialist, leftist national liberation
> movements and states, while Saudi Arabia and to
> some extent Kuwait, Qatar, and the United Arab
> Emirates are likely either to support the status quo
> or actively finance religious, anti-communist move-
> ments. [17]

Because of this geostrategic importance, donor states may also
be attempting to diminish the influence of any other donor states
that attempt to woo the recipients.
   Trinidad/Tobago's policy is influenced by considerations
for maintaining a national and regional environment that enhances,
rather than jeopardizes, its developmental efforts. Any political
turbulence in the region would not be in Trinidad/Tobago's best
interests as far as its economic development process is concerned,
since such turbulence is known to spread with a fair degree of
rapidity from one island to another. Although Trinidad/Tobago
was among the three Commonwealth Caribbean states to establish
diplomatic relations with Cuba, Trinidad/Tobago is somewhat
suspicious about Cuba's activities in the region. Consequently,
states politically and ideologically close to Cuba would not be
likely to be showered with aid. In fact, the new Grenadian
regime headed by Maurice Bishop has not received any aid from
the Trinidad/Tobago government. The question to be posed
immediately is: Why did Trinidad/Tobago give assistance to the
Manley and Burnham regimes, despite their adherence to varying
brands of democratic and cooperative socialism and despite their
closeness with the Castro regime? The answer to that question
lies not so much in the politics and ideology of Messrs. Burnham
and Manley as it does in Bishop's method of coming to power.

This is borne out by Trinidad/Tobago's prime minister's reported refusal to read and reply to correspondence from the Bishop administration, as well as by a lack of interest in discussing areas for economic cooperation.

Trinidad/Tobago's role of aid donor has not gone unnoticed within and outside of the country. Indeed, domestic and external constituencies have certainly tried to influence the government's aid programme. The Antigua Caribbean Liberation Movement (ACLM) and the members of the opposition United Labour Front (ULF) requested that the Trinidad/Tobago government refuse Antigua's application for a TT$136-million loan because of its alleged South African connection. Similarly, opinions expressed via the local media constitute another influence in government's consideration of potential recipients of its assistance. For example, one report queried whether or not Trinidad/Tobago was "wasting money" when it granted loans to "Socialist Jamaica." These inputs, however, do not seem sufficiently strong to influence the government's aid policy. A summation of Trinidad/Tobago's aid policy would state that politics and ideology do play a role in the aid-granting process but that the ideological overtones are not as strong as those of traditional aid donors. Countries on the left or on the right of the political spectrum are not likely to be automatically excluded from aid. Countries that are regarded as steering a moderate course and those on the right will be the recipient of aid without problems. Countries on the left would not be excluded provided that their leftism did not hold that revolutionary fervour that would spread to Trinidad—e.g., Guyana and Jamaica. A country that has the revolutionary fervour and has come into power via the gun would be excluded from aid offers—e.g., Grenada.[18] Given the fact that Trinidad/Tobago recently established a Caribbean Aid Council and that its Facility for Financing Oil, Fertilizer, and Asphalt Purchases is administered by political institutions, it is inevitable that political considerations will constitute a major criterion in deciding who assistance will be extended to. It is important to monitor the activity of third-world donors, in order to ascertain whether or not the objectives of their activity are similar to those of the traditional aid donors. It is of interest to note that most oil exporters have opted for the path of development within the context of global capitalism, and are likely to imitate the behaviour of the metropole in their efforts to move vertically within the system.

The time dimension and geographical scope of the aid programmes of these petrodollar powers constitute other peculiar features of their role and activity as aid donors. Since oil is a wasting asset, it means that the source of this surplus capital, which is being siphoned by the developing world, is being depleted. Moreover, the absorptive capacity of these economies increases with the implementation of capital intensive industrialization programmes; and, as other social and economic policies in the domestic environment demand greater financial commitment, the volume of assistance to other developing states is likely to decline.

Like other oil exporters, Trinidad/Tobago only acquired the capabilities for assuming the status of aid donor in the 1973-74 period. The deluge of petrodollars resulting from the hike in oil prices brought into sharp focus the major contribution of the mining sector to the country's gross domestic product. For example, of a GDP of TT$981.2 million in 1973, the petroleum sector accounted for TT$699.3 million. By 1974, the GDP had risen to TT$2.2 billion, of which that sector contributed TT$1.8 billion.[19] The level of crude oil production also rose in that period, from 60.6 million barrels in 1973 to 68.1 million barrels in 1974.[20] There was also a restructuring of government's system of petroleum taxation, which was expected to increase government's take in 1974 by 190 percent. In fact, the government of Trinidad/Tobago, in rationalizing its interest in assisting its CARICOM partners, noted that the country's lending capacity was indeed a phenomenon of the seventies. According to one official document:

> The life of the [new oil] Facility will be determined
> by subsequent events in the international market
> for petroleum products and by the economic strength
> of Trinidad and Tobago, which, for the foreseeable
> future, is dependent on the former factor.[21]

The fact that this source of surplus capital for lending to states in economic distress is of recent origin, and that the assistance to these states is regarded as crucial to strengthening intra-CARICOM relations and to the viability of the integration movement, all interacted to significantly influence the country's activity. The emphasis has been on "the need for rapid—yet managed—transfer of financial resources to the various CARICOM states. . . ."[22]

Given the reality of this temporary nature of the availability of large surpluses of capital for extending aid, and, in the case of this MDC, the comparatively limited resources for doing so, the geographical scope of the country's activity has been confined to the CARICOM subregion.

MECHANISMS FOR ADMINISTERING AID

Following the massive inflow of petrodollars, members of OPEC, cognizant of the need to maintain third-world support for the organization's hike in oil prices, hastened to commit funds to be siphoned by the developing world.

Trinidad/Tobago is not a member of OPEC, but, as the only English-speaking Caribbean state with petroleum resources, it was in the position to embark on aid programmes within the scope of its subregion. Aid is administered primarily on a bilateral basis through the buying of government bonds and the giving of direct balance-of-payments and budgetary support to the MDCs. The channels through which this financial assistance is administered can be classified as political institutions. Inputs and influences from political groups and business interests are taken into consideration while the cabinet and the decision of the political leadership are crucial determinants of which application gets aid. For example, it was stated:

The Trinidad and Tobago Aid Project will be required to:
(a) Operate on the basis of guidelines laid down by Cabinet;
(b) Report to Parliament through the Auditor General. [23]

The Central Bank and the Ministry of Finance were the agencies through which funds were made available to these applicants. Loans totaling TT $37 million were also raised on the Trinidad/Tobago capital market for use in CARICOM countries.

In 1974, US $25 million was given to Jamaica, repayable as follows:

Date	Amount
December 31, 1976	US $2.0 million (repaid)
December 31, 1977	US $5.0 million
December 31, 1978	US $8.0 million
December 31, 1979	US $10.0 million

In that same year, a loan of US $20 million was made to Guyana, repayable as follows:

Date	Amount
December 15, 1976	U.S. $45.0 million (request to convert into bonds)
December 15, 1977	U.S. $5.0 million
December 15, 1978	U.S. $5.0 million
December 15, 1979	U.S. $5.0 million

Barbados received a loan of U.S. $10 million in 1974, to be taken up in 1977. Fifty percent of this sum was drawn on January 10, 1977, and the loan is repayable in four equal installments beginning January 31, 1979. The interest rate on all these loans is figured on an average of three-month treasury bills of four Central Banks.[24] Fixed deposits of U.S. $10 million with the Bank of Jamaica have also been made, through the Trinidad/Tobago Central Bank, as well as promissory notes worth U.S. $55 million, with an interest rate of 8.85 percent, repayable in five equal installments at the end of the third year (i.e., 1979-83).[25] The assistance listed in Table 6.5 has also been extended to some LDCs, again on a bilateral basis and conducted through the Central Bank.

The feature that stands out in this country's aid administration is the bilateralism that characterizes the receipt, processing, and finalizing of applications for assistance, and the lack of institutionalized mechanisms, at the national level, for handling disbursements. Unlike Venezuela, for example, which has the Fondo de Inversiones de Venezuela, the Central Bank, the Ministry of Finance, and the Instituto de Comercio Exterior, through which funds for specific projects and programmes are disbursed, this MDC relies heavily on the Ministry of Finance and the Central Bank for administering aid to applicants. Moreover, in the early period, the heads of state convened, discussed, and finalized agreements for assistance. On June 6, 1976, the political leaders of the four MDCs met in Port of Spain to finalize an agreement on which there had been previous discussions at bilateral level.[26] Prior to that, these leaders had, in 1974, met to discuss the ways in which the adverse effects of the energy crisis could be dealt with on a collective basis, and Trinidad/Tobago had given loans of TT$25 million to Jamaica, U.S. $20 million to Guyana, and U.S. $10 million to Barbados. This MDC is the largest contributor and the only nonborrowing member of the Balance-of-Payments Mutual Support Interim Facility.

Prior to 1977-78, there were no attempts at combining multilateral approaches to existing methods of administering aid to

TABLE 6.5. Assistance to LDCs

Country	Term	Amount ($TT)
Grenada		
7 percent debentures	1972-83	450,000
6 1/2 percent debentures	1976-81	400,000
Government treasury bills due	6/27/74	700,000*
7 1/2 percent bonds	1982-83	300,000
		1,850,000
Saint Lucia		
7 3/4 percent bonds	1981-83	50,000
Dominica		
7 1/2 percent bonds	1980-82	50,000
Dominica treasury bills due	3/16/77	700,000
		750,000
Saint Vincent		
7 1/2 percent bonds	1982-83	50,000
8 percent bonds	1987-88	300,000
		350,000

*These Grenada government treasury bills have not been rolled over but are still outstanding.

Source: Accounting for the Petrodollar (Port of Spain: Government Printery, 1977).

CARICOM, nor was there any specialized agency to deal specifically with this activity. Government technocrats were marshaled to deal with applications for loans on an ad hoc basis.

In 1977, Trinidad/Tobago's policymakers demonstrated a willingness to get involved in a multilateral arrangement in collaboration with industrialized states and those agencies which have been traditional aid donors to members of the Anglophone Caribbean. In fact, Eric Williams is credited with having proposed to the visiting U.S. Secretary of State, Cyrus Vance, that a regional aid consortium be established. Two months later, when the U.S. ambassador to the United Nations, Andrew Young, went on his extended tour of the Caribbean and Latin America, it became apparent that efforts were being made to get Venezuela actively involved in the proposed consortium. Trinidad/Tobago, having already expressed its concern over the political implications of Venezuela's interest in assisting members of the subregion, decided to play a passive part in the Caribbean Group for Cooperation in Economic Development.

What is noteworthy is the fact that the preference for using bilateral arrangements for the directing of aid to other developing states is not peculiar to Trinidad and Tobago. One official source noted:

> The preponderant use of bilateral channels for directing the OPEC countries' concessional aid flows to other developing countries [88 per cent in both 1974 and 1975] resembles the pattern set by the OECD countries which channelled more than 80 per cent of their official development assistance bilaterally as late as 1971 and were still channelling as much as 83 per cent bilaterally in 1974.[27]

Nevertheless, it has been noted that oil-producing donors, while they do not want to totally relinquish the significant amount of political influence they could wield through bilateral arrangements, have been making use of certain multilateral channels, and of the expertise to be found within UN and regional institutions. While Trinidad/Tobago has avoided the use of multilateral channels for the administering of financial assistance, the political leadership has nevertheless stated its intention to "consult regularly with the International Monetary Fund [IMF] in respect of its Assistance to the Caribbean countries, provided the IMF so agrees."[28] Similarly, when it was decided that a Special Facility for Financing Oil, Fertiliser, and Asphalt Purchases should be established, it was reported that discussions on this were to be held with officials from the World Bank and the IMF. Like other OPEC aid donors, this state has been taking steps to make use of the expertise in these multilateral lending agencies. Nevertheless, there is the marked preference to carry out its own aid programme.

Aid is tied to projects and procurement. Under the initial guidelines of the Caribbean Aid Council, project aid applications were not being expeditiously processed and financed, for a variety of reasons. There were, however, applications received for this type of aid from Antigua and Saint Vincent up to the time of publication of the White Paper on CARICOM 1973-1978.

> Antigua applied for a loan of EC$150.26 million for
> projects covering infra-structure, industry, tourism,
> agriculture and purchase of property.
>
> St. Vincent applied for an additional TT$5.0 million
> to finance its sugar factory.[29]

Government officials subsequently noted that "loan approvals
and disbursements under this Facility have been modest primarily
because of constraints following from the project-oriented nature
of lending."[30] The problem of shortage of personnel to carry
out feasibility studies as prerequisites for approval and disbursement of funds was a major constraint to the effective functioning
of the programme. While project aid is still an integral part of
the country's aid programme, procurement aid is an even more
salient characteristic of it. Applications for loans to buy goods
and services from the donor state had been submitted by
Dominica, Guyana, and Jamaica up to the time the White Paper
on CARICOM was published.[31] While the Jamaican application
was withdrawn, to date, the Trinidad/Tobago government has
disbursed funds to Saint Vincent, Antigua, and Guyana in the
form of procurement aid.

The disbursements of procurement aid noted in Table 6.6
have been made to date (mid-1980).

The government of Trinidad/Tobago has developed a specific
division for dealing with the economic and functional cooperation
with CARICOM members: the division for CARICOM affairs, with
Senator Mervyn de Souza as minister. The Caribbean Aid Council, as a mechanism for processing loans, particularly for projects,
was plagued with a shortage of personnel to carry out feasibility
studies; and, as the shortage of foreign exchange to finance
imports became more severe in the region, another mechanism
to meet this demand was devised. In March 1980, a committee
headed by Euric Bobb, deputy governor of the Central Bank,
began working on the guidelines for this new facility, which is
devised as a purely programme type of assistance. The government of Trinidad/Tobago opened a special CARICOM Oil Facility
Account to be operated by the Central Bank as agent, and the
state has accepted responsibility for incremental costs of commodities (oil, fertiliser, and asphalt), using as a base the prices
of the products effective from December 26, 1978. With the
CARICOM region using an estimated 80,000 barrels of petroleum
products per day, and with importing territories in serious debt,
the minister of CARICOM Affairs reasoned that this MDC was
concerned with the issue of "how to supply members of CARICOM

TABLE 6.6. Disbursements of Procurement Aid

Country	Disbursement (TT$)
Antigua: loan in 1979 for the purchase of factory shells	456,490.58
Antigua: loan in 1979 for the purchase, supply, and installation of approximately 2.5 to .5 mw of generating plant for Antigua, and for purchase of replacement parts for existing generating equipment	3,822,917.00
Guyana: grant in 1978 for the supply of foodstuffs and toiletries from Trinidad and Tobago, to relieve a serious shortage caused by electricity failure	801,969.80
Total	5,081,377.38

Source: Trinidad and Tobago Ministry of Finance, "Aid to CARICOM Countries, Total Disbursements to Date" (Port of Spain, 1980).

with very favourable terms to provide them with their oil requirements."[32] The emphasis in the Caribbean Aid Project is on the granting of project and programme aid, while the Facility for Financing Oil, Fertiliser and Asphalt Purchases is geared to fulfill more urgent and immediate import needs, while indirectly ameliorating balance-of-payments problems, as less foreign exchange goes toward payments for these products. Loans under this deferred-payment facility will be for a 15-year period, with a three-year grace period and with an interest rate of 3 percent for the MDCs and 2 percent for the LDCs.[33]

An important aspect of this facility is its projected duration of about three years in this initial stage. This time span of aid projects set by developing oil-exporting territories is another characteristic that is peculiar to the activity of these emergent donors that are dependent on hydrocarbon resources and the revenue deriving therefrom, as the base of their role and initiatives as donor.[34]

Trinidad/Tobago is using petrodollar and resource diplomacy in conducting its activity as regional aid donor. For example, bilateral arrangements continue to predominate,[35] and efforts at institutionalizing channels at the national level, for dealing with loan applications and disbursements, are being undertaken. There is a propensity, in the granting of financial assistance, to transact arrangements on a government-to-government basis, while the regional development bank (the Caribbean Development Bank) is not utilized as a major agency for such activity. For example, to date (mid-1980), loans on a bilateral basis, in the form of project and procurement aid, total TT$8.7 million.[36] This includes neither balance-of-payments support nor emergency relief in times of natural disaster, nor the buying of government bonds. In contrast, loans raised on this MDC's capital market for extension to CARICOM states, through the Inter-American Development Bank, were TT$25 million and, through the Caribbean Development Bank, TT$12 million up to 1978. The purchase of World Bank bonds for use in CARICOM countries was valued at TT$12 million, and it is clear that the focus has been and will be on bilateral arrangements.[37] Efforts at strengthening such mechanisms as the Caribbean Aid Project (under the Caribbean Aid Council), and the Facility for Financing Oil, Fertiliser and Asphalt Purchases are likely to continue. It is evident that this MDC is not keen on collaborating with Venezuela and/or Mexico in conducting an aid programme for the subregion. President Perez's suggestion in 1978, and the speculation that Trinidad/Tobago ought to join these two states in their oil-facility project that recently came on stream, have not produced any indication of interest in participating in such joint ventures.

CONCLUSION

Trinidad/Tobago's aid programme was conceived as a potential instrument for profitably making use of the unprecedented wealth for which the domestic economy did not have an adequate absorptive capacity. The fact that the aid is tied to the purchase of this country's domestic exports also illustrates that it is expected to broaden avenues for the exporting and regional marketing of commodities. As the only aid donor among CARICOM states, this MDC is in a position to fulfill the role expectation of its CARICOM partners, and to buttress its status as regional economic leader. In other words, the aid programme would serve to counterbalance Venezuelan initiatives in assuming the role of major aid donor in the Caribbean community. The aid programme has within it certain provisions that will enable this state to fulfill certain economic objectives (i.e., promotion of BWIA as regional carrier; ruling out of construction of oil refineries in other states). The state, as the principal source of capital for loans to the region, will also be well poised to assume the status of regional financial center. As aid donor, Trinidad/Tobago will be in a position to indirectly influence economic and political developments in the recipient territory, thereby creating conditions that will not militate against efforts at consolidating intra-CARICOM relations. The aim is to ensure that projects are not duplicated; that institutions likely to compete with existing regional ones are not financed; and that tensions caused by outstanding debts to exporters are mitigated. Certain aspects of developments in the domestic politics of applicants could also be influenced, as there are specifications that loans must not be used for purchasing arms and ammunition or to transact arrangements with South Africa and Rhodesia. Such economic developments as the establishment of offshore banks and tax havens, and even the abolition of the income tax, negatively affect decisions by policymakers in the donor state to grant loans to states in which certain conditions exist. There has been an obvious refusal to enter into loan agreements with the Grenadian regime for political-cum-ideological reasons. The Grenadian government seems to possess more revolutionary zeal than the Guyanese government does or the Manley regime did. Its vote on Afghanistan and its closeness with the Nicaraguan regime testify to that. When these actions are compounded with rumours of Trinidadians being trained in Grenada as revolutionaries, one can understand the reluctance of the Trinidad/Tobago government to enter into loan agreements with the Grenadian government.

Trinidad/Tobago's lending philosophy has been influenced by both domestic and external factors. An important domestic factor is that oil is a wasting asset and its presence has to be employed to spark the development of other sectors of the economy that would sustain the country when the oil runs dry. The nature of the international economic order, requiring South-South states to collaborate to their fullest possible extent, is a strong impetus encouraging Trinidad/Tobago to play the role of aid donor. An examination of the mechanism employed for aid disbursement at the national level indicates that agencies for such disbursement have been created on an ad hoc basis in the Ministry of Finance, and only recently a ministry has been formed to deal with this matter. Lack of personnel is a major problem adding to the portfolios of government functionaries in these agencies.

Of decided interest is the bilateral nature of the aid and the avoidance of the use of regional institutions to disburse such aid.

Some of the characteristics of Trinidad/Tobago's aid giving are its limited geographic scope; the avoidance of multilateral institutions for aid disbursements and a preference for bilateral arrangements; the paucity of aid personnel; and the generosity of the aid given within the framework of the UN call for fulfillment of certain basic needs. Further, recent figures released by the Trinidad/Tobago government indicate that Trinidad/Tobago's contribution of aid for 1978 and 1979 has reached over 2 percent of its GDP; there is the political and ideological nature of the aid, and, finally, the objective of using such aid to strengthen the regional integration movement.

In summary, while members of CARICOM are likely to continue to supplement loans from this MDC with loans from aid agencies as well as other oil exporters in this hemisphere, CARICOM states, particularly the LDCs, can be expected to appreciate and make use of facilities made available to them by this geographically proximate donor. The donor, in turn, is likely to continue in its efforts to conduct a regional resource-based diplomacy, which, given the stress under which the integration movement is operating, may be one of the ways to maintain one important aspect of intra-CARICOM economic interaction.

NOTES

1. K. J. Holsti, International Politics: A Framework for Analysis (Englewood Cliffs: Prentice-Hall, 1972), p. 355.

2. "Excerpt from 'The Economics of Nationhood' on the financial Relationships between the Federal and Territorial Governments and on the Economic Development and Integration of the Area," published by the government of Trinidad and Tobago, September 1959. Documents on International Relations in the Caribbean, ed. Roy Preiswerk (Port of Spain: Institute of International Relations, University of the West Indies, and San Juan: Institute of Caribbean Studies, Puerto Rico University, 1970), p. 341.

3. An address by Eric Williams, prime minister of Trinidad and Tobago, to the 14th National West Indian Jaycees Convention, October 1, 1974 (Port of Spain: Office of the Prime Minister of Trinidad/Tobago, Public Relations Division, 1970), p. 6.

4. Guyana Chronicle, June 16, 1976.

5. Caribbean Task Force, Report of the Caribbean Task Force (Port of Spain: Government Printery, 1975), p. 37.

6. Review of the Economy, 1978, p. 42.

7. Government of Trinidad/Tobago, Facility for Financing Oil, Fertiliser and Asphalt Purchases by CARICOM States from Trinidad and Tobago (Port of Spain: Ministry of Finance, June 1980), p. 1.

8. Ibid., p. 6.

9. Ibid., p. 6.

10. Ibid., p. 7.

11. Report of the Committee To Review Government Expenditure (Port of Spain: Government Printery, 1978), p. 32.

12. Government of Trinidad/Tobago, White Paper on CARICOM, 1973-1978 (Port of Spain: Government Printery, 1979), p. 16.

13. A breakdown of the country's financial assistance to CARICOM was presented in an official document in which the government accounted for the ways in which the petrodollars were being utilized. See government of Trinidad and Tobago, Accounting for the Petrodollar (Port of Spain: Government Printery, 1977), pp. 36-37.

14. Kamaluddin Mohammed, Caribbean Integration (Port of Spain: Government Printery, 1969), p. 20.

15. Facility for Financing Oil, Fertiliser and Asphalt Purchases, p. 7. See also Provision 7:2 on p. 6, which deals with the same issue.

16. Paul Gordon Clarke, American Aid for Development (New York: Praeger, published for the Council on Foreign Relations, 1971), p. 74.

17. Abdo I. Baaklini, "Patterns of Aid: Kuwait, the Middle East and the Developing World," in OPEC and the Middle East: The Impact of Oil on Societal Development (New York: Praeger, 1977), pp. 161-62.

18. For example, in March 1980, Grenada's deputy prime minister complained of not being afforded the opportunity to discuss, with Trinidad/Tobago government officials, nine proposals for closer economic and function cooperation between the two states. The extent to which this MDC's leadership is adverse to the conduct of the new Grenada regime came out in the response by the minister for CARICOM affairs, Senator Mervyn De Souza, when he said, ". . . they [Grenada's proposals] may be contained in the letters we have not opened." See Express, March 14, 1980. On the other hand, Grenada, under the Gairy administration, received financial assistance from Trinidad/Tobago. See White Paper on CARICOM 1973-1978, p. 16.

19. Government of Trinidad/Tobago, Review of the Economy, 1978 (Port of Spain: Central Statistical Office Printing Unit, 1979), p. 80.

20. The production levels of crude are listed in the same publication; ibid., p. 76.

21. Facility for Financing Oil, Fertiliser and Asphalt Purchases, p. 2.

22. Ibid., p. 1.

23. White Paper on CARICOM, 1973-1978, p. 16.

24. Accounting for the Petrodollar, pp. 36-37.

25. Ibid., p. 36.

26. White Paper on CARICOM, 1973-1978, Appendix VI, p. 46.

27. UNCTAD Secretariat, Financial Solidarity for Development, TD/B/627 (New York: United Nations Publications, 1977), p. 7.

28. White Paper on CARICOM 1973-1978, p. 16.

29. White Paper on CARICOM 1973-1978, p. 17.

30. Facility for Financing Oil, Fertiliser and Asphalt Purchases, p. 1.

31. White Paper on CARICOM, 1973-1978, p. 17.

32. Trinidad Guardian, March 21, 1980.

33. Facility for Financing Oil, Fertiliser and Asphalt Purchases, p. 2.

34. Ibid., p. 2.

35. There have been discussions about bilateral financial assistance, and functional cooperation, with Barbados in April 1979; with Antigua in June 1979; and with Saint Vincent in May 1979.

36. Ministry of Finance, "Aid to CARICOM Countries: Total Disbursements to Date" (Port of Spain: Ministry of Finance, 1980). The breakdown is as follows: Saint Vincent, TT$3,600,000; Antigua, TT$4,279,407.58; and Guyana, TT$801,969.80.

37. See White Paper on CARICOM, 1973-1978, p. 16.

7

EMPLOYMENT AND THE UNPERCEIVED
ADVANTAGES OF BEING
A LATECOMER

Myron J. Frankman

Some 65 years ago, Thorstein Veblen spoke of the advantage of being a latecomer.[1] The latecomer can "borrow" from the pioneer and may well be able to overcome the latter's early lead. Building on this insight of Veblen, Wendell Gordon urged the Latin American countries in the mid-1960s to "jump to the technological frontier"—to speed their development by acquiring the most modern productive facilities available.[2] Such counsel tends to be contrary to the current writing on development by many economists, who urge labor-abundant, poor countries to spurn modern labor-saving equipment lest their employment problems be exacerbated. To turn one's back on capital-intensive technology requires, in one view, a radical delinking from the world capitalist economy,[3] while in another, more common view, it requires altering the relative price of labor and capital so as to encourage labor absorption in industry.[4]

More recently, Albert Hirschman has mused about the disadvantages of "late-late industrialization."[5] From a not altogether different perspective, the writers of the dependency school have sketched in detail the difficulties confronting the very late latecomer in a highly articulated, transnational, corporation-dominated world capitalist economy.[6] Both Hirschman and the dependency

---

This is a slightly revised version of a paper presented at the Carleton University symposium on Latin American prospects for the 1980s, in Ottawa in November 1980. I should like to thank Barbara Haskel and William Watson for helpful comments.

school have questioned the ability of late-late industrialization
to provide jobs. It is my contention that jobs are indeed being
provided; the fact that the bulk of these jobs are being created
outside of industry and agriculture should not of itself be a
cause for concern, but may well be essential to the creation of
thoroughly modern, internationally competitive national economies
in Latin America and elsewhere.

A numerical example of structural change in employment
during the 1960s in two sets of countries, whose identity will
remain hidden for the moment, highlights the nature of recent
job creation, albeit at the highly aggregative level given by the
customary threefold division of agriculture, industry, and services. It seems clear from the absolute changes in labor-force
structure that the sample-B countries have not advanced as far
in their structural transformation as the sample-A countries:
In the sample-B countries, agriculture had not yet experienced
absolute declines in its labor force and additions to service employment were a little more than double the increment in industrial
employment (see Table 7.1). The sample-A countries as a group
would appear to have experienced the stereotypical distortions
of rapidly urbanizing, rapidly industrializing countries in which
incentives are heavily tilted in favor of the acquisition of capital-
intensive, labor-saving machinery and equipment. I note that
in group A, the increase in service employment was equal to
96 percent of the growth of the total labor force. We shall return
to group A and group B later.

Marshall McLuhan has decried what he terms "rear-view
mirrorism": walking into the future looking resolutely backward.[7]
I would suggest that much of the development literature is guilty
of just such rear-view mirrorism. The approach to closing the
gap between the rich and poor countries can be compared to the
marksman who endeavors to hit a moving target by shooting
either at the target's location during the current moment or at
where it was yesterday or even last week. Clearly, a direct hit
requires aiming at the point in the trajectory that the target is
expected to reach. Employment- and investment-policy prescriptions that take as their point of departure the comparisons of
employment patterns in less developed countries, today, and in
industrial countries, when they had a comparable degree of urbanization or per capita income, are patent examples of rear-mirrorism.
Alternatively, one might argue that the source of our error is
not in our looking backward, but, rather, that we base ourselves
on an inadequate understanding of the past. As recently as
1970, the noted Oxford economic historian R. M. Hartwell spoke
of the obvious importance of the growing service sector of Eng-

TABLE 7.1. Change in Labor-Force Structure for Two Eleven-Country Samples, 1970 Relative to 1960

Sector	Changes in Employment (millions)		Changes in Labor-Force Shares (percentage points)	
	Sample A	Sample B	Sample A	Sample B
Agriculture	-4.28	2.66	-3.5	-6.8
Industry	5.12	4.60	-2.1	1.7
Services	20.39	9.30	5.6	5.1
Total labor force	21.24	16.57	5.6	5.1

Note: Agriculture includes agriculture, forestry, hunting and fishing. Industry includes mining, manufacturing, construction, electricity, water, and gas. Services includes all others.

Source: Derived from International Labour Organization, Labour Force Estimates and Projections 1950-2000, 2d ed. (Geneva: ILO, 1977).

land's economy during the industrial revolution,[8] and observed
that "the history, measurement and analysis of economic change
in the tertiary sector of the English economy during the industrial revolution remains a largely unexplored and important area
of research for the economic historians."[9]

In contrast, policy prescriptions that take, instead, as
their point of departure the supposed relative labor abundance
and capital scarcity are not even aiming at a point in someone
else's past, but, rather, are making a quantum leap from an
ahistorical static-equilibrium model, the resemblance of which
to reality in the smallest measure is likely to be the purest of
chance. To provide just one example, I draw your attention to
the following statement of Marcelo Selowsky of the World Bank:

> Additional efforts for factor costs to reflect relative
> scarcities must be made. This is well known. . . .
> A special effort is made to assess the payoff of im-
> proving labor market functioning so that increases
> in labor demand can be translated into stronger in-
> creases in employment.[10]

Selowsky spoke of this as a "tricky" matter,[11] and seemed to
suggest that getting prices right would go no further than shifting the burden of social security taxes away from employers
and to general tax revenues.[12] It doesn't require much imagination to guess what kinds of actions the economist's technical
counsel "to improve labor market functioning" is likely to suggest
to a military government.

Factor costs that reflect relative scarcities are supposed
to be the key to expanding industrial employment. Indeed,
Selowsky's only table relating to employment is addressed to
industrial employment and apparently to getting prices right.[13]
He went on to discuss the satisfaction of basic needs in terms
of the cost in percentage of gross national product, but not in
terms of the required expansion of service employment: namely,
health-care personnel, teachers, employees in transportation
and distribution, and public service employment. The economist's
plea that relative scarcities be properly reflected derives from
a static theoretical model that predisposes him to consider primarily or exclusively activities like agriculture and industry,
which produce tangible outputs, and to overlook, downgrade,
or scorn service-sector employment.

If the main objective of forcing the absorption of labor in
industry is to provide income to individuals, then I suggest
that there are far more efficient and effective ways to do this.

I would further suggest that those who advocate measures for
adjusting prices to account for relative scarcities may well have
overlooked the potential that modern techniques have for reducing
toil and for freeing the human spirit for less alienating, more
ennobling activities. The free-market and Marxist economists
seem to converge in their disdain for capital-intensive machinery
(one speaks of factor proportions, and the other speaks of technological dependence). Paradoxically, both would seem to support
an outcome in which the alienation of the worker would be increased.

A proper answer to the question "development for whom?"
would seem to be an essential starting point. I offer an answer
provided by Nicholas Georgescu-Roegen:

> . . . the true "product" of the economic process is
> not a material flow, but a psychic flux—the enjoy-
> ment of life by every member of the population. It
> is this psychic flux which . . . constitutes the
> pertinent notion of income in economic analysis.[14]

If enjoyment of life and reduction of toil are our clear desiderata,
I believe we must conduct our search for solutions in a distinctly
different manner.

I should like to suggest that the Latin American countries
would do well to continue to take advantage of their historic
opportunity by borrowing selectively all the best and most advanced technology, practices, and institutional arrangements
from the industrial countries. The agenda for modernization
through implantation and adaptation of foreign methods should
not stop at agriculture and industry. (I note that a recent
inter-American Development Bank report on Economic and Social
Progress in Latin America comments separately only on the
agricultural, industrial and energy sectors, in its account of
general economic trends. The growth of the service sector
apparently did not warrant comment.)[15] The agenda must continue to encompass the service sector and must give a key role
to professional development and public administration, including
relevant tax measures and welfare programs. I should like to
stress the need for tax measures and welfare programs, in that
problems of underemployment and/or low remuneration can perhaps only be dealt with in the short run through redistributive
programs that provide access either to discretionary purchasing
power or directly to selected goods and services.

If it is reasonable to expect that employment patterns in
developing countries and industrialized countries may eventually

converge, then we are well advised to consider the direction in which employment is heading in the industrialized countries. I shall not provide exhaustive support for my reading of the already observable trends, but will, I hope, give sufficient indication to support my contention that if the less developed countries, or more particularly the Latin American nations, wish to build internationally competitive economies, they should continue to promote investment in the most productive types of facilities available. Remedies for unemployment and underemployment and for skewed income distribution must be found elsewhere; they should not be sought by endeavoring to increase the labor-to-capital ratio in industry.

SERVICE-EMPLOYMENT GROWTH

Let us consider first the changes in the shares of labor force employed in agriculture, industry, and services in the industrialized countries between 1960 and 1978, as reported by the World Bank in its World Development Report, 1980. For the 18 countries identified as industrialized, the average labor-force share in agriculture fell from 17 percent to 6 percent, with the change reaching almost revolutionary proportions in Finland, Italy, and Japan, where labor-force shares in agriculture dropped from 36 to 14 percent, 31 to 13 percent, and 33 to 13 percent, respectively.[16] Each of these three countries registered increases in the share of employment in industry, but without exception the increase in service employment was greater. In Finland, which registered the largest percentage-point decline in agricultural employment, industrial employment increased by six percentage points, while service employment increased by 16 percentage points. For the industrial countries as a group, industrial employment increased by only one percentage point, from 38 to 39 percent, while service employment increased by ten percentage points, from 45 to 55 percent.[17] A different perspective on what might well be regarded as the long-run future role of industrial employment may be provided by considering the countries presently in the avant-garde in the historical movement to remove man from the soil. If we arbitrarily divide the industrialized countries into two categories, those which had 20 percent or more of their labor force in agriculture in 1960 and those which had less, we notice a very striking pattern: Of the 11 countries in the latter category, eight registered declines in the share of employment in industry and, during the decade of the 1960s, two recorded absolute declines in indus-

trial employment (Belgium and Sweden; industrial employment
in the United Kingdom rose by less than one-tenth of 1 percent).[18]
By now it should be clear that these 11 countries are my sample-
A countries.[19] It is important to stress that having almost
reached the limit as far as the departure of the labor force from
agriculture is concerned, they are now experiencing relative
declines in the industrial labor force and may well all experience
before long the net expulsion of labor from industry. The basic
fact of life that the bulk of future employment throughout the
world will be service employment must be fully understood by
policymakers and by society at large.

My sample-B countries, the 11 Latin American countries
whose populations exceeded 5 million in 1978, have yet, as a
group, to experience an absolute decline in agricultural population
(although this has begun in four of the 11: Argentina, Chile,
Colombia, and Venezuela).[20] Together these 11 countries have
over 100 million people living in rural areas.[21] In the 1980s
and 1990s we can reasonably expect to witness an absolute decline
in agricultural population in Latin America and, with it, an explosive growth in service employment. Woe betide both the
remnants of democracy and the hopes for its restoration in Latin
America if earnest attempts are made to expand industrial employment much beyond the rate at which it is likely to grow in any
event.

Dennis Gabor, a Nobel Prize winner in physics, has offered
a guess as to the structure of employment in advanced industrial
countries in the year 2000. He sees only 20 percent of the population working as production operatives, leaving 80 percent to
be engaged in supplying intangibles.[22] This may well under-
estimate the changes directly ahead of us.

Rather than engage in such flights of fancy, I would suggest
that a detailed breakdown of service-sector employment in any
of the advanced countries will provide an instructive clue to
emerging employment patterns in Latin America. For this purpose,
I have looked at the structure of U.S. service employment, a
breakdown of which appears in Table 7.2. While total employment
grew by 20.1 percent over the period 1970 to 1978, equivalent
to an average annual compound rate of 2.3 percent, eight categories of service employment grew more rapidly. Of those eight,
employment in the following six grew at an average annual compound rate greater than 4.0 percent (or 36.9 percent for the
period): welfare and religious agencies (84.4 percent for the
period); health services (69.4 percent); business services (51.8);
automobile services (45.6); entertainment and recreation (42.2);
and finance, insurance, and real estate (37.1). Note that the

TABLE 7.2. U.S. Service Employment

Service	Employment		Total Change (percent)*	Employment in 1978 per 1,000 of Total Population
	1970 (millions)	1978 (millions)		
Transport, communications, and other public utilities	5.3	6.2	15.9	27.9
Wholesale and retail trade	15.0	19.3	28.4	87.0
Finance, insurance, and real estate	3.9	5.4	37.1	24.3
Business services	1.4	2.1	51.8	9.5
Automobile services	0.6	0.9	45.6	4.1
Personal services†	4.3	3.8	-10.5	17.5
Private households	1.8	1.4	-21.6	6.3
Hotels and lodging places	1.0	1.1	9.9	5.0
Entertainment and recreation	0.7	1.0	42.2	4.5
Professional and related†	12.9	18.3	42.1	83.8
Hospitals	2.8	3.8	33.1	17.1
Health services	1.6	2.8	69.4	12.6
Education	6.1	7.2	17.2	32.4
Welfare and religious agencies	0.8	1.5	84.4	6.8
Public administration	4.5	5.0	12.2	22.5
Total employed				
Services†	49.0	62.5	27.6	285.8
All sectors	78.6	94.4	20.1	431.5

*Percentages are calculated from data to the nearest thousand that appear in source.
†Includes activities not shown separately.

Source: U.S. Department of Commerce, Bureau of the Census, Statistical Abstract of the United States 1979 (Washington, D.C.: Government Printing Office, 1979), p. 403.

only category that registered a decline in number employed was that of personal services, with 86 percent of that decline represented by the fall in personal services in households.[23]

The table indicates the number employed in each activity per thousand of the total U.S. population. This kind of calculation might well be useful in a consideration of employment policy in Latin America. Let us take just one example from the health-care area: If Colombia were to have increased the number of physicians and nursing persons recorded as the 1977 average in the industrialized countries, it would have had to add in 1980 approximately 28,900 to its stock of doctors and 100,000 to its stock of nursing personnel.[24] These two increments alone would have accounted for at least 1.4 percent of Colombia's total 1980 labor force.

This same kind of exercise could be repeated, inter alia, for education, both in terms of teachers required and the expected increase in number of students: The latter would represent a decrease in the total labor force and is probably the most effective cure for youth unemployment. Just as late marriage was once a principal approach to limiting population, late entry into the labor force is today one of society's main techniques for dealing with potential unemployment and should quite unashamedly be recognized as such.

A further word or two about basic needs would seem appropriate at this juncture. The 1980 World Development Report of the World Bank focuses on human development and the task of abolishing absolute poverty. It gives special attention to education, health, and nutrition. Improvement in all three areas would require substantial increases in service employment and concomitantly in the current, as distinct from capital, expenditures of governments.[25] Certainly any advice from the bank's sibling, the International Monetary Fund, that government-budget growth should be kept in check is clearly going to be at cross purposes with the World Bank's concern for human development.

I would like to conclude by suggesting that we relieve industrial expansion of principal responsibility for resolving the employment problem (but not of paying its fair share of taxes), and focus our attention more directly on the challenge of increasing the enjoyment of life for every member of the population. An employment policy that is clearly centered on the recognition of the key role of the service sector is, I believe, a means to this end.

NOTES

1. Thorstein Veblen, Imperial Germany and the Industrial Revolution (New York: Macmillan Co., 1915), pp. 17-41.
2. Wendell C. Gordon, The Political Economy of Latin America (New York: Columbia University Press, 1965), pp. 290-91.
3. Frances Stewart, International Technology Transfer: Issues and Policy Options, World Bank Staff Working Paper No. 344 (Washington, D.C., July 1979), p. 108.
4. Michael P. Todaro, Economic Development in the Third World (New York: Longman, 1977), pp. 181-84.
5. Albert O. Hirschman, "The Political Economy of Import-Substituting Industrialization in Latin America," Quarterly Journal of Economics 82 (February 1968), pp. 2-32.
6. Norman Girvan, "The Development of Dependency Economics in the Caribbean and Latin America: Review and Comparison," Social and Economic Studies 22 (March 1973), p. 26.
7. Marshall McLuhan and Quentin Fiore, War and Peace in the Global Village (New York: Bantam Books, 1968), pp. 126-27.
8. R. M. Hartwell, The Industrial Revolution and Economic Growth (London: Methuen & Co., 1971), p. 212.
9. Ibid., p. 224.
10. Marcelo Selowsky, "Income Distribution, Basic Needs and Trade-Offs with Growth: The Case of Semi-Industrialized Latin American Countries" (Address given at Conference on "Latin American Prospects for the '80s: What Kinds of Development?," Carleton University, Ottawa, November 13, 1980).
11. Ibid.
12. Ibid.
13. Ibid., table 4: Annual growth rate in employment and wages in the industrial sector, for 1963-72 (in percentages), was as follows:

Country	Employment	Real Wages
Brazil	4.1	2.8
Colombia	4.2	2.7
Ecuador	5.8	2.5
Mexico	1.9	6.9
Peru	1.0	3.7
Unweighted average	3.6	3.7

14. Nicholas Georgescu-Roegen, The Entropy Law and the Economic Process (Cambridge: Harvard University Press, 1971), p. 284.

15. Inter-American Development Bank, Economic and Social Progress in Latin America: 1978 Report (Washington, D.C.: n.d.).

16. World Bank, World Development Report, 1980 (New York: Oxford University Press, 1980), p. 147 (hereafter cited as WDR, 1980).

17. Ibid.

18. Ibid.

19. Sample A: Australia, Belgium, Canada, Denmark, the Federal Republic of Germany, the Netherlands, New Zealand, Sweden, Switzerland, the United Kingdom, and the United States. Since the mid 1960s, the absolute level of employment has also fallen in Austria (not included in sample A), Germany, the Netherlands, Switzerland, and the United Kingdom. Angus Madison, "Economic Growth and Structural Change in the Advanced Countries," in I. Leveson and N. Wheeler, eds., Western Economics in Transition: Structural Change and Adjustment Policies in Industrial Countries (Boulder: Westview Press, 1980), p. 48.

20. Sample B: Argentina, Bolivia, Brazil, Chile, Colombia, the Dominican Republic, Ecuador, Guatemala, Mexico, Peru, and Venezuela.

21. WDR, 1980, pp. 110-11, 148-49.

22. Dennis Gabor, The Mature Society (New York: Praeger, 1972), p. 93.

23. By way of historical footnote, R. M. Hartwell has observed that between 1801 and 1851, domestic service in England was one of the largest occupational groups. It has declined continuously in proportion since 1890. Hartwell, pp. 223-24.

24. WDR, 1980, pp. 152-53. The comparison for 1977 follows:

	Per 1,000 of Population	
	Physicians	Nursing Persons
Colombia	0.5	0.8
Industrial countries (average)	1.6	4.5

25. It is the present writer's conviction that some of the poorest countries may well be incapable of making the necessary expenditures unless a system of automatic international financial transfers is established. On this latter point, see the report of

the Independent Commission for International Development Issues
(Brandt Commission), North-South: A Program for Survival
(Cambridge: MIT Press, 1980), pp. 244-45, and Myron J. Frank-
man, "Financing International Cooperation: An Immodest Proposal"
(Revised version of a paper presented at the meetings of the
Canadian Economics Association, Winnipeg, June 1970).

8
CENTRAL AMERICAN
ECONOMIC INTEGRATION
Gert Rosenthal

Central America has been in the headlines lately as a region facing dramatic changes: revolution, increasing polarization of its societies, and acute economic difficulties. Rarely does the topic of economic integration crop up as an important ingredient in these events, yet the Central American Common Market continues to be a significant factor in the economic development of every country. In fact, one of the more interesting aspects to watch in the region is whether the economic-integration process can resist—or, rather, adjust to—the changes taking place.

In the 1960s, the Central American Common Market (CACM) was held up as one of the more successful experiments of its kind. After a period of trial and error in the previous decade, reflected in bilateral trade agreements and studies on ways of best furthering economic integration, the governments adopted an audacious commitment in 1960, with the signature of the General Treaty. According to this treaty, unlimited free trade for all goods produced within the region, plus an external common tariff on all third-country goods, were to be adopted within a period of five years. The institutional framework for the common market was established, including the creation of a Central American clearing house for reciprocal payments in domestic currencies, and a highway network was initiated to facilitate the physical movement of goods between countries.

The results of these ambitious agreements were not long in coming. Trade grew spectacularly—from around $30 million in 1960 to $130 million in 1965. New industrial projects flourished—the ratio of industrial value added to total GDP grew from 12.9 percent to 15.1 percent for the region as a whole during the same period. And the common market became an increasingly important element in the economic growth of the countries.[1] The impetus gained in the achievement of the original commitments—by 1965 the free-trade zone and the common external tariff had virtually been completed—and the goodwill and camaraderie that prevailed in the meetings of the intergovernmental bodies of the common market, were additional assets that furthered the cause of integration and heightened international interest in what was widely regarded as the most successful experiment of its kind within developing countries.[2]

Some of the salient characteristics of the economic-integration process in Central America during these formative years of the common market can be summarized as follows:

1. The common market was at the service of five economic systems that typified what the ECLA has described as "peripheral capitalism": basically market economies with a relatively modern and dynamic, export-oriented agricultural sector evolving with a backward subsistence type of farming, while in the urban areas, modern services and a tiny manufacturing sector contrasted with growing numbers of unemployed or underemployed poor, all giving rise to highly skewed income and consumption patterns. It is true that the common market helped to perfect the functioning of these neocapitalistic economies, contributing to an expansion of an urban middle class, through the promotion of industrial development, but it is equally true that it did not alter the basic functioning of these five economies, nor did it make major inroads in reducing critical poverty in the region. What is more, it would have been unfair to ask the integration process to alter the style of development in the five countries, since, integration being one more tool of development, it is logical that the governments involved would use that tool to further their own image of development. Thus, what one would conventionally catalog as the left in Central America criticized, and continues to criticize, the integration process for not solving the countries' major structural problems in development. What should really be the object of their ire is the national development policies followed by each country, and not the integration process per se, which was only a logical reflection of those national development policies.

2. For the reason mentioned above, market forces were relied on as the primary—if not the only—means of allocating resources within the expanded regional market. Although the Economic Commission for Latin America had proposed—and the governments had initially accepted—a mechanism to establish

what, in effect, amounted to legal monopolies, to be more or less evenly distributed between countries, both organized business groups and the government of the United States mounted a vigorous attack against this so-called Régimen de Industrias de Integración; they argued that the common market would make its greatest contribution to economic growth if market forces would indicate the optimum location for each new industry, and that competition within the regional market would allow only the fittest to survive.[3] This dogmatic insistence on avoiding any interference with market forces contributed greatly to a concentration of new activities induced by the common market in the relatively more developed countries of the region, given their greater domestic markets and their relatively more developed physical and human infrastructure.

3. Perhaps due to the relative degree of homogeneity in the political systems—with the notable exception of Costa Rica, a country that conspicuously dragged its feet, during the early years of the common market, in joining the others in adopting regional commitments—economic integration was successfully separated from the other spheres of foreign policy of each country. Thus, even when political differences cropped up from time to time, they usually did not spill over into the arena of the common market. For example, the intergovernmental bodies of the integration process were made up of representatives of the ministries of economy, while the ministries of foreign relations conducted their largely ritualistic discussions on possible future political integration under the aegis of the now all-but-defunct Organization of Central American States (ODECA).

4. While the integration process touched on many areas of national economies and societies, most formal commitments were related to the creation of a customs union, wherein all goods produced in the region had unlimited free movement within the region, and a common tariff was applied to all goods from outside the region. In that respect, it would be fair to describe Central America's integration process as an integration of markets, or a commercial integration.

5. The conceptual framework behind the common market was very much inspired by writings coming out of the academic world in industrialized Western countries.[4] Thus, it was generally believed that the common market would spill over, in a linear and ever-broadening manner, to other sectors, until eventually the five economies would merge into a single economic unit—the customs union was regarded as a first stage toward this distant but final objective—with not only a unified market and free movement of goods, capital, and labor, but also unified economic policies.

MEETING THE COMMITMENTS

By 1965 the original commitments undertaken by the countries had been met, and an increasing level of economic interdependence was becoming a fact of life in each country. However, while this interdependence continued to grow during the second half of the 1960s—at least as measured in terms of regional trade, which grew from $130 million in 1965 to $300 million in 1970—sometime during this period, the impetus of previous years began to be muted. For one thing, the benefits of integration were being distributed in what some governments perceived to be a highly inequitable manner, to the benefit especially of Guatemala and El Salvador, and to the detriment especially of Honduras. For another, while the countries had experienced a period of strong growth in their traditional exports during the first half of the decade, they faced increasing balance-of-payments difficulties during 1966-67 due to a slump in the international prices of the main export commodities; and thus all countries—with differences of degree—faced global balance-of-payments and fiscal difficulties. Instead of utilizing integration as a means of common defense vis-à-vis the rest of the world, some governments (notably those of Nicaragua and, later, Costa Rica) tried to limit their global imports, and this policy came into conflict with their integration obligations, which included unlimited free trade for all goods produced within the region. It has to be pointed out that, although some of those obligations were violated, the customs union, in general, withstood the strains associated with balance-of-payments constraints. However, in the light of these new difficulties, governments were loath to undertake new commitments that would further economic integration along the linear path that some of the ideologues of the process had foreseen.

Other difficulties cropped up. The decision-making process of the common market turned out to be cumbersome, and when corrective actions for specific problems were required, by the time those actions were actually applied, the circumstances that had originated them had usually reversed themselves. For example, the modification of the common external tariff, either to raise it to protect certain industries or to lower it to defend the consumer, would require extended negotiations and parliamentary ratification in each country, all of which took several years. In the same vein, the Common Industrial Incentives Agreement, signed in 1962, entered into effect until 1969. Finally, the CACM had a very reduced constituency throughout this whole period—academics, technocrats, and the more enlightened elements of the industrial sector—but it never really captured the imagination of large groups of Central Americans. Thus, the economic-integration process tended to be regarded by most people as something peripheral to what was really important for the economic development of each country.

Then, in 1969, a singular event took place: Two countries of the common market had political differences that rapidly escalated into an armed conflict. This is not the place to examine the origins of the 100-hour war between El Salvador and Honduras, but the fallout of this conflict greatly exacerbated the cumulus of problems that the common market was facing. It should be pointed out that the fact that the whole integration process did not come apart after such an extreme disagreement between two member states is a testimony to the degree of economic interdependence reached by 1969. Although Honduras severed its economic relations with El Salvador after the war, it did not withdraw from its multilateral obligations until the end of 1970, when negotiations aimed at giving that country special provisions failed. In other words, even in the midst of an armed conflict, economic integration was largely isolated from events in the political arena; and it was only 18 months after the conflict that political and military events spilled over into the economic sphere, and the normality of a customs union of five countries was interrupted.

In sum, the spectacular progress and momentum gained in Central American integration during the first half of the decade was not kept up during the second half. While a high degree of economic interdependence was maintained, the linear progress of previous years was not, and, after the 100-hour war, it even suffered a regression.

A NEW PHASE

Thus, the 1970s marked a new phase for the economic-integration process in Central America. For those who had postulated that the degree of economic interdependence would expand in ever-widening arcs, or in a linear fashion, the process was in a crisis, notwithstanding the fact that in spite of the armed conflict between two countries, the CACM continued to provide the scenario for over 20 percent of the countries' total foreign trade. For the less demanding observer, the degree of interdependence had leveled out—reached some point of equilibrium—but continued to show signs of vitality. After all, the value of regional trade continued to grow, reaching the $1-

billion mark by 1978, and the original commitments undertaken
by the countries involved in the General Treaty were still, to
a very large degree, being observed. Even Honduras had
returned to the fold by 1973, through the expedient of bilateral
treaties with all countries except El Salvador.

However, it cannot be denied that throughout the 1970s,
the CACM began to languish—at least in comparison to its dynamic
performance in the 1960s—and that a general sense of malaise
pervaded the discussions of regional forums. No longer was
the CACM held up as a model to be imitated, and talk of the
need to "restructure" the process cropped up in the beginning
of the decade and continued to intensify as time went on.[5]

It might be useful to characterize the main elements of this
general sense of malaise. In the first place, as pointed out above,
while it is true that the customs union continued to be preserved,
the abnormal functioning of the free-trade agreements after
Honduras's withdrawal from its multilateral obligations, added
to periodic restrictions applied by several countries to the un-
hampered movement of goods, introduced an element of instability
and uncertainty to the future of this common market. This, in
turn, greatly deterred new investments geared to the regional
demand, and, in fact, gave rise to a process of national industrialization designed to curb intraregional imports.[6] Partly as
a result of these phenomena, the level of intraregional trade
grew at lower levels than in previous years. For example, while
during the 1960s, trade expanded at average annual rates of
30 percent, both in nominal and real terms, in the 1970s this
rate dropped to 15 percent in nominal terms and to only 5 percent in real terms. The relative participation of this trade in
total foreign trade dropped from 25 percent in the late 1960s to
around 20 percent at present.

At the same time, while in 1968 almost 25 percent of the
gross value of industrial production of the region as a whole
participated in intraregional trade, by 1978 this proportion had
dropped to a little over 10 percent. This figure underscores
both the intraregional import substitution that occurred in the
1970s, as well as an incipient but growing trend toward exporting
manufactured goods to third countries.[7]

Another negative characteristic of integration in the 1970s
was a gradual erosion of mutual confidence and of the sense of
solidarity that had prevailed in previous years, added to a growing skepticism about the potential of the CACM. The camaraderie
referred to earlier has largely disappeared in later years, and
with the loss of this vital ingredient, the mood of integration
in Central America has considerably soured. Although it is

hard to quantify this characteristic, it is obvious both in the
way that intergovernmental forums conduct their business and
in the way that public opinion perceives the integration process.

Finally, the regional institutions of the CACM have been
both the object and the subject of the malaise discussed above.
On the one hand, governments have been loath to give political
and financial support to these institutions (although they continue to assign ever-expanding obligations to them), thus
curtailing their effectiveness. On the other hand, these same
institutions have lost their best people, due to the lack of stimuli—
which has weakened their capacity to respond to the new challenges posed by Central American economic integration. The
imaginative proposals that some governments perhaps sought in
the regional institutions so as to overcome some of the difficulties
the CACM faced in the 1970s were simply not forthcoming.

In sum, it would not have been appropriate to say, by the
end of 1978, that the CACM was in a "crisis," unless this term
was applied to the expectations that some observers harbored
during the formative years of the common market. Rather,
the process was at a halfway house between those expectations
and stagnation, showing signs of vitality and malaise simultaneously.

In 1979, exactly ten years after the conflict between El
Salvador and Honduras, a second major event shook Central
America and its integration movement: the downfall of the
Somoza dynasty, and the rise of a new government born out of
an armed insurrection. This event took place in an increasingly
turbulent and polarized atmosphere, with ramifications in all
countries, but especially in El Salvador and Guatemala.

The new government of Nicaragua is made up of a broad
coalition, whose major, if not only, common denominator was
opposition to the Somoza regime. After Somoza's fall, the new
leadership has been extremely cautious in defining its specific
goals, in order to avoid provoking premature divisions in a
coalition whose main raison d'être had already disappeared.
However, the mere fact that Somoza's Guardia Nacional was
swept away with him marks a major realignment of forces in
Nicaragua, especially since the only armed force remaining in
the country is totally dominated by the Frente Sandinista de
Liberación Nacional (FSLN). Although both economic and political
policies followed during the first year of the national government
of reconstruction have been relatively moderate (in spite of a
more radical stance in the official rhetoric), for Central America's
more conservative elements, that country has already been lost
to "international communism," while in the economic sphere,

important differences have, in fact, appeared between the type of laissez faire neocapitalism postulated—with differences of degree—in most countries and the more interventionist, mixed-economy approach postulated by the new government in Nicaragua.

The immediate question that this new state of affairs raises for the CACM is whether, in addition to the difficulties that have been piling up over the years, as described above, economic integration can persist in the face of this highly heterogeneous situation. Certainly some of the previously enumerated difficulties are exacerbated. It should be recalled that what has conventionally been called the left in Central America has always criticized the integration process as one more tool of "imperialism" and as the means of enhancing the already dominant positions of the economic establishment and the transnational enterprise. Now that the left has actually reached a position of political responsibility, will it continue to participate in a movement much reviled in the past?

Now that there are governments that postulate different paths to development, can the common market be equally responsive to heterogeneous and possibly even contradictory objectives of economic policy? Can the governments continue to rely on the market mechanism as the main allocator of activities within the common market, when at least one of them wishes a greater degree of intervention to regulate economic activities? In a common market where private investment is still dominant, won't all future investments flow to those countries where private investors feel relatively more secure, to the detriment of Nicaragua, which at least at present is considered—perhaps unfairly—a hostile environment for private enterprise? Will the governments be able to continue to separate economic integration from the political sphere, under the pressure of increasingly acute differences? Nicaragua lately has had border incidents with Honduras and Costa Rica, while leaders of the governments of Guatemala and El Salvador have alluded to the dangers of "another Cuba" in their midst. Even worse, while there are mutual recriminations of intervention in each country's affairs— Guatemala claiming that Nicaragua is aiding its domestic guerrilla movement, and Nicaragua claiming that Guatemala is aiding Nicaraguan counterrevolutionary activities in the region—what is to prevent political differences from spilling over into the economic arena and ending the CACM, at least as a regional grouping of five countries? Can the regional institutions preserve enough distance and neutrality so as not to be suspect to some governments and to have equal acceptance by all?

It would be equally harsh to state that the new heterogeneous situation establishes irreconcilable differences, which mark
the doom of the integration process, as it would be to ignore
these differences, which certainly mark a new era in the region.
So far, the course of events actually offers room for optimism.
The new government of Nicaragua did not interrupt its commitments within the CACM, as some observers had expected it to
(and, no doubt, the more radical elements in the new alignment
of forces in Nicaragua wanted it to). In fact, the level of trade
in 1980 actually increased, due, in part, to the fact that the
central banks of Guatemala, El Salvador, Honduras, and Costa
Rica extended credit lines for over $100 million to Nicaragua
during the reconstruction period of its civil war. Over one-
third of Nicaragua's total imports during the first semester of
1980 originated in Central America; in absolute terms, those
imports grew from $49 million during the first semester of 1979
to $121 million during the same period of 1980. [8] Nor have the
political differences spilled over into the economic sphere, at
least up to now. All governments continue to give lip service
to the need for restructuring the integration process, and are
participating in various forums that are exploring this possibility.
Nicaragua also continues to participate actively in the maintenance
of all regional institutions, and it has been an important bene-
ficiary of financing on the part of the Central American Bank
for Economic Integration.

So while it is too early to tell how the appearance of a
revolutionary government in Central America will affect the
integration process, it is clear that the new situation of hetero-
geneity poses novel and difficult problems. In the best of
circumstances, the conceptual framework for economic integration
will have to be overhauled to correct some of the secular problems
mentioned above and to respond to the new circumstances described. In the worst-case scenario, political differences will
spill over into the sphere of economic integration, either ending
or radically modifying this 20-year-old experiment in international
economic cooperation.

If the latter can be avoided, it is probable that some type
of integration will survive—possibly even flourish—given the
high level of economic interdependence that persists in the region.
The potential for continuing joint industrial development, as
well as joint activities to solve common problems—such as increasing exports to third countries—also is high, in spite of heterogeneous political, economic, and social systems. What must be
abandoned once and for all is the vision of the 1960s: that eco-

nomic integration will eventually lead to the formation of a single economic unit, with unified economic policies, free movement of all factors, and joint institutions with some degree of supranationality.

Thus, if one cannot report at this time that economic integration in Central America is alive and well, one can, at least report that it is alive, with the possibility of even making it well. How well, and when, and under what circumstances? Only time will tell.

NOTES

1. See; William R. Cline, "Benefits and Costs of Economic Integration in Central America," in Economic Integration in Central America (Washington, D.C.: The Brookings Institution, June 1978).

2. It was no accident that during the formative years of the CACM, it was analyzed by many U.S. academics. See, for example: S. Fagan, Central American Economic Integration: The Politics of Unequal Benefits (Berkeley: Institute of International Studies, 1970); R. Hansen, Central America: Regional Integration and Economic Development (Washington, D.C.: National Planning Association, 1967); H. Hinrichs, "Growth without Development in Guatemala," in Fiscal Policy for Industrialization and Development in Latin America (Gainesville: University of Florida Press, 1974); K. Holbik and P. Swan, Trade and Industrialization in the Central American Common Market: The First Decade (Austin: Bureau of Business Research, University of Texas, 1972); D. McClelland, The Central American Common Market: Economic Policies, Economic Growth and Choices for the Future (New York: Praeger, 1972); J. Nugent, "Empirical Investigations in Central American Economic Integration" (Los Angeles: University of Southern California, mimeographed, 1973); J. Nye, Central American Regional Integration (New York: Carnegie Endowment for International Peace, 1967); P. Schmitter, "Central American Integration: Spill-Over, Spill-Around, or Encapsulation, in Journal of Common Market Studies, September 1970.

3. For an interesting description of the above-mentioned experience, see D. Ramsett, Regional Industrial Development in Central America: A Case Study of the Integration Industries Scheme (New York: Praeger, 1964).

4. Typified in the realm of political science, by, for example, E. B. Haas and Philippe C. Schmitter, "Economic and Differ-

ential Patterns of Political Integration: Projection about Unity
in Latin America," in International Political Communities: An
Anthology (New York: Anchor Books, 1966); and in the realm
of economics by Bela Balassa, The Theory of Economic Integration
(Homewood, Ill.: Richard D. Irwin, 1961).

5. To this end, the Secretariat of the CACM prepared an
overall proposal in 1972, which was followed by a second, even
more ambitious draft treaty prepared in 1976. See SIECA, El
desarrollo integrado de Centroamérica en la presente década
(Guatemala City: SIECA/72-VII-6/36, October 1972); and Comité
de Alto Nivel para el Perfeccionamiento y la Reestructuración
del MCCA, Proyecto de Tratado Marco (Guatemala City: SIECA,
March 1976).

6. An interesting example of the deliberate nature of this
phenomenon is that while the Central American Agreement on
Fiscal Incentives for Industrial Development provides certain
incentives to new industries at the regional level, the countries
continue to apply the criterion of "new" industries at the national
level.

7. It should be pointed out that this intraregional import
substitution is evolving under more or less competitive conditions,
since, as already pointed out, there are virtually no restrictions
on trade of Central American goods. Thus, this new trend is
not necessarily a bad thing, although it may be contributing to
excess capacity in a number of activities.

8. On the export side, Nicaragua did not fare so well,
due largely to the fact that many of the industries oriented to
the regional market were destroyed during the civil war preceding
Somoza's downfall, while others still face raw-materials shortages
and general disruptions. The already abnormally low level of
exports during the first semester of 1979—$55 million—fell to
$32 million during the same period of 1980.

PART III
PROCESSES OF AND OBSTACLES TO GENUINE DEMOCRATIZATION

9

POLITICAL DEMOCRACY IN LATIN AMERICA:
AN EXPLORATION INTO THE NATURE
OF TWO POLITICAL PROJECTS

Jorge Nef

INTRODUCTION

Since the 1960s, American perceptions of Latin America
have experienced several changes. These have been reflected
in the dominant social science paradigms[1] for the area of Latin
American Studies.[2] In its early phase—that of the Alliance for
Progress—the main theme was the espousal of reformist movements under the aegis of the middle class and the "progressive
bourgeoisie."[3] In the middle 1960s, with the passing of the
Kennedy administration, the emphasis shifted toward the "young-
educated-technical-elites,"[4] and their vanguards—the Christian
Democratic parties. Nixon's response to the Latin American
challenge—the latter is expressed in the Consenso de Viña del
Mar[5] and other manifestations of growing political and economic
nationalism—would be the National Security Doctrine[6] and Rockefeller's "new military."[7] In the late 1970s, under the spell of
the trilateral doctrine,[8] the paradigm appeared wrapped in a
new vocabulary: "Human rights," military withdrawals, and a
return to a sort of "limited democracy" substituted for the harsher
overtones of "Pentagonism."[9] After the swing to the right under
Reagan, a resurgence of counterinsurgency and national security
is ostensible. Despite the apparent discontinuity in policy,
there seems to be a remarkable persistence of the mainstream
U.S. visions of Latin America. A comparative analysis of these
seemingly different policies reveals two fundamental and consistent traits. One is the overall epistemological and ideological
continuity of the paradigm, expressed in the major concern for
developmentalism and stability.[10] The second, related trait is

the close association between area studies and official policy.
In this sense, the aforementioned paradigm involves compelling
ideological postulations along with explicit policy prescriptions
and implicit value assumptions regarding an optimal state for
Latin America. It is in this context that the prospects for military
withdrawal with democratisation and for the remilitarisation of
the hemisphere under Reagan must be analysed.

The objective of this essay is not to concentrate on the
changing paradigm proper, but to assess the fit of its most
recent mutations to the politics of the region. Three main
questions will be discussed: What are the conceptual and ideological underpinnings of the two most recent U.S. models,
focusing on military withdrawals with limited democracy and on
resurgent militarism in Latin America? What is the feasibility
of these scenarios as real alternatives? And as a sort of conclusion, what are the implications of the Reagan regime for Latin
America? Because of its brevity, this presentation will merely
scratch the surface of a complex and unfolding debate about
the governability of Western democracies, whose implications
go beyond the geographical confines of this chapter.[11] Moreover, this essay is intended to be a highly polemic and inter-
pretative synthesis, not a dispassionate explanation or a highly
elaborate research piece.

The central thesis of this essay is that the characterisation
of contemporary Latin America as a region undergoing a change
toward increased democratisation—liberal, populist, or socialist—
is an intellectual hallucination. The concepts of "military withdrawal," "limited democracy" (as presented by the Carter
administration), and Reagan's "responsible right" mask the
objective consequences of the ideology and policy of "developmentalism."[12] This means the maintenance, albeit under changing
garments, of a continuous pattern of satellising dependence.
As Helio Haguaribe argues, the latter is rationalised by two
core values that "feature a false consciousness, a self-protective
adulteration to soften reality. This first [is] . . . anti-communism
and its correlates of moralism, the supremacy of order and
authoritarianism. The second in vogue among the bourgeoisie
and the satellizing intelligentsia is the theory of interdependent
development illustrated by the idealized case of Canada."[13]

The latter point deserves to be properly stressed. The
serious debate about the core assumptions of developmentalism
is extremely relevant for both Canada and Latin America. Especially in light of the current rhetoric of "continentalism," it is
a kind of issue that could affect us all in the decades to come.
For Canadians, in particular, an analysis of the developmentalist

ideology may serve to highlight some of the structural traits and
functional contradictions extant in the pattern of satellised dependence, as well as its operational limits. In this respect, a
Brechtian alienation may provide the medium—and thus the
message—through which critical awareness can ensue. The
implications of the Alliance for Progress's notion of development
as counterinsurgency and the National Security Doctrine have
been explored in a previous article.[14] Therefore, the present
study will concentrate on two more recent developments: the
now defunct Carter Doctrine and the new hawkish outlook toward
Latin America of the Reagan regime.

TRILATERALISM: MILITARY WITHDRAWAL
AND "RESTRICTED DEMOCRACY"

We will begin by concentrating on the assumptions under-
lying the Carter type of "revisionism" of U.S. policy toward
Latin America. On August 19, 1979, an editorial in the Miami
Herald characterised the "new mood" in the following terms:

> Historians in the future will note that the Summer
> of 1979 marked a remarkable turning point in Latin
> America. It is a period when, on the eve of a new
> decade, new seeds of democracy are sprouting after
> the long, authoritarian 70's.[15]

The abovementioned statement portrayed rather closely the main
thrust of Carter's blueprint for a U.S. policy toward Latin
America—the Linowitz Report.[16] This policy, attempting to
remove the nastier overtones of the Nixon doctrine, called for
a "new political order,"[17] including a "peaceful end to military
rule,"[18] and a number of replacement formulas (fórmulas de
recambio). In fact, it constituted the Trilateral Commission's
position for a revised North-South dialogue in the context of
the whole Latin American region.[19]
Several Latin American scholars have pointed out that since
the inauguration of the Carter administration, U.S. policymakers
have "reviewed (at the light of the trilateral doctrine) their
relationships with Latin American militarism. They have concluded
that . . . [the National Security regime] is not the most effective
system to generate, both at the present and in the near future,
the kind of development which could adequately serve the economic interests of the trilateral countries."[20] Such a policy did
have some limited success. It should be given "credit for the

democratic trend in the Andes," according to a New York Times
editorial of July 4, 1979. The article, focusing on Bolivia, indi-
cated that "the Carter Administration has persistently pressed
for the end to military rule."[21] It also suggested that "the same
impulses should also pave the undoing of the military juntas now
ruling Argentina, Chile and Uruguay." This appeared as a
major policy shift: "From positively favoring military governments and subverting democratic ones under Nixon and Kissinger,
the U.S. government came out demonstratively in favor of the
transition from authoritarian to democratic rule."[22]

On the academic front, this refurbishing of the developmentalist paradigm popularised a new phraseology. Catchwords
such as "complex interdependence"[23] substituted for the more
blatantly authoritarian overtones of the Rockefeller Report.
The new semantics attempted to muffle—and, for that matter,
even trivialise—the most dissonant concepts of the Latin American
counterparadigm: terms such as dependencia, exploitation, and
class conflicts. Dependence was thus presented as misperceived
interdependence; neocolonialism, as "multiple linkages"; and
class conflicts, as "ungovernability."[24] A recent article represented the abovementioned view in an unequivocal way:

> One advantage of viewing Latin American politics
> from the lens of complex interdependence is that it
> might help to counterbalance the traditional highly
> conflictual paradigm of Latin American politics.[25]

In a footnote to the text, the same author complements his assertion in even more explicit terms: "This conventional paradigm
is partially based on Latin American realities and partially based
on the paramount position of Marxism as a theoretical perspective
and tool of analysis."[26] There are a number of flaws in the
argument. The conflictual model is not the "conventional
paradigm"—at least not in North America. "Developmentalism" is
still the conventional wisdom of which "complex interdependence"
is an intellectual mutation. By the explicit admission of its
authors, "complex interdependence" has been formulated, amongst
other reasons, to counteract "heretic" views. At a more ambitious
level, interdependence intends to bridge the epistemological gap
between mainstream international relations (dominated by the
conflict model of the realist school) and national politics (dominated
by the ideology of the liberal consensus). It suggests a new
"global consciousness"—a unified consensus theory of politics
in direct and explicit opposition to the unified conflict theory
of dependentistas and Marxists alike.

One problem with relabeling, however, is the generalised
proclivity toward linguistic fetishism. Some may assume that
because we name things differently, the undesirable properties
of the concrete phenomena they portray will just wither away.
Conversely, we may run the risk of a sort of intellectual self-
hypnosis: the belief that by calling something a name, the concept will be reified in the real world. Because we rechristen
an objective condition does not mean the nasty features of the
original reality will vanish. That is, by renaming the institutionalisation of repression, and calling it "democratisation" or
"military withdrawals," we will not necessarily accomplish much
in the search for political, social, and economic democracy.

Whilst the latent function[27] of the trilateral doctrine can
be characterised as the spread of "perpetual capitalism" (as
opposed to "capitalism within one country"),[28] its major moral
justification is the ideology of "human rights." The latter are
defined in the narrowest possible terms, to mean absence of
physical abuse and torture. For instance, with regard to the
Southern Cone, the stated[29] goal of the Linowitz recommendation
was "to halt the most flagrant violations of human rights."[29]
This was to be done, however, as one observer noted, without
challenging the underlying social system that has brought about
the violations.[30]

> The Carter team has calculated that some liberaliza-
> tion (controlled elections, for example) would not
> only enable the United States to improve its image,
> but also make the internal contradictions of these
> regimes less explosive.[31]

This linking of human rights with American foreign policy was
not just a reaction against the Nixon doctrine, though. It was
an attempt to provide an ideological and policy linkage between
two increasingly conflictual forces in Latin America: those of
liberal capitalism and of participatory democracy. This discrepancy seriously worries many proponents of the liberal-democratic
hybrid. In the words of a prestigious contributor to Trialogue,
the Trilateral Commission's official organ: "Once a widespread
incompatibility (between democracy and capitalism) were generally
recognized, human rights would be seen to threaten both the
ideological and material interests of international capitalism."[32]
This, of course, runs counter to the most manifest ideological
objective of American cold-war policies: the defense of democracy.

This new phase of the paradigm contains a number of
specific structural prescriptions for producing a balance between

democracy and order. Nevertheless, the Huntingtonian premise that an "excess of democracy" is at the core of decay—and subsequently of praetorianism[33]—remains central to the analysis. It should be remembered that this postulation was also the fundamental tenet of the Rockefeller Doctrine. Thus, the main concern in the Carter model appears to have been to stop the "vicious cycle of praetorianism" leading eventually to institutional "decay"[34] and to revolution. In order to accommodate a number of ideally typical conditions specifically relevant to the Latin American scene, the construct of the "trilateral doctrine," as suggested by Alan Wolfe,[35] has been expanded here. It contains a basic redefinition of bourgeois democracy in the context of an interdependent world. Its main characteristics are as follows.

Peaceful Transition

The project stresses the importance of a negotiated transfer of power to civilian hands,[36] leading to a constitutional regime, with the United States playing a central role in the negotiations.[37] Whilst the cases of Spain, Portugal, and Greece (the Karamanlis formula) are often cited as examples of the reversibility of "authoritarian" regimes,[38] the major Latin American test cases have been the Dominican Republic, Panama, and, most importantly, Peru, Bolivia (before the García Meza coup), and Ecuador.[39] Even Brazil's amnesty programme and subsequent "decompression" and aberturia (opening) have been perceived as a viable model.[40] Military withdrawal is seen necessarily as an orderly retreat— not a chaotic collapse à la Iran or Nicaragua, with a sudden decline of American influence.

Military Guardianship

The peaceful return to the barracks serves to secure the integrity and de jure extraterritoriality of the security forces. In fact, they are to remain as a constitutionally enshrined insurance policy against future "democratic excesses" and hypermobilisation.[41] This legal formula not only guarantees the untouchability of the military establishment, but also legitimises future interventions without resort to the suspension of the constitution or to illegal coups d'etat. The principle of mutual reversibility—from military to political power, and vice versa—is thus legalised. Counterterrorism replaces national security as a more circumscribed, police-like operation to combat challenges to the status quo.

Transnationalisation

Structural reforms are to be undertaken to secure an appropriate milieu for the operation of modern transnational capitalism.[42] In the context of interdependence, supranational cooperation[43] will harmonise economic policies to secure international movements of resources, finance, and technology, thus facilitating the spread of development.[44]

Modernisation of the Mode of Production

Together with the influx of modern technology through transnational corporations, a thorough reform of the area of labor[45] and production systems is to be undertaken. The strengthening of the economic order is aimed at "securing . . . a sustained and equalitarian rate of growth geared at increasing . . . the purchasing power of the population in conjunction with a more or less competitive industrial expansion."[46] Modern economies, inspired by postwar Germany and Japan, are thought to assure the survival of the capitalist mode of production on a global scale.

Institutionalisation

A special concern for the restoration of "the shell, not the actual content of democratic government,"[47] is present in the notions of "restricted," "balanced," or "limited" democracies. Such limitation means the reduction of the scope and size of the political arenas (political markets) where the power intercourse takes place.[48] This is to be accomplished through four main institutional reforms: the revitalisation of "pragmatic" (as opposed to ideological) parties,[49] the strengthening of political leadership,[50] a "revised" type of corporatism,[51] and symbolic populism.[52] The latter two are of paramount importance. While symbolic populism provides an ideological mechanism for legitimation, corporatism secures the continuity of the megemonic project under uncontested elite control. Orlando Fals Borda has used the term "democracy limited"[53] to refer to a rather artificial political system where "civilian governments and formal democracy . . . favor both some degree of prosperity among the middle class, small industrialists and the dependent commercial groups and a relatively equitable distribution of income"[54] amongst them. However, this design contains specific built-in mechanisms that preclude the conversion of political power into actions geared toward legally altering the rules of the socioeconomic order. In fact, the key economic agencies, such as the Central Bank and planning agencies—and the same is the case with security policy—

are to retain metapower outside the arena of acceptable political debate. For Rui Mauro Marini, these are to be "stable regimes with some measure of popular support and respect for democratic liberties and with a certain degree of institutional legitimacy."[55] Beyond democratic formalism, however, autonomous grassroots participation is discouraged.[56] As for the regime's ideology, the human-rights issue involves only the removal of the most ostensible forms of physical repression, not a rallying cry for "social justice."[57] That is, the model favors growth, not redistribution, as the key mechanism for consensus building. Should the latter fail, the option always remains to revert to the estado de excepción by impeccable legal means.

THE PROSPECTS FOR MILITARY WITHDRAWAL

Latin American political processes do not operate in a vacuum. Nor do inter-American relations. They are profoundly affected by changing circumstances intertwining in a concrete historical context. The prospects for democratisation in individual countries and in the region as a whole should be seen as one of a number of multiple possible outcomes of the aforementioned process. In this vein, Douglas Chalmers has proposed a linkage model for analysing Latin American politics, "not only as a whole, through the responsible elite, but also through the manifold linkages that exist between groups and institutions within and outside the area."[58] He has suggested four dimensions for studying such linkage patterns: the character of the international system, the external linkage groups, the internal linkage groups, and the character of the polity. We will explore the prospects for a return to democracy by reference to the above categories.

Continental Imbalance and Penetration

One fundamental aspect to be remembered here is the distinctively unipolar nature of the inter-American system. Only subparamount actors (i.e., Mexico, Brazil, and Venezuela) exist with some degree of autonomy outside the American-centered system. Ideologically, the international environment is still dominated by cold-war themes. Often, national aspirations for self-determination are purposely distorted in a constraining matrix of East-West confrontation. During the 1950s, it was Guatemala; in the 1960s, Cuba, the Dominican Republic, and Brazil; and the 1970s, Chile. All should provide lasting reminders that détente has never been an accepted component in hemispheric relations. With very few exceptions, American foreign policy is, and will continue to be, a fundamental determinant in the region's domestic politics. Economic dependence is a dominant leitmotiv but security considerations have been equally important. Since economic nationalism and international nonalignment have been constant themes resulting from expanding political participation, Latin American governments that are more responsible to mass internal constituencies would pose, in the short run, a threat to U.S. domination. The American response, under different administrations, has been predictably an interventionist one.[59] Only repressive-authoritarian regimes appear to safeguard the American national interest in Washington's eyes.

U.S. Foreign Policy: Continuities, Discontinuities, and Manifold Linkages

If one examines the prospects for democratisation from the standpoint of Chalmers's second level of analysis, the external linkage group, American foreign policy toward Latin America cannot be seen as a monolithic whole. For instance, the Carter line on human rights was quite explicitly stated in the Linowitz report:

> Our mutual concerns in the hemisphere center not
> on military security, but rather on the central issues
> of economic and political security in an uncertain
> world.[60]

This is ostensibly different from General Haig's posturings in Central America. Indeed, variations of style and content of policy do take place; change in orientation and in bipartisan continuity obtains. It can be suggested that U.S. policy toward the area could be seen as the outcome of a composition of several forces. Each one constitutes a specific "external linkage," in Chalmers's terminology. These sectors of U.S. foreign policy are the official, the economic, the military, and the intelligence-clandestine sector. Each sector can be seen, at least in theory, as having specific and often conflictual institutional objectives—a definition of "the national interest," and their own intelligence and transnational connections. In this perspective, U.S. policy toward Latin America as a whole or toward a specific country can be seen as a result of a conjunctural alliance amongst these sectors. Consensus, congruence, logrolling, passing, opposing, or sabotaging may take place regarding initiatives, countries, or time periods. In the formal structure of the U.S. government, the White House retains the final power to set the agenda, adjudicate intersectorial conflicts, and veto initiatives. However, this is possible only when it possesses the time, level of information, and determination to take political risks. This is especially true in crises (e.g., the Bay of Pigs invasion).

A cursory examination of U.S. policy over the last 20 years reveals a shifting pattern between coherence and incongruity amongst the policy sectors. Generally, during the recent Republican administrations (Eisenhower and Nixon-Ford), the policy has been internally consistent in all four areas. Conversely, during Democratic administrations, incoherence amongst the diplomatic, economic, military, and clandestine components appears to increase. The Alliance for Progress under Kennedy and Johnson[61] (and Carter's "human rights") has generally followed an indecisive and contradictory mold.[62] Indeed, no moral judgment is implied in analysing the content or the instrumentalities of the policy. All that is being suggested here is that conservative diplomacy is more readily acceptable by the State Department bureaucracy, business, and the military and clandestine sectors within the Washington political establishment. The opposite is true with the more liberal initiatives. In fact, it appears as if the Alliance and Carter's human-rights initiatives were severely watered down by realpolitik considerations before they became acceptable. In this regard, an observer commented:

> . . . of course, there are conflicts within the Carter
> administration over how the human rights thrust
> should be carried out, but the struggle is between
> those who favor a hard-line position and those who
> favor an even harder one.[63]

The shift toward a hardening posture was noticeable even during the conservative administration of Gerald Ford. At the time of the 1976 election,

> militants in the Republican Party were not satisfied;
> the further right that Ford moved, the more right
> Reagan had to go in order to outflank him. The
> result was a 1976 Republican foreign policy plank
> that criticized Ford's own reactionary administration
> for not being hawkish enough.[64]

All these considerations seem to point toward a very practical constraint in the implementation of a serious policy of military withdrawal and democratisation. The current right-wing trend in American politics can only accentuate the aforementioned tilt.

Latin American Elites and the Transnationalisation of the State

The prospects for democratisation must be seen, as well, from the standpoint of the Latin American elites, the "internal linkage" group. The most salient trait of the Latin American power elites has been their high degree of transnationalisation, paradoxically accompanying a growing degree of state autonomy. Unlike the predepression era, when the linkage role was monopolised by the landed and commercial oligarchy, since the 1950s, the military and the technocracy have developed linkages with transnational constituencies. This process has resulted in both a growing alienation from possible internal constituencies and an increased reliance on external supports from metropolitan clients. The transnationalisation of the military and its insertion into the hemispheric security system has been the most dramatic illustration of this trend. More often than not, its role has shifted from the maintenance of territorial sovereignty to that of a facilitator for external penetration, a sort of native occupying force for its own territories.

The few attempts at building an independent project have soon run into the unrelenting opposition of what has been called "reactionary coalitions."[65] These encompass alliances of both domestic and external forces intent on maintaining order by violent means if necessary. The well-known manifestation of these reactionary coalitions has been the spread of the national-security regimes in the 1970s. For its proponents, in the global struggle against communism, democracy offers no safeguard. Only a highly centralised state would secure a solid defence for capitalism. This is not just a question of ideological principle; it is also a pragmatic consideration for good business. Here, the Huntingtonian premise of the analysis of "overparticipation"[66] becomes tautologically correct. In dependent, underdeveloped economies, like those of Latin America, political regimes that allow for genuine political participation are bound to challenge the status quo, both the domestic and international. Moreover, for the proponents of national security, even the mildest attempts at military withdrawal would open the door to catastrophe. This hard-line position is exemplified by the Confederación Anticomunista Latinoamericana. In September 1980, the organisation met in Buenos Aires. The meeting had representatives from high places from most repressive regimes and was hosted by the Argentine government, which presented its keynote speaker, Argentianian General Carlos Suárez Mason. The conference

> outlined a programme for halting the Brazilian
> abertura, blocking Uruguay's projected "democratic
> plans," wiping out the ligas agrarias in Paraguay
> and giving whole-hearted support to the García Meza
> regime in Bolivia.[67]

In fact, Nicaragua and Iran are perceived from this viewpoint as
the undesirable consequences of letting reliable regimes down,
not as the outcome of long-run U.S. intervention and protracted
repression by the local elites. The events in Bolivia in 1980
point in the direction of a revitalisation of national security as
a viable option for domestic elites.[68] Chile as well, with its
mixture of institutionalisation and repression, seems to stand as
an example where a stable formula for intraelite power sharing
is at work. National security is not only the dominant pattern
of Latin American politics, but "resurgent militarism"[69] could
become a nasty mutation of the repressive 1970s.

Legitimacy Crisis and State Terrorism

Let us, finally, assess the prospects for democratisation
by concentrating upon the internal factor: the nature of the
contemporary Latin American state.

The hegemonic crisis that Quijano and Nun[70] quite eloquently
described in the 1960s is still an unfolding process in Latin
American political institutions. Four factors underpin the
crisis: the inability of the state to accommodate conflicting
demands, the very limited degree of political choice, restricted
sovereignty, and a relatively low level of economic capabilities.
Keeping political participation down, under conditions of constant
social mobilisation (e.g., migration, urbanisation, and literacy)
has only compounded the long-run problems repression was
thought to prevent. The combination of transnational integration
(economic, military, and bureaucratic) of the Latin American
elites into one U.S.-centered hegemonic project, and a growing
marginalisation and alienation on the part of the bulk of the
internal constituencies, has brought about an acute crisis of
legitimation. In the absence of tangible rewards to buy off
legitimacy, violence (insurgent, repressive, or institutionalised)
becomes the most common political currency. Not only repression,
but plain state terrorism, evolve into a distinct style of conflict
management.

Under these circumstances, revolution often turns into a
self-fulfilling prophecy, as the perceived alternative to repression. The shrinkage of political spaces tends to reduce the
generally multifaceted power intercourse to a simple first-degree

military equation: power equals force. The ongoing tragedies in El Salvador, Guatemala, or Argentina are undoubtedly related to an accelerated reduction of any middle ground for compromise or negotiation. Nicaragua and Chile illustrate, at both ends of the spectrum, the models available. When consensus fails and inflationary politics exhausts its bag of tricks, authoritarianism and revolution are always there. The question is, of course, one of the acceptable social cost, for the ruling coalitions.

Perhaps in this context, the cases of Ecuador or Peru (and, for that matter, the Dominican Republic) cannot be seen, after all, as the start of a trend but as exceptions, fragile and temporary experiments in a sea of authoritarianism.

CONCLUSIONS AND POSTSCRIPT

The cursory exploration undertaken above regarding the prospects for military withdrawal seems to point not only in the direction of stagnation but also toward the reversal of the trend. It is possible to suggest that the authoritarian trend of the 1970s will not be reverted. Worse, a new wave of repression is not unlikely. In each of the four levels of analyses explored, it appeared that the question of military withdrawal was, at best, problematic, even the "limited-democracy" concept advocated by the Linowitz Report. The single most important factor behind the trend toward restricted (and formal) democracy was the existence of a political coalition of U.S. transnationals and the White House that supported this project. This coalition, identified with the Trilateral Commission, was receptive to the rhetoric of human rights—not the content—voiced by the Latin American churches and other human-rights organisations.

The Reagan victory undoubtedly shattered the aforementioned coalition. Even before the election, the Council of the Americas, a business group that voices the Rockefeller interests (and that widely espoused the Trilateral views on the region) returned to the political discourse of the Nixon years. In July 1980, it issued a policy paper outlining a desirable direction for the new decade:

> The document avoids direct criticism of the administration's human rights policy but it urges the government to refrain from using economic measures for political ends. It argues that restrictions unrelated to national security erode U.S. competitiveness overseas, send conflicting signals to U.S. exporters and foreign buyers . . .[71]

In its most crucial part, however, the document recommended, in no unequivocal terms, "expanded sales of military equipment and the furnishing of security training programs for governments throughout Latin America."[72] Since Nelson Rockefeller's Pentagonistic recommendation in 1969, the policy went a full circle—through human rights, with restricted democracy, to new authoritarianism. The symbol of this new policy was General Haig's appointment as secretary of state.

For one thing, even ruling out complicity or intent, the change of presidents was perceived by Latin American hard-liners as a green light to unsheathe their long knives—witness the assassination of President Roldos in Ecuador and the mysterious accident that removed General Torrijos from the Panamanian political scene. A weakening of the Carter stand certainly gave the Bolivian generals a clue. The same thing is true in a toughening of the repression in both Argentina and Chile. Once again, we are faced with the well-known dictum that when things are defined as real, there are real consequences.

Moreover, if one goes by the record regarding a Reagan policy toward Latin America, a number of disturbing propositions could be advanced. A new institutional variable is the absence of political constraints in the U.S. Congress. The defeat of moderate and liberal senators opened the gate to a new breed of right-wing militants, further to the right of Reagan, and certainly of Vice President Bush. The moderating role that a liberal Senate exercised in past U.S. foreign policies is thus curtailed. Another well-known fact is the ultraconservative ideological bent of both the president and his Latin American team: Roger Fontaine and Pedro San Juan, not to mention the secretary of state himself. Also well-known are the ideological stands of the major think tanks (the Georgetown Center for Advanced Strategic and International Studies, and the American Enterprise Institute [AEI])[73] behind the Republican foreign policy.

A preelection interview with Roger Fontaine in the Miami Herald highlighted some clues regarding the Reagan position. He suggested, in no uncertain terms, that there was going to be "a rather striking difference"[74] with Carter's approach to the region. For one thing, reference was made to a "Truman doctrine" for Latin America, an explicit reminder of the U.S. stand in the Greek civil war in the 1940s. Regarding the role of repressive regimes, especially in Central America, Fontaine left no room for ambiguity: "It means that they need military advisors. . . . It means that they need military training. . . . You don't fight terrorists and guerrillas with non-lethal aid."[75] This stands in sharp contrast to the tone and the content of the

Carter policy—e.g., Treasury Secretary Michael Blumenthal's statement at an Inter-American Development Bank meeting in Guatemala in May 1980:

> We do not believe that the philosophy of using terrorism as a means to fight terrorism is a policy that can succeed over the long-run.[76]

On the subject of direct military intervention, Fontaine stated that "the use of military force is an option any nation, in terms of its vital national interest, has to maintain as a possibility."[77] Another most alarming concept is that referring to an operational definition of the Marxist "enemy": "Part of the definition is in what their friends are."[78] In fact, under this concept, any discrepancy with U.S. designs could do (e.g., the Panama Canal or Mexican Oil). On the subject of dictatorships, however, is where the policy is most explicit in stating "that turbulent countries going through a period of turbulence are going to have that sort of thing, at least for a period of time."[79] These statements must be taken seriously. The Reagan regime's test case for its Latin American policy has been El Salvador. There, the U.S. military appears to have been given a relatively free hand in dealing with its local clientele—the Salvadoran army—even against the wishes of the then national security adviser, Richard V. Allen, the CIA, and numerous State Department officials.[80] In November 1981, General Haig conducted a purge in the latter organisation. The action was unprecedented since the loss of China in 1949.[81] At the same time, he pushed for a military solution to the crisis, involving not only direct action in El Salvador but also a contemplation of armed attacks at "the source of the problem,"—in the general's view, Nicaragua and Cuba.[83]

Without even attempting to draw too close a parallel between Indochina and Central America, a similar American military response seems to be taking shape. This involves at least two all-too-familiar themes: the oversimplification of an indigenous and complex political problem into the equation of military force and Communist aggression; and the belief that only the continentalisation of the conflict offers the United States a chance for a decisive military victory—a last stand of sorts.

In a different historical setting, Antonio Gramsci wrote a commentary that may well describe the current predicament of Latin America:

The crisis consists precisely in the fact that the old
is dying and the new cannot be born; in this inter-
regnum a great variety of morbid symptoms appear.[84]

NOTES

1. This concept is used here in the sense given by Kuhn,
to mean "some implicit body of intertwined theoretical and methodological belief that permits selection, evaluation and criticism."
Cf. Thomas S. Kuhn, The Structure of Scientific Revolutions,
Second ed. (Chicago: University of Chicago Press, 1970), pp.
15-17.
2. Cf. Susanne Bodenheimer, "The Ideology of Developmentalism: American Political Science Paradigm—Surrogate for
Latin American Studies," Berkeley Journal of Sociology, No. 15
(1970), pp. 95-137.
3. See Rodolfo Stavenhagen, "Seven Fallacies About Latin
America," in James Petras and Maurice Zeitlin (eds.), Latin
America. Reform or Revolution? A Reader (Greenwich: Fawcett,
1968), pp. 22-23. Cf. John P. Gillin, "Ethos Components in
Modern Latin American Culture," in D. Heath and R. Adams,
Contemporary Cultures and Societies of Latin America (New York:
Random House, 1965), pp. 514-15.
4. A characteristic treatment is Seymour M. Lipset and
Aldo Solari (eds.), Elites in Latin America (New York: Oxford
University Press, 1967).
5. The Consenso was the report on the Committee of
Ministers of Foreign Relations and Economics held at the Viña
del Mar resort in Chile in 1969. The stand taken there was
clearly one of economic nationalism, largely accepting the ECLA
thesis of structural dependencia, whilst still looking favorably
upon foreign aid. Cf. Jerome Levinson and Juan de Onís, The
Alliance that Lost its Way. A Critical Report on the Alliance for
Progress (Chicago: Quadrangle Books, 1970), pp. 183-84.
6. Cf. A. Weil, J. Comblin, and J. Senese, The Repressive
State: The Brazilian National Security Doctrine and Latin America
(Toronto: Latin American Research Unit Studies, c. 1976),
Document 3, No. 2, pp. 36-63.
7. Nelson Rockefeller, The Rockefeller Report of a United
States Presidential Mission for the Western Hemisphere (Chicago:
Quadrangle Books, 1969), cited in W. Raymond Duncan and James
Nelson Goodsel (eds.), The Quest for Change in Latin America.
Sources for a Twentieth Century Analysis (New York: Oxford
University Press, 1970), pp. 542-49. Senator Frank Church,

"Toward a New Policy for Latin America," in Richard B. Gray (ed.), Latin America and the United States in the 1970's (Itasca, Ill.: F. E. Peacock Publishers, 1971), p. 347.

8. Cf. Arturo Siat and Gregorio Iriarte, "De la Seguridad Nacional al Tri-Lateralismo," Cuadernos de Christianismo y Sociedad (Buenos Aires, May 1978), pp. 17-30.

9. The term has been coined by former Dominican President Juan Bosch. Cf. Juan Bosch, Pentagonism: A Substitute for Imperialism (New York: Grove Press, 1969).

10. Bodenheimer, op. cit., pp. 95-102. Also, Donal Cruise O'Brien, "Modernization, Order and the Erosion of a Democratic Ideal, American Political Science 1960-1970," Journal of Development Studies, No. 8 (July 1972), pp. 351-78.

11. Cf. Michel Crozier, Samuel P. Huntington, and Joji Watanuki, The Crisis of Democracy, Report on the Governability of Democracies to the Trilateral Commission (New York University Press, 1975), pp. 1-5, 169.

12. Bodenheimer, loc. cit.

13. Helio Jaguaribe, "Dependency and Autonomy in Latin America," in Joseph S. Tulchin (ed.), Latin America in the Year 2000 (Reading, Mass.: Addison-Wesley, 1975), p. 197.

14. Cf. J. Nef and O. P. Dwivedi, "Development Theory and Administration. A Fence Around an Empty Lot?," International Journal of Public Administration, Vol. 27, No. 1 (January-March 1981), pp. 42-66.

15. "Ecuador's New Tool Lifts Freedom in Latin America," The Miami Herald, August 19, 1979.

16. "A New Quest for Stability," NACLA Report on the Americas, Vol. 12, No. 2 (March-April 1979), p. 29.

17. "Democracy Climbs the Andes Again," New York Times, July 19, 1979.

18. Miami Herald, loc. cit.

19. Cf. Richard Gardner, Saburo Okita, and B. J. Udink. A Turning Point in North-South Economic Relations, The Triangle Papers: 3 (New York, 1974), pp. 9, 11.

20. Siat and Iriarte, op. cit., p. 23.

21. Editorial, New York Times, July 4, 1979.

22. Washington Office on Latin America, Latin America Update, Vol. 5, No. 5 (September/October 1980), p. 1.

23. Cf. Mansbach, Lampert, and Ferguson, The Web of World Politics: Non-State Actors in the Global System (Englewood Cliffs: Prentice-Hall, 1976), pp. 2-45, 273-79; also, Robert O. Keohane and Joseph S. Nye, Power and Interdependence. World Politics in Transition (Boston: Little, Brown, 1977), pp. 3-37. In Keohane's and Nye's words, under conditions of

complex interdependence "we can imagine a world in which actors other than states participate directly in world politics in which a clear hierarchy of issues does not exist and in which force is an ineffective instrument of policy." The model is supposed to challenge both state-centric "realism" of "power politics" and "international dependency," the ECLA doctrine. Cf. Keohane and Nye, op. cit., p. ix, especially footnote 4. See also, Steve C. Ropp, "Concepts Drawn from Contemporary International Relations Theory of Analysis of Latin American Politics: "Regime" and "Complex Interdependence" (Paper, 1980 Annual Meeting of the Southwestern Political Science Association, Houston, Texas, April 2-5, 1980), p. 16.

24. Crozier et al., The Crisis of Democracy; also, Alan Wolfe, "Capitalism Shows its Face," The Nation, November 29, 1975, p. 559.

25. Ropp, op. cit., p. 16.

26. Ibid., p. 22.

27. The term is used in the Mertonian sense of "consequences." Cf. Robert Merton, Social Theory and Social Structure (New York: Free Press, 1966), pp. 60-64.

28. Alan Wolfe, "The Two Faces of Carter," The Nation, December 18, 1970, p. 651. He sees "Trilateralism" as a response to the "American first" policy of the Nixon years (1972), which provoked much antipathy in both Europe and Japan.

29. NACLA Report, March-April 1979, pp. 3, 30.

30. Ibid.

31. Ibid., p. 6.

32. Tom J. Farer, Trialogue, No. 19 (Fall 1978), p. 14.

33. Cf. Samuel P. Huntington, Political Order in Changing Societies (New Haven: Yale University Press, 1968), pp. 194-98.

34. Ibid., pp. 78-92, 198.

35. Cf. Wolfe, "Capitalism Shows Its Face," pp. 557-63.

36. Cf. Miami Herald, August 19, 1979; Siat and Iriarte, op. cit., p. 23; also, Washington Post, June 13, 1979, states, with reference to the Nicaraguan crisis: "Since last September, U.S. policy-makers openly have taken the position that Somoza should give up the presidency and allow his moderate opposition from Nicaraguan business and professional classes to prepare the country for a transition to democracy."

37. NACLA Report (March-April 1979), pp. 9, 29, 30, 33.

38. Interview with Henry Kissinger in Trialogue, No. 19 (Fall 1978), p. 3.

39. See, for instance, Washington Post, June 6, July 21, 1979; Miami Herald, July 19, August 9, 1979, August 19, 1979; and New York Times, July 4, October 30, 1979.

40. NACLA Report, op. cit., p. 30.

41. Ibid., p. 31

42. Wolfe, "The Two Faces," p. 651; also; "El ABC de la Comisión Trilateral," Prisma, June 2, 1977, pp. 2-4.

43. Wolfe, "Capitalism," p. 559; also, Gardner, Okita, and Udink, The Triangle Papers, No. 3 (1979), pp. 9-11; Farer, op. cit., p. 16. An article in No. 20 (Summer 1979) of Trialogue, entitled "Industrial Policy and International Economy," is quite illustrative of the abovementioned position: "[Our] industrial policy should complement market mechanisms, rather than work against the underlying forces of the market. . . . Positive industrial policies . . . [should] stimulate viable activities and help move resources [amongst nations] . . . [Such] policies often had to be combined with more 'defensive' measures to secure 'socially acceptable' peace and the required adjustments. [Our] nation's policies [have] tended to be exclusively 'defensive', thereby failing to meet the need for truly adaptive strategies and exacerbating international frictions."

44. Wolfe, "The Two Faces," p. 651.

45. Wolfe, "Capitalism," p. 559.

46. Siat and Iriarte, op. cit., p. 24.

47. Wolfe, "Capitalism," p. 561.

48. Ibid., p. 559.

49. Ibid.; NACLA Report, op. cit., p. 30.

50. Ibid.

51. Wolfe, "The Two Faces," p. 650-51.

52. Ibid., p. 650.

53. Orlando Fals Borda, cited by June Carolyn Erlick, "Columbia is a Democracy," World Press Digest, Vol. 1, No. 4 (January 1979), p. 19.

54. Siat and Iriarte, op. cit., pp. 24-25.

55. Quoted in Siat and Iriarte, ibid., p. 27.

56. Ibid., p. 28.

57. Ibid.

58. Douglas A. Chalmers, "Developing on the Periphery: External Factors in Latin American Politics," in Yale H. Ferguson, Contemporary Inter-American Relations. A Reader on Theory and Issues (Englewood Cliffs: Prentice-Hall, 1972), p. 12.

59. Cf. C. Neal Ronning, Intervention in Latin America (New York: Alfred A. Knopf: 1970), pp. 3-23; also, Yale H. Ferguson, "Reflections on the Inter-American Principle of Non-intervention," in Ferguson, op. cit., pp. 84-103.

60. Commission on United States-Latin American Relations (Sol Linowitz, chairman), The Americas in a Changing World (New York: Quadrangle Books, 1975), p. 60.

61. Cf. Levinson and de Onis, op. cit., pp. 323-31.

62. Paul Pickering, "Carter's Double Standards," The New Statesman, Vol. 99, No. 2552 (February 15, 1980), pp. 1-2; also, Latin America Weekly Report, February 15, 1980, "Baptism of Fire for New Washington Policy."

63. Council for Hemispheric Affairs (COHA), COHA Press Release, June 15, 1977, p. 1.

64. Michael T. Klare, "Resurgent Militarism," IPS Issue Paper (Washington, D.C.: Institute for Policy Studies, December 1978), p. 11.

65. Cf. Liisa North, "Development and Underdevelopment in Latin America," in J. Nef, Canada and The Latin American Challenge (Guelph: Ontario Cooperative Program on Latin American and Caribbean Studies, 1978), p. 79.

66. Cf. Samuel P. Huntington, Political Order in Changing Societies (New Haven: Yale University Press, 1968), pp. 47-59.

67. Latin America Weekly Report, September 19, 1980, p. 5.

68. General Jorge Videla, then president of Argentina, explained Argentina's support for García Meza in the following terms:

> The formally correct thing . . . would have been for a government resulting from elections to have taken power, but [it] represented for us a high degree of risk because of the possibility that it would spread ideas contrary to our way of life and the permanence here of a military government.

69. Klare, op. cit., p. 1.

70. José Nun, "A Latin American Phenomenon: The Middle-Class Coup," in J. Petras and M. Zeitlin (eds.), Latin America. Reform or Revolution? A Reader (Greenwich: Fawcett Publications, 1968), pp. 145-185.

71. Business Latin America, August 20, 1980, p. 267.

72. Ibid., p. 269.

73. For an AEI perspective on U.S.-Latin American relations, cf. Edmund Gaspar, United States-Latin America: A Special Relationship? (Washington, D.C. and Stanford: AEI/The Hoover Institution, 1978).

74. Miami Herald, August 24, 1980.

75. Ibid.

76. COHA Press Release, June 2, 1977, p. 1.

77. Miami Herald, loc. cit.

78. Ibid.

79. Ibid.
80. Cf. New York Times, November 5, 1981, pp. A1, A8.
81. New York Times, November 3, 1981, p. A9.
82. New York Times, November 5, 1981, p. A8.
83. Ibid.
84. Antonio Gramsci, quoted in Susanne Berger, "Politics and Antipolitics in Western Europe," Daedalus, Vol. 108, No. 1 (Summer 1971), p. 51.

10

THE AUTHENTICITY OF
PARTICIPATORY DEMOCRACY IN CUBA
Archibald R.M. Ritter

". . . at this moment, the Revolutionary Government transfers to the National Assembly the power it has held up to now. Thus the Council of Ministers invests this assembly with the constitutional and legislative functions it exercised for almost 18 years, the period of the most radical and deep political and social transformations in our country's life."

> Fidel Castro, Inaugural Speech at the Founding Session of the National Assembly, December 2, 1976, Granma Weekly Review, Havana, December 12, 1976, p. 3.

INTRODUCTION

Cuba's political system has undergone a major transformation since 1974. In the 1960s, the system was characterized by

---

I wish to thank the Humanities and Social Sciences Research Council of Canada for funding which facilitated a visit to Cuba in February 1979, when some useful materials for this essay were collected.

This revised version originally appeared as "Los Organos del Poder Popular and Participatory Democracy in Cuba: A Preliminary Analysis," in December 1980, Social and Economic Studies. Used with permission.

Fidel Castro's charismatic "ad hocery"; by a lack of formal representational mechanisms in the governance of the state; by a lack of democratic controls in the civil organs of society; and by the monopolistic central role of what became in 1965 the Communist Party of Cuba. However, partly in response to some of the difficulties encountered in the latter half of the 1960s, a reexamination of the political as well as the economic system was conducted by the revolutionary leadership. This resulted in some revitalization within the trade unions and the party, the convening of the First Congress of the Communist Party in December 1975, and the adoption of a constitution by referendum in 1976. Of greatest significance in Cuba's new political system is the installation of a set of representative assemblies at the municipal, provincial, and national levels—the organos del poder popular, or organs of popular power (OPP).

The objective of this essay is to examine the functioning of the representative assemblies in the new institutional system. It must be emphasized immediately that such an examination can only be tentative at this time, because of the relatively short period in which the system has been operating and the consequent lack of information on it. Nevertheless, some questions concerning the relations between the OPP and the Party are taken up here. The key question relates to how effective power is shared between these groups. What powers do the OPP institutions at different levels actually possess? To what extent, and in what senses, do the new assemblies constitute effective initiative-taking and decision-making bodies? What is the role of the Communist Party in the assemblies, and is it compatible and/or incompatible with genuine democratization?

In order to examine the extent to which the new system is authentically democratic, one must first provide a definition of the terms "democracy" and "democratic participation." I will not enter a political-philosophic discussion of the meaning of these terms, however. Nor will I deal with the ideological debate between Western pluralistic and Communist conceptions of democracy. The criterion I will employ for "democratic participation" will be the influence or degree of control that ordinary citizens exercise over the selection of those in leadership positions, and over the policies and procedures adopted in the relevant collectivities.[1] It might be noted that in certain situations, some control may be exercised by a citizenry over policymaking, through referenda, through consultative processes concerning new legislation, or through other means, without direct control over the selection of leaders. Similarly, it is possible that a citizenry might have substantial control over leadership selection, but relatively little direct or indirect influence over policy formulation. To what extent do the citizens of Cuba exercise control over who is selected for the municipal, provincial, and national assemblies? To what extent do they influence decision-making processes and policies in Cuba?

A definitive treatment of these issues is still not possible as the new political institutions have indeed been functioning only since late 1976. Source materials currently available include only basic documents such as the constitution and the First Party Congress Resolution on the Organs of People's Power; reports in the Cuban press concerning elections and the meetings of the National Assembly; and some of the main speeches presented at the National Assembly. Indeed, there are, so far, few fragmentary visitor impressions that can be pieced together in an attempt to arrive at an overall analysis.

There have been some studies on the functioning of the new system, however. Of these, two were based mainly upon the experimental Matanzas elections of 1974.[2] A more recent study by W. Leogrande focused upon political participation in general terms, including some discussion of the OPP and their effects upon the participatory opportunities available to the Cuban people—which, he concluded, have expanded significantly.[3] In his major work, J. Dominguez devotes some attention to the electoral procedures within the OPP as well as to the unions and some mass organizations.[4] One conclusion he reaches is that while electoral procedures are meant to broaden popular participation, the system in law, and as practiced, limits electoral competition and permits the Party to exercise substantial control over electoral processes.[5]

This essay also attempts to gauge the authenticity of the participatory democracy inherent in the functioning of the OPP. It begins with a brief survey of the nature of participation in the 1960s. The new political structures are then outlined. Information on the general role of the Party in the OPP, on the functioning of the local OPP, on the National Assembly, and on its Council of State, is presented in order to permit a preliminary assessment of the nature of political participation through the OPP.

Perhaps it should be emphasized here that the task attempted in this essay is especially difficult, owing to the immense and treacherous ideological overburdens and undercurrents around the concept of democracy. Many observers from the Western world would quickly reject the notion that political democracy could exist in a system characterized by a monopolistic political party; monopolistic control of all organs of communication by that party; intense purveying of a single ideology and party line, through the educational system and the media; and thorough penetration and substantial manipulation of the civil organs of society by the party. On the other hand, other observers would just as quickly reject the notion that authentic democracy could exist in Western systems characterized by highly unequal owner- ship and control of financial resources by citizens, generating unequal capabilities for manipulation of the system; the presence of large and vociferous private business establishments, with disproportionately large powers to shape legislative processes and policy formulation; private ownership and financing of the communications media; and mass deformations of character en- gendered by capitalism.

In this essay, I will attempt to sidestep these ideological debates by assuming what seems to be a reasonably straight- forward concept of democracy, as presented earlier—namely, the extent to which citizens control and influence the selection of their representatives and leaders in the political system, and the extent to which they control and influence the formulation of public policies.

THE POLITICAL SYSTEM OF THE 1960s

When the revolutionary army under Fidel Castro seized power in 1959, it moved into the institutional vacuum left by the deposed Batista regime. The ultimate authority from the start was Fidel Castro as initiator of the rebellion and commander of the successful revolutionary army. Castro's legitimacy was won not through any electoral system, but through the displacement of a regime that was perceived by most Cubans as being illegiti- mate (having come to power by the coup d'etat immediately before the 1952 election that Batista was bound to lose).

As the eliminator of the old regime and the embodiment of the new, Castro's authority was charismatic in nature, being based upon the personal relationship between him and the people. A constitution did exist, however—the Ley Fundamental de la Revolución (Fundamental Law of the Revolution) of February 1959. This was implemented by the Council of Ministers set up by the Dirección Nacional del Movimiento 26 de Julio (National Board of the July 26 Movement), which was controlled by Castro. It then legitimized the Council of Ministers as the supreme organ of the state, with constitutional, legislative, executive, and other administrative powers.[6] But the constitution did not provide for the creation of representative institutions or for the election of public officials.

Throughout the 1960s, the essence of the political system was the direct relationship of Castro with the people. The mass rallies were perhaps the most important media for such communication. As Ché Guevara described it:

> At the great mass meetings, one can observe something like the dialogue of two tuning forks whose vibrations summon forth new vibrations in each other. Fidel and the masses begin to vibrate in a dialogue of increasing intensity until it reaches an abrupt climax crowned by cries of struggle and victory.[7]

Premier Castro also listened directly to people's views on his frequent tours and visits throughout Cuba. Castro's intimate contact with the rural people of the Sierra Maestra from 1956 to 1959 probably had a lasting impression as well. These, then, were perhaps some of the major media through which people could affect the content and processes of policy formulation.

The mass organizations had some potential in the 1960s as institutions through which democratic participation could have occurred. This potential was largely unrealized, however. Organs such as the labour unions, the National Association of Small Farmers (ANAP), and youth organizations operated largely as transmission belts from top to bottom—indeed, transmitting orders, exhortation, and discipline downward, and representing the interests of the entire nation as perceived and defined by the revolutionary leadership. Their roles were not to aggregate, articulate, and defend the sectional interests of their constituencies. Instead, they were arms of the state, designed in large part to coopt, orientate, coordinate, and integrate people so that their behaviour and actions would further the national interest as seen by the leadership. For example, the absence of a representational function for the labour unions from the mid-1960s to 1970 is well known. In the words of Labour Minister Jorge Risquet (July 31, 1970):

> There is no one to defend him [the worker]; . . . the party has become so involved with the management that in many instances it has ceased to play its proper role, has become somewhat insensitive to the problems of the masses. . . . The trade union either does not exist, or it has become the vanguard bureau. . . . Local unions are weak, their importance has been downgraded.[8]

What had happened was that in viewing themselves as media for manipulating the work force at the enterprise and plant levels, in the pursuit of national objectives, the unions were not in a position to defend the sectional interests of the workers. The pre-1970 situation in the unions was understood by Premier Castro, who stated, in the September 1970 speech in which he announced forthcoming union elections:

> We are going to trust our workers and hold elections
> in all locals . . . right away. They will be absolutely
> free and the workers can choose the candidates. . . .
> If a worker has really been elected by a majority
> vote of all of his comrades, he will have authority;
> he won't be a nobody who has been placed there by
> decree. [9]

The situation in other mass organizations was likely as nonrepresentational as in the unions, and their functions also were more for coordinating and manipulating people's actions than for the defense of their sectional interests.[10] The Communist Party continued to be a centrally controlled organization.

The political system throughout the 1960s, and especially in the latter half of that decade, can be considered to be democratically representative neither in the sense that mechanisms were used or even existed for the popular selection of the leadership, nor in the sense that people were able to influence policymaking through formal mechanisms. It is very important to emphasize, however, that despite this, policies were formulated that were highly beneficial to the large majority of the population. With surprising success, these policies redistributed income, reduced urban-rural disparities, virtually eliminated "open" unemployment, and achieved universal access to education and public health as well as sports.[11] The political system that brought about these results has been aptly labeled "revolutionary paternalism" by Nelson Valdés.[12] Presumably, the system generated beneficial results because of the identification of the revolutionary leadership with the interests of the bulk of the population and with its commitment to improve the material well-being of the people, and perhaps also because of the communication between the leaders and the people in the years of guerrilla warfare in the 1956-58 period, in the mass meetings, and through continuous informal contact.

In the latter half of the 1960s, and especially from 1968 to mid-1970, the nonparticipatory nature of the political system aggravated other difficulties encountered by the revolution. It is very difficult to disentangle the impacts of the political system from economic factors such as excessive centralization, heavy reliance upon nonmaterial incentives, and the fixation on the 10-million-ton sugar-harvest target. The lack of representational machinery in the state, the party and the mass organization, together with a lack of other means for influencing policy formulation, such as ready access to communications media, likely contributed to growing public apathy in the face of the strenuous exhortation to work harder and to accept intensified austerity. If people had no meaningful input into the formulation of national objectives or plant-level targets, could it be expected that they would behave as the planners desired, on the basis of exhortation and moral incentives rather than according to their perceptions of their own costs and benefits? The symptoms of the difficulties arising from a lack of meaningful participation (and other factors) were high levels of absenteeism, low on-the-job productivity, and "indiscipline."[13] When exhortation and moral appeals did not successfully mobilize public effort, the alternative, in the absence of effective material incentives, was to use more coercive activation devices. Increased reliance was thence placed upon conscripted (military) labour, and upon increased pressures on workers to shift to agriculture or to extend working hours. The imagery and symbolism of the mobilization drive from 1968 to 1970 became militaristic; workers were exhorted to work as if their lives depended on it, to defend Cuba from imperialism, and to uphold the honour and prestige of the revolution.[14] The organization of part of the work effort in agriculture was a quasi-militaristic activity reflected also in the lack of concern for costs. This transformation of the mobilization system, together with the widespread movement of military personnel into civilian positions, was part of the basis for the observation that Cuban society had become "militarized." Some authors have stressed the critical choice that the Cuban revolution faced by 1970: between heightened centralization, perhaps accompanied by repression, on the one hand; and more democratic forms of societal organization, on the other.[15]

By mid-1970, the shortcomings of the existing system were apparent to the revolutionary leadership. A decision was made to establish institutional mechanisms through which participatory democracy could function. Democratization and institutionalization became the hallmarks of the system that was to be constructed. Movement toward a new system began with some public discussion of the problems of the late 1960s, and continued with public consideration of new pieces of legislation (such as the Anti-Loafing Law), with elections in the labour unions, and with work on the drafting of a new constitution.

THE BASIC OUTLINE OF THE NEW POLITICAL SYSTEM

The organos del poder popular were launched on an experimental basis in the province of Matanzas in 1974 and 1975. The
definitive blueprint for the new political system was then outlined
in Cuba's new constitution, which was approved by the First
Congress of the Communist Party of Cuba in December 1975, and
which then received a 97.7 percent majority vote in the national
referendum of February 15, 1976. The new constitution articulated the main social, political, and economic principles of Cuban
society; recognized freedom of expression, religion, association,
and the press so long as these were in harmony with the objective
of socialist society; specified the rights and duties of citizens;
and outlined the framework for the electoral system. [16]
The new political structure consists of a five-tiered set of
assemblies beginning at the neighbourhood level, and moving
through the circunscripción (district) electoral level, the municipal level, and the provincial level to the national level.
At the level of the neighbourhood, citizens select, by a
show of hands at a general public meeting, a secretary and
president, whose task is to run the nomination proceedings for
the rest of the meeting. Potential candidates for the later elections at the circunscripción level are then nominated from the
floor. Of the several potential candidates (the minimum being
two), one is elected at the meeting, again by a show of hands.
The individual chosen then becomes the neighbourhood nominee
for the circunscripción election. In these elections, one representative is selected by secret ballot in enclosed voting booths
and, by a simple majority (with a runoff, if necessary), to represent the circunscripción in the Municipal Assembly.
The municipal assemblies, and not the citizens directly,
select the delegates to the 14 provincial assemblies (one delegate
for every 10,000 inhabitants and for a portion of people greater
than 5,000) and the deputies for the National Assembly (one for
every 20,000 inhabitants and for a portion exceeding 10,000).
Circunscripciones electorales may select candidates from outside
the relevant area. Similarly, the municipal assemblies may choose
delegates to the provincial assemblies and deputies for the
National Assembly who are neither delegates to the municipal
assemblies, nor residents of the relevant municipalities. [17]
The structure of the new electoral system—excluding the
neighbourhood level—is illustrated in Figure 10.1.
On October 11, 1976, some 10,725 delegates were elected
in the national elections for the 169 municipal assemblies. These
assemblies then elected 1,084 delegates to the provincial assemblies

FIGURE 10.1. Structure of the Organs of People's Power, 1979

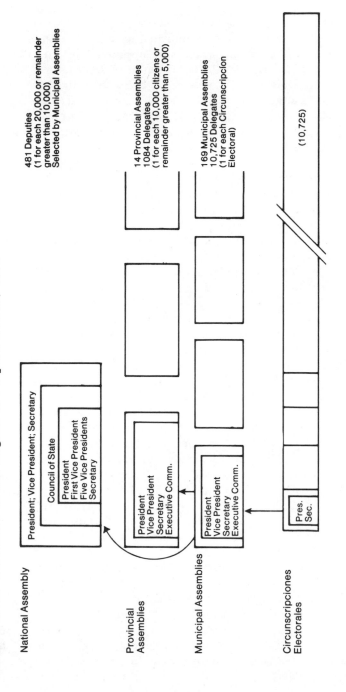

National Assembly

President; Vice President; Secretary

Council of State

President
First Vice President
Five Vice Presidents
Secretary

481 Deputies
(1 for each 20,000 or remainder
greater than 10,000)
Selected by Municipal Assemblies

Provincial
Assemblies

President
Vice President
Secretary
Executive Comm.

14 Provincial Assemblies
1084 Delegates
(1 for each 10,000 citizens or
remainder greater than 5,000)

Municipal Assemblies

President
Vice President
Secretary
Executive Comm.

169 Municipal Assemblies
10,725 Delegates
(1 for each Circunscripcion
Electoral)

Circunscripciones
Electorales

Pres.
Sec.

(10,725)

Sources: "Cuba: Su Institucionalización Histórica," in Cuba Internacional: Suplemento Especial
(Havana, 1976), and Granma, February 16, 1979, p. 4.

190

and 481 deputies for the National Assembly.[18] In the National Assembly, a Council of State was selected, with Fidel Castro as president and Raul Castro as first vice president; five other vice presidents, a secretary, and 23 other members were named.

The modes of operation and the responsibilities of the municipal and provincial assemblies and the National Assembly and of the Council of State were outlined in the constitution. According to the constitution, the National Assembly is the ultimate and supreme organ in the political system. It selects the Council of State, and is also the ultimate constituent and legislative body. It is the supreme economic authority, being empowered to discuss and approve the national economic and social plans, the state budget, and the nature of the economic-management system. It is the foremost authority on such matters as the general outline of foreign and domestic policy. It selects the members of the Supreme Court and the attorney general. It also "exercises the highest supervision over the organs of state and government."[19]

The executive body of the National Assembly is the Council of State, which represents the former when it is not in session, and which is charged with overseeing the implementation of its decisions. However, another body, the Council of Ministers is the highest-ranking administrative and executive organ and in fact constitutes the government. Members of this body are appointed by the president of the Council of State and approved by the National Assembly. The Council of Ministers includes the president, vice president, and secretary of the Council of State, together with all ministers, the head of the Junta Central de Planificación (JUCEPLAN), and some others.

At the provincial and municipal levels, the assemblies are charged with overseeing and controlling the administrative leadership and local enterprises in their relevant jurisdictions, with aiding in plan formulation and implementation in their relevant areas, with upholding the constitution, and defending the rights of citizens and socialist property, and with other legal and appointive tasks.[20] The municipal and provincial assemblies do not possess independent revenue-raising capabilities, however.

Two important mechanisms exist to ensure that delegates to municipal and provincial assemblies and deputies for the National Assembly continue to be in close contact with their constituents and responsive to their needs, suggestions, and criticisms. First, delegates must be "accountable" to their electors. In practice, this means that they must meet every four months with their electors, and listen to complaints, grievances, and proposals they then may transmit upward.

They also report back to their constituents on their own activities and those of their respective assemblies. Municipal-assembly delegates are required to set aside a specific time every few weeks for consultation with constituents, although often this consultation apparently occurs also on a much more informal and frequent basis. The Cuban Communist Party (PCC) is charged with the responsibility of ensuring that such accountability processes function effectively:

> It must be the Party's constant and primary concern to ensure that the process of rendering account to the electors, at every level, take place regularly and systematically, and that they are free from any routine or formalism, and are so organized as to guarantee the true and effective participation of the masses and the free expression of views and suggestions.[21]

Second, delegates and deputies are subject to recall by their electors. If a delegate or deputy is thought to have been negligent in his or her duty, those, and only those, who elected that delegate or deputy can remove that person from office and select another representative. The PCC is also charged with the responsibility of ensuring that this mechanism works:

> . . . the Party must see to it that the masses in the constituencies and the delegates of various levels can, whenever necessary, fully exercise the power of recalling the representatives elected by them.

> The principle according to which only electors can recall those they have elected should be ensured without exception, and it should always be guaranteed that those being subjected to the process of recall are given the opportunity to freely address the assembly of those who elected them.[22]

THE NEW INSTITUTIONS: HOW DEMOCRATIC
ARE THEY IN PRACTICE?

The organs of popular power are designed to be highly democratic in the sense in which that term is being used in this essay. They are meant to provide citizens with direct control over the selection of members of municipal assemblies, and indirect control over provincial assemblies and the National Assembly. Each level of the representative institutions has clearly defined powers, as outlined earlier. Electoral procedures, which are followed rigourously, together with the practices of accountability sessions and recall may be seen as ensuring that the control exercised by the citizenry over selection of representatives, and ultimately over policy making, is indeed genuine.

There can be no doubt that the new political institutions constitute an improvement in terms of providing citizens with mechanisms and procedures through which they can participate in the selection of their political leaders and in the process of policy formulation. There is little comparison between the "vibration technique" of elitist-mass communication plus the informal itinerant visitations of Premier Castro among the people, as these occurred before 1970, and the current electoral system.

The Role of the PCC in the Organs of Popular Power

Some queries concerning the authenticity of the practice of participatory democracy arise from the role of the Communist Party in the organs of popular power. On the one hand, the Party is meant to provide a substantial degree of guidance for or control over the OPP. As stated in Article 5 of the constitution:

> The Communist Party of Cuba, the organized
> Marxist-Leninist vanguard of the working class,
> is the highest leading force of the society, which
> organizes and guides the common effort toward
> the goals of the construction of socialism and the
> progress toward a communist society.[23]

Also, the text of the First Party Congress Resolution on the Organs of Popular Power contains the following statement:

> The Party must guide, promote and control the
> work of state organs, control the policy for the
> promotion and training of cadres and perfect the
> mechanisms of the state; but the Party should
> never replace the state in the exercise of its power
> and functions.[24]

It would thus appear that it is the responsibility of the Party not only to ensure the correct functioning of the OPP, but also

194 / Latin American Prospects for the 1980s

to ensure that leadership selection and policy formulation are consistent with, and further the progress of the development of, the Communist society. However, Party and UJC members are supposed to participate in the OPP purely on a personal basis, and not as representatives of the Party.

It is worth noting again that the Party continues to possess a pure monopoly over organization for political action, over the media, over other civil organs of society, over the formulation and dissemination of a world view and of ideology, as well as over crucial policy areas such as education. The Party and its junior affiliate, the Unión de la Juventud Comunista (UJC), constitute the only organized groups participating in the OPP. These groups undoubtedly contain many, and probably the large majority, of the politically activist, better-connected, and ideologically certified citizens. Therefore, it would be surprising indeed if Party and Juventud members were not prominent in the functioning of the OPP.

While the Party is charged by the constitution with the important "sheep-dog" function discussed above, it is also exhorted to respect the supremacy of the OPP institutions: "We must bear in mind that the Organs of People's Power are the highest state authority on the territories under their jurisdiction."[25] Chapters VIII and IX of the constitution also emphasize the National Assembly as the supreme organ of state power, while the municipal and provincial assemblies are vested with the "highest authority for the exercise of their state functions in the areas under their jurisdiction."[26]

But ambiguity emerges again from the First Party Congress Resolution on the Organs of People's Power, in which the Party, and notably the Central Committee of the Party, is made responsible for defining and adjudicating the relationships and demarcation of powers between the OPP and the other mass organizations:

> The Party must see to it that the relations between the Organs of People's Power, the U.J.C., and the various mass organizations develop normally and coherently in keeping with their functions, tasks and responsibilities within the structure of the guidance of our society.[27]

This implies that the Party stands over and above the OPP and other mass organizations in its capacity as allocator and coordinator of roles, functions, and responsibilities.

One further mechanism of control exercised in part by the Party operates through the procedures for the selection of the

executive committees of the assemblies. While the delegates to
the assemblies elect the president, vice president, secretary,
and other members of the executive committees, the candidates
are screened by a special committee presided over by "a representative of the Party's leading organ at that level," and formed
by representatives of the leadership of the Unión de la Juventud
Comunista, and of the mass organizations, such as ANAP. In
viewing this device, E. Gonzalez concluded:

> As gatekeeper to executive office, therefore, the
> PCC is in a position to promote politically reliable
> as well as competent leadership in local government,
> thereby helping to ensure the latter's compliance
> with national policies and directives.[28]

The Local Levels of the OPP

The preliminary and experimental elections held in 1974 in
the province of Matanzas were a means of trying out electoral
institutions as a pilot plan to help with the constitutional archi-
tecture involved in designing the OPP as they would be outlined
ultimately in Cuba's constitution. In this election, it turned
out that approximately 59 percent of the successful candidates
were members of the Communist Party or of the Unión de la
Juventud Comunista. At the provincial level, approximately
75 percent were Party or UJC members.[29] Unfortunately, comprehensive information on the characteristics of candidates or
elected delegates at the municipal level in the elections of October
1976 or April 1979 does not seem to be available. A few fragments
have been made public, however. Of all the candidates nominated
throughout Cuba for the municipal elections of 1976, 56 percent
were Party members, and 24.4 percent were UJC members. In
the six municipalities of Ciudad Havana (the province of metropolitan Havana), Party and UJC members accounted for from a
minimum of 78 percent of total elected delegates to 88 percent
in Marianao and in Plaza de la Revolución, respectively. At the
level of the province, Party and UJC members constituted 71
percent of the total elected delegates to the assembly of Ciudad
Havana and 90 percent of those for Havana Province excluding
the city.[30]

Whether this phenomenon of party dominance at the local
OPP levels is due mainly to superior individual characteristics
of party and UJC members, or to implicit or explicit collusion
among members of the sole political machine, is hard to know
for sure. One suspects, however, that collusion is not improbable in view of the organizational monopoly of the Party and its

junior affiliate, together with the old-boy networks it nurtures, and the certification of good character and ideological correctness it provides.

There are, however, a number of mechanisms that facilitate the work of the Party in shaping electoral outcomes. First, no uncontrolled campaigning is permitted before the municipal-level public votes occur, or before the indirect selection of provincial delegates and national deputies. Instead, election commissions write up and distribute biographies of all candidates at the local level. While the makeup of these commissions is not known for sure, it is unlikely that the roles of the Party, the UJC, and the mass organizations therein would be very different from their roles in the commissions that scrutinize and approve or disapprove of nominees for the positions of provincial delegate or national deputy. Under these circumstances, it is highly unlikely that a candidate with a questionable background, of a noncompliant disposition, or openly hostile, would let his or her name stand as a nominee, thereby risking public embarrassment or humiliation.[31] Inherent in this arrangement is a strong bias in favour of yes-men (or women) and of certified Party or UJC individuals.

A second important factor in the apparent Party/UJC predominance at the municipal level arises from the organization of the elections. Each of the four-to-eight neighbourhoods within a circunscripción selects a nominee for the election. Because of the organizational and media monopoly of the Party, any support for noncompliant nominees is likely to be of a neighbourhood favourite-son nature. With no possibility of overt campaigning, and great obstacles to covert political action, support for noncompliant nominees is likely to be fragmented and neighbourhood specific. On the other hand, the Party/UJC machine, of course, continues to function during elections, and can ensure without difficulty that its members throughout the circunscripción support the certified candidate(s).

There do not yet seem to be available detailed studies of the functioning of the neighbourhood, circunscripción, municipal, or provincial assemblies. In a visit to Cuba, I was able to gather some impressions from a number of neighbourhood nomination meetings held between February 5 and 21, 1979, for the municipal elections of April 1979. While general conclusions concerning the participatory nature of local electoral processes obviously cannot be drawn on the basis of four cases from central and old Havana in the province of Ciudad Havana, two of these cases at least suggest the range of possibilities.

In all of the meetings at the neighbourhood level that I attended, correct procedures were followed scrupulously, as

far as I could tell. The meetings only commenced when it was
assured that more than 50 percent of the eligible citizens were
present; two members of the Comisión Electoral Municipal (CEM)
of Havana initially chaired each session until a new president
and secretary for the meeting were selected; the CEM members
monitored and corrected the procedures thereafter.

In one of the neighbourhoods, I acquired the distinct impression that a small group of individuals were successfully
manipulating the proceedings, with the fairly passive agreement
or acquiescence of other citizens. What happened was that a
teniente-colonel in the armed forces, who was also a Party member, nominated both the president of the meeting (who was a
UJC member) and a nominee (again a member of the UJC) who
then won against another opponent with ease. The Party and
UJC activists appeared to dominate the meeting and played vital
roles.

In another meeting I attended, the results appeared to be
different. In this case, after an officer of the Fuerzas Armadas
Revolucionarias (FAR) declined the nomination because of the
likelihood that he would be moving out of the neighbourhood
and perhaps the country, the person who had previously been
the delegate for the circunscripción was renominated for a second
term; this candidate was a major in the armed forces, and lived
outside the neighbourhood. Following this, there was some
shuffling and stalling. After an exhortation to nominate a second
candidate, as there must be two candidates for this position,
some spontaneous interaction among a few citizens occurred,
and a second candidate was then nominated. This candidate
was not a member of the PCC, the UJC, or the armed forces.
When the vote was taken, the second candidate was favoured
by a vote of 63 to 53. Since 63 votes did not constitute one-
half of the people present, a second vote was taken and very
carefully counted. This time it was over 80 to 58 in favour of
the second candidate. The electors casually had replaced the
incumbent, who had PCC and FAR credentials, with a local man
without such credentials, who would run in the circunscripción
elections as the neighbourhood nominee.

These cases suggest that while a small clique of Party and
UJC members may be able to seize the initiative and dominate
such nomination meetings, citizens can overcome such groups
and throw out incumbents supported by the machine. But as
argued earlier, success in ousting a machine candidate at the
neighbourhood level may augment the chance of electoral success
for another machine nominee from another part of the same circunscripción, if Party/UJC members and mass-organization

activists throughout the circunscripción support a machine candidate.

The mechanism of the recall or revocation has also been employed to some extent. By February 1979, 108 out of 10,725 municipal-level delegates had been recalled. For at least a few others, recall proceedings had been initiated but the relevant body of electors had refrained from voting the delegates out of office.[32] While the recall may help to ensure that delegates are responsive and responsible to their electors, it is possible that this mechanism could be used to induce conformity and, in the extreme, to weed out troublemakers and upstarts. Because any member of an assembly can propose that recall procedures be carried out against individual delegates or deputies, the consequences of getting out of line may be severe. Whether a recall of this sort has been carried out is not yet known. In any event, the electors who initially vote the delegate or deputy into office continue to have the ultimate power to recall or to keep the delegate.

On the basis of the highly fragmentary evidence available, I would venture to conclude that at the municipal level, citizens do have some control over the selection of their delegates, subject to the qualification that groups of Party and UJC members may exercise disproportionate influence. This, of course, is their constitutional responsibility.

The National Assembly

Deputies for the National Assembly are selected by the delegates to the municipal assemblies, and not directly by the people. Information on some of the characteristics of the members of the National Assembly is presented in Table 10.1. The most striking feature illustrated in the table is the predominance of the Party in the National Assembly. Party militants or aspirants and UJC members constituted fully 96.7 percent of the membership in December 1976, leaving only 3.3 percent without such affiliation. It is also of interest to note that 44.5 percent of the members were not delegates to the municipal assemblies, although they were selected by the latter.

While it is difficult to know exactly why such Party/UJC dominance exists, one can infer how it is generated. To begin with, a substantial proportion of municipal-assembly delegates are Party or UJC members. Indirect selection of National Assembly deputies permits the municipal delegates to select their Party superiors, both from within and from outside the municipal assem-

TABLE 10.1. Characteristics of Members of the National
Assembly, December 1976

Characteristic	Number	Percent
Political affiliation		
PCC members or candidates	441	91.7
UJC	24	5.0
No party affiliation	16	3.3
Total	481	100
Municipal-assembly membership		
Members	267	55.5
Nonmembers	214	44.5
Total	481	100
Sex		
Male	374	77.8
Female	107	22.2
Total	481	100
Occupation		
National leaders in the economy, politics, science, or culture	59	12.3
Local leaders in the economy, politics, science, or culture	140	29.1
Members of the armed forces	35	7.3
Workers in production, services, and education	144	29.2
Peasants	7	1.5
Technicians in industry, agriculture, and services	38	7.9
Others	58	12.0
Total	481	100

Source: Granma Weekly Review (Havana), December 12,
1976. See also, C. Mesa-Lago, Cuba in the 1970's: Pragmatism
and Institutionalization (Albuquerque: University of New Mexico
Press, 1978), p. 81.

blies. It is likely that in view of the role of the Party in providing a certification of good behaviour and of ideological rectitude
for its members, Party members, rather than nonmembers, are
likely to be chosen by other Party members.

The result of this overwhelming presence of Party members
in the National Assembly is that a clear separation between the
Party apparatus and the organs of the state has not been
achieved, as some observers had hoped and expected.33 What
appears to have happened instead is that the OPP, especially
the National Assembly, are providing a public and legitimate
forum for discussions and decision making by the Party. The
National Assembly is likely to have only as much participatory
democracy as the Communist Party itself. The internal politics
of the Party are not open to public scrutiny, but "democratic
centralism" is the characterization of its internal politics used
by the Party itself.

The Council of State and the Central Committee

The permanent executive organ of the National Assembly
is the Council of State, the members of which are elected by
the Assembly. It is of interest to note that of the 31 members
of the Council of State, 30 are also members of the Central Committee obtained a position in the Council of State, including the
positions of president, first vice president, secretary, and the
five vice presidents. This overlap in the membership of the
Council of State and the Central Committee is outlined in detail
in Table 10.2.

Perhaps it should not be surprising that Party heavyweights
occupy virtually all the Council-of-State positions, in view of
the Party predominance in the National Assembly. What seems
to have happened is simply that Party members in the Assembly
have selected their Party superiors for the leadership positions
in the Council of State. This table also illustrates some of the
overlap that exists between the Council of Ministers, the Central
Committee, and the Council of State; as well as the incorporation
of the leadership of the mass organizations—such as the Confederación de Trabajadores Cubanos, the Comités por la Defensa
de la Revolución, the Asociación Nacional de los Agricultores
Pequeños, and the Federación de Mujeres Cubanos—into both
the Central Committee and the Council of State.

In view of the fact that virtually all Council-of-State members are also members of the Central Committee of the Party,
with key Council positions being occupied by Politbureau members,
it is difficult to envisage how the National Assembly could take
any initiatives or adopt any policies that had not been decided

upon previously within the higher echelons of the Communist Party.

The predominance of the Party in the National Assembly should help assure that serious debate on difficult issues occurs before the legislation reaches the Assembly for approval. One would anticipate that the National Assembly should have little problem in dealing with the large number of pieces of legislation that are likely to come before it, in its three-day sessions each year.

The Functioning of the National Assembly, 1976-80

The National Assembly appears to be designed by the constitution to be a surprisingly amateurish legislative body. However, the information available on the functioning of the Assembly generates both optimism and some skepticism regarding its potential to be and to become a powerful initiative-taking and decision-making organ.

The Assembly meets twice annually, in June and/or July and in December and/or January. Its sessions lasted for three or three and one-half days each from 1976 to 1978, and two days each in 1979 and 1980. Each session had a very heavy workload, with substantial pieces of legislation, state budgets, and socio-economic plans to approve; with numerous reports to consider; with important appointments to approve; with decree-laws, passed by the Council of State between sessions of the Assembly, to approve; and, from 1976 to 1978, with various matters, raised at the initiative of deputies, to consider. Partly as a result of this heavy workload, together with the relative brevity of the sessions, the discussions on some important items seem to have been extremely brief.

A second factor that may well limit the potency of the National Assembly (and perhaps also the provincial assemblies) is the part-time nature of the deputy's position. According to the constitution, deputies continue to hold their regular jobs, and are given leave from these when their work as deputies demands.[34] (Deputies are given leave without pay from their regular tasks, but receive as deputies a daily allowance equivalent to their regular salary plus expenses.) There also appear to be insufficient time, support staff, and financial resources to permit individual members to scrutinize problem areas, pieces of legislation, and reports independently and carefully, or to take major initiatives in the Assembly independently.

The activities of the first five years of sessions of the National Assembly are summarized briefly in Table 10.3. The heavy workload and the high productivity of the sessions, in

TABLE 10.2. Party, Government, and State Leadership in Cuba

Person	The Party — Politbureau	The Party — Secretariat	The Party — Central Committee	National Assembly Council of State	Council of Ministers	Other Positions
Fidel Castro Ruz	First Secretary	First Secretary	Member	President	President*	Commander in Chief, FAR
Raúl Castro Ruz	Second Secretary	Second Secretary	"	First Vice President	First Vice President, Minister, FAR*	General, FAR
Juan Almeida Bosque	Member	Secretary		Vice President	Vice President*	
Guillermo García Frías	Member			VP	—*	
Blas Roca Calderío	Member	Member		VP		
Carlos Rafael Rodríguez Rodríguez	Member	Member		VP	VP*	
Celia Sánchez Manduley	—			Secretary	—	
Ramiro Valdés Menendez	Member	—		VP	VP*	
Pedro Miret Prieto	Member	Member		—	—	
Osvaldo Dorticos Torrado	Member			Member	VP*	
Armando Hart Dávalos	Member		"	"	Minister of Culture	
Sergio del Valle Jiménez	Member		"	"	Minister of the Interior	Division General, FAR
Jose Ramón Machado Ventura	Member		"	"	—	
Arnaldo Milián Castro	Member		"	"	—	
Diocles Torralba González			Member	"	VP*	
Belarmino Castilla Mas			"	"	VP*	
Flavio Bravo Pardo			"	"	VP*	
Joel Domenech Benítez			"	"	VP*	
Luis Orlando Domínguez Muñiz			"	"		First Secretary, UJC
Roberto Veiga Menéndez			"	"		Secretary General, CTC
Jorge Lezcano Pérez			"			National Coordinator, CDR
Vilma Espín Guilloys			Member	Member		President, FMC
José Ramírez Cruz			"	Member		President, ANAP
Haydée Santamaría Cuadrado			"	"		Director Casa de las Americas
Osmany Cienfiegos Gorriaran			"	"	Secretary	
Severo Aguirre del Cristo			"	"		
Reynaldo Castro Yedra			"	"		
Marta Deprés Arozarena			—	"		

202

Serén Casras Rogueiro		Member	Division General, FAR, First Vice Minister, MINFAR
Abelardo Colome Ibarra		"	Division General, FAR, First Vice Minister, MINFAR
Raul Roa		"	Minister of Foreign Affairs
Isidoro Malmierca Peoli	Member		
Jorge Risquet	"	Member	
Antonio Pérez	"	"	
Raul García		"	
José Ramón Fernández Alvarez		"	Minister of Education
Marcelo Fernandez Font			Minister of Foreign Trade
Rafael Francia Mestre			Minister of Agriculture
Antonio E. Lussón Battle			Minister of Transport
Zoilo Marinello Vidaurreta			State Committee for Science and Technology
José A. Naranjo Morales		"	Minister of the Food Industry
Arnaldo Ochoa Sánchez		"	Commander, Cuban forces in Ethiopia
Faustino Perez Hernandez		"	JUCEPLAN
Hector Rodríguez Llompart		"	State Committee for Economic Collaboration
Fernando Vecino Alegret		Member	Minister of Higher Education
Anibal Viera Suaréz		"	Minister of the Fishing Industry
Serafín Fernandez Rodríguez		Alternate Member	Minister of Domestic Trade
José A. Gutierrez Muniz		"	Minister of Public Health
		Plus 66 other members and 10 alternate members	

*Indicates members of the Executive Committee, Council of Ministers.

Sources: Granma Weekly Review (Havana), January 4, 1976, p. 12; Granma Weekly Review, December 12, 1976, p. 5; E. Gonzalez, "Institutionalization, Political Elites, and Foreign Policies," in C. Blasier and C. Mesa-Lago (eds.), Cuba in the World (Pittsburgh: University of Pittsburgh Press, 1978).

TABLE 10.3. Main Activities of the National Assembly, 1976-78

Session	Laws Approved	Other Matters
Inaugural session, December 2-4, 1976		Founding of the Assembly Election of president, vice president, and secretary of the Assembly Inaugural speech by Fidel Castro Election of Council of State Designation and approval of Council of Ministers Salutes by mass organizations, UJC Speeches by visiting delegations Closing remarks by the president of the Assembly
First regular session, July 12-14, 1977	Law No. 1—Law on the Preservation of Cultural Heritage Law No. 2—Law on National and Local Monuments Law No. 3—Law on Military Courts Law No. 4—Law on the Organization of the Judicial System Law No. 5—Law on Criminal Procedure Law No. 6—Law on Military Penal Procedure Law No. 7—Law on Administrative and Labor Civil Procedure Law No. 8—Law on the Organization and Functioning of Work Councils Law No. 9—Law Modifying the Family Code	Approval of composition of working commissions Discussion of regulations by municipal assemblies Reports on international activities Discussion of matters raised by delegates Closing speech by President Castro
Second regular session, December 22-24, 1977	Law No. 10—Law on the Integral Plan for Economic and Social Development for the Year 1978 Law No. 11—Law on the State Budget for the Year 1978 Law No. 12—Law against Creation of New Historical Salaries	Approved report of the Council of State Ratification of nine decree-laws, passed by Council of State Designation of court officials and attorney general Reports on international matters Housing Report (referred to Politbureau of PCC

Third regular session, June 28-30, 1978	Law No. 13—Law on Work Protection and Hygiene Law No. 14—Law on Copyright Law No. 15—Law Modifying the Law on the Politico-Administrative Division	Four reports on local matters Matters raised by delegates Closing speech by President Castro
	Law No. 16—Code on Children and Youth Law No. 17—Law on the System of Decorations and Honorary Titles Law No. 18—On the Demarcation of Provincial and Municipal Boundaries (Tomes I and II)	Renaming the Isle of Pines as the Isle of Youth Consideration of 13 reports, including reports on the work of the Supreme Court, crime, local OPP, Cattle Purchase Policy, and international activities of Cuban state Matters raised by delegates Speech by President Castro
Fourth regular session, December 28-30, 1978, January 1, 1979	Law No. 19—Law on the Integral Plan for Economic and Social Development for the Year 1979 Law No. 20—Law on the State Budget for the Year 1979 Law No. 21—Penal Code Law No. 22—Law on Military Offenses Law No. 23—Law on Municipal Museums	Reports on international activities Reports from the Commission on Construction and Construction Materials Report by Commission on Complaints and Suggestions Matters raised by delegates; Twentieth Anniversary Speech by President Castro
First 1979 ordinary session, July 4-5.	Law No. 24—Social Security Law	Debate on methodology for rendering accounts and handling issues raised by electors Report and debate on account rendered by Attorney General's Office Report on provincial assemblies' account rendering Ratification of decree-laws issued by Council of States Discussion of report on passenger transportation Proposal to transfer housing to local OPP Approval of reports on tourism traffic problems, the expenses of the National Assembly, and Its international activities

(continued)

Table 10.3 (continued)

Session	Laws Approved	Other Matters
Second 1979 ordinary session, December 26-27.	Law on the State Budget for 1980 Law on the Integral Plan for Economics and Social Development for 1980 Law on the Establishment of the Great Sierra Maestra National Park (plus two or three additional laws)	Report on the international activities of the National Assembly Ratification of decree-laws issued by the Council of State Consideration and approval of reports on sewers of urban drainage, agricultural drainage, and road maintenance Report on activities for the International Year of the Child Closing speech by President Castro
First 1980 ordinary session, July 2-3.	Organic Law on the State Budgeting System	Report on international activities of the National Assembly Reports on rendering of accounts by the Supreme Court, Attorney General's Office, and the provincial assemblies Ratification of decree-laws issued by the Council of State Election of some judges Closing speech by President Castro
Second 1980 ordinary session, December 26-27.	Law on the 1981-1985 Five Year Plan Law on the Integral Plan for Economic and Social Development for 1981 Law on Environmental Protection and Rational Use of Resources	Report on international activities of the National Assembly Report on the Soviet/Cuban space flight Presentation of the report on rendering of accounts of the Council of State Closing speech by President Castro

Sources: Granma Weekly Review, December 12, 1976; July 24, 1977, p. 1 and p. 9; January 1, 1978, pp. 1-5; January 8, 1978, p. 2; July 9, 1978, pp. 2-3, January 21, 1979, p. 3; July 15, 1979, January 6, July 13, 1980; and "Cuba: Su Institucionalización Histórica," Cuba Internacional, Suplemento Especial (Havana, 1976), pp. 1-16.

terms of laws approved and reports considered, are apparent.
This raises some question concerning the seriousness of the
discussion of major pieces of legislation. In a three-day session,
is it possible to devote sufficient amounts of time to discussions
of from three to nine major new laws plus numerous reports,
appointments, and matters raised by delegates, not to mention
the speeches by President Castro? On December 22, 1977, for
example, the first day of the second regular session of the
Assembly, the following work was conducted:

1. A report by the Council of State was submitted and approved.
2. Nine decree-laws on the settling of territorial, commercial,
   and other matters were approved.
3. Two vacancies in the Assembly were filled by a vote.
4. The state budget was presented, amended with a motion by
   Osvaldo Dorticos, and unanimously approved.
5. The 1978 Integrated Plan for Socioeconomic Development was
   presented by the minister of the Junta Central de Planificación and was passed unanimously.
6. The Law on the Noncreation of New Historical Salaries was
   presented, debated for two hours by 36 deputies, and was
   passed unanimously with four amendments. [35]

This heavy agenda would not allow much, if any, time for a
careful appraisal of, for example, the state budget and a critical
discussion of it by the deputies. There thus has been a tendency
for the Assembly merely to approve the legislation presented to
it, usually unanimously, although some laws have been amended
and some, but not all, have been discussed at greater length.

Despite its heavy workload and the time constraints within
which the Assembly must operate, there are two important factors
that may prevent the Cuban National Assembly from becoming a
rubber-stamp organ, merely ratifying decisions made within the
Party. These are the working commissions, and the deputies'
question period in which deputies can raise questions and discuss
problems at their own initiative.

Twenty working commissions have been established, dealing
with such issue areas as Child Care and Women's Rights; Culture
and Art (chairman: Nicolas Guillen); Defense and Internal Order
(chairman: Brigadier-General Sixto Batista); Constitutional and
Legal Affairs; Work, Social Security, Social Prevention, and Aid;
Young People and Children; Construction and Construction
Materials; and Complaints and Suggestions. [36] Judging from
the accounts of the Assembly proceedings in the Cuban press,
these commissions play an active role. [37] The commissions are

charged with examining drafts of legislation and proposing modifications for discussion and approval at the assemblies. They
also are charged with following and reporting upon the particular
issue areas with which they are identified by their names. This
was done, for example, with considerable effectiveness by the
Transportation and Communications Commission, whose report
on the national passenger-transportation service was presented
and debated in the July 1979 meeting of the Assembly. Its
report appears to have been comprehensive, thorough, and
highly critical of the transportation system and, by implication,
the Ministry (and minister) of Transportation. After some heated
debate, the report was approved and submitted for action by
the Executive Committee of the Council of Ministers.[38] This
type of scrutiny of a particular aspect of Cuba's socioeconomic
system may turn out to be invaluable as a means to put the heat
on parts of the economic bureaucracy, in order to improve performance from the standpoint of citizens in their position as
consumers. The commissions may come to play an important role
in permitting the views and interests of the public on specific
issue areas to find expression in the National Assembly.

In at least the first four regular sessions of the National
Assembly, some time was set aside for deputies to bring up
problems for discussion at their own initiative, or on instructions
from their electors. In the third regular session, for example,
the matters raised by the deputies included problems of "broken
water mains which are repeatedly discussed at grass-roots assemblies but not solved"; problems relating to gas service, urban
transportation, the quality of bread, and the domestic distribution of goods; and "buck-passing" from one official to another,
among other things.[39] Again, however, time constraints on this
part of the Assembly's sessions have been severe. Usually only
one portion of one day's meetings is devoted to matters raised
by the deputies. There does not seem to have been time allotted
to matters raised by delegates in the sessions of 1979 and 1980.[40]

It appears that the societal priorities inherent in the state
budget and in the Integrated Plans for Socioeconomic Development, for example, cannot be seriously questioned or reshaped
in the sessions of the Assembly, due in large part to time constraints. The opportunity deputies had to raise matters in the
Assembly may have had an impact on shaping the Assembly's
agenda in future sessions, and on future budgetary and plan
priorities. For example, the questions and proposals pertaining
to housing, urban transport, the distribution system, and official
buck-passing in the first four regular sessions likely had a
reinforcing impact upon how the problems and priorities are

perceived by the Junta Central de Planificación, which constructs the annual socioeconomic plans.[41] It is, therefore, unfortunate that the delegates' discussion period seems to have been terminated.

CONCLUSION

The objective of this essay has been to examine Cuba's new political system in order to estimate the extent to which it is authentically democratic. The essay began with an examination of the system of the 1960s and a brief explanation of why new institutions were installed in the 1970s. The structure and some of the procedures of the new organos del poder popular were then outlined. Finally, a highly tentative assessment of the authenticity of the participatory democracy in the OPP was put forward, the criterion for democracy being the degree of control exercised by citizens over the selection of those in leadership positions at different levels, and over policymaking in the relevant political organs.

There can be no doubt that the new organs constitute a great improvement over the pre-1970 political system in terms of permitting active participation and more control by the public in leadership selection and policy formulation. While the distributional impact of the policies adopted in the 1960s era of revolutionary paternalism were beneficial to the bulk of the population, there were no adequate means for the public to participate either in leadership selection or policymaking.

Empowered by the constitution to perform a pervasive and primordial sheep-dog function in Cuban society, the Party seems to be very important at the local and municipal levels, and predominant at the level of the National Assembly. It would be somewhat exaggerated to view the OPP only as a front to be used for legitimizing the actions of the Party and for improving the efficiency with which the decisions of the Party can be implemented in Cuban society.[42] However, the Party so far does seem to be fulfilling its constitutional responsibilities within the OPP quite well.

Despite the monopoly position of the Party, I conclude, tentatively, that at the local level, where citizens directly elect neighbourhood leaders, and at the municipal level, where citizens select candidates and directly elect their representatives, democracy defined in terms of control over leadership selection exists to some degree. Accountability and recall reinforce the influence of the electors, although recall conceivably could be employed to keep elected delegates in line with Party policy. Direct elections, the importance of neighbourhood and circunscripción electoral meetings, and the practice of accountability sessions appear to operate so as to ensure some responsiveness on the part of elected delegates to their electors' wishes. Unfortunately, no estimates as to the authenticity of participatory democracy could be reached for the provincial assemblies because of lack of information.

At the National Assembly, the role of the Party is paramount, with 96.7 percent of the deputies having had a Party or a UJC affiliation from 1976 to 1980. The Council of State is dominated by members of the Central Committee of the Party. The key executive positions within the Council of State are all filled by members of the Politbureau of the Central Committee of the Party. The predominance of the Party within the National Assembly would lead one to conclude that the democratic centralism, as practiced within the Party, is simply transferred to the Assembly. Separation of powers between the Party and the national-level organ of people's power has not been achieved.

Assembly deputies are not directly elected by citizens but are chosen by the municipal assemblies. It would seem that municipal delegates select party members and superiors for the National Assembly; and that deputies for the latter select their Party leaders for Council-of-State positions.

So far, the National Assembly has had a heavy agenda and only four-to-six days each year to complete its tasks. Undoubtedly the workload and time constraint have limited discussion on new legislation, reports, budgets, development plans, and matters raised by deputies. This lends support to the conclusion that the National Assembly is not an organ within which independent initiatives can be taken.

However, the formation of some 20 working commissions and their active work so far, in and between assemblies, generate some optimism that the Assembly might acquire an activist dynamic of its own. The question period for deputies appears to have been of some significance in affecting problem perceptions and developmental priorities, but this question period seems to have been terminated in 1979.

At present, then, I conclude that at the level of the National Assembly, a large proportion of the processes of leadership selection and policy formulation is carried out by the Party within the shell or framework of the Assembly. The National Assembly could conceivably evolve into a more independent, powerful, and self-activating organ, at least to some extent. The working commissions, the complexity and number of issues brought up by delegates, and the overcrowded agenda might necessitate some increases in the duration of the Assembly's sessions. Direct elections, with choices among candidates, would likely intensify the responsiveness of deputies to their electors. But direct election for Assembly deputies is not likely to be established in the foreseeable future. And as long as the Party monopoly over the aggregation and articulation of citizens' interests, over the media, and over the formulation and dissemination of world views and ideology continues, Party domination of the National Assembly undoubtedly will continue.

NOTES

1. This definition is borrowed largely from W. R. Schonfeld, "The Meaning of Democratic Participation," World Politics, Vol. 28, No. 1 (October 1975).

2. C. Bengelsdorpf, "A Large School for Government," Cuba Review 6 (September 1976); and L. Casals, "On Popular Power: The Organization of the Cuban State during the Period of Transition," Latin American Perspectives, Vol. 2, No. 4 (1975).

3. W. M. Leogrande, "Mass Political Participation in Socialist Cuba," in J. A. Booth and M. A. Seligson, Political Participation in Latin America, Vol. I (New York: Holmes and Meier, 1978).

4. J. I. Dominguez, Cuba: Order and Revolution (Cambridge: Harvard University Press, 1978).

5. Some of the discussion in the July 1979 issue of Cuban Studies, "Forum on Institutionalization," is peripherally, but not directly, relevant to the issue dealt with in this essay.

6. L. de la Cuesta, "The Cuban Socialist Constitution: Its Originality and Role in Institutionalization," Cuban Studies/ Estudios Cubanos, Vol. 6, No. 2 (July 1976), pp. 20-21.

7. R. E. Bonachea and N. P. Valdés (eds.), The Selected Works of Ernesto Guevara (Cambridge: MIT Press, 1969), p. 157.

8. J. Risquet, "Sobre Problemas de Fuerza de Trabajo y Productividad," Granma (Havana), August 1, 1970.

9. F. Castro, speech of September 7, 1970, Granma Weekly Review, September 20, 1970, p. 5.

10. C. Mesa-Labo, Cuba in the 1970s: Pragmatism and Institutionalization (Albuquerque: University of New Mexico Press, 1978), pp. 87-111.

11. See A. Ritter, The Economic Development of Revolutionary Cuba: Strategy and Performance (New York: Praeger, 1974), for substantiation of this statement.

12. Nelson P. Valdés, "Revolution and Institutionalization in Cuba," Cuban Studies/Estudios Cubanos, Vol. 6, No. 1 (January 1976), p. 12.

13. A. Ritter, op. cit., pp. 282-94.

14. See, for example, F. Castro, speech of October 27, 1969, in Granma Weekly Review, November 2, 1969: And every worker—as if he were a soldier acting as he would while in a trench defending his country, as he would in the face of an enemy attack—should feel like a soldier in a trench, with a rifle in his hand, fulfilling his duty.

15. C. Ian Lumsden, "The Future of Castroism," International Journal, Vol. 24, No. 3 (Summer 1969), pp. 545-58, concludes his essay with the statement: "It therefore becomes all the more urgent for Cuba to proceed with the democratization of its institutions and the liberalization of its political climate." See also Nelson P. Valdés, "Cuba: Socialismo democratico o burocratismo collectivista," Aportes, No. 23 (January 1972).

16. "Constitution of the Republic of Cuba," Granma Weekly Review, March 7, 1976.

17. See First Congress of the Party, "Resolution on the Organs of People's Power," ibid., January 11, 1976, and Granma, February 16, 1979, p. 4.

18. "Cuba: Son Institucionalización Historica," Cuba Internacional, Suplemento Especial, 1976, and Granma, February 16, 1979, p. 4.

19. "Constitution, op. cit., Chapter VIII.

20. Ibid., Chapter IX.

21. First Congress, "Resolution," op. cit.

22. Ibid., p. 9.

23. "Constitution," op. cit., Chapter I, Article 5.

24. First Congress, "Resolution," op. cit., p. 9.

25. Ibid.

26. "Constitution," op. cit., Chapter IX, Article 102.

27. First Congress, "Resolution," op. cit., p. 9.

28. E. Gonzalez, "The Party Congress and Poder Popular; Orthodoxy, Democratization and Leader's Dominance," Cuban Studies/Estudios Cubanos, July 1976, pp. 9-10.

29. L. Casals, op. cit., p. 83.

30. J. I. Dominguez, op. cit., p. 290.

31. Ibid.

32. Granma, February 16, 1979, p. 4.

33. See, for example, L. Casals, op. cit., p. 81, and the Economist Intelligence Unit, "Cuba, the Dominican Republic Haiti and Puerto Rico," Quarterly Economic Review, 1977, p. 1.

34. "Constitution," op. cit., Article 80.

35. Granma Weekly Review, January 8, 1978, p. 2.
36. Granma Weekly Review, July 24, 1977, p. 9.
37. Ibid.
38. Granma Weekly Review, July 15, 1979, p. 3.
39. Granma Weekly Review, July 9, 1978, p. 3.
40. Granma Weekly Review, July 15, 1979, pp. 2-3, January 6, 1980, July 13, 1980, and January 11, 1981.
41. The candid discussion of these problem areas by the head of the Junta Central de Planificacion, Humberto Perez, in February 1979, might be a response to this type of pressure in the National Assembly, as well as to other factors. See "Lo Que el Pueblo Debe Saber," Bohemia, 17, No. 7, 16, 1979.
42. Evidence for this point of view is not entirely absent. One of the advantages initially envisaged by Premier Castro in having democratically elected union officials, instead of appointees, was that the former would be in a better position to advocate and implement policies adopted by the "revolution." He said: "He [the official] will have the moral authority of his election, and when the revolution establishes a line, he will go all out to defend and fight for that line" (Fidel Castro, speech of September 2, 1970, p. 5). Democratic unions were not seen as means of defending the sectional interests of the workers, but, instead, as means of improving the efficiency with which workers' actions could be harmonized with societal objectives.

11

PROBLEMS OF DEMOCRATIZATION
IN PERU AND ECUADOR
Liisa L. North

INTRODUCTION

Both Peru and Ecuador, following a period of authoritarian
military rule in the 1970s, are now governed by popularly elected
civilian governments. In Ecuador, President Jaime Roldós
Aguilera of the Concentración de Fuerzas Populares (CFP) and
his Christian Democratic vice-presidential running mate, Osvaldo
Hurtado, took office in August 1979, following a landslide electoral victory in which the team obtained 62 percent of the vote.
This impressive victory was interpreted as a strong popular
mandate for the reforms promised during the campaign. The
presence of a flurry of distinguished foreign visitors at the
inauguration ceremonies (including Rosalynn Carter, then
Secretary of State Cyrus Vance, and most of the world's Christian
Democratic leaders), reflected strong U.S. and international
support for this return to democracy. (Hurtado's ascension to
the presidency, following Roldós's death in a plane crash in
May 1981, followed constitutional procedures.)

In Peru, the expectations surrounding the inauguration
of Fernando Belaúnde Terry of Acción Popular (AP), in July
1980, were more muted. In an election with a 38-percent abstention rate, the president had won 42 percent of the popular vote,
and his party had obtained a majority in the House of Deputies,
although not in the Senate. The Accion Popular victory was
somewhat ambiguous also because many Peruvians tended to
perceive Belaúnde as the lesser evil on two counts: with reference to his opponents in the presidential race, and with reference
to the military government by which he had first been overthrown
in 1968 and which he now replaced.

In July 1980, Bolivia, the third Andean country that was expected to follow the example of her neighbors, instead experienced a brutal coup d'etat followed by a widespread and murderous repression that continues to the present date. By the fall of 1980, the international situation had also changed inauspiciously for the strengthening of the democratic process, with the election of Ronald Reagan as president of the United States and with all that the change of administration would imply.

The contrast with Bolivia underlines the significance of formal democracy. Nevertheless, the nature and degree of democratization, as well as its viability in Peru and Ecuador, need to be examined. Although the period of formal democracy covered here is short, the intention is to uncover the long-run and basic political-economic structural blockages to democratization in both countries.

To begin, a distinction has to be made between those classes and sectors of classes that are organized to participate in the political process (however unequal their capacity to influence policy making may be) and those who are not organized. In general terms, the organized are integrated into the modern and expanding sectors of the economy, while the unorganized are made up of those sectors of the population that have been excluded by the patterns of economic growth that have taken place in these two countries since World War II and even earlier. The marginal ones constitute the majority in both Peru and Ecuador.

It must be noted that the military regimes replaced by Roldós and Belaúnde began as radically reformist, albeit authoritarian, regimes intending to carry out structural reforms that would incorporate the mass of the population into the development process. The Peruvian variant of the military-regime-sponsored reform was considerably more radical, but both military regimes momentarily enjoyed popularity and the support of sectors of the political left. Reformist goals in both cases were abandoned not only due to economic failures but also due to the strong opposition of capital and of vested interests in general. Widespread popular opposition then developed pari passu with the conservatization, increasing repressiveness, and corruption of the military regimes. Thus these regimes were incapable of formulating a viable economic-development strategy or constructing a political base at the moment when progressive sectors inside and outside the military institutions held the initiative. In fact, any broadly redistributive impact that could have been expected from the agrarian and other reforms of the 1970s was counteracted or negated by the income-concentrating consequences of the economic-development strategies chosen by the military reformers, i.e., their emphasis on capital-intensive urban industrialization and the mechanization of agriculture. The effect of those policies was the further concentration of income in the modern sector of the economy and the deepening marginalization of the approximately 50 percent of the labor force that is unemployed or underemployed.

The economic policies and programs of the succeeding civilian administrations do not promise any substantial alteration of the income-concentrating economic policies of the previous military governments. Judging from their pronounced socioeconomic goals and legislation carried out through early 1981, these civilian regimes, in fact, were less reform oriented than their predecessors during their initial years in power. In this sense, Ecuador's and Peru's democratically elected governments represent formal political democracy only; they do not represent a movement toward a broad democratization of social and economic relationships.

In the long run, political democracy may permit the political organization of the marginated and thereby provoke political conflicts leading to the breakdown of these regimes and to the reimposition of authoritarian rule. The short-run fragility of political democracy in Peru and Ecuador, however, arises from conflicts among those classes and sectors of classes that have been integrated into the economic-development process and are already organized. Formal democracy permits liberty of political action for parties, unions, and other modern-sector popular organizations whose demands represent a threat not only for domestic and foreign capital but also the middle classes. Popular demands for redistributive measures cannot be met without affecting their interests. Income and access to services, after all, are also very unequally distributed among the integrated.

In different degrees (given differing levels of political mobilization, and differences in the economic resources available to the state and in political resources available to the president), the democratic regimes in both countries are faced with the choice of either coercing/pressuring established interests in order to carry out the redistributive measures demanded by popular organizations or, alternatively, repressing those organizations. In either case, the level of political conflict will tend to increase, destabilizing the democratic regime. Both regimes, mutatis mutandis, may follow the sequences of initial diffuse support and then a disintegration into the generalized opposition experienced by their military predecessors.

Having outlined the general argument, I will briefly examine the dimensions of marginalization and its relationship to the economic-development strategies adopted during the past two decades; and the formal and fragile character of the democratization represented by the elected civilian governments. I will conclude with some general considerations on the historical roots of the contemporary situation and the potential political alliances that might be forged to transform it.

DEVELOPMENT STRATEGIES AND MARGINALIZATION

In Peru the data on the distribution of income and services and on the availability of employment demonstrate the gross inequalities between the rural and urban sectors and, within them, between their modern and traditional subsectors. With reference to the general income-distribution profile, Richard Webb (currently president of Peru's Central Bank) found that in 1961 the top 1 percent of income earners received 25 percent of national income, the top 20 percent received 64 percent, and 80 percent of the population managed on 36 percent. The share of the bottom 20 percent, almost all subsistence peasants in the highlands, was 2.5 percent (Webb, 1975, p. 82; Thorp and Bertram, 1978, p. 10). In 1973, following the first Belaúnde presidency and five years of reformist military rule, the income distribution profile was even more skewed. No absolute improvement had taken place in the living standards of 15-25 percent of the population while "the overall distribution of income worsened" and "most of the rural population . . . [became] relatively porrer" (Webb, 1975, pp. 89, 93). While the military government's reforms did not promote greater equality in the basic income-distribution profile, the agrarian, industrial, mining, and fishing laws did improve the positions of some categories of unionized labor in the modern sector. Figueroa (1976, p. 171) notes that, to

> summarize the redistributive impact of the military
> government's reforms, altogether they apply to
> 45% of national income, and they transfer between
> 3% and 4% of it to approximately 18% of the country's
> labour force. This transfer takes place entirely
> within the wealthiest income quartile [to which organ-
> ized modern-sector workers belong].

Access to industrial employment and educational opportunities, the enforcement of labor laws, and access to basic services, such as sewage and safe drinking water, are almost exclusively urban phenomena (Doughty, 1976). And Lima, by itself, concentrates the nation's economic activity, and access to reasonable living standards, to a remarkable extent as noted by Cabieses (1980, p. 17):

> Metropolitan Lima concentrates a third of the national
> population, but two thirds of the Economically Active
> Population. More than half of GDP is produced in
> Lima. . . . More than three quarters of industrial
> establishments, of industrial workers, of the gross
> value and of value added in industrial production
> are concentrated in Lima. Three fifths of electrical,
> gas and water services, commerce, banking, insurance,
> transport, communications, communal and social serv-
> ices are also centralized in Lima. 90 per cent of taxes
> are recovered in Lima and 65 per cent of public ex-
> penditures are located in this department.

In 1971, "as an average, each person active in agriculture [47 percent of the labor force in 1970] worked less than 100 full days per year," while the exodus from the miserable conditions in the rural areas to the shanty towns surrounding the major cities worsened urban unemployment and underemployment, calculated by sample survey at 7.8 percent and 28.0 percent, respectively (Cebrecos Revilla, 1979, pp. 418-19).*

In addition to the profound social problems arising from the above, the Belaúnde administration inherited the consequences of Peru's worst economic crisis since the Great Depression. Without attempting to analyze that crisis (apparent by 1974 and certainly related to the military government's incapacity to force the economic sacrifices necessary for implementing its reforms in any sector of the population), suffice it to note that by 1980, so-called economic-recovery policies had reduced real salaries to 51.5 percent of their 1973 levels. The sharpest rate of decline took place after 1976, with the imposition of the IMF "shock" recovery recipe (Actualidad Económica, May-June 1980).

---

*The IBRD estimated overall unemployment and underemployment in 1971 (a good year in general economic performance) at 4.4 and 44.4 percent, respectively (IBRD, 1973, p. 7).

These were not auspicious circumstances for the establishment of a democratic regime. The economic policies of the second phase of the military government (1975-80) had radically reduced the salaried incomes of organized modern-sector workers and employees, while levels of underemployment and open unemployment had increased in a country whose socioeconomic structure was already defined by extreme inequality. Moreover, the austerity measures, imposed with a heavy dose of repression, followed upon a reform process that had dramatically raised popular expectations and levels of political mobilization.

Turning to the situation inherited by Roldós in Ecuador, a World Bank report (1979, p. 16) on the country's development prospects presents the income-distribution profile of the country (see Table 11.1). Similar to Peru, during the 1970s some redistribution of income took place within the urban sector but it did not benefit the lowest-income groups. According to the Bank report (1979, p. vi) between 1968 and 1975,

the 55 per cent of the urban population situated immediately above the poorest 20 per cent, which includes besides the middle class proper also some of its poorest strata, increased its share of income by more than 6 percentage points of total income. . . . Of this, as much as 5.8 percentage points were taken away from the most privileged quartile of the urban population. However, 0.4 percentage points came from the poorest 20% of the population.

In Ecuador, these changes in urban income distribution were less the product of reformist policies and more the consequence of rapid economic growth fueled by petroleum exports. What needs to be emphasized is that even in the boom conditions of the 1970s, the relative position of the lowest 20 percent of income earners declined and "52 per cent of the urban economically active receive[d] less than the minimum salary" (World Bank, 1979, p. 7).

While the above suggests that the income from the activities generated by petroleum earnings did filter down to a relatively broad spectrum of the urban population (through the rapid expansion of employment in construction, the public bureaucracy, and the service sector), the condition of the great majority of the rural population either deteriorated or remained static. Export agriculture and modern pastoral, dairy, and poultry production did grow impressively in the 1970s. However, production in the subsistence sector (where the majority of the

TABLE 11.1. Distribution of Income from Labor, Urban Areas Compared to Rural, 1975

Quartile	Annual Income per Employed[a]		Annual Income Per Capita[a],[b]		Percentage of Income Held		Urban over Rural (share of income = 1.00)
	Urban	Rural	Urban	Rural	Urban	Rural	
First	312	97	94	29	4.3	3.0	1.43
Second	918	290	278	88	14.6	8.9	1.64
Third	1,520	596	461	181	23.6	18.1	1.30
Fourth	3,715	2,295	1,126	695	57.5	70.0	.82

[a]Data are in Peruvian soles; S/25 = $100.
[b]Calculated on the basis of one employed person supporting 2.3 persons.
Source: World Bank (1979).

rural population is located) grew hardly at all (World Bank,
1979, p. v). Thus between 1970 and 1975, "the real minimum
vital wage for rural workers, who made up 56.7 [percent] of
the labour force in 1970, declined by 8.4 per cent" (World Bank,
1979, p. 19).* Not unexpectedly, the majority of the 39.7 percent of Ecuadorian children, like that of the 44.5 percent of
Peruvian children, under five, who suffer the effects of protein-
calorie malnutrition are located in the rural areas (Inter-American
Development Bank, 1978, p. 138). Moreover, both Peru and
Ecuador have been importing ever-increasing quantities of food
sold at subsidized prices for urban consumption and thereby
further prejudicing the subsistence peasantry's capacity for
improving its living standards. In fact, per-capita food production in Ecuador declined by 8.5 percent during 1976-77 and then
grew modestly by 1.2 percent in 1977-78; in Peru, a decline of
3.8 percent in 1976-77 was followed by a 9.8 percent decline in
1977-78 (Inter-American Development Bank, 1978, p. 19).

Just as the income-distribution profiles of the two countries
are similar, including the worsening trends for the lowest-income
earners in general and the subsistence peasantry in particular,
so their industrial- and agricultural-development strategies
have shared common features. Through a wide variety of explicit
incentive programs and implicit subsidies, both countries have
promoted capital-intensive urban industrialization, and the
mechanization of agriculture. In both countries, but particularly
in the case of Ecuador, the new industries are weakly linked to
the natural-resource base. In the mid 1970s, "imported inter-
mediates accounted for 80 per cent of all inputs used by [Ecua-
dorian] industry" (World Bank, 1979, p. ix). Capital intensity,
coupled with other factors, has prevented the expansion of
industrial employment. Despite a 10-percent average annual
growth in industrial production between 1970 and 1977, industry's
share in employment in Ecuador, according to the World Bank
(1979, p. 219), remained static at approximately 15 percent from

---

*Value added per worker in agriculture, as a percentage
of value added in manufacturing, declined from 40.5 percent
in 1972 to 28.3 percent in 1976. Value added per worker in
agriculture as a percentage of value added in services, however,
rose from 40.9 to 51.2 percent during the same period (World
Bank, 1979, p. 19). The relative improvement with reference
to services reflects the conversion of rural misery, through
migration, into urban marginality.

the early 1960s to 1977. According to figures provided by Carrón (1980, p. 514), the manufacturing industry's share in employment declined steadily from 23.8 percent in 1950 to 14.6 percent in 1962, and to 11.8 percent in 1974. These figures may also reflect the disintegration of small-scale, labor-intensive artisan production in the highlands. Peru's performance in generating industrial employment was hardly better; the labor force in manufacturing added up to 13 percent of the total labor force in 1950, 13.5 percent in 1961, 13.2 percent in 1961, and 14.5 percent in 1970 (Thorp and Bertram, 1978, p. 259).

The above data, together with data (which cannot be reviewed here) on the prominence of MNCs and on the character of the export sectors of both countries, suggest a process of "peripheralization" as defined by Arrighi (1979, p. 163). That is, "a process in which the increase in the density and connectedness of the networks that link [a country's] units of production to the 'outside' world . . . is matched by a smaller increase (or by a decrease) in the density and connectedness of the networks that link the same units within themselves."

A critique of the ineffectiveness of the development-planning system, published by the Ecuadorian Junta Nacional de Planificación (JUNAPLA) in 1972, continues to be relevant for the present and for both countries. Its authors argue (pp. 4-5):

> The first conclusion that arises . . . [relates] to the lack of political decision for carrying out a legitimate agrarian reform process in a country essentially of agrarian character where rural problems are the basic problems . . .*
> On the other hand, the process of import substitution, . . . promoted through [industrial] Promotion Laws, followed the traditional pattern, without succeeding [in] escap[ing] industrial infantilism which, on the one hand, generates an excessive social cost, and on the other hand, a low level of productivity, at the same time that it creates increasing rigidity in the balance of payments as imported inputs become more important each day. . . .

---

*Although the Peruvian military government carried out an extensive land-redistribution program, it was not accompanied by other measures that could have converted it into a viable agrarian reform.

Simultaneously, it is a sector with a low potential
for absorbing employment.

A second conclusion . . . would be that the expectations for the expansion of the industrial process
will die in a structurally strangled market. . . .

Two additional factors contribute to accentuate
the crisis of the planning systems: the external disequilibrium and the growing fiscal deficits.

The external disequilibrium is not simply the
expression of the various tendencies registered by
the expansion of exports and imports. . . . [Rather],
that disequilibrium reflects the structural behaviour
of the Ecuadorian economy and society—the unequal
distribution of income which generates a very diversi-
fied demand for goods and services, based on the
consumption patterns of the groups with the highest
incomes. That is to say that the distribution of income has tended and tends to shape the structure
of demand and supply, or what adds up to the same
thing, to orient investment and, in this way, to stimulate the emergence of commercial and financial gaps.

The report concludes that the basic source of the planning
system's incapacity to confront these problems arises from the
structure of political power within the country.

THE FRAGILITY AND SUPERFICIALITY
OF CURRENT DEMOCRATIZATION PROCESSES

Given their apparently broad bases of popular support,
could the new civilian administrations be expected to successfully
promote economic policies that would begin to deal with unemployment and underemployment, rural misery and urban marginalization, and a pattern of industrial growth that deepens dependency?
Can these democratically elected governments address the growing
inequalities between the marginated and integrated in their
access to reasonable standards of living? How might they deal
with conflicts among those unequally integrated into a modern
sector that grows but excludes the majority from the benefits
of growth?* Both governments claim to have learned from the

---

*For a discussion of the exclusionary character of peripheral
capitalism, see Prebisch (1980, pp. 19-27).

mistakes of their predecessors and have appointed respected
technocrats and economists to key policymaking positions.

In fact, the electoral support obtained by Roldós and
Belaúnde could not be translated into an effective power capability. Although the traditional political parties of the right
were routed in Ecuador's 1979 elections, Roldós's party, the
Concentración de Fuerzas Populares (CFP), consisted of an
extremely loose and heterogeneous coalition of sharply diverging
tendencies. Already, before assuming office, the president-
elect was faced with a split in his own party that then materialized
in Congress into a majority alliance of the traditional right with
the anti-Roldós faction of the CFP. The president's agrarian,
tax, and other reform proposals were thus effectively blocked
and it was not until a congressional realignment took place in
August 1980 that the executive branch obtained the minimum
support for moving ahead, however slowly, with its program
(Nueva, August 1980).

The congressional realignment, however, provided the
necessary but not the sufficient, political base for reform implementation in this democratic context. The CFP party machinery,
for whatever it was worth, was in the hands of Roldós's opponents
and the president was incapable of organizing an alternative
party base for himself. Nor did his political group have strong
working relationships with existing unions or with peasants'
and shantytown dwellers' associations, which, moreover, are
at a low or incipient level in their organizational development.

Specifically, it is difficult to visualize how an effective
land reform could be implemented without the political mobilization
and organization of the peasantry that is needed as a counter-
weight to the existing economic and political power of landowners
who have direct access to the highest levels of the political system, individually or through their associations. Presuming the
implementation of agrarian reform, how would unionized urban
labor react to the elimination of subsidies for food—a measure
necessary for increasing rural agricultural incomes? (This was
a measure not taken in Peru during the course of the military
government's agrarian-reform program and, therefore, it was
one of the important causes of the bankruptcy of the agricultural
cooperatives that were created.) How can employment in industry
be expanded without dismantling subsidies that promote the substitution of capital for labor?* However, wage increases for

---

*According to Eduardo Villagaran, the president of the
Cámara de Industriales of the Province of Pichincha (one of the

unionized labor can also promote greater capital intensity. In this respect, it is not surprising that the wage increases introduced by Roldós in August 1980 were quickly identified as one of the causes of increasing underemployment in urban areas (Latin America Regional Reports—Andean Group, January 23, 1981).

In sum, the appropriate policy package for reversing the inequities of the system is not easily formulated or politically implemented.* The Roldós administration was mandated to carry out broad structural reforms, but it had no organic ties to mass organizations whose coherent and sustained support, loyalty, and even willingness to suspend corporatist claims for immediate material gains are the preconditions for carrying them out. Thus the executive's reform proposals were not simply blocked in Con-

---

two most powerful associations of industrialists in Ecuador), the generous tax exemptions of the Industrial Promotion Laws "should be understood more as an abstention or a fiscal investment rather than as a 'sacrifice,' given that the State would never arrive at collecting taxes if it did not first facilitate their installation." Villarán also argued that 43 percent of the labor force depended on industry, most of them through the multiplier effect of industrial activity (El Tiempo, July 15, 1980).

*Problems of capital-versus-labor intensity, rural exodus, and employment creation also plague the socialist economies. Tepicht (1975, p. 264) writes: "In recent years Polish economists have been suffering from a kind of schizophrenia. On the one hand they want to be very modern, so have aimed at a form of industrial development which is very modern, that is, labour saving or capital intensive and so on. On the other hand, there is mass rural exodus, with generations of rural migrants knocking at the factory gates, which imposes a policy of labour intensive employment. So far there has been no way out of this vicious circle. To underline the social effect of this, I want to remind you that labour saving industry is in general in the interests of the old sections of the working class, of skilled, more qualified workers, and of technicians and so on. The labour intensive form of employment, on the other hand, corresponds with the interests of the great masses from the countryside. So this is not just an academic discussion: it is a question of latent social conflict." Socialism may be necessary but it is not sufficient per se for resolving the problems of Polish or Ecuadorian or Peruvian development.

gress; they were blocked by the fragmentation and incoherence of political society.

In Peru, Belaúnde did not promise major structural reforms; in one way or another, his military predecessors had experimented with just about every alternative that had been proposed by the country's reformist parties since the 1930s (Pásara, 1980). But what he did promise was no less ambitious: the rationalization of the economy, to ensure growth with greater equity, i.e., a progressive democratization of the socioeconomic system. The specific policies made or discussed have included the elimination of some of the exorbitant subsidies provided to industry (especially to producers of nontraditional exports); the elimination of subsidies for foodstuffs; the creation of free zones and the promotion of an artisan industry, along with the reactivation of the construction sector, to increase employment (Dancourt and Pásara, 1980, p. 5); and, in general, greater reliance on the market, a drastic reduction of state intervention and ownership in the economy, and a greater openness to foreign capital.

The new administration has been put to the task of explaining how these policies differ fundamentally from those adopted by Chile and Argentina, with their well-known income-concentrating characteristics. The elimination of subsidies for foodstuffs will certainly help local agricultural production but, if not coupled with measures to provide credit, storage, and marketing facilities for the highland peasantry, the benefits will go primarily to mechanized modern enterprises on the coast. Moreover, the government has not proposed compensatory measures for the urban marginal population that can't afford the new prices; thus "government critics have forecast a sharp rise in infant mortality rates as . . . [these] policies increase malnutrition and poverty" (Latin America Regional Reports—Andean Group, February 27, 1981). In short, those most in need do not benefit from the policies proposed or implemented, and the announced goal of greater equity does not emerge as a primary concern.

It is revealing that while the food-price increases have been decreed, the government found it difficult to disentangle the industrial-tariff-and-subsidy structure due to the opposition of capital. This is not to say that the government has acceded to the demands of capital on every count. Manufacturers in early 1981 were "furious with the labour ministry's maintenance of the military government's labour laws which restrict[ed] their freedom to sack workers and close down plants" (Latin American Weekly Report, February 20, 1981).

The implementation of food-price increases and other similar measures, which introduced a greater reliance on market forces,

were accompanied by protests and strikes, as could be expected.
To these the government was able to respond quite effectively
through a combination of moderate wage increases and some
repression. A certain balance between contradictory goals
was thus maintained. In accord, a tripartite labor-business-
government commission for discussing wages and industrial
disputes was organized (Latin America Regional Report—Andean
Group, April 3, 1981). However, the unpopularity of the
government's measures and the bankruptcy of the representative
system were reflected in the fact that Congress in early 1981
absolved itself of responsibility in policy making, by delegating
special powers to the executive for 90 days. During those 90
days, propped up by the patriotic fervor created by Peru's
late-January 1981 border clashes with Ecuador,* the government
decreed an antiterrorist law. It was described in the Latin-
American Weekly Report of March 20, 1981:

> It provides for 10- to 20-year sentences for persons
> found guilty of "acts which could endanger life,
> health or property or which aim to damage or destroy
> public or private buildings, roads, and means of
> communication or transport." Acts which threaten
> public peace or state security are also included.
> Particularly controversial are articles five, six and
> seven, which make the law applicable to organizations
> and persons who "count on" terrorism, who incite
> terrorist acts, and who publish "apologias" for acts
> of terrorism.

The capacity of the Belaúnde government to continue balancing
the demands of organized urban interests and neglecting the
conditions of the marginated, without recourse to open repression, is doubtful.
    Unlike Roldós, Belaúnde faced a politically mobilized popula-
tion. The popular sectors' level of organization, however, varies
greatly. Industrial labor, labor in the export-agriculture and

---

*Similarly, Roldós took the opportunity to enact one of the
first items on his energy-policy agenda by tripling petroleum
prices and also raising the prices on other fuels, necessary
measures that had been postponed because of the government's
political weakness (Latin America Regional Reports—Andean
Group, April 3, 1981).

mining sectors, private and public employees (with bank clerks and schoolteachers prominent among them) are the most strongly unionized. It is these groups that are potentially capable of engaging in or coordinating unified political action. In short, union organization among those integrated into the modern sector of the economy has reached a high level. Nevertheless, highland peasants did form active associations during the years of military reformism, and urban marginals, who have voted heavily for the revolutionary left, have also reportedly set up a myriad of associations and councils in the shantytowns surrounding Lima and other major urban centers.

Belaúnde's Acción Popular party has no organic links to these mass organizations, although many of their members may have voted for him since the left, with its five presidential candidates, did not offer an alternative. Moreover, as Cotler (1980, p. 96) puts it, Belaúnde,

> distinguishing himself from his competitors, was neither a "búfalo" [the candidate of APRA],* nor a "boss" [the Christian Democratic candidate] but a man of "dignity" . . . "who knew how to speak well"; he was neither a "sectarian" nor a "patrón"; he was a liberal and pluralist professional.

The cadres and militants of the mass organizations owe no loyalty to Belaúnde and can't be expected to accede naturally to government policy. On the contrary, many of these organizations were established by, or under the control of, the revolutionary left during the period of military rule.

The question is whether or not these organizations can act as a bloc to oppose government policy or propose viable alternatives. Are there issues that can unify them for collective action? The record of conflict and fragmentation on the left suggests that, at the maximum, general unity may be obtained on purely defensive issues related to the preservation of political/formal democracy (e.g., the antiterrorist law and the arbitrariness with which it is likely to be implemented). Unity on wage and price policies may also be obtained among workers and employees in the modern sector. But it is difficult to conceive a unified program of action that could also incorporate and alleviate the

---

*APRA, Peru's oldest reformist party (founded in 1931), has been tainted with strong-arm tactics and a closed organizational behavior.

condition of the marginated in the urban areas (their basic need is for jobs) and in the rural areas (a need for credit, higher prices for agricultural products, etc.). In fact, wage demands may contradict the possibilities for expanding employment, given the present structure of the economy.

While neither Roldós's nor Belaúnde's program represented a threat to capital, neither administration received its unqualified support. Even modest efforts to rationalize the economy and promote employment and salary levels that would actually expand the national market are resisted. Capital's narrow interests lie in the preservation of the existing structure and, consequently, policies designed to modify it are rejected out of hand. The correlation of political opinion and socioeconomic vision within the military also favors capital. Thus, if the Roldós and Belaúnde administrations had tipped their balancing scales toward effective structural reforms, they would have quickly faced the threat of military intervention. Similarly, if mass organizations manage to unify around a coherent leftist political and economic program as an alternative, military intervention (with the support of capital and most of the middle class) can be expected in both countries. The prospects for substantive democratization, in sum, are negligible, and even formal democracy is fragile in both countries. Both the character of the bloc in power and the contradictions among the subordinated sectors suggest that the current impasse will not be overcome in the short or medium term.

HISTORICAL ROOTS OF, AND PROSPECTS FOR, ECONOMIC AND POLITICAL POWER STRUCTURES

The contemporary contours of the socioeconomic and political power structures of these two societies derive from post-World War II policies of industrialization and modernization that tended to disregard the agricultural sector,* and to view rural society as a backward traditional obstacle to development. More fundamentally, they are rooted in the general evolution of class relationships since the constitution of these societies as primary-export economies in the late nineteenth century.

To begin with post-World War II policies, Anderson (1967) was among the first, from a critical perspective, to draw attention

---

*For a discussion of rural neglect, see Lefeber (1980, pp. 93-103).

to the "urban bias" (p. 105) of Latin American political systems.
He noted an "obsession with industrialization" (p. 52) and "the
most advanced model" (p. 15) in use among the region's statesmen. Latin American policy makers, he argued, "looked to the
political and economic theories, to the institutional framework,
of Western Europe and North America in clarifying their problem,
in delineating their goals" (p. 38). Since the beginnings of
rapid export expansion during the second half of the nineteenth
century, he noted (p. 34),

> the modernizing elites—concentrated in the capital
> city, the bureaucratic groups, the new middle classes
> called forth by the heightening of a transactional
> economy—demanded, and by and large received,
> public policies designed to create for them an urban
> environment similar to that of their Western counter-
> parts on whom their aspirations were modeled.

Whether we see these policies as part of a "development strategy"
or as a generalized outlook on the world, they involved closing
off rural reality as irrelevant or "extraneous" to the process of
transformation, he noted:

> Coping with demands that are [considered] "inappro-
> priate" to the strategy of change may imply that one
> simply ignores part of the environment. This is par-
> ticularly suitable when the demands ignored are not
> linked to any power capability that makes them appear
> as a threat to the stability of the governing coalition.
> Thus many Latin American decision-makers have long
> possessed a capacity "not to see" the rural subsistence
> sector as part of the environment, and have visualized
> and worked with the political economy as including
> only the modern sector.

Rather than simply not "seeing" the rural reality, one can
argue that policymakers, particularly in countries such as
Ecuador and Peru, with large Indian populations, saw it as the
realm of "barbarism," an unfortunate stain on the fabric of
national society.* It is worth recalling the description of the

---

*It is revealing that the southern Peruvian departments,
with a majority Indian population, are popularly known as the
"mancha India."

Argentine intellectual and president, Sarmiento, of the city and countryside, in his Civilización y Barbarie (1845):

> All civilization, whether native, Spanish or European, centres in the cities, where are to be found the manufactories, the shops, the schools and colleges, and other characteristics of civilized nations. Elegance of style, articles of luxury, dress-coats, and frock-coats, with other European garments, occupy their appropriate place in these towns.
>
> I mention these small matters designedly. . . . The inhabitants of the city wear European dress, live in a civilized manner, and possess laws, ideas of progress, means of instruction, some municipal organization, regular forms of government, etc. Beyond the precincts of the city everything assumes a new aspect; the country people wear a different dress, which I will call South American, as it is common to all districts; their habits of life are different, their wants peculiar and limited. The people composing these two distinct forms of society do not seem to belong to the same nation. Moreover, the countryman, far from attempting to imitate the customs of the city, rejects and disdains its luxury and refinement; . . . Everything civilized which the city contains is blockaded there, proscribed beyond its limits . . .*

Sarmiento was also the most prominent nineteenth-century advocate of European immigration to Argentina, but his ideas were echoed elsewhere on the continent, as Burns has recently documented in his The Poverty of Progress (1981). During the second half of the century, all over Latin America, first the European and then the North American came to be identified with technical and economic progress. Simultaneously, the native population "came to be regarded as a hindrance and was condemned to backwardness" (Sánchez-Albornoz, 1974, p. 148) as the emerging positivist intellectuals of the dominant classes adopted and perfected racist variants of social Darwinist thought.

---

*For a discussion of the theme of city and countryside, European and native, in Latin American literature, see Brotherston (1977).

In Ecuador and Peru, as well as in Latin America, profoundly racist and, thereby, antidemocratic forms of thought continue to permeate the attitudes of broad sectors of the urban population, in particular as regards the Indian and the peasant agriculturalist. However, what is more important for the argument being developed here concerning the urban bias of politics and economic policy making, the European-North American-modernity-technology-industry-progress-city phenomena became associated as terms.

This set of associations was not limited to the groups that Anderson names the "modernizing elites," but included those that can be more precisely identified as the export oligarchies, and the urban commercial and financial interests with which they were allied. The radical movement that developed after World War I and grew rapidly in the depression years of the 1930s shared the same set of associations. Those movements originated in the cities or in export enclaves. In both cases, the middle and working classes that formed them did not question the fundamental superiority of the new, the modern society being created, or the typification of the traditional rural order as backwardness, tout court.* Rather, they challenged the limited distribution of the new society's rewards and its exploitative economic and political power structures.

In this, the radical movements were also the inheritors of nineteenth-century European socialism. Not unfairly, Nisbet (1970, p. 67) has argued that for Marx,

> socialism (in structure) is simply capitalism minus private property [over the means of production]. Socialism is seen by Marx, however dimly, as consonant with and as emergent from the organizational categories of capitalism: the industrial city, factory, machine, working class and so on.†

---

*These orientations can be found in the early-twentieth-century novel, A la Costa, of Ecuadorian Luis A. Martínez.

†Marx's abhorrence of "rural idiocy" is well known. Nevertheless, his rationalization of England's imperial policies in India in terms of long-run historical good is worth citing (from "The British Rule in India," in Feuer [1959], pp. 480-81):

> Now sickening as it must be to human feeling to witness those myriads of industrious patriarchal and

Engels's strongly negative reaction to anarchist condemnation of the factory system, reflecting the same position, is quoted by Nisbet (1970, p. 30):

> Wanting to abolish authority in large-scale industry is tantamount to wanting to abolish industry itself, to destroy the power loom in order to return to the spinning wheel.

With the prominent exception of Peruvian socialist José Carlos Mariátegui, Peruvian and Ecuadorian radicals tended to follow the lines of thought that had already become dominant in the European tradition of socialism. To the extent that they incorporated indigenismo (nativism) into their programs, the education and civilization of the Indian—his incorporation into modern society—were the primary considerations.

---

inoffensive social organizations disorganized and dissolved into their units, thrown into a sea of woes, and their individual members losing at the same time their ancient form of civilization, and their hereditary means of subsistence, we must not forget that these idyllic village communities, inoffensive though they may appear, had always been the solid foundation of oriental despotism, that they restrained the human mind within the smallest possible compass, making it the unresisting tool of superstition, enslaving it beneath traditional rules, depriving it of all grandeur and historical energies. We must not forget the barbarian egotism which, concentrating on some miserable patch of land, had quietly witnessed the ruin of empires, the perpetration of unspeakable cruelties, the massacre of the population of large towns. . . .

England, it is true, in causing a social revolution in Hindustan, was actuated only by the vilest interests, and was stupid in her manner of enforcing them. But that is not the question. The question is: Can mankind fulfill its destiny without a fundamental revolution in the social state of Asia? If not, whatever may have been the crimes of England, she was the unconscious tool of history in bringing about the revolution.

In sum, a number of mutually reinforcing political-ideological tendencies and social processes (only some of which have been sketched in their broadest outlines here) converged to structure the context in which all sectors of modern society identified urban industrialization as the strategy par excellence for the resolution of society's ills. From the perspective of radicals, it would promote the development of a national bourgeoisie that would contest the dominance of and dependency on foreign capital, destroy feudal relations in the rural areas, and pave the way toward an eventual transition to socialism by creating its class antagonist, the proletariat. Potential entrepreneurs were motivated by more mundane considerations. The new middle classes—professional and technical categories—saw it as the path to progress, to reducing dependence on primary exports, and to forging independent and progressive national societies with the type of sustained economic growth that had already taken place in Western Europe and North America.

These professional and technical groups, often supported by the political left, played a critical role in the elaboration of policies for promoting industrialization. Given the weakness of national industrial capital and the dependency on the advanced capitalist centers, they proposed and obtained a strong measure of state intervention in the process. Following World War II, a number of regional organizations, with the UN Economic Commission for Latin America (ECLA) most prominent among them, also helped design industrial-promotion laws and national-planning institutions. It was in the 1950s and 1960s that Ecuador and Peru began to follow this path, legislating an indiscriminate series of incentive, subsidy, and other such measures. And indeed, the industrial-growth rates of both countries were very impressive during the 1960s and the 1970s.

This impressive growth, however, did not aid in resolving the basic socioeconomic problems of these societies. In fact, the characteristics of that industrialization, as argued earlier, have deepened problems of dependency, income inequality, marginality, and so on. Moreover, rural transformation was neglected. Although landlord power has been contested (to different degrees) in both countries, the subsistence peasantry and landless agricultural labor have not obtained access to productive property, employment, or sufficient income so as to constitute themselves as part of an expanding national market. In other words, the rural conditions that permitted capitalist industrialization elsewhere (e.g., Japan, Canada, and France) to elevate living standards for all sectors of society (albeit unequally) were not obtained in Ecuador or Peru.* Moreover, the international and technological conditions in which capitalist development is taking place in the periphery areas are also unfavorable vis-à-vis those conditions as they existed for center economies.

Many, but certainly not all, of the planners, technocrats, and economists who participated in the elaboration of industrial-promotion laws and in the organization of planning agencies were at least partially aware of the importance of the agrarian transformation. Such policies, however, could not be pushed in the Peruvian or Ecuadorian context without generating opposition and conflict. Thus they appear to have adopted an incrementalist approach—doing the possible, adopting low-political-risk strategies. Unfortunately, their praxis eventually contributed to rigidifying the current structure of inequality, making fundamental change all the more difficult, given the ways in which middle classes and organized urban labor were integrated into the exclusionary modern sector. Analyzing a similar process in the context of Central American economic integration, Cohen Orantes (1972, p. 83) writes:

> By suggesting import substitution as the solution
> to their backwardness, [ECLA's proposals] . . .
> assured [member governments] . . . that something
> was going to be added to what already existed without requiring major transformations in their societies,
> as would have been the case if the experiment had
> started with the agricultural sector of their economies.
> It can be argued that these limited goals were proposed as a device for obtaining a preliminary consensus that would allow, with the passing of time,
> a gradual application of more relevant measures in
> more controversial sectors. This argument can be
> supported by the fact that these preliminary measures were in line with the reformism cherished by
> the ruling elites to which they were being proposed.
> But further sacrifices to achieve more results were
> avoided with equal assiduousness. . . .

---

*See Cueva (1977) for a discussion of the reactionary character of Latin American capitalism, especially pp. 66-68 and 79-100.

The behavior of the nation-states in the Central American context finds parallels in the behavior of the different sectors of the new industrial groups and, more generally, in that of the dominant classes in Peru and Ecuador. Cohen Orantes (1972, p. 83) notes:

> The avoidance of "high" costs that characterized the Central American integrative experience affected the gradual emergence of a larger political entity among the participants. Instead of learning to upgrade the common interest, the members learned to put in practice those measures whose economic consequences could be lessened by foreign assistance and that, consequently, demanded a minimum of sacrifices from them. Instead of the gradual transfer of expectations to a larger entity, each participant pursued the satisfaction of his individual interests. . . . In other words, the process became one in which short-term benefits were more important than any long-term expectation.

In Peru and Ecuador, as in Central America in the 1950s and 1960s, and still today, the emphasis on industrial promotion effectively "excluded the [interests of] the largest sectors of the population" (Cohen Orantes, 1972, p. 84) from being directly addressed by national planning policy. Technocrats and planners thus provided the theoretical rationalization and expertise for the reformism of sectors of the national elite and they continue to do so under the present civilian administrations in both countries. They aim for carefully delimited goals within the power structure as it is, and understandably so—their power capability as a group is low. But one wonders, while recognizing important geopolitical and other differences, whether or not the social and political conflicts in these two Andean countries (as well as Bolivia) will eventually peak to the level they have now reached in Central America.

The question is not posed facetiously. Although the picture is far from clear, what seems to have emerged in Nicaragua, and currently appears to be emerging in El Salvador, is a coalition of revolutionary forces in which mobilized marginated sectors from the urban and rural areas are playing a critical role. Simultaneously, the traditional left and organized labor appear to have taken a back seat in the revolutionary vehicle propelled by a new left that organized itself and a significant sector of the marginated population during the 1970s.

BIBLIOGRAPHY

Actualidad Económica, May-June 1980.

Anderson, Charles W. Politics and Economic Change in Latin America: The Governing of Restless Nations. Princeton: D. Van Nostrand Co., 1967.

Arrighi, Giovanni. "Peripheralization of Southern Africa, I: Changes in Production Processes." Review, vol. III, no. 2 (Fall 1979).

Brotherston, Gordon. The Emergence of the Latin American Novel. Cambridge: Cambridge University Press, 1977.

Burns, E. Bradford. The Poverty of Progress: Latin America in the Nineteenth Century. Berkeley: University of California, 1981.

Cabieses, Hugo, et al. Industrialización y Desarrollo Regional en el Peru. Lima: Ediciones Economía, Política y Desarrollo, 1980.

Carrón, Juan M. "La Dinámica de Población en la Sierra Ecuatoriana: Los desplazamientos de Población y su Evolución Reciente." In Barsky et al., Ecuador: Cambios en el Agro Serrano. Quito: FLACSO/CEPLAES, 1980.

Cebrecos Revilla, Rufino. "Employment and Underemployment in Peru." In Juan J. Buttari (ed.), Employment and Labour Force in Latin America: A Review at National and Regional Levels. An ECIEL study. Washington, D.C.: OAS, 1979.

Cohen Orantes, Isaac. Regional Integration in Central America. Lexington: D. C. Heath and Company, 1972.

Cotler, Julio. Democracía e Integración Nacional. Lima: Instituto de Estudios Peruanos, 1980.

Cueva, Agustín. El desarrollo del capitalismo en America Latina (México: Siglo veintiuno, 1977).

Dancourt, Oscar, and Luis Pásara. "La Política y la Economía del Señor Ulloa" (an interview). La Revista (Lima) no. 3 (November 1980).

Doughty, Paul L. "Social Policy and Urban Growth in Lima." In David Chaplin (ed.), Peruvian Nationalism: A Corporatist Revolution. New Brunswick: Transaction Books, 1976.

El Tiempo (Quito), July 15, 1980.

Feuer, Lewis S. Marx and Engels: Basic Writings on Politics and Philosophy. Garden City: Anchor Books, 1959.

Figueroa, Adolfo. "The Impact of Current Reforms on Income Distribution in Peru." In Alejandro Foxley (ed.), Income Distribution in Latin America. Cambridge: Cambridge University Press, 1976.

Inter-American Development Bank. Economic and Social Progress in Latin America, 1978 Report. Washington, D.C.: Inter-American Development Bank, 1978.

International Bank for Reconstruction and Development. The Current Economic Position and Prospect of Peru. Washington, D.C.: IBRD, 1973.

JUNAPLA. La Década del Sesenta. Algunos Aspectos de la Economía Ecuatoriana. Quito: JUNAPLA, 1972.

Latin America Regional Reports—Andean Group, January 23, February 27, April 3, 1981.

Latin America Weekly, February 20, March 20, 1981.

Lefeber, Louis. "Spatial Population Distribution: Urban and Rural Development." In Louis Lefeber and Liisa North (eds.), Democracy and Development in Latin America. Toronto: CERLAC-Latin American Research Unit, 1980.

Nisbet, R. A. The Sociological Tradition. London: Heinemann, 1970.

Nueva (Quito), August 1980.

Pásara, Luis. "Política-afflición: ¡Que hemos elegido!" La Revista, no. 2 (July 1980).

Prebisch, Raúl. "The Dynamics of Peripheral Capitalism." In Louis Lefeber and Liisa North (eds.), Democracy and Development in Latin America. Toronto: CERLAC-LARU, 1980.

Sánchez-Albornoz, Nicolás. The Population of Latin America: A History. Berkeley: University of California Press, 1974.

Tepicht, Jerzy. "A Project for Research on the Peasant Revolution of our Time." Journal of Peasant Studies, vol. 2, no. 3 (April 1975).

Thorp, Rosemary, and Geoffrey Bertram. Peru 1890-1970: Growth and Policy in an Open Economy. New York: Columbia University Press, 1978.

Webb, Richard. "Government Policy and the Distribution of Income in Peru, 1963-1973." In Abraham F. Lowenthal (ed.) The Peruvian Experiment: Continuity and Change under Military Rule. Princeton: Princeton University Press, 1975.

World Bank, Ecuador: Development Problems and Prospects. Washington, D.C.: World Bank, 1979.

12

MECHANISMS OF SOCIAL CONTROL
OF THE MILITARY GOVERNMENTS
IN BRAZIL, 1964-80
Maria Helena Moreira Alves

INTRODUCTION

There have been many important works written about the
origins of the authoritarian states in Latin America.[1] Most of
the works deal with the establishment of such states and explore
the political, historical, and economic underpinnings of their
emergence.[2] The literature is rich and varied, for it has been
a highly controversial question that elicited a number of debates.
Thus, I cannot hope here to provide even a brief overview of
the work of so many authors. I shall limit myself to the analysis
of the institutionalization process of one such state—that of
Brazil.

In this chapter I shall concern myself with the anatomy of
Brazil's distinct type of state since 1964. The wider context of
my research is an attempt to understand the building up of this
type of capitalist state and the characteristics that makes it
distinct from other authoritarian states—such as Mexico—as well
as from totalitarian states. I shall point out the factors that
enable one to term it the "national-security state" in order to

The study resulting in this essay was made under a fellow-
ship granted by the Social Science Research Council and the
American Council of Learned Societies. This grant supported
research for a Ph.D. dissertation in political science at the
Massachusetts Institute of Technology. However, the conclusion,
opinions, and other statements in this article are those of the
author and are not necessarily those of the councils.

express fully a kind of state that has been raised upon the foundations of a particular mode of production, has its own ideology, and has important comparative aspects in different countries of Latin America. Since Brazil is the first such state, and has been the longest-lasting one, it is relevant that one should pay close attention to the structures that have emerged through time and that characterize it.

The main thrust of my research is the analysis of how the structures of the national-security state were created through time and built up largely as a result of constant pressure from the opposition. Thus, it is a central thesis that the national-security state is dialectically related to the opposition. The very need to control the society creates a dynamic by which the structures and mechanisms of control must be changed constantly in order to bring about a new conformity. A further important theoretical point to understand is that this situation is one of inherent instability and weakness. Since the national-security state must constantly build new structures of coercion and new mechanisms of social control, it falls into three traps. First, it is prone to bureaucratic overgrowth in such a way that it may lose control of its own bureaucratic, repressive apparatus. It is sufficient here to point out that successive Brazilian governments have been unable to control the repression apparatus that it set up in order to maintain a high degree of coercion. In fact, the repression apparatus tends to become a parallel power to that of the executive. Second, it is completely unable to eliminate opposition. It merely displaces opposition from one sector of civil society to another. In the very attempt to modify the structures in order to control a specific sector of the opposition, the state creates new opposition. The very process of coercion induces other sectors to engage in opposition while it does not tend to eliminate the original opposition it attempted to control. Thus, the mechanisms of control are constantly shifting in order to handle opposition expressed through the electoral process, through the political parties, the judiciary, the universities, the trade unions, the Catholic movements, the press, and even the military itself. In its attempt to handle the different sectors, the national-security state does not eliminate the opposition—for it does not solve the conflicts that create such opposition—but merely coerces it into temporary silence. Thus, the resulting "displacement of contra-dictions,"[3] where the state merely displaces conflict from area to area, from sector to sector, of society. Therefore, the national-security state does not reach stability, for it never solves conflict, never reaches legitimacy through consensus.[4]

Third, because of the displacement effect, the national-security state is inherently unstable and tends to become progressively isolated in a circle, closed within itself. In fact, it has a long-range tendency to become eventually the state of a small group that controls civil society and even its own ranks with increasing force, but is haunted by constant opposition and by unsolved contradictions. Its very isolation from civil society brings about a stalemate and a constant state of institutional crisis.

The Brazilian state has adopted a particular model of economic development. This model is highly dependent on foreign capital and on the necessity for establishing a secure and attractive climate for foreign investment. Thus, it has in practice meant the establishment of a series of fiscal incentives for foreign investment—benefits for credit and profit remittance as well as tax rebates. This economic model of development has also meant a progressive concentration of income, with the consequent impoverishment of large sectors of the population and the increasing wealth of a few. The model also has resulted in a skewed pattern of industrialization—favoring durable consumer goods produced for the higher brackets of the population—characterized by capital-intensive industries and the consequent dependency on foreign technology. The results of the model have been the subject of an increasingly vivid debate in the past 15 years.[5] Consequences of the model shall be discussed further in the concluding part of this essay. However, my main concern here is with a different implication of the Brazilian economic model: its effect in generating a political opposition that has, in turn, required continuous redefining of the state in its (unsuccessful) pursuit of stable institutions that can keep such a model of development functioning.

Against this brief theoretical framework, it is the purpose of this work to present the main mechanisms of social control that the military governments have set up in Brazil since the onset of the national-security state. This is not the place for deeper analysis; thus, the considerations will be largely schematic and shall be meant to provide a graphic and summarized view of the general legislation of control as well as of the specific structures of control per area of the opposition.

GENERAL MECHANISMS OF SOCIAL CONTROL

The general mechanisms of social control can be considered to be of two kinds. The first is the body of laws that provides the judicial basis for control of the society—in a general way—

and that provides the framework that empowers the executive to rule by decree and pass decree-laws and complementary acts meant to control some specific areas of society. This body of laws and regulations is to be found in the series of institutional acts the military governments have passed since 1964. The second is the repressive apparatus of the state, encompassing the National Information Service (SNI), all of the information divisions in the ministries of the government, in all the state-owned corporations and agencies, and in federal universities. This is the informational network that includes as its active side the various police and military organizations.

Legal Structures

The military governments of the national-security state launched in Brazil in April of 1964 have passed a total of 17 institutional acts, nearly 80 complementary acts, and hundreds of decree-laws based on these acts.

The institutional acts are considered a foundation of force, of exception, of "revolutionary power," that allows for rule by the executive in the form of decrees that are independent of the legislative branch of government. Thus, they are the coercive foundation of the rule of force, the judiciary under-pinning for a de facto power.

Institutional Act Number One, passed on April 9, 1964, by the High Command of the Revolution,[6] begins with a manifesto "to the nation" and puts this question forward clearly:

> Today's Institutional Act could only be drafted by the Commanders-in-Chief of the Army, the Navy and the Air Force who, in the name of the victorious revolution and with the support of the majority of the Nation, now propose to begin a new government and provide it with the indispensable institutional framework with which to carry forth its mission of the economic, financial, political and moral recon-struction of Brazil. . . . The victorious revolution needs to institutionalize itself. . . . Only the victorious revolution may make the rules and the regulations which will constitute the new government and provide it with the powers and juridical instru-ments which will ensure its effective power to rule in the interests of the country.
>
> To demonstrate that we do not intend to radical-ize the process of revolution, we have decided to

> maintain the Constitution of 1946, and have limited
> ourselves to amending it in the part which deals with
> the powers of the President of the Republic. . . .
> In order to reduce further the powers which belong
> to this victorious revolution, we have equally decided
> to maintain the National Congress, establishing only
> certain limitations to its power.
>   Thus, it should be clear that the revolution
> does not intend to legitimate itself through Congress.
> On the contrary, it is Congress which is legitimized
> by this Institutional Act which could only result
> from the inherent and revolutionary exercise of
> Constituent Power.[7]

Thus, in effect, the institutional act vested the High Command of the Revolution with virtual power to legislate and build the legal framework for coercion, thereby laying down the foundation of the national-security state. The most important provisions of this Act Number 1 were the establishment of indirect election, by the National Congress, of the president and the vice president of the republic; the establishment of a procedure known as <u>decurso de prazo</u>, whereby the president is empowered to present law projects to Congress, which has only 40 days to consider them, after which they are legally and automatically approved; a provision by which Congress could no longer legislate on matters of budget—this becoming the exclusive prerogative of the executive; and the elimination of all constitutional guarantees of individual rights for the period of six months. Similarly, all guarantees of tenure and of job stability were suspended so that people considered to be subversive or sympathetic to the deposed government could be summarily dismissed from their jobs. According to Marcus Figueiredo,[8] Institutional Act Number One was responsible for the punishment of more than 2,900 Brazilian citizens.

Indeed, this first phase of the institutionalization process of the national-security state was mainly concerned with purging the state apparatus, and political life in general, of any people who could be remotely considered to be either sympathetic to the previous government or a threat to the new government; thus, the velocity and ferocity of the use made of the powers of the institutional act.

As time went on, however, internal contradictions within the new forces of the state forced the government to proceed with further measures for political control. This pattern becomes evident in our historical perspective and has been consistent in the last 16 years of military rule in Brazil.

Institutional Act Number Two, passed on October 27, 1965, was the result of a bitter governmental defeat in the gubernatorial elections of two of the most important states of the country: Rio de Janeiro and Minas Gerais. Thus, one of its most important measures was to ensure that such mishaps would no longer happen, by extending the mechanisms of indirect election by the federal Congress to cover the governors and vice governors; from then on, all state governors and vice governors would be indirectly elected. Institutional Act Number Two also abolished all the 13 parties then in existence and regulated the conditions under which new parties could be formed. In practice, it created the biparty system of the National Renovating Alliance (ARENA—the government's party) and the Movimento Democratico Brasileiro (MDB—the opposition party) that lasted until 1979.

Institutional Act Number Two maintained the provision of the decurso de prazo and gave the president explicit power to pass complementary acts and decree laws. It dealt specifically with the judiciary and stipulated that crimes against national security and political crimes would be tried by a military court. This act extended the powers of the president, giving him unlimited powers to declare a state of siege, to close the federal Congress and state and municipal assemblies, and to rule by decree during periods of intervention. The president was also empowered to intervene in states and municipalities, to remove governors and mayors from office, and to appoint intervenors. It further empowered the president to cancel the political rights of anyone for ten years. Those who suffered such punishment would be unable to vote or to participate in any electoral process (be it governmental, associative, or syndicalist) for the period of ten years. They were also prohibited from speaking publicly on any subject dealing with politics and were liable to be put on parole when the government considered it necessary. The act empowered the president to dismiss, put in reserve, or forcefully retire any public employee, civil servant, or military person. It allowed the president to cancel the electoral mandate of any elected official, whether at the federal, state, or municipal level.[9] Under the act, 305 people were punished.[10] However, the act also had limited legal power. Its last article stipulated that it would no longer be valid after March 15, 1967.

It is important to note at this juncture that pressure from groups opposing these two acts began to challenge the state. Groups which had originally supported the military takeover now moved into the opposition—at first because of the powers of the executive under Institutional Act Number One, its limitations on Congress, and its provision for indirect election; and then increasingly because of widespread denunciations of torture

and police violence against political prisoners.11 Institutional
Act Number Two thus had the effect of increasing the force of
the opposition. Furthermore, the government was beginning
to implement its economic model, imposing strict measures aimed
at reducing inflation and passing two highly controversial bills:
a law to regulate (and virtually prohibit) strikes (known as the
Lei de Greve), and a wage-freeze law (known as the arrocho
salarial). The latter stipulated that thenceforth, salaries could
no longer be negotiated freely, but would be raised automatically
by decree once a year and according to a percentage calculated
from a formula held as a state secret.

Thus, 1966, 1967, and 1968 were years of ferment, of
opposition organization, and of a growing public outcry against
the budding national-security state. Despite the losses from
the large number of representatives who were removed from
office, opposition groups in Congress reorganized and, in 1966,
new and combative congressmen were elected by the new opposition party, the MDB. They used the congressional floor to
denounce the authoritarian structures and demand investigation
of tortures perpetrated against political prisoners. The students
also began to reorganize, after a first period of despair caused
by the banning of their national organization (União Nacional
dos Estudantes—UNE) and the burning of the student organization's headquarters in Rio de Janeiro, followed by imprisonment
of hundreds of student militants. By 1968 the student movement
was sufficiently reorganized to stage large demonstrations in
Rio de Janeiro and in São Paulo principally. Finally, the labor
unions also began to build up opposition to the strike law and the
wage-freeze law, and in 1968—in spite of the overt prohibition—
the metalworkers of Osasco (in São Paulo) and Contagem (in
Minas Gerais) went out on strike and occupied their factories.

Although the controls of the authoritarian state had been
severe, they were insufficient to counter the growing opposition.
In fact, they created new opposition groups within the ranks of
those who had originally supported the military takeover in the
belief that it would guarantee democratic institutions. The
executive power purged politicians, intervened in trade unions,
and abolished all previous political parties; it gave itself the
right to rule by decree, to pass institutional acts and complementary acts, to intervene in state and municipal governments
and state and municipal assemblies, to fire, retire, and expel
people without a trial, and to cancel electoral mandates and
cancel the political rights of important leaders. A great deal
of force was employed in implementing such acts, and denunciations of torture were more and more frequent; police brutality

and invasion of people's residences, of schools and universities, and of trade unions were frequent. Arrests were sometimes made in massive doses—cleanup operations that involved the arrest of hundreds of people. The very force of the repression, in fact, created new opposition.

Within the national-security state, the contradictions on how to handle dissent—between the hard-liners and the legalists—became unmanageable. Institutional Act Number Five was passed on December 13, 1968.[12] Of all the legislative pieces of the national-security state, this was the most important one and the most repressive and longest-lasting one (1968 to 1979). In it the president regained the power to close Congress, and state and municipal assemblies, and to reconvene them at will. In fact, Costa e Silva, then president, did indeed close Congress, and it was only reopened at the end of 1969 and in order to elect a new president after Costa e Silva's death. The president also regained the power to intervene in states and municipalities and to remove officials from office. Institutional Act Number Five reestablished the right of the president to cancel the electoral mandates of elected representatives and cancel their political rights for ten years. It again allowed the president to fire, put on reserve, or forcefully retire civil servants or military people, to intervene in the judiciary, and to rule by decree-law. It enabled the executive to pass more complementary acts, decree-laws, and other institutional acts. In fact, this act was a repeat of Institutional Act Number Two in many of its most repressive articles. It had, however, the aggravating feature of establishing no time limit for its own validity—being considered permanent and having finally been revoked, under great pressure, by a decree-law in 1979. It also had the further and important aggravating circumstance of removing all constitutional guarantees indefinitely and, especially, the right of habeas corpus for crimes against the National Security Law. It should be pointed out that these repression figures reflect only the published cases—in the Diário Oficial de União. In fact, the extent of the repression was much greater since it involved inquiries into the activities of people in private enterprises, private universities, and all state and municipal bureaucracies as well. Not all these cases were published in the Diário Oficial da União and not all the cases were legally justified. Often, people were simply dismissed without the formality of a reason or charge. The figures are an indication of a much harsher reality.

Under the period of rule of Institutional Act Number Five, the national-security state proceeded to lay its other judicial

and repressive framework. In the ruling periods of the two
subsequent governments, there were another 12 institutional
acts passed. These were meant to establish the specific controls
over different sectors of civil society. The national-security
state became concerned with ensuring the legislative support
that would provide a basis for mechanisms of control over all
potential sources of opposition. We shall deal with each individually later.

One further piece of general control legislation needs to
be considered at this point: the National Security Law. The
National Security Law of 1969, established as Decree-Law Number
898, was passed on September 29, 1969, by the military junta
that ruled in the period between Costa e Silva's death and the
inauguration of President Médici. This law was in effect until
December 17, 1978, when Geisel passed Decree-Law Number
6,620, known as the New National Security Law, and modified
it for the last time. I shall analyze its content, which is consistent throughout the two versions. The prison terms in it
varied and the modifications by Geisel dealt strictly with the
reduction of the years of imprisonment given as a penalty for
each crime; I would refer the reader to the legislation for an
examination of the particular penalties for each crime. I shall
deal here with the main articles in the National Security Law.

First, what constitutes a crime against national security
is loosely defined as those acts that lead to "psychological warfare," "subversive warfare," or "any threat or pressure of any
form or nature which has an effect on the country."[13] Furthermore, the concept of national security itself includes the definition of the enemy as existing within the nation and, thus, that
the repression of internal pressures and of social dissent is a
necessary part of defending the security of the nation.[14]

Psychological warfare is further defined in the law to be
"the employment of any propaganda, information or action, in
political, social, economic or military affairs, which may negatively influence public opinion and cause a reaction against the
national objectives."[15] Crimes against national security include
the dissemination of any information that will "indispose the
population against the constituted authorities";[16] demonstrations,
rallies, forbidden strikes, and distribution of pamphlets, books,
magazines, newspapers, or journals that preach subversive
warfare;[17] attempts to reorganize a political party or an association that had been dissolved by force of the institutional acts;[18]
actions that "offend the honor or the dignity of the President,
the vice-President, the President of the Senate and the House,
of the Supreme Court, the ministers of state, the governors of

of states and territories and the mayor of the Federal District";19
actions that "incite people to subversion of the political and
social order, to civil disobedience, to animosity between the
people and the Armed Forces or between the different branches
of the Armed Forces, to engage in class struggle, to paralyze
public services or essential activities";20 actions that "morally
offend those who exert authority, for motives of sectarianism
or political-social inconformity";21 actions that "attempt to sub-
vert the status quo or the political social structure now in effect,
in order to establish a class dictatorship."22

The National Security Law has a number of articles directed
specifically at control of the press. Some of the above-mentioned
articles also include specific penalties if the crime is published
in any of the media or committed by a journalist or a person
responsible for newspapers, radio, or television. I shall deal
with these more particularly later. The National Security Law
also specifically prohibits strikes under Articles 38, 39, and 45.
The penalty for such crimes varies from two to 30 years. For
other crimes, the penalty—under the 1969 National Security Law—
could be life imprisonment or even death. The modifications
introduced by President Geisel in the 1978 version of the National
Security Law abolished the death penalty and life imprisonment
and established, as the highest penalty, 30 years of confinement.
It should be emphasized, however, that the articles of the
National Security Law of 1978 have remained virtually the same.
The law is still in effect.

It should be emphasized also that all crimes committed
against the National Security Law are judged by a military
court—not by a civilian and regular judicial process. Since all
judges of the military court are appointed by the executive, one
can readily see that civil-rights guarantees are minimal and the
chances for what is known as fair-trial procedures are very
small. The strength of the control force of the National Security
Law, because of its coercive power, is maximum. In fact, during
the years of life of the Institutional Act Number Five (1968-79),
this was compounded by the fact that political prisoners charged
under the National Security Law had no right to habeas corpus.
The regaining of this right has been an important event and a
victory for the opposition group of lawyers who worked with
the Brazilian Bar Association for ten years in order to pressure
the executive to revoke the act and establish the right of habeas
corpus once again. The National Security Law, however, still
stands with its full coercive power.

The Repression Apparatus

The National Information Service—Serviço Nacional de Informações—was created by a decree-law passed on June 13, 1964. Thus, it was one of the first acts of the new government and showed its concern with the institutionalizing of an apparatus capable of controlling information and providing support for the policies of purges and coercion. The SNI was created as an organ of the presidency, and was to be responsible to the president and the National Security Council of the executive. It is stated in the law that the SNI must cooperate with the National Security Council in "all subjects pertaining to National Security."[23] It had as its established purpose the collecting and analysis of information pertinent to national security, of counterinformation, and of information on internal subversive affairs. It is the equivalent of the FBI and the CIA put together. In fact, the SNI has been the locus of a de facto power, perhaps even parallel to that of the executive. It is sufficient to point out that all the chiefs of the SNI have been extremely powerful men within the national-security state. General Golbery do Couto e Silva, its creator and first chief, is considered to be the most powerful man behind the scenes and the ideologue of the state. Other chiefs have become president, as is the case with the present president, João Batista Figueiredo, who left the SNI to take office.

Since 1964 the SNI has grown to be an effective agency of information and of political control. By law, it has one Central Agency in the Federal District of Brasília and regional agencies in each state. In fact, it is more than that. As can be seen in Figure 12.1, the SNI is at the top of the repression apparatus, the convergence point for the entire security system. All data collected by the so-called community of information (comunidade de informação) end up in the SNI. The National Information Service has been estimated to employ close to 2 million people, including informants. Ultimately, the chief of the SNI has direct control of all the information gathered and analyzed by the entire system. Therefore, one can readily see that the power of such a position is enormous, and parallel to that of the powerful president. In fact, this has proven to be one of the problems of the national-security state: It has created such a beast that the SNI now stands next to the executive, as a parallel force, not always obedient and often imposing its own will upon the executive to which it is supposedly subordinated. All of the progressively more repressive institutional acts were passed under the pressure of the system—the sistema—which is variously

FIGURE 12.1. The Repression Apparatus

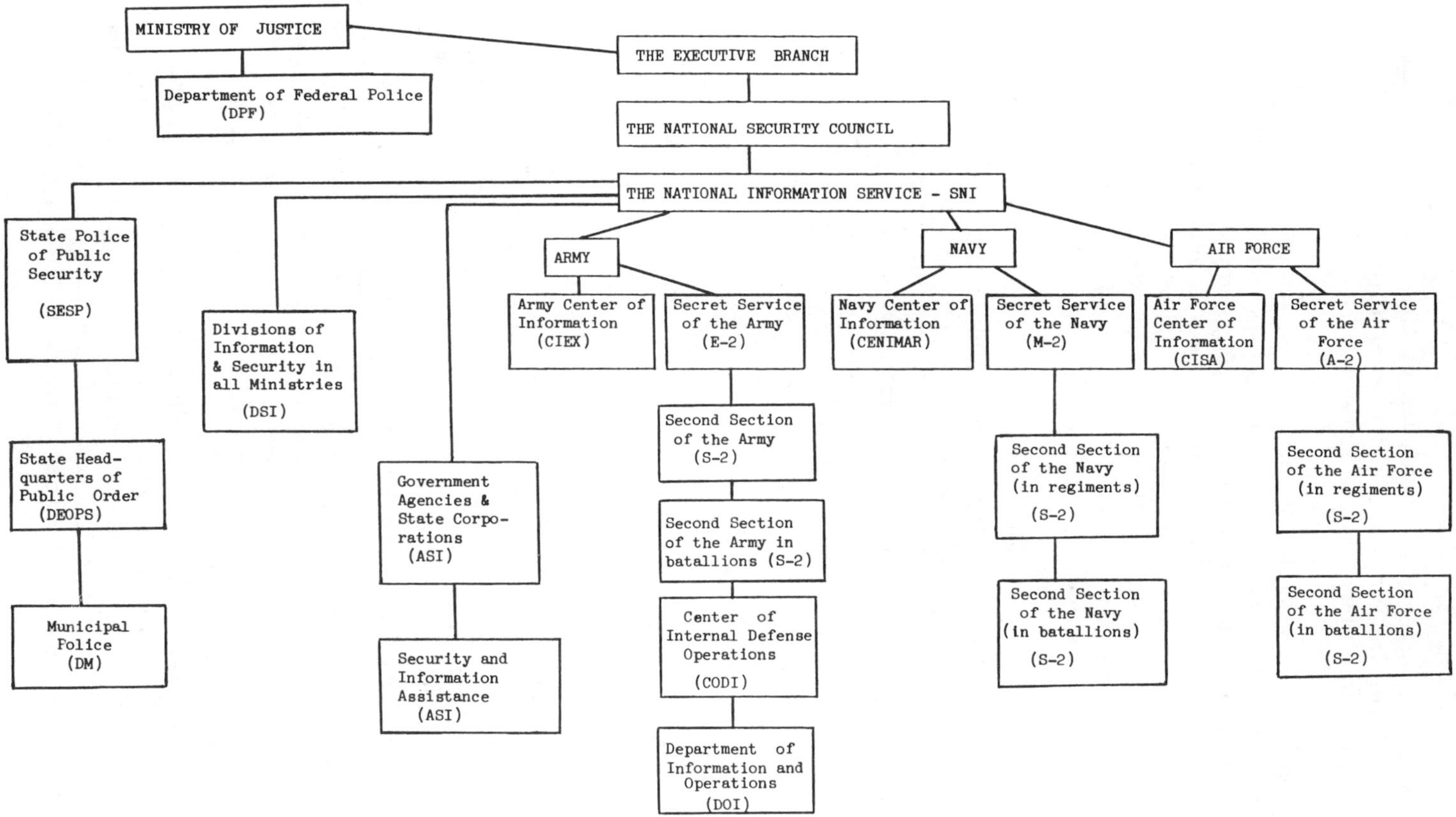

THE EXECUTIVE BRANCH

MINISTRY OF JUSTICE

Department of Federal Police (DPF)

THE NATIONAL SECURITY COUNCIL

THE NATIONAL INFORMATION SERVICE – SNI

State Police of Public Security (SESP)

State Head-quarters of Public Order (DEOPS)

Municipal Police (DM)

Divisions of Information & Security in all Ministries (DSI)

Government Agencies & State Corpo-rations (ASI)

Security and Information Assistance (ASI)

ARMY

Army Center of Information (CIEX)

Secret Service of the Army (E-2)

Second Section of the Army (S-2)

Second Section of the Army in batallions (S-2)

Center of Internal Defense Operations (CODI)

Department of Information and Operations (DOI)

NAVY

Navy Center of Information (CENIMAR)

Secret Service of the Navy (M-2)

Second Section of the Navy (in regiments) (S-2)

Second Section of the Navy (In batallions) (S-2)

AIR FORCE

Air Force Center of Information (CISA)

Secret Service of the Air Force (A-2)

Second Section of the Air Force (in regiments) (S-2)

Second Section of the Air Force (in batallions) (S-2)

credited, in the press and even by the presidents themselves, with being behind every major move to the right.[24] And the SNI is the pinnacle of the sistema.

The SNI has a very specific mission: to promote and carry forth the "evaluation and integration of information," to disseminate such information among the various branches of the government, to establish all the necessary ties with state and municipal governments, and with private and state enterprises, and to draw up certain plans, which include the planning of strategic information; the planning of internal security; and the "planning of counter-intelligence."[25]

The figure demonstrates how the repressive apparatus works for the control of Brazilian society and how it converges to the SNI, the National Security Council, and the executive. The left side of the figure, essentially, shows the apparatus that is meant for the collection of information and the control of the civilian population. The Secret Service network in the military also is used to collect information on civilians and has often been the locus of torture—particularly the army's CODI-DOI and the navy's CENIMAR.[26] One should note the far-reaching network of such controls. At the extreme left, the figure shows the police departments, at regional, state, and municipal levels (the SESP, the DEOPS, and the municipal police). Next, it shows the Divisions of Information and of Security (DSI) that exist in all ministries and are meant to collect information not only about civilians who come under the jurisdiction of each particular ministry, but also about its own public employees. Thus, for example, university professors and students are watched at four levels: by the state—police level; by the military secret services; by the Divisions of Information and Security of the Ministry of Education, and, finally, through the Security and Information Assistance (ASI) departments at the university itself. The figure also demonstrates the ramification of the Security and Information Assistance departments. Such departments exist in all state agencies and state enterprises as well as in federal universities and autarchic institutions. Private firms and private universities do, as well, often have Security Divisions that report on people and keep tabs on their activities.

The right-hand side of the figure shows the control of the military itself. The repressive apparatus for the military is no less severe than it is for civilians. Besides the existence of a Center of Information for the army (CIEX), for the navy (CENIMAR), and for the air force (CISA), the figure also shows the connections involved in the internal repression: For each branch of the armed forces, there exists a general Secret Service

(the E-2 for the army, the M-2 for the navy, and the A-2 for
the air force). There is also an agency known as the Second
Section (Segunda Seção, or S-2). This is tied to each regiment
and even to each battalion. Therefore, the military, also, does
not escape the far-reaching grasp of the repressive apparatus
that has been set up to support the national-security state. In
fact, counting again only the published cases, this apparatus
has been responsible for the punishment of 4,787 officers since
1964.

The CODI-DOI (the Centro de Operações de Defesa Interna
and the Destacamento de Operações e Informações) have a substitute unit, the OBAN (Operação Bandeirantes), which was
created in January of 1970 and was subordinated to the local
command unit of each of the armies. For example, the OBAN
of Sao Paulo was subordinated to the Second Army; that of Rio
de Janeiro, to the First Army; and of Rio Grande do Sul, to the
Third Army. The OBAN was created in order to repress and
destroy the growing guerrilla warfare of the years between 1969
and 1974 and became well known for its brutality and for the
torture of political prisoners.

It is important to note as well that the Military Police force
has been made subordinate to the army, and is also tied to the
general system of repression. The Military Police is responsible
for the overt and explicit job of repression of demonstrations,
rallies, public meetings, strikes, or other popular manifestations
of dissent. It is the Military Police officers, and rarely the
army, who throw tear gas, break up meetings, and invade universities, churches, and trade unions. This keeps the armed
forces in the background of the repressive system and allows
public anger to be more centered on the Military Police—thus
freeing the armed forces from direct and overt responsibility
in its most visible forms. The subordination of the Military
Police, however, has a more important reason: It was originally
created as an independent force and could perhaps challenge
the national-security state. By subordinating it to the armed
forces, establishing that its commander must be a general of
the army, and providing it with the Second Section to deal with
its own membership, the national-security state ensures its
docile compliance with the rules.

As to the State Police forces, they have equally been subordinated to the federal government, under Institutional Act
Number Two. This was considered to be important in case the
opposition should win the election for the gubernatorial posts.
Some states have a police force that is potentially large enough
to challenge the federal powers. São Paulo, for example, in

1965, had a police force of 20,000 men. It now has a police force of close to 40,000 men. As is the case with the Military Police, the State Police forces also have security sections to watch their membership.

The repressive apparatus of the national-security state has sufficient independence to make its presence felt even to the point of being a parallel government. President Geisel, at the onset of his "decompression" policy, ran into a direct confrontation with the comunidade de informações and was forced to remove the Second Army commander from his post. Other attempts have been made by all the presidents—from Castello Branco to Figueiredo—to limit the use of torture, but the strength of the apparatus becomes apparent with each recurrent case of torture.

Recently, the use of torture as a mechanism for the obtaining of information from political prisoners has in fact diminished. Torture of common prisoners has been a constant in Brazilian society since at least the 1930s and, under an authoritarian state, it tends to be encouraged due to the impunity of police officers. In fact, torture is an essential part of the institutionalized repression of the national security state. But due to a great deal of internal and external pressure, the present government has not made use of it on political prisoners—however, the potential for torture has remained the same. None of the officers who were publicly connected with the torturing were either punished or removed from their jobs. The entire apparatus of repression is intact and effectively maintained and ready for action at any moment—if the national-security state becomes unduly threatened. Moreover, the actual exercise of coercive violence has continued in new forms: In the past years the activities of paramilitary groups—widely suspected of being connected to the repressive apparatus—have increased.[27] In fact, violence is a necessary part of the national-security state and widespread use of terror an intrinsic part of its nature. The cleanup operations continue—although disguised as the search for bandits—and extreme police violence is a part of everyday life.[28] The power of the repressive apparatus is the center of the dilemma of the national-security state. It needs to increase the power of its repressive apparatus constantly in order to control the various sectors of society. In so doing, it indeed creates a parallel force that applies constant pressure on the executive and brings about increasingly unbearable contradictions.

SPECIFIC CONTROLS PER AREA OF OPPOSITION

We have seen where the general mechanisms of control affect specific areas of civil society and the military itself. I shall now briefly deal with the specific mechanisms that have been brought to bear for each area.

The Control of the Judiciary

The first direct intervention in the judiciary by the military executive took place in 1965, with the passage of Institutional Act Number Two. In this act, ministers of the Supreme Court were increased from nine to 13, to be appointed by the executive. The reason for this extension was that the hard-liners of the military felt that the Supreme Court was being too lenient in its decisions on political cases.[29] Not only did it increase the size of the Supreme Court, but the act also specified a special military court for the trials of political prisoners. Until 1965, only military personnel were judged by the military tribunals, hierarchized so that at the top of the pyramid is the Supreme Military Court (STM). All civilians were tried by the civil tribunals, the highest court of which is the federal Supreme Court (STF). Then under Institutional Act Number One, which began the period of trials for political crimes, the federal Supreme Court began to deal with cases that were, in essence, crimes of conscience. But the hard-line military felt that the STF was not dealing with these cases with sufficient severity and, thus, interfered in the judicial system by establishing that political crimes of civilians also would thenceforth be tried in the Supreme Military Court. The Supreme Military Tribunal also had its size regulated under Institutional Act Number two. Its size was increased to 15 judges, with life tenure, to be appointed by the president—without consultation with Congress—and to be chosen in the following manner: Four judges had to be active-duty generals of the army, three judges had to be active-duty generals of the air force, and five judges could be civilians.

Institutional Act Number Five increased the controls over the judiciary. To begin with, it suspended legal guarantees and suspended the right of habeas corpus for crimes against the National Security Law. Furthermore, it suspended the constitutional guarantees of judges: lifelong tenure and nontransferability. From then on, judges could lose their position or be transferred from court to court if their opinions on cases diverged with those of the government, or if they were believed to be liberal, or too lenient, in political trials.

In my interview with the president of the Brazilian Bar Association (OAB), Eduardo Seabra Fagundes, this problem was discussed at length.[30] He pointed out that it is impossible for the judiciary to remain independent and a power equal to the executive, once it is so trampled on and interfered with. The guarantees of job stability, of lifelong tenure, and of un-removability, Seabra Fagundes emphasized, are essential to the proper functioning of the judicial system. Not only is it essential to ensure fair trials, but it is necessary in order to protect judges from those who hold power so that they can freely exercise their function without pressure. These guarantees are also essential for the maintenance of an uncorrupted judicial system. What has been observed in Brazil is that judges are often punished and threatened with punishment if they do not acqui-esce with the will of the powerful on civil suits as well as on political suits. This fact has greatly affected the independence of the judiciary and has undermined the constitutional guarantees of equal power among the three branches of government.

Finally, it should be pointed out that 146 members of the judiciary, including Supreme Court judges, were punished by the force of Institutional Acts Numbers One, Two, and Five.[31] Again, these are the published cases of judges whose removal was justified directly under one of the three major acts. According to Seabra Fagundes, and others whom I interviewed on the question of the judiciary, it is impossible to know just how many judges did in fact lose their position because of political ideas or were transferred and pressured in other ways. The important point is that once the legal and constitutional guarantees are removed, then repression takes place, and even if at times it is not actualized, the demonstration effect of fear is always present.

Lawyers have been persecuted also and have suffered arrests and even torture because of their political position or for their defense of political prisoners. One of the most active lawyers in defense of political prisoners, now Congressman Modesto da Silveira, from Rio de Janeiro, has suffered a number of death threats, and was actually kidnapped once while enforc-ing a judge's order for the release of three 16-year-old girls who were being held in one of the prisons. His is not a unique case. Raymundo Faoro, past president of the Brazilian Bar Association—and himself active in defense of civil-rights guarantees—told me that he no longer pays any attention to telephone calls or to mail threats, for he receives so many

death threats that he believes it is essential to ignore them and
show no sense of intimidation. Airton Soares, now congressman
for São Paulo, and Luis Eduardo Greenhalg—both São Paulo
lawyers who have defended political prisoners—had their office
machine-gunned on one occasion and have also been victims of
threats and of a bomb. José Carlos Dias and Dalmo Dallari, of
the Justice and Peace Committee of the archdiocese of São Paulo,
have been threatened many times and have been arrested once.
Dalmo Dallari, in July of 1980, was kidnapped and seriously
injured with a knife. These are just examples of a situation
that is fairly widespread and is certainly an added factor in
the control and repression of the judiciary system. For a number of years, the intimidation was so violent that few lawyers
were brave enough to take on the defense of political prisoners.
It is necessary to regard these better-known cases as samples
of the daily life of lawyers who defy the powers-that-be. It is
clear that the repressive system works both in legal ways and
in underground, paramilitary forms. They counterbalance one
another and increase the demonstration effect of terror and
intimidation that is the foundation of the national-security state.

One should mention here as well the ten-year-long campaign
that was waged to bring under control the Brazilian Bar Association. The military governments tried for many years to break
the resistance of the powerful lawyers' association and to bring
it under the direct control of the Ministry of Labor. These
efforts were effectively resisted and the Brazilian Bar Association showed itself to be sufficiently strong to remain independent.[32] It has not, however, escaped threats and attacks from
paramilitary groups. The OAB has been bombed twice during
the last 16 years; the last bomb, at the end of 1980, killed the
secretary to the president of the association. It was a letter
bomb that had been addressed to Seabra Fagundes. None of
the attacks on lawyers or on the Brazilian Bar Association have
ever been seriously investigated and, certainly, those responsible
have never been punished. Leads indicate, however, that they
were members of extreme right groups that have been known
to work closely with the so-called comunidade de informações
and are often members of the repressive apparatus.

Control of Political Representation

I here define control of political representation to include
controls of the national congress, of state and municipal assemblies, as well as the control of political parties and the electoral

system. Controls in this area impede the free flow of political representation and of forms of government that are an integral part of representative democracy. These controls have been many and varied, and, at times, highly imaginative. I shall begin with the structural controls on the legislative branch.

The national Congress, state assemblies, and municipal assemblies were purged many times, particularly after Institutional Acts Numbers One, Two, and Five.[33] As may be seen in Table 12.1, 595 political representatives at the federal, regional, and municipal levels have been purged between 1964 and 1980. If one added up the votes of all those purged members, one could say that with the last purge, that of Congressman Alencar Furtado, the total number of votes that could be said to have been canceled by decree reached 7,938,274 votes.[34]

Institutional Act Number Five alone was responsible for the purge of 110 federal congressmen, six senators, 161 state congressmen, and 22 aldermen.[35] Furthermore, the institutional acts also purged 11 governors and 57 mayors.[36] Under the institutional acts, an elected representative who is punished (cassado) loses his or her electoral post and that place is not filled by a substitute. Thus, Congress becomes smaller with each documented case of punishment (cassação), and the majority held by the governmental party is increased. In Fact, I have counted only 28 congressmen of the ARENA party (the government's) who were ever punished by the institutional acts. And most of the ARENA representatives who were punished were hit by Institutional Act Number Five when they sided with the opposition MDB party and voted against the executive in an unusual show of independence. Moreover, according to Marcus Figueiredo, only 1.7 percent of those who were cassado did not also lose their political rights for ten years.[37] The great majority were effectively eliminated from all political activities for ten years. For, in accordance with the institutional acts and a complementary act known as the Estatuto dos Cassados, those who lose their political rights cannot vote, cannot be voted for, and cannot join political parties or express political opinions in public or in printed form. Thus, they are politically dead for the duration of the period.

Naturally, the mechanism of cassação has been an extremely effective way to control opposition and limit the influence of opposition sectors at all levels of political representation. It has been used widely to ensure executive control. In fact, in at least one documented occasion (Rio Grande do Sul in 1967 on the occasion of a possible electoral victory for the opposition in the gubernatorial election), three state congressmen lost

TABLE 12.1. Control of Political Representation: Elected Representatives, Mayors, and State Governors Purged (breakdown by governmental period)

Branch of Government	1964-66— Castello Branco	1969-71— Costa e Silva and Military Junta	1971-73— Médici	1974-79— Geisel	Total
National Congress	76	105	0	8	189
State assemblies	100	178	10	2	290
Aldermen	11	36	0	2	49
State governors	10	0	0	0	10
Mayors	27	30	0	0	57
Total	224	349	10	12	595

Source: Diário Oficial da União, April 1964 to December 1979.

their electoral mandates only to ensure that ARENA would have
the majority in the state assembly, which was to choose the
governor. The institutional acts have also been used at times
to remove specific opposition politicians who were considered to
be an actual or a potential threat to the military governments.
This was the case, for example, of three ex-presidents—João
Goulart, Jânio Quadros, and Juscelino Kubitschek. Carlos
Lacerda, a powerful politician and ex-governor of the state of
Guanabara (now Rio de Janeiro), also lost his political rights
for the same reasons. Other politicians lost their rights for
ten years only to keep them from becoming candidates in a
local or state election.

The national Congress suffers further restrictions that
limit its legislative ability. First, Institutional Acts Numbers
One, Two, and Five took away many of the constitutional prerogatives of the legislative branch that make up part of what is
referred to as the constitutional checks and balances that ensure
the equality of powers among the three branches of a democratic
state. It should be noted that the revoking of the institutional
acts has not changed the situation, and that Congress remains
highly controlled and has not reacquired any of its constitutional
prerogatives.

With Institutional Act Number One, and again later under
Institutional Acts Numbers Two and Five, Congress lost the
power to legislate on budgetary matters. The procedure known
as decurso de prazo is equally still in effect. Under the period
of control of the institutional acts, the time period allowed for
Congress to examine executive-drafted laws was 30 days. Now
this time period has been increased to 40 days. This mechanism
allows the executive branch to make sure that all its legislation
will be eventually approved, for it only needs to filibuster for
the 40 days and prevent Congress from voting on the measure.
After that it is automatically approved. As can be readily seen,
this, in practice, has proven to be an effective way to get controversial legislation passed by Congress even against its will.
To illustrate this point, I shall mention only some of the most
recent and highly controversial legislation the executive saw
approved: the Amnesty Bill of 1979; the law which abolished
the MDB and the ARENA—known as the Party Reform Law; and,
finally, the law known as the Estatuto dos Estrangeiros—the
Foreigners' Law—passed in August of 1980. The Foreigners'
Law was a particularly controversial bill, for it was the target
of widespread charges that it aimed principally at the control
of the church (which has been variously estimated to have 40-60
percent of the foreign missionaries in the country) and of the

Latin American political exiles who have sought refuge in Brazil. Knowing that this would be a particularly difficult bill to push through, the executive took advantage of one further control it has over Congress: Since Institutional Act Number Five, Congress does not have the right to reconvene itself from recess for examination of a particularly important issue. Only the executive may reconvene Congress from its scheduled recess. Thus, the government introduced the Foreigners' Bill at the very end of June, thereby taking advantage of the 30-day recess period of July. When Congress was reconvened on August 2, it had only a few days to discuss and vote on the bill before the period of decurso de prazo ended. It was automatically approved as it stood.

Other controls of Congress that are still in effect include the following. Congress cannot hold more than five congressional investigations per session. This is an enormous limitation, for one of the most important functions of Congress is its power to investigate, and act as a counterbalance to the power of, the executive. It is supposed to have the right to supervise the acts of the executive and investigate whatever Congress feels has been an act of abuse of power. A Congressional Investigation Committee (CPI) that Congress may use, furthermore, cannot spend more than a limited amount of money (decreed by the executive). The committee cannot pay for traveling expenses of members outside Brasília. Thus, as Congressman Modesto da Silveira told me, a CPI that is investigating, for example, the activities of Jari Corporation in the Amazon cannot finance the expenses of travel to the site. The members of the committee who wish to see for themselves must pay out of their own pocket the cost of their endeavor to discover the truth. Besides, the Investigating Committee does not have complete power to enforce its request that government officials come in to give testimony to Congress. Recently, for example, the CPI that investigated the German-Brazilian Nuclear Treaty petitioned a colonel—reputed to be an important member of the comunidade de informações—to testify before the committee. The simple reply was that he would not come and that the committee could hear only the testimony of the minister of planning. Once more, the comunidade showed its real power and Congress felt its own impotence.

Finally, and most important, after Institutional Act Number Five, congressmen and senators lost their constitutional right to parliamentary immunity. This meant that because of comments made on the floor of Congress, elected representatives could lose their mandates and have their political rights canceled automatically, without a formal charge and a trial. After Institutional Act Number 5 was revoked in 1979 this was modified. Now, if an elected representative is felt to have incurred offenses against the National Security Law, he is charged with the crime and tried by the Supreme Court. The punishment is still the loss of mandate. Thus, parliamentary immunity has only been partly regained; at least now the elected official has the right to defend himself. And this power of the executive is already being used: In the middle of 1980, two congressmen were indicted and are now being tried—Congressman João Cunha of São Paulo and Congressman Genival Tourinho of Minas Gerais.

These considerations allow us to see the complete power the executive branch of the state holds. It virtually controls the judiciary and the legislature. Thus, one can say that one strong characteristic of the national-security state is the rule by executive power, with tight controls established wherever political representation may infringe upon and change policies, soften the force of the repression, or share in the exercise of power. This is an added factor of contradiction, for the extreme isolation of the executive branch of the state—which is separated from civil society and even from the state itself—is the seed of its instability. External conflicts and pressures are not resolved but, rather, are brought into the state itself, thereby undermining its legitimacy even from within.

The nature of the electoral controls and the mechanisms that control political parties can be summarized as follows. First, and most important, the executive clearly has the power to create and to abolish parties at will. In fact, it has done so on two occasions in the past 16 years. In 1965, Institutional Act Number Two abolished all the 13 parties then in existence. The act also set the ground rules for the creation of a biparty system that resulted (as noted earlier) in the birth of two parties—one, the ARENA, to be the government's support party; and the second, the MDB, to be the "responsible" opposition.[38] Over time, however, the opposition party became a representative vehicle of dissent and acted as a unified front for different opposition groups. In fact, it began to win important elections and to threaten the power of the groups that control the national-security state. Table 12.2 presents the electoral results from 1966 to 1978, which demonstrate the growing electoral strength of the MDB party.[39]

In November 1979, the Party Reform Bill (Reforma Partidária) was forced through Congress under the threat of the decurso de prazo. This bill abolished the ARENA and MDB parties and detailed the strict conditions under which new parties could be

TABLE 12.2. Federal and State Elections in Brazil from 1966 to 1978

Election	1966	Percent	1970	Percent	1974	Percent	1978	Percent
Senate								
Total number of votes	17,259,598		22,406,624		28,925,792		37,601,641	
Total number of valid votes	13,630,743		16,123,219		24,544,673		30,770,038	
Total votes for ARENA	7,719,382	56.63	9,898,694	61.4	10,068,810	41.0	13,239,418	43.0
Total votes for MDB	5,911,361	43.36	6,224,525	38.6	14,579,372	59.3	17,530,620	56.9
Total blank votes	2,014,579	11.6	4,955,167	22.1	2,665,818	9.21	3,783,550	10.0
Total void votes	1,614,276	9.3	1,328,238	5.9	1,705,296	5.89	3,048,053	8.1
Seats won by ARENA	48		40		6		15	
Seats won by MDB	14		6		16		8	
House of Representatives								
Total number of votes	17,285,556		22,435,521		28,981,015		37,553,882	
Total number of valid votes	13,647,108		15,645,741		22,820,958		29,792,217	
Total votes for ARENA	8,731,638	63.9	10,867,814	69.4	11,866,482	51.9	15,024,298	50.4
Total votes for MDB	4,915,470	36.0	4,777,927	30.5	10,954,440	48.0	14,767,919	49.5
Total blank votes	2,461,523	14.0	4,690,952	20.9	4,112,973	14.2	5,042,955	13.4
Total void votes	1,176,925	6.0	2,098,828	9.3	2,047,084	7.06	2,718,710	7.2
Seats won by ARENA	277		233		203		231	
Seats won by MDB	132		87		161		189	

State assemblies

Total number of votes	17,260,382		22,405,624		28,867,300		37,447,839
Total number of valid votes	14,044,039		16,382,966		23,393,263		30,222,386
Total votes for ARENA	9,005,278	64.1	11,442,894	69.8	12,184,240	52.0	15,410,073	50.9
Total votes for MDB	5,038,761	35.8	4,940,072	30.1	11,209,023	47.9	14,812,313	49.9
Total blank votes	2,088,927	12.1	4,129,835	18.43	3,487,546	12.08	4,632,604	12.3
Total void votes	1,127,416	6.5	1,893,823	8.45	1,986,491	6.89	2,592,849	6.9
Seats won by ARENA	—		493		457		492
Seats won by MDB	—		208		330		353

Note: Percentages are of total valid votes for the ARENA and MDB parties (without blank and void), and percentages of blank and void votes are of total votes.

Sources: Dados Estatísticos, Volume 9: Eleições Federais Estaduais realizadas no Brasil em 1970 (Tribunal Superior Eleitoral, Departamento de Imprensa Nacional, 1973); Dados Estatísticos, Volume 11: Eleições Federais e Estauais realizadas no Brasil em 1974 (Tribunal Superior Eleitoral, Departamento de Imprensa Nacional, 1977); Márcio Moreira Alves, "As Eleições no Brasil 1978," in Revista Critica de Ciência Sociais.

formed. The party legislation was drafted in such a way that
it is extremely difficult to organize a party independent of
strict state controls in Brazil. The law included, as well, two
clauses so as to discourage the most promising opposition parties.
The first clause established that the word "party" necessarily
had to be included in the name of whatever organization was to
be formed. This was meant to avoid the implementation of the
MDB's plan to be "reborn from its ashes like the Phoenix,"
including the utilization of the same name. The second clause
prohibited the organization of a party that appealed to issues
or was composed of one particular class. This aimed at avoiding
the formation of the Workers' Party, the Partido dos Trabalhadores (PT), which was in the process of organization.

However, the actual effect of these clauses has been nulli-
fied by the implementation efforts of the two main opposition
parties. The Partido do Movimento Democrático Brasileiro (PMDB)
avoided the first clause simply by adding the word "party" in
front of the old name. As to the Workers' Party, it won an
important judicial decision that accepted the interpretation of
the party as an elastic coalition of salaried people, peasants,
and middle-class members. Thus, it was granted the final registration by the Electoral Tribunal. On the other hand, other
stipulations of the law remain in effect and may cause a great
deal of difficulty for the opposition in the future elections.

Electoral controls are implicit in the controls of Congress
and of the party system. There are some specific ones, however, that should be emphasized. Whenever the military executive
noticed the possibility of an opposition victory in gubernatorial,
congressional, or municipal elections, it would change the rules
of the elections and the legislation pertaining to them. A recent
important example can illustrate such a practice. Soon after
the surprising and overwhelming victory of the MDB party in
the congressional elections of 1974, it became obvious that in
the next elections, the opposition party might win the majority
in Congress. Therefore, in 1977, then President Ernesto Geisel—
using the powers of Institutional Act Number Five—closed Congress temporarily and passed a set of decree-laws known as the
April Package Laws (Pacote de Abril). These laws established
two very important changes in the electoral system. First, it
changed the number of seats available in the House of Representatives for each state of the union. Until that time, each
state had the number of seats proportionate to the number of
eligible voters in the state. Geisel changed this rule to read,
"proportionate to the population of the state." This seemingly
minor change has had an immense political importance and did,

in fact, make the difference in the maintenance of the ARENA's majority in Congress. This is because eligible voters in Brazil must be literate. The MDB had been traditionally strongest in urban areas and in more developed areas with a higher percentage of educated people, who were better informed and more politicized. These were not, however, the most populous states but had a smaller illiteracy rate. Since the MDB-controlled states had most voters but fewer people, it made great political sense to change the electoral rules in order to make seats proportionate with the population of the state rather than the voters. Thus, the MDB-controlled states of the center-South lost seats and the ARENA-controlled states of the Northeast and the North gained seats. Second, the April Package Laws created the colloquially called "bionic senators." By this decree-law, one-third of the Senate would thenceforth be indirectly elected (as is the case with governors and the president). In practice this means virtual appointment by the executive. The bionic senators also had a mandate of eight years, longer than the mandate of senators who are elected by popular vote. Thus the popular nickname "bionic"—for they are created from the top, are artificially made, and cannot be beaten. The bionic Senators have played an important role in the phase of political decompression. They are the government's insurance that all of its laws will pass through Congress, because, if by any chance the opposition should succeed in gaining the majority of the House of Representatives, all their endeavors could still be effectively blocked when the legislation reached the floor of the Senate.

As we have mentioned already, however, the opposition is proving to be able to be able to possibly overcome the difficulties imposed upon it by the technicalities of the decree-laws. The national-security state may have to remake its regulations again in order to control the growing opposition and bring it into line. It is clear that the executive holds enough power to play with the rules of the game and restructure the entire party system and the electoral system whenever it sees fit. The problem is that every time it does so, it loses credibility, loses legitimacy, creates conflict within its own ranks, and adds to the institutional crisis in which it is constantly immersed.

The Control of Information

The control of information must be considered in its three forms: the control of information and learning—involving control of teaching, or professors in universities, and of the activities of students; the control of the press, radio, and television; and the control of culture and information transmitted through theater, literature, cinema, and music.

First, professors and students have been the center of some of the strictest controls of the national-security state. The National Union of Students was prohibited and its headquarters burned in 1964. An analysis of the archives existent in the National Council of Churches in New York showed that the incidence of documented evidence of arrest and torture is greatest among students and workers. Universities were often invaded by the Military Police or other organs of the repressive apparatus that were in search of student activists. Two of the best-documented invasions occurred in 1968 (in Rio de Janeiro and in Brasília) and resulted in serious injury and death. These invasions triggered mass demonstrations of protest that were also violently repressed. Students were subjected not only to the National Security Law but, after 1969, to two auxiliary articles known as 477 and 288, which prohibited explicitly political manifestations and commentary. The penalties ranged from suspension to expulsion with the stipulation that those who infringed the articles and were thereby expelled from a university would be prevented from studying anywhere in the country for a period of five years. The prohibition also affected the structure of the student's organizations, tying them closely to the Ministry of Education. Professors had to contend with two types of direct repression. In order to get a job, they were frequently required to obtain from the Security Police a document known as the atestado ideológico. This document contained an ideological green light from the Security Police, establishing that the bearer was not sympathetic to groups deemed to be subversive; this in fact meant most of the opposition to the government. Furthermore, within the classroom there frequently were known police agents who would carefully note comments or statements considered critical of the government's policies. Professors were also included in the articles 477 and 288 and, if found guilty of infringement, were expelled and prohibited from teaching in any institution of learning (even a private one) for a period of three years. Thus, the penalty, in effect, withdrew from professors the right to earn a living for three years. Teachers were subject to the investigations of the Security Police, the watching of the various departments of security, and were dismissed without trial, under Institutional Acts Number One, Two, and Five. Since 1964, 312 university professors were punished by the institutional acts and expelled from universities. The total number of those punished or fired for their political

beliefs is much higher but it is not possible to assess, for it
was often done under orders and is not easily documented.
These two types of punishment are called cassação (referring
to the documented cases of punishment under the institutional
acts) and cassação branca (which refers to the process of dis-
missal under orders of the Security Police, but which remains
undocumented).

In 1979 President Geisel revoked the Institutional Act Number Five and the auxiliary decrees 477 and 288. The form of
control within the universities was modified to conform to the
policies of decompression. The clear intention of the government was to devise new mechanisms of control that were less
overt and to establish more subtle and sophisticated types of
control. Geisel's government recognized the problem that overt
repression results in stronger opposition and, as a consequence,
clearly deemphasized violence, torture, and mechanisms of explicit control. The modifications in the area of the universities
implied a decreasing use of the mechanism of cassação and an
increased use of cassação branca. This has been particularly
true since the return of the exiled intellectuals and after passage
of the Amnesty Bill.[40] Many of the control mechanisms in the
revoked decrees 477 and 288 were included in the statutes and
disciplinary codes of the individual universities.

These mechanisms have not been able to completely control
either the student movement or the process of information and
learning. Students reorganized in 1967 and 1968, went underground and joined the various guerrilla groups between 1969
and 1974, after the passing of the Institutional Act Number
Five, and surfaced again as a widespread movement in 1977.
They have succeeded in reshaping the National Union of Students
and in holding direct elections for the board of directors in
1979 and 1980. The UNE has held two national meetings in the
last two years and exists as a de facto national organization—
although it is still legally prohibited. The students reorganized
through parallel institutions at the university level—at both the
regional and national levels; these are the free academic centers
that exist everywhere. Professors have also organized a national
union and staged a nationwide strike that involved all of the
federal universities and close to 40,000 professors. The strike
was aimed at pressuring the government to provide more educational funds for universities and at establishing promotional
and professional guarantees for university professors. Students
and university professors have followed a similar opposition
strategy to that of the leaders of the new trade union movement:
to create de facto alternative organizations that press for legal

changes in a more liberal direction. So far, with the movement in the universities, the reaction of the military government in the decompression years since 1976 has been to have a dialogue and to avoid explicit repression. The one time this was not done—with the student demonstrations in São Paulo in 1977 and the repression by the police, coupled with the armed invasion of the Catholic University—the result has been highly unfavorable for the government. The public outcry was strong enough to pressure the government into more quiescent policies. This has by no means been the case with the trade union movement, which has been consistently and strongly repressed, as we shall see later.

The control of the press has been important in the overall logic of the national-security state. Censorship has been, and still is, widely used to obtain social control and keep large sectors of the population uninformed and thereby unable to participate politically in effective ways. Censorship in Brazil is carried out in two forms: a priori censorship, with orders being transmitted to the media that prohibit public information on certain subjects or events or even people; and a posteriori censorship, which involves the prohibition of the sale of newspapers or magazines, and of the transmission of taped programs for television and radio. A priori censorship (censura prévia) usually takes four different forms. First, a censor is present who oversees all materials and may cut out any parts or all of the material; this censor is a bureaucrat, usually of the Ministry of Justice. Second, journalistic enterprises are forced to send finished material—texts, stories, facts, illustrations, films, and tapes— to a government department (usually physically within the Ministry of Justice) in the same city or even in Brasília. The material that is not approved cannot be published or aired. This process means a considerable financial burden for the enterprises and has caused at times the economic death of an enterprise particularly targeted by the government. This was the case, for example, of one large traditional newspaper, the Correio da Manhã and one weekly paper, Opinião. Third, the government also has the power to close down a journalistic enterprise entirely. Fourth, legal controls and a threat of imprisonment to journalists, editors, or even owners of newspapers are contained in the National Security Law and in a special law known as the Press Law. The articles in these laws prohibit the publication of material deemed to be subversive or threatening to the national-security interests. Journalists, editors, and media owners are personally considered liable and have in reality been often arrested and/or indicted under either

the National Security Law or the Press Law. A posteriori
censorship tends to take similar forms: the seizure of the entire
edition of a printed work or the prohibition of the airing of a
program. A systematic implementation of this control usually
means the economic death of the enterprise. The government
may also just close down a firm's operations after an act of
disobedience in response to an a priori order of censorship.
The firm may have its license revoked or temporarily suspended.
Finally, a threat, an arrest, and indictment, under the National
Security Law and the Press Law, have occurred in cases where
censorship orders were disobeyed or in cases where the material
published passed the censor but irritated the central government. These direct forms of state censorship have led to a
great deal of self-censorship in the press and in television and
radio—principally in the last two, where the threat of cancelation
of the operation license and economic loss is greater. 41

        After 1976, there was a progressive easing of direct censor-
ship of the written media. The physical presence of censors,
and the requirement that materials be previously analyzed by
the Ministry of Justice, elicited a strong press campaign for
freedom of the press. As a consequence of the increasing
pressure, censors were removed from two of the country's
major papers, the conservative Estado de São Paulo and the
more liberal Folha de São Paulo. Censors remained present for
a period at other papers but were gradually removed even from
the alternative-press papers (smaller opposition papers that
have mushroomed as a means of disseminating prevalent opposition views). In 1977, then Press Secretary Toledo Camargo
established the government's new policy: Only radio and television would remain controlled. This is clearly because the largest
newspapers in the country have, at most, 300,000 daily copies.
Radio in Brazil reaches an estimated 85 million people, and television an estimated 45 million, and the written press does not
reach more than 20 million. 42 In a country where 40 percent
of the population is still illiterate and where, of the educated
people, only a small number can afford to purchase products
of the written press, it is clear that the power of radio and
television is comparatively much more politically significant.
Both the a priori and the a posteriori forms of censorship,
therefore, have remained for radio and for television. In fact,
they are also subjected to a further law, known as the Lei Falcão
(named after the minister of justice who decreed it). This law
establishes the conditions under which television must portray
the political candidates for an election. This law was passed
after the MDB electoral victory of 1974—widely believed to have

been achieved principally because, for the first time, the opposition party had been granted free access to television and was thus able to express its views on a variety of issues. Also, it must be emphasized that the restrictions included in the National Security Law and in the Press Law (Lei de Imprensa) are still in effect. The violent forms of control also have increased: 1980 was a year of widespread attacks both on the offices of alternative newspapers and on newsstands that sell them. Bombs and incendiary weapons have exploded in the offices of two different newspapers and burned newspaper stands all across the nation.

Theater, literature, cinema, and music have all been subjected to strict censorship controls. Plays are subjected to both a priori censorship, when the censor reads and cuts out material from the text, and to the presence of censors at the performance. A theater or cultural performance must provide four free tickets to censors so that they can attend the show or the play and testify that what was said is in conformity with the previously censored text. Songs have to be subjected to prior censorship and if the words are not approved by the Federal Police, then the song can only be played, and not sung. The same is true for the cinema. Books have been often censored and publication prohibited. In 1976 a further law was passed by the then Minister of Justice Armando Falcão, whereby books, magazines, newspapers, and journals received from foreign countries would be subjected to censorship. Culture became identified with opposition views and, as such, cultural activities have been considered suspect and are often repressed and censored. Since 1976, the overt acts of repression—such as invasion of a play or cultural activity—have ceased. Censorship, however, has not ended or even diminished. It is now a regular part of the bureaucracy and all works must be cleared through the Federal Police Censorship Department. Censors have been more lenient in their judgment and some previously prohibited works have since been approved for publication. But the process of the censorship stays the same. [43]

The Control of the Trade Unions

Because of the strength of the organized trade union movement prior to the takeover by the military, this has been an important area of control. [44] One of the definitive choices made by those in power, right from the beginning, has been the pursuit of a particular model of economic development very much

dependent on foreign capital investment. The consequence of
such a choice was the need to make sure that there was security
for foreign investment and an exceptional investment climate.
Translated into political language, this meant an apparatus for
the control of dissent and conflict as well as specific legislation
and regulations to control wages. Thus, one of the first actions
of the new government in 1964 was to pass a law that has now
become known as the belt-tightening law. This legislation established that all salaries were thenceforth to be raised by decree
only, once per year, according to a percentage rate to be stipulated by the federal government (the índice oficial) and added
to the salary of all workers. The rate of increase has been consistently kept below the rate of inflation. A DIEESE study
published in May 1980 showed that the metalworkers of São
Bernardo, for example, should have asked for a 240-percent
raise in salary if they expected to regain the salary lost from
below-inflation raises since 1965.[45] One should point out here
that these are among the best-paid workers in the country.
Because of this law, trade unions cannot engage in direct collective bargaining with employers and discuss freely the question
of salary.

Workers also had their right to strike severely limited. I
have already mentioned the clauses included in the National
Security Law that prohibit strikes. Besides these, the executive
passed Decree-Law Number 4,330, on June 1, 1964. This law
regulates the situations under which workers may legally declare
a strike. The regulations are such that in practice the only
strikes that have occurred since 1964 and have been considered
legal involved crass exploitation—such as nonpayment of the
workers for three or more months. This law's Article Number 23
established that strikes would be absolutely prohibited in activities deemed essential: water, energy, light, gas, sewage,
garbage, communications, transport, port work, funeral work,
hospitals, maternities, sale of foodstuffs, pharmacies, hotels,
and basic and essential industries for national defense.[46]
Government workers, at all levels, were already prohibited from
striking under the National Security Laws. In 1979 another
decree-law extended the sector of essential services to include
bank workers.

It is clear that the legislation is meant to ensure the silence
of the working population and establish the secure investment
climate necessary to attract foreign investment and implement
the particular economic model chosen. One of the most important
ways of ensuring silence, besides overt and direct repression,
is to control the trade unions. Here, the military that took

power in 1964 found a ready-made body of legislation: The
Brazilian Labor Code, under its Article V, which deals with
the organizational structure of trade unions, is a literal copy
of Mussolini's Labor Code. Passed under the period of dictatorship of Getúlio Vargas, in 1943, this legislation has been left
unchanged through all of these years, its main control mechanisms surviving even during the periods of democratic government. It is the world's only living piece of fascist legislation
still in effect. The military left it largely untouched, making
only some further changes that increased its power of control.
One such change stipulates that the union may have its operating
license suspended, or even dissolved altogether, if the union
leaders make comments critical of the government's economic
policies. This line was added to an existing article dealing
with the conditions under which the government may cancel
the union's registration and close it.[47] Other changes include
Article 530, which deals with the occasions when a person is
considered to be ineligible, i.e., unable to run for office. This
article was changed on February 28, 1967, to include in the
prohibitions the candidacy of those who had lost their political
rights and of those "who publicly defend the program or ideas
of an abolished political party or belong to an association or
organization which has been considered to be against the national
interest."[48] This article also considers to be "ineligible" all
those who have been removed from an administrative office or
from their trade union post.[49] This article began a policy of
requiring atestado ideológico (ideological clearing) for those
who desired to run for office at any level in the trade union
structure. Thus, its power of control was made pervasive,
and it effectively cut out from trade union activities any budding
leadership or established leadership that proved challenging.
Article 549 deals with the budgetary controls of the trade unions
and establishes that "the budget of unions, federations, and
confederations must be spent as established in their annual
report." This line was added in 1976 to emphasize the importance
of the presentation of the annual budget to the Ministry of
Labor. Article 553, which establishes the penalties for infractions (ranging from a fine to suspension of the directors for
30 days, to removal from office or even a closing down of the
union altogether). Decree-Law Number 925, of October 10,
1969, added two paragraphs to it: The first read that penalties
for the administrators personally would not imply that the
association itself could not be penalized or vice versa. The
second stated that officials could be removed from office as a
preventive measure taken upon the filing of a formal charge.[50]

To summarize, the most important control mechanisms
established by the Labor Code are the following: First, the
government can intervene and has the right to remove union
officials from office simply through a governmental decree-law
of the Ministry of Labor. Second, an official who has been
removed from his post cannot hold elected office at any level
of the trade union structure for the rest of his life. This is
why trade union leader Luis Ignácio da Silva (called Lula),
president of the Metalworkers' Union of São Bernardo do Campo
and Diadema, told me in an interview that this article of the
code is the "Institutional Act Number Five of the worker."[51]
The intervention in a union accomplishes the cassação of the
removed official. In 1979, when the Metalworkers' Union of São
Bernardo and Diadema suffered its first intervention, Lula's
return to his post was only possible with a decree-law that
revoked the intervention. It was the first such occurrence and
came as a surprise. Third, the government has final say on
the recognition of trade unions and has the ability to create
trade unions on its own; these are called "ghost unions" and
are important for reasons I shall discuss below.[52] The government's power to cancel the registration and to close down a
union is also a strong deterrent to free union activity. Fourth,
the government determines which professions shall be included
in one union and the territorial boundaries of the union. This
article has been widely used by the military governments to
break up a trade union that was highly organized and to divide
it into two or more professional unions, thus weakening the
strength of the organization. Indeed, because of the power of
the São Bernardo do Campo and Diadema Metalworkers' Union,
which carried out three massive strikes, each involving 200,000
workers (in 1978, 1979, and 1980), the minister of labor is now
considering breaking it up into three or four unions. Sometimes
the opposite is done, but for the same reason, with the purpose
of diluting the strength of a small but well-organized and effective union. Some of the labor leaders I interviewed have emphasized this aspect of the Labor Code as being most important.

Finally, the structure of trade union organization is established in Articles 533 to 539 of the Labor Code's Title V. It
follows a typical corporative pattern: In it, trade unions are
to be established by category and with preestablished territorial
boundaries. The various local trade unions may form a federation for their particular profession at a state level. The many
state federations for a profession may then form a confederation.
This pyramidal structure is an important mechanism of social
control for the following reasons. Trade union officials are

elected directly by union members at the local union level. The ballot includes two names to fill posts for federative representation. Thus, each trade union has the right to two representatives at the federative level. All of the trade unions of the profession, independently of the number of members represented by the union, have the right to two representatives at the federative level, but only one vote. The federations of all professional groups elect the confederation officials. In practice, this works as follows: The Metalworkers' Union of Rio de Janeiro, for example, which represents 250,000 metalworkers, has the same voting voice that the Metalworkers' Union of Niterói, which represents only 9,000 metalworkers, has, or that even smaller trade unions, with as little as 100 workers, have. It is here that the government's ability to create the ghost unions becomes politically important. The government has created a large number of small unions throughout the country. This structure enables the government to maintain a tight control over the small unions, since the government also controls budgets. The small unions are also a guarantee of governmental control of the federations and of the confederations. Therefore, it is rare indeed that you will find a federative union official (and especially a confederation union official) who in fact represents the workers or even who represents the viewpoint of the largest and most representative trade unions. It is extremely difficult to have any real influence at both the federation and the confederation levels of the union structure or to remove any official from office. In fact, some federation and confederation officials have held their posts for 30 years and are practically immune to dissent and pressure from below.

An important feature of this pyramidal trade union structure (see Figure 12.2) is that it prevents collective organization across professional groupings. It is against the Labor Code for trade unions to meet at a local level and to establish formal coordinating-organization structures. An interunion central is prohibited. Thus, a metalworker-union official cannot coordinate activities with a bank worker, or a transport worker, or any other professional groups. He may meet only other metalworkers affiliated with his federation. The federations, similarly, cannot coordinate actions among themselves. They may coordinate functions only at the confederation level. The penalty for infringement is governmental intervention and removal of the elected officials from office.

In addition, the structure of the labor unions prevents any form of horizontal organization across job categories. This aspect is demonstrated in Figure 12.3, which presents the

FIGURE 12.2. The Pyramidal Structure of Labor Unions

FIGURE 12.3. The Representational Structure of the Labor Unions

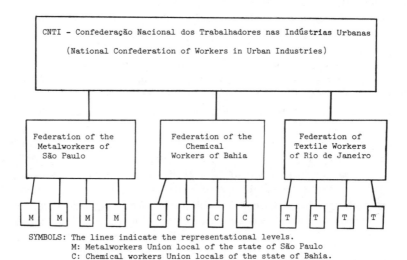

SYMBOLS: The lines indicate the representational levels.
M: Metalworkers Union local of the state of São Paulo
C: Chemical workers Union locals of the state of Bahia.
T: Textile workers Union locals of the state of Rio de Janeiro.

Note: The confederation and federation names are examples that apply only to these industries.

representational structures of the unions; the lines indicate
representation levels. As one can see, the entire organizational
structure is vertical so as to ensure a maximum degree of centralization at the federation and confederation levels. The
Ministry of Labor, at the top of the pyramid, controls vertically
the representation structure of labor. This is an inherent part
of Section V of the Brazilian Labor Code, following closely an
established corporative pattern.

Another important mechanism of control of the trade unions
is the budgetary control by the government. The budget of
the unions in Brazil comes, for the most part, from a deduction
in the salary of all Brazilian workers and from an enforced union
contribution from employers; this is considered a tax and is
known as the imposto sindical. The salary deduction is equivalent
to one day's salary per year and is taken from all salaried
workers, whether or not they are unionized. This fund goes
to the Ministry of Labor, which is then responsible for the
distribution of the fund among all of the unions. In the act of
distributing the union tax fund, the government ensures its
control of trade unions: Budgets have to be carefully drawn
up and submitted to the Ministry of Labor each year. They
must conform to conditions carefully established in the Labor
Code. A trade union must follow the legally defined percentage
of spending for various activities: medical care for union members, dental care, complementary adult education, judicial
assistance, day-care centers, and cooperatives. When added
up, the health and education assistance that the government
requires trade unions to provide consume the largest part of
the total budget. In fact, trade unions have been transformed
by the military into organizations of social welfare, rather than
organizations set up to defend the economic interests of the
union members. They have been made to take on a burden that
in reality should belong to the federal and state governments.
The budget a union submits must be approved by the Ministry
of Labor. Violations can be punished with fines, a suspension
of directors, intervention, or even dissolution of the union.[53]
Perhaps even more serious is the fact that trade unions must
deposit all of their income, whether it comes from the salary
tax or from union dues or any other source, in one particular
bank account. This bank account may be blocked by the government when it sees fit—for instance, when it decides that some
of the budgetary percentages have been violated. Many of the
trade union leaders whom I interviewed pointed to this control
as being terribly important and effective in ensuring total compliance with governmental wishes.

In spite of the strict controls, the trade union movement
has grown increasingly independent and organized. The main
demand is, of course, for freedom from direct control of the
Ministry of Labor. The new trade union movement is concerned
with the issues of trade union autonomy, the right to have direct
bargaining with the employers, the right to strike, and the right
to coordinate interunion activities and to set up contacts with
international union organizations, without prior governmental
approval.[54] The question of the wage policy of the government
has also been a major point in the trade union list of demands.
In response to growing pressures, the military government
passed a decree-law in 1979 that established that salaries are
now to be raised twice per year and that unions may negotiate
directly with their employers for an increase proportionate to
the productivity rate.[55] This has not been a satisfactory issue
and has elicited another series of debates. The government
also has taken the initiative in proposing major changes in the
Labor Code itself and has drafted a law project to that effect.
The trade unions, however, have been against this project,
for it incorporates many of the same control mechanisms of the
present Labor Code. Through much of 1979 and 1980, the
unions active in the new union movement have held assemblies,
and promoted conferences and study groups, to analyze the
government's proposed modifications to the Labor Code. As a
result of their endeavors, they have come up with a consensus
position and drafted an alternative Labor Code to present to
Congress and to the federal government.[56] This has, so far,
been ignored by the authorities. It indicates, however, the
degree of maturity and of organization of the new trade union
movement. The government's consistent refusal to even engage
in dialogue with the trade unions, and its responding with
repression instead of negotiation, have increased tension in
the area and has brought the new trade union movement into
direct confrontation with the federal government.

The Control of the Military

As has already been mentioned, the military did not escape
the general network of control established by the national
security state. Marcus Figueiredo points out in his work that
the military actually suffered more punishments from the institutional acts than did the civilian bureaucrats.[57] The national-
security state has had to mount a vast apparatus for the control
of the military itself. Military personnel on active duty are not

allowed to express dissent or to make public political comments.
Table 12.3 presents the total number of military personnel
punished by the institutional acts. Table 12.4 presents the
number of those who suffered other kinds of punishment, including arrest and suspension. Again, it must be emphasized
that these data indicate only those cases that were published
or personally known to military personnel who were interviewed.
They are a sample of the degree of coercion that the national-
security state must apply to control dissent within the military
itself. The incompleteness of the data results from the problem
of compiling information which often is unpublished.

In the interviews I conducted with military personnel, one
of the most common points emphasized was the importance of
the number of military personnel who were punished.58 It
showed, they pointed out, that they themselves are divided,
that they are not all in favor of brutality, of torture, of repression, and of economic injustice. It, furthermore, shows that
those who are not in favor are sometimes also brutally repressed.
And yet, many have been brave enough to face the consequences
of their defiance. It was further emphasized that they, as a
part of society, often coming from the middle classes, are also
deeply influenced by prevailing public opinion. Many seemed
to have been particularly influenced by the positions of the
Catholic church.

The military, however, is subjected to an aggravating
punishment. Once a member of the military has been punished
by any of the institutional acts or their complementary acts, he
is declared to be legally "dead." This means essentially that
he loses all the benefits he has gained as a military person—such
as pensions, retirement benefits, promotion pay, health and
education benefits, and aid to children. But a wife gets a
widow's pension. This has often been a source of trouble, for
there were some cases of separation where the punished military
man was left with no source of income at all. A punished military
man who has been declared "dead" has great difficulty finding
even a civilian job. According to a general who was cassado,
the limitations are so severe that just about the only remaining
right is to pay income tax. He added, smiling, that for 16 years,
he has written across his income tax form: "I am dead."

Needless to say, this exotic mechanism for the control of
the military is a powerful deterrent to opposition within the
armed forces. It should be emphasized that the repressive
apparatus reaches into the military as well, through the Second
Sections of each of the three branches of the armed forces,
through the Military Police, and the naval fusiliers. Since these

TABLE 12.3. Control of the Military: State Action and Punishment Based on Institutional Acts Numbers One, Two, and Five (1964-80)

Branch of the Armed Forces	Expelled and fired	Put on Reserve	Total
Army			
Higher officers	32	163	195
Sergeants and lower officers	79	174	253
Corporals and soldiers	12	0	12
Total	123	337	460
Navy			
Higher officers	16	12	28
Sergeants and lower officers	16	272	288
Corporals and sailors	196	167	363
Total	228	451	679
Air force			
Higher officers	26	103	129
Sergeants and lower officers	241	79	320
Corporals and soldiers	47	0	47
Total	314	182	496
Naval fusiliers			
Higher officers	8	2	10
Sergeants and lower officers	21	22	43
Corporals and soldiers	23	2	25
Total	52	26	78
Military Police			
Higher officers	19	10	29
Sergeants and lower officers	2	5	7
Corporals and soldiers	41	15	56
Total	62	30	92
Total number of military punished by institutional acts			1,805

Sources: Diário Oficial da União; data from interviews, and data compiled by the Central Computer System of the Brazilian National Congress. The data gathering took place between 1978 and 1980.

TABLE 12.4. Control of the Military: Other Punishment,
Including Disciplinary Arrests and Suspension

Branch of the Armed Forces	Number of Published Cases
Army	
Higher officers	2
Sergeants and lower officers	15
Corporals and soldiers	12
Total	29
Navy	
Higher officers	2
Sergeants and lower officers	3
Corporals and sailors	4,707
Total	4,712
Air force	
Higher officers	2
Sergeants and lower officers	6
Corporals and soldiers	9
Total	17
Naval fusiliers	
Higher officers	0
Sergeants and lower officers	3
Corporals and soldiers	5
Total	8
Military Police	
Higher officers	5
Sergeants and lower officers	0
Corporals and soldiers	16
Total	21
Total punished	4,787

Sources: Data are based on interviews and on research in
Veja, Isto É, Journal do Brasil, Movimento, Tribuna da Imprensa,
O Globo, Folha de Sao Pualo, and O Estado de São Paulo; as
well as on data gathered by the Associaçao Brasileira pela Defesa
dos Atingidos Pelos Atos Institucionais. It should be pointed
out that these are incomplete data, based only on what is published or known to political actors.

Second Sections are organically structured down to the regiment and the battalion level, one can readily see that the degree of control is extremely high.

The military officers are ruled by a special Military Code that establishes the legal structure and the penalties to be decided by military courts. Besides the regulations of the Military Code, they are subjected to the Internal Disciplinary Regulations (Regimento Disciplinar Interno) in each of the branches. These are statutes that control the political activities of the members by prohibiting, among other things, public comment or political expression.

It is interesting to note here, as a sign of growing discontent within the military, that President Figueiredo found it necessary in 1979 to pass a decree-law that extends to those military officers now in the Reserves the same prohibitions that used to be in effect only for active-duty officers. This decree came as a response to a growing number of political expressions of disapproval coming from officers in the Reserves. It clarifies the divisions among the officers themselves and the nature of the isolation of the military group that controls executive power.

CONCLUSION: PROSPECTS FOR THE 1980s

What have been the economic, social, and political consequences of the model I have described? What are the prospects for Brazil, in the 1980s, considering the entire structural apparatus that comprises the national-security state and has been developed over the past 16 years?

First, the economic model that has been pursued—decidedly geared for the achievement of a position of power within the context of geopolitical considerations, rather than for the fulfillment of basic needs—has now reached a bottleneck. The early deflationary policies of the governments of Castello Branco and Costa e Silva reduced the rate of inflation temporarily. However, it has slowly climbed since 1975, until, at the end of 1980, it had reached Brazil's highest rate of inflation in history: a total of 113 percent.[59] In addition, the alarming escalation of the foreign debt, demonstrated in Table 12.5, has caused a serious drain in the total gross national product due to the constantly increasing percentages of total export income that must be spent simply to service the foreign debt. By 1980 the service of the foreign debt cost Brazil a total of close to $13 billion.

As a consequence of the escalation of the foreign debt and the inflation, the economic policies of the government have be-

TABLE 12.5. Brazil, Foreign Debt and Reserves, 1964-80

Year	Debt (in millions of dollars)	Reserves (in millions)
1964	2,942	244
1965	2,400	—
1966	2,956	421
1967	3,372	199
1968	3,917	257
1969	4,403	656
1970	5,295	1,187
1971	6,622	1,723
1972	9,521	4,183
1973	12,572	6,416
1974	17,600	5,267
1975	22,300	4,071
1976	25,985	6,500
1977	32,000	6,700
1978	42,000	12,000
1979	49,000	9,600
1980	58,500	6,900

Sources: Marcos Arruda, Herbet de Souza, and Carlos Afonso, Multinationals and Brazil: The Impact of Multinational Corporations in Contemporary Brazil (Toronto: Brazilian Studies, Latin America Research Unit, 1975); Veja, October 15, 1975, p. 22; Veja, November 17, 1976, p. 134; Veja, July 6, 1977, p. 96; Isto É, July 7, 1978, p. 82; Movimento, February 9-15, 1981, p. 15.

come reduced to desperate attempts to increase exports while, at the same time, applying the brakes upon the economy so as to reduce imports, lower inflation rates, and try to balance the budget. The resulting deep recession has added to the already enormous problems of the economy and the society.

Furthermore, the economic model pursued by the military national-security state provided specific advantageous conditions for the penetration of multinational capital.[60] This has created a pattern of consistent denationalization of the economy—a factor which now aggravates the economic problems, for major decisions

are not made in Brasília (in spite of all the emphasis there upon
centralized planning) but, rather, are made in New York, Detroit,
Japan, Germany, and Canada, to name only some of the major
investors. Table 12.6 presents the tripartite alliance of foreign
multinational corporations, private national capital, and state
capital per sector of industry. As may be seen, the most dynamic
modern sectors of the economy are predominantly under the
majority control of multinational capital. The effects of decapital-
ization of the Brazilian economy may be seen in Table 12.7, which
shows the ratio of capital brought to Brazil to capital remitted
out of the country either in the form of profits, or payments
for technology.

The most important consequences of the economic model
pursued by the national-security state under the protection of
the system of control of dissent have been the social costs and
the increasing impoverishment of the majority of the population.
The economic model is based upon a high rate of exploitation
and upon a greatly unequal distribution of income.

The worsening distribution of income has been apparent
since the period of economic growth known as the economic
miracle. This has become a more marked characteristic of the
model, as may be seen in the data presented in Table 12.8, which
gives the distribution of income from 1960 to 1976.

The majority of Brazilian workers are paid monthly salaries
that range in between two and three minimum salaries. The
minimum salary is regularly used in statistical analyses of the
real income of the economically active population and in measure-
ments of distribution of income. In 1979, as may be seen in
Table 12.9, a total of 67.6 percent of the economically active
population in Brazil earned up to three minimum salaries. Only
5.9 percent of the population earned more than the equivalent
of ten minimum salaries per month. In dollar terms for 1979,
this means that the majority of the population earned only $41.65
per month and that only 5.9 percent earned over $400 per
month. [61]

In addition, a study by the DIEESE, on the evolution of
the minimum salary, reached the conclusion that by 1976 the
real minimum salary in Brazil had only 31 percent of the value
it had held in 1959. [62] Therefore, workers had to work a greater
number of hours so as to earn a sufficient salary to purchase
the minimum food basket legally considered to be necessary for
survival of the worker and his family. In 1965, just after the
implantation of the national-security state, a worker needed 88
hours and 16 minutes to buy food for a month for his family.
By 1978, according to a DIEESE study, it was necessary to work

TABLE 12.6. The Role of Private-National, Multinational, and
State Firms in the Various Sectors of the Brazilian Economy, 1978

Sector	Private-National (percent)	Multi-national (percent)	State (percent)
Predominantly National Firms			
Civil construction	100.0	—	—
Communications	100.0	—	—
Supermarkets	98.3	1.7	—
Furniture	97.4	2.6	—
Clothing, shoes	96.9	3.1	—
Retail business	90.0	10.0	—
Heavy construction	88.7	8.5	2.8
Printing and publishing	73.8	26.2	—
Food	66.6	33.4	—
Pulp and paper	59.9	32.9	7.2
Nonmetallic minerals	58.0	42.0	—
Predominantly Foreign Firms			
Wholesale business	41.4	42.2	16.4
Machinery	41.5	48.8	9.7
Transportation equipment	37.7	53.6	8.7
Heavy vehicles	45.2	54.8	—
Petroleum distribution	11.0	60.8	28.2
Electronics	33.6	66.4	—
Textiles	31.8	68.2	—
Cleaning products	27.2	72.8	—
Plastics and rubber	21.5	76.1	2.4
Beverages and tobacco	23.6	76.4	—
Pharmaceuticals	15.6	84.4	—
Office equipment	13.8	86.2	—
Automobiles	0.6	99.4	—
Predominantly State Firms			
Public services	—	—	100.0
Chemicals and petrochemicals	5.0	15.8	79.2
Steel	27.1	7.9	65.0
Minerals	29.5	12.0	58.5
Transportation	49.6	—	50.4

Sources: "Melhores e Maiores," Exame, September 1979, p. 125; these figures refer to the sales of the 20 largest firms in each sector. Also, Sylvia Ann Newlett, The Cruel Dilemmas of Development: 20th Century Brazil (New York: Basic Books, 1980).

TABLE 12.7. Transnational Companies in Brazil, January 1965-July 1975

| Company | Total Capital Brought into Brazil, Including Years before 1965 | Their Impact in U.S. $ Million | | | | | Ratio of Surplus Generated in Brazil to Capital Brought into Brazil |
		Reinvestment	Profits and Dividends Remitted Abroad	Remittances in Payment for Technology	Total Remittances Abroad	Surplus Generated in Brazil	
Volkswagen	119.5	72.8	70.6	208.5	279.1	351.9	2.94
Rhodia	14.3	108.7	39.9	20.7	60.6	169.3	11.84
Exxon	1.8	67.7	44.5	—	44.5	112.3	62.33
Pirelli	28.7	37.8	41.5	19.8	64.9	102.7	3.58
Phillips	9.9	51.2	5.0	9.4	14.4	65.6	6.63
Firestone	4.1	44.5	48.1	2.1	50.2	94.7	23.1
General Electric	13.9	32.2	19.4	4.3	23.7	55.9	4.02
Souza Cruz	2.5	129.5	81.3	1.0	82.3	211.8	84.7
Johnson & Johnson	0.7	28.2	16.8	—	16.8	45.0	32.14
Brazilian Light	102.0	86.4	114.7	0.6	115.3	201.7	1.98
Total	298.8	693.0	502.4	272.1	774.5	1467.7	4.91

Sources: Report of the parliamentary investigation into MNCs in Brazil in 1975, published in Diario do Congresso Nacional, No. 79 (supplement), July 1, 1976; Floriano Gomes da Silva, "National Security and Foreign Capital in Brazil" (Master's thesis, University of Texas, Austin, 1980), p. 126. The same table appears in Sylvia Ann Hewlett, The Cruel Dilemmas of Development: 20th Century Brazil (New York: Basic Books, 1980), p. 229, where, however, the last column is miscalculated.

TABLE 12.8. Income Concentration in Brazil, 1960-76
(in percentages of GNP)

Economically Active Population	GNP Share per Year		
	1960	1970	1976
Poorest 50 percent	17.71	14.91	11.6
Next poorest 30 percent	27.92	22.85	21.2
Middle 15 percent	26.60	27.38	28.0
Richest 5 percent	27.69	34.86	39.0

Source: Isto É, August 9, 1979, p. 65.

TABLE 12.9. Distribution of Income (by minimum salary)
in Brazil, 1979

Salary per Month	Percentage of Economically Active Population, 1979
Number of minimum salaries received	
Less than 1	11.5
Between 1 and 2	38.0
Between 2 and 3	18.1
Between 3 and 7	22.3
Between 7 and 10	4.2
More than 10	5.9
Total	100.0

Note: One minimum salary in 1979 was Cr$ 2,166. The exchange rate in December 1979 was Cr$ 52 per U.S. dollar.
Sources: Ministério do Trabalho, Relação Anual de Informações Sociais (Brasília, 1979); also published in Isto É, December 17, 1980.

137 hours and 37 minutes so as to purchase the same amount of basic foodstuffs. [63] Table 12.10 shows the consequences of the deterioration of the real salaries of workers in terms of total number of working hours needed to purchase sufficient food for survival.

One of the most serious consequences of the falling living standards of the majority of the working population, since the military takeover in 1964, has been the increase of child labor as a result of extreme poverty. As may be seen in Table 12.11, a Congressional Investigation Committee, analyzing the situation of children in Brazil in 1975, came to the alarming conclusion that a total of over 15 million needy and abandoned children existed in the country. In order to complement the family income for survival, an increasing number of children must work between 29 and over 40 hours per week. In 1976, out of 13,748,646 children between ages 10 and 14 in the country, a study conducted under the auspices of the Catholic church concluded, as many as 2,533,122 children worked out of a need to supplement the family income. Of these working children, a total of 68 percent had to labor over 40 hours a week to earn a sufficient salary to pay for transportation and food. [64]

Clearly, such a situation of plight and social injustice has profound social ramifications. In order to maintain such a long-term rate of exploitation, the successive governments have been forced to build a comprehensive system of social and political control designed to stifle dissent, protest, and legitimate interest-group pressure. In spite of the variety of mechanisms of control, however, the disparities of income have been the real roots of consistent and growing opposition. For an extreme general framework of social-economic inequality and poverty breeds dissent and conflict that surpass the ability of the state to regulate, suppress, or eliminate them.

Therefore, in spite of the control mechanisms imposed by the state in all areas of civil society, a large social movement of opposition has been fueled by the inequality and surfaced at the forefront of the political arena, particularly after 1974.

By 1979 Brazil had an unprecedented number of strikes for better pay and working conditions; in the course of the year, there were an estimated 113 strikes, with more than 3 million workers actively involved. These were met with severe governmental repression and intervention in a number of trade unions or associations. However, the government recognized the real social roots of the strikes and modified the salary legislation to provide for twice-a-year salary increases that would somewhat offset the effects of the high rate of inflation.

TABLE 12.10. Minimum Salary and Minimum Monthly Food
Ration: Work Time Necessary to Purchase the Minimum Food
Ration (as defined by decree-law 399 of April 30, 1938)
per Year

Year	Work Time Needed	Index
1959	65 hours and 05 minutes	100.00
1960	81 hours and 30 minutes	125.22
1961	71 hours and 34 minutes	110.47
1962	94 hours and 48 minutes	145.66
1963	98 hours and 20 minutes	151.09
1965	88 hours and 16 minutes	135.62
1966	109 hours and 16 minutes	167.86
1967	105 hours and 16 minutes	161.74
1968	101 hours and 35 minutes	156.08
1969	110 hours and 23 minutes	169.69
1970	105 hours and 13 minutes	161.66
1971	111 hours and 47 minutes	171.75
1972	119 hours and 08 minutes	183.05
1973	147 hours and 04 minutes	225.97
1974	163 hours and 32 minutes	251.27
1975	149 hours and 40 minutes	229.96
1976	157 hours and 29 minutes	241.97
1977	141 hours and 49 minutes	217.90
1978	137 hours and 37 minutes	211.45

Note: In the entire period, there were two moments in
which the value of the minimum salary reached its peak in
purchasing power: in July of 1956 and in January 1959. If one
should calculate the minimum salary of July 1956 in 1979 currency,
the minimum salary of 1956 would be, in 1979 money, Cr$
4,963.00, or three times the value of the minimum salary of
1979. One can obtain a measure of the purchasing power of the
minimum salary also by calculating the cost of purchasing the
minimum daily essential foodstuffs for one month. As the minimum salary lost its purchasing power, the worker had to work
more hours to earn enough to purchase the same food basket.
In 1959 the median monthly work time hours necessary to purchase the minimum food basket was 65 hours and 5 minutes. By
1978 this same food basket cost the worker a total of 137 hours
and 37 minutes of work time.
Source: Departamento Intersindical de Estatísticas e Estudos
Sócio-Econômicos, Separata da Revista do DIEESE, April 1979.

TABLE 12.11. Abandoned and Needy Children in Brazil, 1975

Region	Abandoned		Needy	
	Number	Percentage	Number	Percentage
Northwest	58,284	30.0	536,142	4.0
Northeast	776,200	40.7	5,104,203	37.7
North	854,849	44.8	5,052,617	37.3
Center-West	157,178	8.2	2,353,586	17.4
South	63,059	3.3	495,960	3.6
Brazil (total)	1,909,570	100.0	13,542,508	100.0

Note: Although the Congressional Investigation Committee of the Minor officially reached the estimate of 15 million abandoned and needy children in Brazil (in 1975), the CPI concluded that the correct number of children without the most minimal basic needs approaches the total of 25 million. The Investigation Committee also concluded that the cause of the abandonment of children is the extreme misery of the population, brought about by the concentration of income in the country, where, according to data of the committee, in 1975, 50 percent of the poorest received 11.8 percent of the income and the richest 5 percent of the population received up to 39 percent of the total income.

Source: Data are from the Comissão Parlamentar de Inquérito do Menor (Brasília), and published in A Situação da Criança no Brasil (Rio de Janeiro: Edições Muro, 1979), p. 23.

In 1980 the total number of strikers went down to 675,700, partly as a result of the new salary policy combined with the repression. Significantly, however, in the countryside the activity of peasants organized for better working conditions and higher salaries increased. Sugarcane workers in Pernambuco organized a vast, coordinated rural movement involving the church's basic community groups and 31 rural trade unions, so as to press for a series of longstanding demands. A two-day strike by an estimated 250,000 sugarcane workers was victorious in achieving some of the most important demands of peasants.

The Catholic church has moved into the forefront of the opposition, taking a firm position in support of the rights of the workers, denouncing the inequality and social injustice, and the repression of workers and peasants. This support led the state to develop specific legislation for control of foreign missionaries, the Foreigners' Law, passed in 1980.

In turn, the Foreigners' Law has increased and intensified both the church-state conflict and the isolation of the state from civil society.

This isolation has become manifested and instrumentalized in the growth of opposition parties that challenge the national-security state's majority control of the federal Congress in important votes. The Party of the Brazilian Democratic Movement, the largest of the opposition parties, has been able to organize more municipal directories in the short period between the end of 1979 and the end of 1981 than its parent MDB had organized in its entire existence. The Popular Party, a center-conservative party, is showing impressive growth in the midstate of Minas Gerais, where the government's party was believed to predominate. The Workers' Party is now the third largest opposition party and has been catapulted by an informal alliance of church activists and trade unionists in both the urban and rural areas. It has been able to gather the support of 300,000 affiliates in the period of slightly over one year since it won its judicial recognition. The smaller parties of the opposition have also been able to complete all the intricate legal requirements of the Party Law. It was expected that, between them, the opposition parties would win the gubernatorial posts in Rio de Janeiro, Minas Gerais, Paraná, São Paulo, Rio Grande do Sul, Pernambuco, Santa Catarina, and Mato Grosso, if the elections of November 1982 were in fact freely held.

Perhaps the most impressive development of the past few years has been the growth of the grassroots organizations of the neighborhoods and the movement of peasants and squatters in the countryside. The variety of forms of organization and the widespread nature of the militancy promise to provide an interesting alternative of political participation in decisions of government, by pushing for reforms from below. The strength of the social movement demands a transformation of the economic model so as to provide for the basic needs of the majority of the population.

However, the military people, who have become isolated at the top of the structures of the National-security state, do not seem to be willing to either consider structural reforms in the economic model or even to give up a part of their monopoly of power. In fact, they may be willing to employ a great deal of renewed violent coercion so as to bring the population under control through fear. For it must be pointed out that the entire framework of repression is intact and ready for use. Although the national-security state is inherently unstable, lacks legitimacy, and is beset by contradictions that create a constant state of institutional crisis, the power of coercion is not—by any means—diminished.

There is a crisis in the economy—a runaway inflation and foreign debt, wage controls, and the repressive controls that are still in effect. However, the growing opposition incorporates new groups and pushes the state into further isolation from civil society. This is a situation that will lead the country to troubled times.

Brazil has reached a critical point where it is clear that deeper changes in the model of development itself must be made. These reforms must touch the root of inequality and injustice and reverse the pattern of income distribution. The strength of the population's organizational structure may be tapped for developmental projects capable of answering to the basic needs of the poor. An enlargement of political participation in the decision making of government could be the key to change from within the policies of development, so that programs conform to the needs and desires of the population.

If, on the other hand, the demands for participation are met with repressive force in a new cycle of coercion, Brazil may become immersed in a diffused and difficult civil and social strife that will tear the fabric of society. For the opposition to unjust policies that cause extreme social inequality and poverty is not likely to be permanently subdued by the simple application of physical violence. A dialectic of violence could be unleashed in a process of pushing large numbers of the population beyond the brink of tolerance—to a point where they have nothing else to lose. Even if extreme violence forces the population into temporary silence, the anger is bound to resurface to provide a different challenge to the national-security state.

The most likely prediction is that a dialectic of state versus opposition, of violence versus abertura (opening up) and liberalization, is likely to continue well into the 1980s. Furthermore, since the dialectical relationship is dynamic and changing—each part affecting the other—the result shall depend upon the process itself.

From the viewpoint of long-term analysis, one concluding remark may be made: If the opposition groups succeed in becoming a unified force, they will have the support of the majority of the population that is needed to put an end to the national-security state and bring a complete transformation of the political, social, and economic model.

If this is to occur through a peaceful transition to democracy, by a slow process of corrosion from below, it depends, to a great extent, upon the acts of the state toward the demands of the opposition for a share of political power and social and economic influence in the state's decision-making apparatus. If force is, once more, utilized to repress all dissent, Brazil may find itself in a position where peaceful transition out of a repressive context becomes impossible. It is to be emphasized that physically violent confrontation in the next few years could throw the country into the trap of violence that would lead it into the dark path followed by Argentina—where state violence is a silent and parallel underground force searching for the enemy within the nation by destroying the population itself.

NOTES

1. The data used in this chapter were compiled from interviews with political actors; from data in Diário Oficial da União, daily issues from April 1964 until July 1980; from articles in Jornal do Brasil, O Estado de São Paulo, A Folha de São Paulo, O Globo, A Tribuna da Imprensa, Ultima Hora, Movimento, Isto É, and Veja; from publications of the Brazilian Council of Bishops (CNBB); church newspapers and bulletins; from trade union newspapers, bulletins, and documents; Brazilian Bar Association (OAB) papers and documents; records in the Anais do Congresso Nacional; documents in the archives of the Brazilian Press Association (ABI) and in the National Council of Churches in New York; and data compiled by the Computer Center of the Brazilian National Congress. Laws and regulations are also available in Atos Institucionais, Atos Complementares e Decretos-lei (Brasília: Diretoria de Informação Legislativa do Senado Federal, 1968), Vols. 1-5.

2. See, for example: Charles W. Anderson, Politics and Economic Change in Latin America: the Governing of Restless Nations (New York: Van Nostrand Reinhold, 1967; David Collier, ed., The New Authoritarianism in Latin America (Princeton: Princeton University Press, 1979); Daniel Cosío Villegas, El Sistema Político Mexicano: Las Posibilidades de Cambio (Mexico City: Editorial Joaquin Mortiz, 1972); Pablo González Casanova, Democracy in Mexico (New York: Oxford University Press, 1970); Kenneth Paul Erickson, The Brazilian Corporative State and Working-Class Politics (Berkeley: University of California Press, 1977); Samuel P. Huntington, "Civilian Control of the Military: a Theoretical Statement," in H. Eulau, S. Eldersweld, and

M. Janowitz, eds., Political Behaviour: A Reader in Theory and Research (New York: Free Press, 1956); Edwin Lieuwen, Generals Versus Presidents: Neo-Militarism in Latin America (New York: Praeger, 1964; Abraham F. Lowenthal, "Armies and Politics in Latin America," World Politics 27 (1974):107-30; Liisa North, Civil Military Relations in Argentina, Chile and Peru (Berkeley: Institute of International Studies, University of California, 1966); Guillermo O'Donnell, Modernization and Bureaucratic-Authoritarianism: Studies in South American Politics (Berkeley: Institute of International Studies, 1973); David Scott Palmer, Revolution from Above: Military Government and Popular Participation in Peru, 1968-1972 (Ithaca: Cornell University Dissertation Series, 1973), No. 47; Philippe C. Schmitter, Interest Conflict and Political Change in Brazil (Stanford: Stanford University Press, 1971); Alfred Stepan, The State and Society: Peru in Comparative Perspective (Princeton: Princeton University Press, 1978); Luis Viana Filho, O Governo Castelo Branco (Rio de Janeiro: Livraria José Olympio Editora, 1976); Jean Marc Von der Weid, Brazil, 1964 to the Present: A Political Analysis (Montreal: Editions Latin America, 1972); Osny Duarte Pereira, A Constituição do Brasil de 1967 (Rio de Janeiro: Editora Civilização Brasileira, S.A., 1967).

    3. I have applied to the political sphere the concept of "displacement of contradictions" developed by James O'Connor in his The Fiscal Crisis of the State (New York: St. Martin's Press, 1973), and subsequently applied in the work of Jürgen Habermas, particularly in his Legitimation Crisis (Boston: Beacon Press, 1973).

    4. For an interesting analysis of the crisis of legitimacy of the Brazilian military governments, see Lúcia Klein, "Brasil Pós-64: A Nova Ordem Legal e a Redefinição das bases de Legitimidade," in Lúcia Klein and Marcus Figueiredo, Legitimidade e Coação no Brasil pós-64 (Rio de Janeiro: Forense-Universitária, 1978).

    5. For more information on the debate on the economic model and on the question of income distribution, see Edmar Bacha, Política e Distribuição de Renda (Rio de Janeiro: Editora Paz e Terra, S.A., 1978); Shelton H. Davis, Victims of the Miracle: Development and the Indians of Brazil (New York: Cambridge University Press, 1977); Helio Jaguaribe, Brasil: Crisis y Alternativas (Buenos Aires: Amorrortu Editores, 1974); Celso Furtado, Development and Underdevelopment: A Structural View of the Problems of Developed and Underdeveloped Countries (Berkeley: University of California Press, 1966); Albert Fishlow, "Some Reflections on Post-1964 Economic Policy," in Alfred Stepan,

ed, Authoritarian Brazil: Origins, Policies and Future (New Haven: Yale University Press, 1973); Álvaro Melo Filho, Teoria e Prática dos Incentivos Fiscais: Introdução ao Direito Premial (Rio de Janeiro: Livraria Eldorado Tijuca Ltda., 1976); Maria de Lurdes Scarfon, Crescimento e Miséria (São Paulo: Edições Símbolo, 1979); Mário Henrique Simonsen, Brasil 2001 (Rio de Janeiro: Apec Editora, S.A., 1969); Paul Singer, A Crise do "Milagre": Interpretação Crítica da Economia Brasileira (Rio de Janeiro: Editora Paz e Terra, S.A., 1977).

6. See Ato Institucional No. 1, in Diário Oficial da União, Ano CII, No. 67, April 9, 1964, p. 3193.

7. Ibid.

8. Marcus Figueiredo, "A Política de Coação no Brasil pós-64," in Klein and Figueiredo, Legitimidade e Coação no Brasil pós-64, op. cit.

9. Institutional Act Number Two (Ato Institucional No. 2), in Diário Oficial da União, Ano CIII, No. 206, October 27, 1965, p. 11017.

10. Figueiredo, op. cit., p. 151.

11. Allegations of torture stimulated a press campaign that forced an investigation in the Northeast. The allegations moved lawyers, and particularly journalists, into the opposition. For a detailed and documented account of torture in this period, see Márcio Moreira Alves, Torturas e Torturados (Rio de Janeiro: Idade Nova Editores, 1966).

12. Institutional Act Number Five (Ato Institucional No. 5), in Diário Oficial da União, Ano CVI, No. 241, December 13, 1968, p. 10802.

13. National Security Law (A Nova Lei de Segurança Nacional), September 29, 1969 (Rio de Janeiro: Gráfica Auriverde, 1973).

14. This concept comes from the National Security Doctrine. The law, in effect, is its implementation. For information on the National Security Doctrine, see Ettore Biocca, Estratégia do Terror: A Face Oculta e Repressiva do Brasil (Lisbon: Iniciativas Editoriais, 1974); José Alfredo Amaral Gurgel, Segurança e Democracia (Rio de Janeiro: Livraria José Olympio, 1975); Edgardo Mercado Jarrín, Seguridad Política, Estrategia (Lima: Ministerio da Guerra, 1974); Arthur D. Larson, National Security Affairs: A Guide to Information Sources (Detroit: Gale Research Co., 1973); Robert S. McNamara, The Essence of Security (New York: Harper and Row, 1968). See also, speeches of the military Brazilian presidents, Humberto Castello Branco, Costa e Silva, Garrastazú Médici, and Ernesto Geisel. The most important data on the National Security Doctrine can be found in the courses

taught at the National War College, the Industrial College of the
Armed Forces, and the Inter-American Defence College, all in
Washington, D.C.; also in Brazil, at the Escola Superior de
Guerra do Brasil; in Argentina, at the Escuela Nacional de
Guerra de la República de Argentina; at the Academia Superior
de Seguridad Nacional, in Chile; at the Peruvian Centro de
Altos Estudios Militares; at Ecuador's Centro de Altos Estudios
Nacionales de Ecuador; and in Bolivia, at the Centro de Estudios
Nacionales de Bolivia.

15. National Security Law, op. cit., Chap. I.

16. Ibid., Article 16.

17. Ibid., Article 45, dealing with subversive propaganda.

18. Ibid., Article 43.

19. Ibid., Article 36.

20. Ibid., Article 39.

21. Ibid., Article 34.

22. Ibid., Article 23.

23. Decree-Law No. 4,341, June 13, 1964, cited in Diário
Oficial da União, Ano CII, No. 113, June 15, 1964, p. 5073.

24. As an illustration, one should mention the difficulties
that President Geisel encountered in his attempt to end the use
of torture for the gathering of information. The confrontation
between the executive and the comunidade de informações reached
its climax in 1975, with the death by torture of journalist Vladmir
Herzog, in the premises of the Sao Paulo DOI-CODI. This death
was followed by the death of worker Manoel Fiel Filho, in similar
circumstances. Geisel retaliated by removing the commander of
the Second Army, General Ednardo D'Avila. This was only a
temporary victory. Other incidents of executive/repressive-
apparatus confrontations have been common in all governments
since 1964.

25. Decree-Law No. 55,194, December 10, 1964, cited in
Diário Oficial da União, Ano CII, Section I, Part I, December 11,
1964, p. 11336. This decree-law regulates the SNI and establishes
formally its structure, organization, budget, and objectives.

26. Torture in Brazil has been the subject of a variety of
documents that describe in detail the kinds of torture that were
used against political prisoners, where they occurred, when,
and to whom. Some documents even give the names and rank
of the torturers; these are too numerous to list. They can be
obtained from the archives of Amnesty International, London,
one of whose documents lists the names of 233 torturers; from
the Association Internationale des Juristes Démocrates, Secré-
tariat, Brussels, especially its Dossier Brésil; and from U.S.,
Congress, report of the Subcommittee on Foreign Assistance,

of the Senate Committee on Foreign Relations, Human Rights Reports, March 1977, and The Status of Human Rights in Selected Countries and the U.S. Response, prepared for the Subcommittee on International Organizations of the House Committee on International Relations, July 25, 1977. See also, documents at the Foreign Affairs and National Defense Division, Congressional Research Service, Library of Congress; at the International Commission of Jurists, Geneva—its document Ill-treatment of Political Prisoners in Brazil; the Documentation Service of the Latin America Bureau of the U.S. Catholic Conference, Washington, D.C.; CIDOC (Centro Intercultural de Documentacion) Cuernavaca, Mexico; documents at the Bertrand Russell Peace Foundation, Nottingham, and its main reports, The Verdict of the Russell Tribunal Session in Brussels, Repression in Latin America: A Report of the Russell Tribunal Session in Rome, and Torture in Brazil: Some Evidence from the Second Russell Tribunal; the archives in the National Council of Churches, New York; archives of the Brazilian National Conference of Bishops (CNBB) in Brasília; archives of the Brazilian Bar Association in Rio de Janeiro and of the Brazilian Press Association in Rio de Janeiro.

27. In 1968 there were a reported nine bomb attacks against six theaters, two schools, and the editorial enterprise Civilização Brazeira. In at least two of the theaters, the press identified 47 members of the CCC (Commando to Hunt Communists, a right-wing organization that has been responsible for a large number of attacks and threats to various people and institutions). In 1976, the AAB (Aliança Anticomunista Brasileira—Brazilian Anti-communist Alliance, another right-wing organization) took responsibility for the majority of the ten bomb attacks that occurred throughout the year. In at least four of them, there was distinct evidence that the members of the security apparatus were involved: The chief of the security forces in São Paulo, Colonel Erasmo Dias, knew at the time who had placed the bomb that exploded in CEBRAP (Centro Brasileiro de Análise e Planejamento), as he has said publicly and has been widely reported as saying in the press. The driver of the car in which Bishop Dom Adriano Hypólito was traveling, when he was kidnapped by terrorists, was left in the place where the Death Squadron usually leaves its victims. The bishop and his nephew were made to wear a hood in the fashion of political prisoners undergoing torture in the DOE-CODI. Witnesses saw and wrote down the license plate of the car that stopped near the newspaper Opinião minutes before a bomb exploded there. Police did not arrest the owner or even interrogate him.

The year 1977 had six terrorist attacks. In 1978, the attacks were centered in Minas Gerais; of the fifteen attacks of the year, 13 were in that state. In 1979 two bombs exploded: at the newspaper El Tempo, in Minas Gerais, and in the car of a trade union leader, president of the Metalworkers' Union of João Monlevade, in Minas Gerais. Finally, since all these incidents of right-wing attacks had remained uninvestigated and those responsible were not punished, the tactic of terror escalated. At the end of 1979, Dom Adriano Hypólito, bishop of Nova Iguaçú, was again threatened with kidnapping several times. The church's walls were painted with the letters of the CCC and insults to the bishop. Finally, just before Christmas, a bomb exploded under the main altar of the Cathedral of Nova Iguaçú. Again, these threats and the bomb attack on the cathedral were not investigated.

In 1980 there was a dramatic rise in terrorist attacks; the year ended with a total of 46 attacks. A new target is the newspaper stand that sells opposition papers and magazines. There have also been kidnappings and beatings, including the kidnapping of jurist Dalmo Dallari, ex-president of the Justice and Peace Committee in São Paulo, who was kidnapped on the eve of the Pope's arrival in that city. Two of the bomb attacks in Rio de Janeiro, in September of 1980, had serious consequences: In the attack on the central offices of the Brazilian Bar Association, a letter bomb addressed to OAB's President Eduardo Seabra Fagundes exploded in the hands of his secretary, Lyda Monteiro da Silva, tearing off her hands and violently killing her. The second bomb of that day exploded in the office of Alderman Antonio Carlos de Carvalho, in Rio de Janeiro's City Hall, and blinded and maimed his uncle who worked in the office. Again, the press has uncovered extensive evidence that points to members of the repressive apparatus and of right-wing terrorist groups widely reputed to work closely with security agencies. President Figueiredo said publicly that he believes these bombs were meant against him, with the policy of slow transition to more democratic forms of government. These incidents also indicate strongly to what degree the comunidade de informações stands as a parallel force to the executive. See Veja, September 3, 1980, for an extensive article on the right-wing attacks. See also: Veja, July 23, 1980; Isto É, July 30, 1980 and September 24, 1980.

28. The Death Squadron (Esquadrão da Morte) is a right-wing paramilitary organization reputed to have as members off-duty policemen of the comunidade de informações. It operates in different states, but is most active in São Paulo, and in Rio

de Janeiro, in the extensive, poor area known as the Baixada
Fluminense. A book that documents the cases of Esquadrão da
Morte executions in São Paulo and in Espírito Santo was written
by a journalist, Ewerton Montenegro Guimarães: A Chancela do
Crime: A Verdadeira História do Esquadrão da Morte (Rio de
Janeiro: Ambito Cultural, 1978). Another book documents the
entire structure and the main components of the organization:
Hélio Bicudo, Meu Depoimento Sobre o Esquadrão da Morte (São
Paulo: Pontifícia Comissão de Justiça e Paz de São Paulo, 1976).
Finally, Adérito Lopes documents each crime committed in São
Paulo by the Death Squadron, from 1968 to 1971, in his book
O Esquadrão da Morte: São Paulo 1968-1971 (Lisbon: Prelo
Editora, Sarl, 1973). Besides these books, the daily press
covers the executions of the Death Squadron in the various
states. It is rare when the press does not mention the discovery
of a new corpse carrying the unmistakable signs of a Death
Squadron execution: The victims are always bound, show the
signs of violent torture, are sometimes hanged, and have a
number of bullets in their bodies. Often a picture of a skull
and crossbones is found on the body or carved into the body
with a knife—it is the emblem of the Death Squadron. According
to the Jornal do Brasil, using data reported by the police, the
Death Squadron has killed in the Baixada Fluminense alone, over
2,000 people (see Jornal do Brasil, June 3, 1979, p. 38). Montenegro Guimarães, in his book A Chancela do Crime, documents
another 20,000 cases of criminal actions of the Esquadrão da
Morte in the state of Espírito Santo. His denunciation of the
crimes won him a trial under the National Security Law and a
prison term of six months; the crimes reported in the book were
not investigated, however (see a report on his imprisonment in
Veja, January 19, 1977). The victims of the Death Squadron
are widely considered to be common criminals, although, in fact,
they have also included trade union leaders, journalists, artists,
and militants in grassroots organizations (see Lopes's account
of this in O Esquadrão da Morte). Since January 1980, the
Death Squadron seems to have changed its name to Mão Branca
(White Hand). From January to June of 1980, I counted 764
executions of the Mão Branca in Rio de Janeiro, all reported in
the daily press.

Besides the organized violence of the Death Squadron and
its successor, the Mão Branca, violence is also used as a daily
routine by the police. Beatings and torture of common prisoners
are reported daily in the press. Some cases have received widespread press coverage, for they involved the suspicious deaths
of suspects. None of the known cases of policemen involved in

brutal beatings or torture resulted in punishment of the police officers. See, for example, the excellent article "It is the Police, Help! ," in Isto É, March 15, 1978. See also: Isto É, March 26, 1980; Isto É, July 2, 1980; Isto É, October 5, 1977; Isto É, October 1, 1980; Veja, June 6, 1979 and Veja, April 12, 1978. All these articles deal with police violence, killings, beatings, and invasion of residences. The violence is so widespread, particularly in the Baixada Fluminense, that its two and a half million residents consider it suicidal to go out after 6 o'clock in the evening.

29. Cited in Luís Viana Filho, O Governo Castelo Branco (Rio de Janeiro: Livraria José Olympio Editora, 1976).

30. Interview with Eduardo Seabra Fagundes, February 8, 1980.

31. See Marcus Figueiredo, op. cit., p. 163.

32. Interview with Seabra Fagundes, February 8, 1980. See also Conselho Federal da O.A.B., As Razões da Autonomia da Ordem dos Advogados do Brasil (Rio de Janeiro, 1975).

33. For a breakdown of the data by federal, state, and municipal areas, see Marcus Figueiredo, op. cit., p. 175-88.

34. For a breakdown of and a list of the names of congressmen and senators purged, and the number of votes each received, see Jornal do Brasil, September 1, 1977, p. 15.

35. For information on this and a list of names, see Jornal do Brasil, July 1, 1977, p. 14.

36. See Jornal do Brasil, December 13, 1977, p. 8.

37. See Marcus Figueiredo, op. cit., p. 175.

38. Popular parlance immediately nicknamed them the "yes" and the "yes sir" parties.

39. The MDB had a surprising victory in the congressional elections of 1974 and then again, despite new electoral controls, in the 1978 congressional elections. It was clearly aiming to win the majority in Congress and perhaps even important gubernatorial posts in the indirect elections.

40. See the documentation on cassação branca compiled by the Committee on Human Rights of the Brazilian Bar Association, in the archives of its central offices in Rio de Janeiro.

41. Paper prepared by journalist Perseu Abramo. I am grateful for the help of the Union of Professional Journalists of São Paulo, which made available to me the material on censorship prepared by its Committee for the Defense of Freedom of the Press, and the papers presented at the National Congress of Journalists in 1976. I have also used data from the Congressional Investigating Committee on Censorship of the Federal Congress, made available to me by Congressman Modesto da Silveira.

42. See the report on censorship in radio and television, presented at the National Congress of Journalists (in Curitiba, Santa Catarina, 1976); and written by Décio Nitrini, Eurenides Pereira, Gabriel Romeiro, Márcia Guedes, Mônica Teixeira, Odair Redondo, Sérgio Leal Maia, and Vera Artaxo. This report can be found in the archives of the Professional Journalists' Union of São Paulo.

43. Information on censorship of cultural activities, as well as a number of documented cases, can be found in the archives of the Brazilian Press Association in Rio de Janeiro; also, in the reports of the Investigating Committee of the Federal Congress; in J. A. Pinheiro Machado, Opinião Versus Censura: Momentos da Luta de um Jornal pela Liberdade (Porto Alegre: L & PM Editores, 1978); and in Index on Censorship: Brazil, Vol. 8, No. 4, July-August 1979, which can be obtained from the Oxford University Press (Journals), London, or from Index on Censorship, New York.

44. For information on the trade unions in Brazil, see, for example: Erickson, op. cit., Latin American Perspectives, Issue 23, Vol. 6, No. 4, Fall 1979; Latin American Perspectives, Issue 24, Vol. 7, No. 1, Winter 1980; Campanhole-Santos, Entidades Sindicais: Legislação, Jurisprudência, Prática (São Paulo: Editora Atlas, S.A., 1978); Boris Fausto, Difel/Difusão Editorial S.A., 1977); Octávio Ianni, A classe Operária Vai ao Campo, Cadernos CEBRAP, No. 24 (São Paulo: Editora Brasiliense, 1976); Leôncio Martins Rodrigues, Trabalhadores, Sindicatos e Industrialização (São Paulo: Editora Brasiliense, 1974); Evaristo de Moraes Filho, O Problema do Sindicato Unico no Brasil: Seus Fundamentos Sociológicos (São Paulo: Editora Alfa-Omega, 1980); Almir Pazzianotto Pinto, Central Unica, Porque não? (São Paulo: Global Editora e Distribuidora, S.A., 1980); Antonio Rezk, A Economia e a Participação Política dos Trabalhadores (São Paulo: Livraria Editora Ciências Humanas Ltda, 1978); José Albertino Rodrigues, Sindicato e Desenvolvimento no Brasil (São Paulo: Símbolo S.A. Indústrias Gráficas, 1979); Francisco Weffort, Participação e Conflito Industrial: Contagem e Osasco 1968, Cadernos CEBRAP, no. 5 (São Paulo, 1972). See also, articles in Coleção Estudos Brasileiros, no. 7 (São Paulo: Editora Hucitec, 1977); Escrita Ensaio, Ano II, no. 4, 1978; Ensaios de Opinião, vol. 2 (Rio de Janeiro: Editora Paz e Terra, S.A., 1979); Revista de Cultura Contemporânea, Ano I, no. 2, January 1979; História Imediata, no. 2 (São Paulo: Editora Alfa-Omega, 1979). See also, documents of DIEESE (Departamento Intersindical de Estatísticas e Estudos Sócio-Econômicos) and of the Frente Nacional do Trabalho, São Paulo.

45. Study by the Departamento Intersindical de Estatística e Estudos Sócio-Econômicos (São Paulo, 1980).

46. Decree-Law No. 4,330, cited in Arthur Cogan, Crimes Contra a Segurança Nacional: Comentários, Legislação, Jurisprudência (São Paulo: Editora Revista dos Tribunais, 1976), p. 120.

47. Article 555 says that a trade union may be closed down if it "does not comply with an order of the President or creates obstacles to the carrying out of the government's economic policy"; cited in Consolidação das Leis do Trabalho: Atualizada para 1978 (Rio de Janeiro: Gráfica Auriverde Ltda, 1978), p. 118.

48. Decree-Law No. 4330, Article 530, p. 109.

49. Ibid. It had been previously established by Decree-Law No. 925, October 10, 1969, and then incorporated in Article 530.

50. Ibid., Article 553, p. 117.

51. Interview with Lúis Ignácio da Silva, September 6, 1978.

52. There are approximately 8,000 trade unions in Brazil, a large number of which were organized under military rule. This does not mean to say, however, that they are all "ghost unions," for the number of actual government-created unions is unknown.

53. The regulations are established in Articles 548 to 557; see Consolidação das Leis do Trabalho, op. cit., pp. 114-18.

54. Ibid., p. 119. Article 505 prohibits affiliation with international organizations without prior approval of the president of the republic.

55. Decree Law No. 6,708, October 30, 1979 (Rio de Janeiro: Gráfica Auriverde, 1980).

56. A copy of this document may be obtained from the union headquarters of members of the new union movement or in the Library of the National Congress in Brasília. It is titled O Anteprojeto de Consolidação das Leis do Trabalho (São Paulo, July 18, 1979).

57. See Marcus Figueiredo, op. cit., p. 162.

58. Because of the high level of coercion, these interviews must remain anonymous. I must remind the reader that military personnel are punished with imprisonment for political comments, even those who are no longer on active duty but have passed to the Reserves.

59. See Isto É, December 10, 1980, p. 79.

60. See Veja, June 23, 1976, p. 85. For more information on denationalization and the activities of multinational corporations in Brazil, see, for example: Marcos Arruda, Herbet de

Souza, and Carlos Afonso, Multinationals and Brazil: The Impact of Multinational Corporations in Contemporary Brazil (Toronto: Brazilian Studies, Latin America Research Unit, 1975); Richard J. Barnet and Ronald E. Müller, Global Reach: The Power of the Multinational Corporations (New York: Simon and Schuster, 1974); Biocca, op. cit.; Jan Knippers Black, The United States Penetration of Brazil (Philadelphia: University of Pennsylvania Press, 1977); Peter Evans, Dependent Development: The Alliance of Multinational, State and Local Capital in Brazil (Princeton: Princeton University Press, 1979); Albert Fishlow, "Who Benefits from Economic Development?," American Economic Review (March 1980, pp. 42-45; Luciano Martins, A Nacão e Corporação Multi-nacional: A Política das Empresas no Brasil e na América Latina (Rio de Janeiro: Editora Paz e Terra S.A., 1975); Kurt Rudolf Mirow, Loucura Nuclear: Os Enganos do Acordo Nuclear Brasil-Alemanha (Rio de Janeiro: Editora Civilização Brasileira, S.A., 1979); Kurt Rudolf Mirow, Condenados ao Sub-Desenvolvimento (Rio de Janeiro: Editora Civilização Brasileira, S.A., 1978). See also, the debate "Empresa Nacional: A Luta Pela Sobrevivên-cia," in Escrita Ensaio Ano I, no. 3, 1977, and U.S., Congress, the report to the subcommittee on Multinational Corporations of the Senate Committee on Foreign Relations, August 1975: Multi-national Corporations in Brazil and Mexico: Structural Sources of Economic and Non-Economic Power (Washington, D.C.: Government Printing Office, 1975).

61. From Isto É, May 7, 1980.

62. See Departamento Intersindical de Estatísticas e Estudos Sócio-Econômicos, Divulgação Número 1/76, April 19, 1976, p. 10.

63. See Departamento Intersindical de Estatísticas e Estudos Sócio-Econômicos (April 1979).

64. The study was conducted at the request of the Arch-diocese of Rio de Janeiro. Based upon official government statistical data, the results of the research were later published in A Situação da Criança no Brasil (Rio de Janeiro: Edições Muro, 1979).

13

ECONOMIC LIBERALISM AND POLITICAL REPRESSION IN CHILE

Jorge Nef

After nearly a decade of military control, it seems clear
that Chile's authoritarian style represents not just a convalescing
period. The state of exception has become the rule. Repression
has been institutionalised into routinised workings of day-to-
day governing. Under this mantle of normalcy, events in Chile—
including the continuous violations of human rights—are no longer
news.

The purpose of this chapter is to assess the possible trends
and directions of contemporary Chilean politics, particularly the
likelihood of a possible return to democracy. The broader
epistemological and ideological context of this theme has been
the object of another essay.[1] Thus, I will limit myself here to
the discussion of the extent to which such a return to democracy
describes a real trend in contemporary Chile. The time frame
of this essay is the period between 1977 and 1981.

To answer this question, two main aspects have to be
analysed: One is the nature of the current national-security
model as a political project, its circumstances and characteristics;
the other aspect is what one can call metaphorically the "composition of forces," that is, the interplay between support for and
opposition to both models—forces for the present status quo
and for the eventual return to democracy. Ultimately, the viability and endurance of either social project will depend upon
this composition of forces. To understand the complexity of
Chile's present power configurations, it should be kept in mind
that, given the penetrated nature of the political system,[2] adequate support will be more than the result of the interaction
between the forces of support and opposition by internal consti-

tuencies alone. The quantum and the intensity of support (or opposition) by external constituencies will be essential as well. Thus, the first analytical task will be to probe into the conditions, both internal and external, that brought about the national-security regime.

PENTAGONISM: HEGEMONIC CRISES AND NATIONAL SECURITY

Even the most cursory examination of the background to the military takeover of September 11, 1973, would suggest a number of persistent traits pointing at the unsubstitutability of the present model. These can be characterised under four major headings.

The Revolt of the Elites

The national-security regime was unequivocally a revolt of the elites that was in response to a challenge to their hegemony.[3] In this sense, the coup—more than an ad hoc response against the "Marxist menace"—was a well-conceived revamping of the elite's hegemonic project. Its central purpose was to maintain and modernise the supremacy of Chile's ruling class and its international linkages.[4]

One intricacy to be dealt with is the coexistence of two apparently contradictory trends: institutionalisation and the repression in the contemporary Chilean state. The maintenance of the regime cannot be explained as a function of repression alone. True, the September counterrevolution, especially in its early phase, included a purely negative and repressive reaction against a perceived threat to Chile's traditional order. But particularly since 1977, a new dimension of the regime—in Manuel Antonio Garretón's terms, a "foundational" dimension[5]—has to be recognised. This entails the coherent formulation of a historical project to modernise and lay the groundwork for the recomposition and reintegration of the capitalist mode of production. This process required a concurrent formulation of a political project—a new state. The consequence has been not just a capitalist restoration to ex-ante conditions, but what Barrington Moore calls a revolution from the top;[6] that is, a planned and conscious effort directed to reorganise Chile's economy, society, polity, and ideology, to serve a streamlined—and, therefore, a more effective—hegemonic coalition. It goes without saying that the completion of the proyecto histórico involves a long-term commitment. As an undoubtedly sympathetic observer commented:

> . . . democratic rule in Chile seems as far away as
> ever. The government's reforms are long-term
> ones. . . . [It] is trying to build up a system of
> "freedom with authority". . . . It aims to provide
> a "protected democracy"—protected, that is, from
> further Marxist adventures. . . .[7]

Demobilisation

Given the degree of mass mobilisation in Chile, repression
became, in the eyes of the elites, the only alternative for clearing the stage of superfluous political actors.[8] Widespread
repression and forceful demobilisation in this light cannot be
dismissed as simple excesses or as temporary dysfunctions.
They were part of a carefully planned strategy to reduce the
internal constituency in Chilean politics.

Transnationalisation

As the internal constituencies decreased, the junta required
the functional incorporation of external constituencies—foreign
consortia, the U.S. defence establishment, and free-world allies—
into the support system of the Chilean state. "Adequate support"[9] for the alliance of military officers, monopoly capital,
and the satellised intelligentsia has ended up relying more on
manifold external linkages than on internal sources. By trans-
nationalising the Chilean state, the inherent contradiction between
accumulation and legitimation[10]—effectiveness and legitimacy[11]—
that affects the territorial state can be resolved. By extending
the domain of support across national boundaries and into those
sectors most benefited by the process of accumulation, the contradiction now is not between accumulation and legitimation[12]
(which occur now at a transnational level), but between capitalism
and nationalism as historically incompatible projects.[13] In fact,
nationalism becomes, in the eyes of the guardians of the state,
synonymous with communism. This interdependence arrangement
of the ruling class induces the transnationalisation of the sources
of opposition as well. So the enemy is forcefully an outsider in
terms of the regime's ideology. Rhetoric and practice need not
coincide, however. In spite of its transnational nature and
doctrine, the ideological discourse of the Chilean military is
still one of symbolic nationalism. This contradiction between
ideology and doctrine is not an uncommon feature in those regimes
that Jaguaribe calls ones of "colonial fascism."[14] We have seen
it in Brazil, Korea, the Philippines, Iran, South Africa, or
Nicaragua. Thus, the regime can—and does—delegitimise its

opposition's members by presenting them as "foreign agents," and as a party to a "worldwide conspiracy against Chile."

Antipolitics

The implementation of the Chilean model precludes the development of any really pluralistic political formula, at least for the foreseeable future. One of the most significant aspects of the military takeover is that it purposely destroyed the mechanisms for political brokerage that had been developed for at least the previous 40 years. Instead, an invertebrate system, with limited political spaces and insignificant channels for socialisation and recruitment into participatory roles, was left behind. Lacking the central conveyor belt—the political party system— only extremely limited conversion of popular social forces into political demands can take place.

SOURCES OF SUPPORT AND OPPOSITION

The second analytical task here is to assess the political viability of both the status quo and its alternative project. From the standpoint of the correlation of forces around either project, it appears that the only relatively coherent coalition so far is that supporting the regime; relative, that is, to its opposition. Perhaps it is not exaggerated to say that it is perhaps the most congruous political alliance in decades, both by design and by default. Not only are the conventional power brokers (parties and associational groups) excluded by reason of force, but the alteration of the rules of the political game have made them ineffectual. In fact, the time-honored political process ceased to be a game in 1973.

A Fragmented Opposition

Whatever chances for articulation were left to groups opposing the regime have been constrained by internal bickering (both amongst and within themselves) over past responsibilities and narrowly doctrinary interpretations of the "correct line."

The Christian Democratic Party is still the largest group in the opposition to Pinochet. It has failed, however, to come to terms with its internal cleavages, let alone with its past rivals. As for the left, it is geographically divided between a small clandestine section and the larger and more visible diaspora and is ideologically fragmented amongst currents and shades.[15] Since its ousting, many of the internal divisions that plagued the Unidad Popular have persisted and new cleavages have emerged.

Although the opposition to the regime appears great, even
mounting, the fracturings mentioned above render it fairly
inadequate to convert feelings, frustrations, and social energies
into political power. It also seems to lack the expertise, even
the will, to seek and create new channels for political expression.
Let us not forget that in a nonelectoral context, other types of
political currencies can substitute for numbers. It is here
where the regime, violencia aguda notwithstanding, has always
maintained an upper hand. The only national power broker
with some degree of clout left has been the Catholic church.
Thus, most political activity has been centered around the relative sanctuary confined to the now limited, yet legitimate, activity
taking place in the temples. Even there, its role is limited to
an almost purely defensive posture, and is not without imminent
risks and uncertainties.

The Many Faces of Fear

The drastic change of the rules of the game has left an
enormous amount of unfulfilled demands outside the confines of
the Chilean state. Although quantitative data in this respect
is hard to get, one could easily estimate that a high degree of
alienation exists. A potentially large volume of discontent and
anomie can be restrained only by physical coercion combined
with an officially sponsored, thin veneer of fatalism and fear.
There seems to be the generalised consensus amongst the ruling
elites that a sudden reestablishment of "market politics" could
bring about an explosive contradiction with the existence of
the new forcefully protected inequities of market economics.
In sum, in the Chilean case, a peculiar kind of self-fulfilling,
row-of-dominoes-like prophecy has been constructed. By reducing opposition to a common denominator, the enemy, the
only alternative to repression becomes revolution—an event that
neither the inner sanctum of the regime nor their associates
can contemplate with much unemotional detachment. For one
thing, there are also broader social sectors who fear revolution,
though they are not directly benefited by the regime's policies.
As for the military, even for those who would rather go back
to their barracks, the booty is too large and the future too
uncertain to simply let go.[16] In this light, both the level of
precoup mobilisation and the subsequent repression by state
terrorism[17] preclude a peaceful transition. Unlike corporeal
enemies, some memories take long to die. In this context, there
seems to be no alternative to repression, except further repression. Fear, both from above and from below amongst the officers,
appears to remain today their most potent ideology. A return

to civilian rule, from the officers' viewpoint, may well mean the
realisation of their worst fears: the end of the present Chilean
military establishment. Thus, military guardianship à la Ecuador
or Peru, even if built into a constitutional formula, would not
provide either sufficient safeguards or a high degree of institutional legitimacy.

A similar attitude prevails amongst the other internal constituencies of the Chilean regime. Widespread fear works in
the same way that the cosmetic dimension of contemporary Chile
does as an ideological component of the regime. Fear does not
necessarily mean the Departamento de Investigaciones Nacionales
(DINA) boogeymen, but something much subtler. There is the
fear that those most benefited will lose their privileges; there
is a fear that those most seriously deprived will agitate. There
are fears of returning to the precoup turmoil. The fears of
one class feed on those of the others and the military-controlled
state specialises in the most professional function of them all:
the "authoritative allocation" of fear.[18] In sum, two fundamental
aspects of the present composition of forces in Chile are basic
in explaining Pinochet's survival record: the atomisation of the
potential opposition and the hegemonic consolidation of a tiny,
but powerful, support group. In a sense, these factors, better
than repression, account for the stability of the present dictatorship.

The Ruling Coalition

As stated earlier, the regime's hegemonic coalition involves
a symbiotic relationship of both internal and external constituencies. The internal coalition is by far the most significant. It
encompasses a clearly identifiable núcleo dirigente—Pinochet,
his immediate entourage, and, most important, the "Chicago
boys." Whilst the former provide the formal hierarchical control
of the repressive apparatus, the latter provide the ideological-
technocratic content for the project. Although by no means
monolithic, internal cohesion within the núcleo is very strong.
Besides those who directly exercise political power, there are
two other identifiable components. One is a support bloc made
up of the armed forces (more properly the officer class) and
the economic clans (those of Larraíns, Vials, or Cruzats).[19]
The other is an ideological zone encompassing the managerial
bourgeoisie linked to financial capital and the upper echelons
of the consumption-intensive middle strata. This latter component of the coalition is largely unified by upward mobility
and high standards of living, but, unlike the support bloc, it
has no direct participation in the material support system of the
new order.

One very important qualification needs to be made here,
though. The congruence between the two components of the
support bloc that are mentioned above is not without contradictions. These are also reflected within the núcleo dirigente.
Although linked by their visceral anticommunism and their
allegiance to the United States, both represent different social
projects in the long run. This has been dramatically illustrated
by the ongoing and behind-the-scenes conflicts between the
economic clans and Colonel Contreras's DINA empire. Since
the Letelier assassination, these contradictions have intermittently
surfaced. For the Chicago boys and the economic elite, repression is only a first step in a long-range strategy. Political
demobilisation, resulting from repression, is a prerequisite to
free the market forces from the strictures of powerful unions,
leftist parties, and the welfare state.[20] These sectors saw that
DINA outlived its purpose by 1977. Worse, it had become a
threat to their liberal and transnational economic model.

DINA's ideology of counterinsurgency, with no small doses
of old-fashioned corporatism, asserted a broader and fundamental
role for the military establishment. That was to draw the terms
of reference for the interplay of social forces. A relatively
autonomous military-bureaucratic state would ensure middle-class
ascendance not unlike the Ibáñez project of 1927.[21] The military
(and more explicitly the security apparatus), were to retain
metapower[22] to arbitrate social tensions within the context of
the national-security doctrine. This model, although by far
more repressive than that espoused by the economic team, had,
nevertheless, statist, even Bonapartist implications. The 1981-
82 debate over the merits of denationalising the state copper
industry (CODELCO) is illustrative of this inner contradiction
between the so-called blandos and duros.

External Constituencies

Both fractions draw support from external (mainly U.S.)
constituencies. By and large, the business sector espouses
an alternative model of hemispheric domination. DINA was
backed by the American military and clandestine establishments
and by their associates throughout the continent. Chilean
finance capital had its global network of economic linkages and
the Trilateral Commission. The latter's position was articulated
by the human-rights concern of the Carter administration. In
the Chilean case, two hegemonic projects—trilateralism and
Pentagonism—were to confront each other. The very survival
of the Pinochet regime depended on the outcome of the confrontation. By 1977, under heavy pressure by the Carter administration

(which was capitalising on the embarrassing Letelier case),
Pinochet was forced to let DINA, and his confidant, Colonel
Contreras, go. DINA's successor, CNI, headed by General
Mena, was subordinated to the rules set by the economic clans,
at least for a while. The aforementioned period—1977 to mid-1980—
was the one in which the most frontal attacks on the regime by
the United States took place. It gave rise to much of the hopeful
discussion on a possible return to democracy.[23] The effort,
however, was ill-fated. The White House and the State Department were strongly opposed by both the American military and
the CIA. Even the bulk of the State Department apparently
did not approve of the move to destabilise a friendly regime.
The U.S. business community followed a pragmatic approach
to reduce risk: It decided to pass until the outcome of the 1980
presidential race. The Reagan victory gave Pinochet a much-
needed lease on life.

In sum, the regime's foreign constituencies have ended up
playing the role of willing hostages. For them, an eventual
collapse of the Chilean model would have undesirable consequences
in both the economic and military spheres. Because of its close
association with (and support from) the U.S. military establishment, the loss of the Chilean connection has been portrayed as
having catastrophic institutional and geopolitical repercussions
for American security. The U.S. military has, in the Chilean
regime, what it had in Iran and Nicaragua and now in El
Salvador—both an unconditional ally (molded in its own image)
and a fundamental external constituency of its own to wage its
power struggles in Washington and beyond. The intelligence
community finds itself in a similar position: having a reliable,
like-minded, though perhaps too eager, friend. As for the
third component of the Chile "lobby"—the world financiers and
economic partners of the Chilean junta—a return even to the
mildest forms of pre-1970 economic nationalism appears to spell
financial havoc. True, they have struck an extremely good
deal. However, their support cannot be explained on purely
pragmatic grounds. In the eyes of international business (as
recent PR campaigns explicitly indicate),[24] the Chilean case
is a fundamental test for the success of the capitalist mode of
development, especially in the midst of a rather bleak global
picture. With its booming foreign reserves,[25] and its Fried-
manian free-market orthodoxy, Chile is the kind of success
story international financiers look upon with great favor. Besides offering them a country for sale at discount rates, it provides the kind of regime most attractive for low-risk ventures.[26]
As two propaganda publications put it:

> Chile offers excellent living conditions to foreign
> investors. They will find personal security, social
> tranquility and business integrity.[27]

> There is a prevailing sense of security in Chile as
> terrorism and street disorders are controlled with
> a strong hand.[28]

The fact that the regime has been successful in its economic
policy should not be underestimated. The reasons are threefold.
First, unlike previous constitutional governments, it has clearly
benefited those sectors it sought to benefit. Second, these
sectors happen to be the most powerful social groups both inside
Chile and in the region. Third, all this coherence is possible
because the size of the constituency—the political arena—has
been forcefully reduced to accommodate only a small number of
actors.

The U.S. foreign policy establishment, broadly defined
(the dominant external constituency), was apparently divided
on the issue of Chile;[29] at least until the presidential election
of November 4, 1980. At the official level, various rhetorical
overtures on human rights[30] were made by the Carter administration. This did certainly change to a much more sympathetic
stand under Reagan. Even the Carter administration's official
policy of commitment without involvement on human rights was
severely criticised amongst important foreign policy circles.
In the words of an influential architect of the Chilean model,
former National Security Adviser and Secretary of State Henry
Kissinger:

> Making [human rights] a vocal objective of our
> foreign policy involves many risks. You run the
> risk of either showing your impotence or producing
> revolutions in friendly countries—or both. . . .
> There is an enormous difference between authori-
> tarian regimes which do not observe democratic
> practices, and totalitarian regimes with universal
> ideological claims. . . . [Between] authoritarian
> military regimes which are trying to produce a
> gradual evolution and totalitarianism, the difference
> is fundamental. . . .[31]

These views carry weight amongst the Trilateral Commission
members in general, and with former National Security Adviser
Brzezinski, in particular.[32] It has been further expanded by

Reagan's representative at the U.N., Jeane Kirkpatrick.[33] The human-rights policy thus has a qualifier: With totalitarian regimes (ditto for Communist ones),[34] the commitment is absolute;[35] with authoritarian ones (such as Chile), the commitment becomes more relative and restricted.

THE PINOCHET FORMULA

What are the implications of the inapplicability of the with-drawal-with-restricted-democracy concept, such as the one outlined during the Carter years for the current Chilean situation? In my view, a number of conclusions can be drawn. One general conclusion is that any attempt at rebuilding democracy in Chile—short of an unlikely armed insurrection—would require the conjunction of Washington with a unified, yet streamlined, opposition within Chile. This appears improbable, to say the least, particularly in the short run, at least not until 1984. Whatever hopes a segment of the Christian Democrats had about the Carter formula, with Eduardo Frei making a comeback à la Karamanlis, have now been definitely shattered.

The Resurgence of Repression

An analysis of trends on the domestic political scene indi-cates that Chile is not moving toward a sort of decompression. Far from it: Since the beginning of 1980, "Chile has witnessed a re-emergence of the types of human rights violations that brought it world-wide attention from 1973-1975."[36] Even the relative sanctuary of the Catholic church has been a new target. As one reporter noted:

> The list of harassments is long and continues to
> grow. The pattern is the same: forcible intrusion
> into meetings demanding inspection of permits,
> etc.; carrying off local leaders for interrogation
> and tortures.[37]

The resurgence of repression and state terrorism seems to correspond to a readjustment of forces within the support bloc referred to earlier; perhaps a "settling of accounts" could be a better expression. Following the suspicious assassination of the director of the School of Army Intelligence, Colonel Roger Vergara, internal rivalries within the military surfaced.[38] "Spontaneous" commandos for the "avenging of martyrs" carried out arrests and persecutions of suspected leftists,[39] and at least

314 / Latin American Prospects for the 1980s

one murder. The objective of this escalation was to force the resignation of the director of the Bureau of Investigations (General Baeza) and the head of the CNI, General Mena.[40] They were both accused of inefficiency.[41] These events happened after both officers expressed public doubts that Colonel Vergara's assassination was a result of leftist terrorism. (It was later found out that the car used by Vergara's murderers came from the presidential palace.)[42] At one level, one could dismiss these events as gang-style vendettas. For instance, Vergara's murder

> has been linked to a $100 million tax fraud involving
> former members of DINA. . . . Gen. Manuel Contreras,
> the retired DINA Chief . . . is also allegedly con-
> nected to the scandals through business dealings
> with Eduardo Romero, who was imprisoned on charges
> of tax fraud. Evidence suggests that at least in
> two cases documents used in fake tax returns be-
> longed to political prisoners who disappeared after
> their arrest by DINA.[43]

Acts such as these, involving official gangsterism, have been by no means rare: Witness the numerous frauds, intimidations, and murders surrounding the bank robbery in Calama in 1979.[44]

At another level, however, there seem to be indications that the issue at stake is not just a few more dollars. At stake is "the power of General Contreras and his friends who remain within the Intelligence Central."[45] As a New York Times reporter suggested:

> Suspicions are widely expressed that the [avenger]
> group has powerful protectors, perhaps including
> General Contreras. . . . He has been operating as
> a private businessman, apparently with plenty of
> money, and is reported to maintain personal contacts
> with General Pinochet's wife and army colleagues.[46]

All this points in the direction of a resurgence of state terrorism, even the nasty varieties of 1973-76.

The Institutionalisation of the Dictatorship

On the institutional front, the plebiscite of September 11, 1980, is an event that deserves some attention. It has been argued that Pinochet's decision to call a plebiscite was "an audacious step to deflect mounting criticism of his regime."[47]

Although there was no doubt about such mounting popular criticism, it appears that the main targets of the referendum were two of the regime's constituencies: the military and foreign business.[48] On the one hand, the plebiscite was an attempt at consolidating personal power and muffling criticism from within the ruling coalition.[49] On the other, it was a PR signal to sympathetic foreign bankers and financiers that "things in Chile were legal." Indeed, the criticism of the plebiscite has been widespread, especially amongst liberal circles.[50] What is important, however, is not its manner of execution, but the fact that the regime's political project was finally unveiled and sactified. In general terms, the referendum approved what could be called an authoritarian-corporatist constitution. Some of its characteristics deserve to be stressed:

1. It is restrictive. "It sets strict parameters in the political realm by allowing only certain types of politicians and political parties to carry out activities and by maintaining tight government control over public expression of political views.[51]

2. It is antipolitical. It provides for the continuity of the regime until 1989 and, in theory, until 1998.[52] "During the period of transition between 1980 and 1989, there will be a political recession and political parties will not be able to operate."[53]

3. It is corporatist. "It seeks a social structure whose axis is the multitude of corporations coordinated and directed from the commanding heights of the state by direct representatives of the groups in power" (Chapter XIII, on "Interval Administration").[54]

4. It is capitalist. A liberal conception of the economy is mixed with the above corporatist philosophy to produce a vision of a benevolent state ruled in an aristocratic and elitist manner.[55]

5. It is authoritarian. It provides "for a strengthened presidency, so that the executive's customary tussles with Congress will come to an end."[56] It also contains provisions "for second-round elections between presidential front-runners, which should keep that office firmly in the hands of right-of-centre candidates."[57]

6. It is technocratic and militarist. The Central Bank and the Superior Council for National Security are vested with effective metapower and put beyond political scrutiny; that is, the economic clans and the military are given a free hand as rulers of last resort. The autonomy of the Central Bank is rationalised on grounds of guaranteeing the maintenance of

"the financial management of the country absolutely free of political influences."[58] The second autonomy (the military's) is justified on grounds that such an arrangement makes it "impossible for . . . [the heads of the armed forces] to be removed through political power."[59]

The extent of fraud present in the referendum is difficult to assess.[60] Even the regime admits that in the weeks before the plebiscite,

> Chileans were constantly bombarded by TV commercials showing newsreel footage of the disorder, violence and scarcity of goods during the Allende government.[61]

However, the fact remains that Pinochet worried enough to engage in propaganda. Moreover, there is another fundamental aspect: The general won the referendum, whatever the means employed. As the Vicariate for Workers of the Church pointed out, the result of the plebiscite

> means for some the definite triumph of a political, economic and social model which has been in gestation since September 11, 1973. . . .
> Those who feel defeated—although most of them never believed their vote could be taken into account—must think of the large number of workers and slum-dwellers, mainly women, who believe, or were made to believe that the model imposed since 1973 is the best. . . . The main question . . . is why so many peasants, so many women of the working class and so many men took the stand they took.
> We believe that it is not enough to be satisfied with a simplistic answer: fraud, fear or the pressures of a wide "campaign of terror."[62]

Indeed, it seems that Pinochet has effectively consolidated his grip on the country, not only by force or domination but through ideological hegemony. It is possible to suggest that endurance may help to explain why Chileans are getting used to the new order. However, there is a more fundamental aspect. For whatever its merits, or lack of them, the regime has been able to present itself—very successfully—as the only clear alternative to an uncertain future.

External Supports

The most relevant external constituencies of the regime that were divided on the issue of the replacement formulas finally agreed on the necessity of supporting it, even before the defeat of the Carter administration. While the State Department and the White House under Carter appeared to have taken a hard line against Pinochet, especially after the Letelier investigation,[63] this stand was neither forceful nor without ambiguity. In no way was it a counterpart of the "quiet diplomacy" of destabilisation of the Nixon era.[64] In fact, Pinochet may be a nuisance for U.S. prestige, but it is one which serves the short-run interests of the U.S. defence establishment and the international business elite rather well. Second, a closer look at the now defunct human-rights stand of the Carter administration reveals that the apparent disagreement between realpolitik and human rights was not as sharp as it appeared to be. Not only are the intellectual and ideological foundations of Pentagonism or the national-security doctrine quite congruent with the assumptions of the trilateral project.[65] The policy of human rights and its commitments to military withdrawal, institutionalisation, and limited democracy, contained in the Linowitz Committee Report, represented, in the Chilean case, only a second phase of a single process whose necessary first stage was repression and forceful demobilisation. The change advocated therefore involved a matter of cosmetics more than one of substance.

Once demobilisation, denationalisation—and, above all, private accumulation[66]—had been induced, at a dramatic rate, by the action of a terrorist state, official repression appeared to outlive its purpose. Then, a political normalisation, with a modernised mold of social and economic relations could take place, and a "governable" polity, in Huntington's terms,[67] could be finally institutionalised. The operational assumptions for this strategy are twofold. One is that the dismantling of the old structure of mobilisation and brokerage has been completed. The second assumption is that normalisation, to be successful, requires both that a technocratic-corporate[68] structure be substituted for the "political" style of interest articulation,[69] and that new mechanisms of legitimation be set in motion. The nonideology of the marketplace can, in theory at least, substitute for politics whilst more subliminal advertising can replace explicit propaganda.

Under the above-mentioned circumstances, institutionalisation can be accomplished only in two cases: if the degree of previous social and political mobilisation has remained relatively low, dis-

continuous, and unstructured (the examples of Ecuador and
Peru come to mind); and if a conscious depoliticisation of an
entire generation had been undertaken.

In the Chilean example—and the same could be said about
Uruguay—the original level of "conscientisation"[70] was quite
high—a thoroughly participatory culture.[71] Therefore, even
after the old order has been torn down, only the uncertain
route of repressive resocialisation into the "politics of antipolitics"[72] may give a modicum of legitimation in years to come.
The latter has repeatedly emerged in the statements by Pinochet
and his cohorts: Only after the war on politiquería has been
completed could some degree of internal "détente" be expected.[73]
As a projunta publication, reporting an interview with Interior
Minister Sergio Fernández, stated:

> Mr. Fernández is unwilling to provide a timetable
> for this hesitant return to democracy. A new
> generation must first be trained, he argued, to
> behave differently from its elders. The political
> parties, Mr. Fernández argues, can manipulate
> uneducated people too easily.[74]

It is not surprising that, whilst other national-security
regimes, such as Ecuador, Peru, Bolivia, or Brazil, stumbled
toward a kind of hastily staged aperturismo,[75] the most traditional bourgeois democracies—Uruguay and Chile—did remain
shrouded in the unsavory garments of repression. Decompression and withdrawal are still too premature a change of gears
to consolidate the novus ordo. In the words of the late Orlando
Letelier, in the "Chilean model,"

> . . . concentration of wealth is no accident . . .;
> it is . . . the base for a social project. . . . [The
> junta's] real failure is not their apparent inability
> to redistribute wealth or to generate a more even
> path of development . . . but their inability to con-
> vince the majority of Chileans that their policies are
> reasonable and necessary. . . . The economic plan
> has to be enforced. . . . While the "Chicago
> Boys" have provided an appearance of technical
> respectability . . . the military has applied the
> brutal force required to achieve those goals. Re-
> pression for the majorities and "economic freedom"
> for small privileged groups are in Chile two sides
> of the same coin.[76]

Whilst the establishment of the withdrawal-with-democratisation
concept may be a relatively progressive and painless step in
more traditional societies, such as Ecuador, it involves much
repression and regressive change in those societies where a
great deal of political participation has already evolved. There,
restricted democracy can only take place after a long period of
forceful demobilisation has safeguarded the continuity of transnational capitalism. Under such conditions, capitalism and
democracy become inherently incompatible. Perhaps the statement by Andres Zaldívar, a former minister of finance under
Frei, summarises the dilemma: "Chileans will have to turn to
violence if they cannot find a peaceful road to democracy."[77]
So far, this is a statement of frustration, not a prediction, at
least for the time being. Finally, as the born-again-hawk
syndrome gained a foothold amongst the U.S. political establishment, with Vietnam and Watergate forgotten and with Iran,
Afghanistan, and El Salvador looming larger than life on the
horizon, it became apparent that even the human-rights rhetoric
had once again downshifted to the realpolitik of the 1970s. Restricted democracy and human rights in Chile proved to be just
temporary mystifications, too early to be considered a practical
alternative. Ronald Reagan's Latin American policy is fairly
unambiguous in this respect. But U.S. support for Pinochet
is not an innovative policy of the present regime in Washington.
By the end of its tenure in office, the Carter administration
had softened its stand on the most controversial issue: its
insistence on a sort of Pinochetismo without Pinochet. A report
prepared by a former critic of the regime, U.S. Ambassador
George Landau, in early 1980, praised the Chilean model in the
following terms:

> In its reliance on market economics, Chile appears
> in the vanguard of a world-wide neoconservative
> response to the menace of growing inflation. . . .
> Most U.S. private-sector observers are inclined to
> believe that the current military regime will be
> followed within ten years by a stable, middle-of-
> the-road government reasonably favourable to free
> enterprise and foreign investment.[78]

His words contain an ominous wishful thinking about a longue
durée—more or less along lines of Pinochet's own Chacarillas
proposal[79]—before a limited political spring may bloom. On the
other hand, his assessment has the familiar accent of déjà vu.
In a different context, I can recall a similar prediction made
about Iran in the midwinter of 1978.

NOTES

1. Cf. J. Nef, "Pentagonism, Trilateralism and Military Withdrawal in Latin America" (Paper presented to the conference on Latin America, Norman Patterson School of International Affairs, Carleton University, Ottawa, November 14, 1980).

2. This concept was first advanced by James Rosenau in "Pre-Theories and Theories of Foreign Policy," and elaborated by Wolfram Hanrieder in "Compatibility and Consensus: A Proposal for the Conceptual Linkage of External and Internal Dimensions of Foreign Policy," in Hanrieder (ed.), Comparative Foreign Policy Theoretical Essays (New York: David McKay Co., 1971), pp. 257-58.

3. Cf. José Nun, "The Middle Class Military Coup," in Claudio Véliz, The Politics of Conformity in Latin America (London: Oxford University Press, 1967), pp. 86-88; also, Anibal Quijano, Nationalism and Capitalism in Peru. A Study in Neo-Imperialism (New York: Monthly Review Press, 1971), pp. 6-12.

4. Cf. Barbara Stallings, Class Conflicts and Economic Development in Chile 1958-1973 (Stanford: Stanford University Press, 1978), pp. 238-39.

5. Manuel Antonio Garretón, lecture to Latin American Research Unit, Toronto, April 16, 1980; also, in Garretón, "Institutionalización y Oposicion al Régimen Autoritario Chileno," mimeographed, February-March 1980.

6. Cf. Barrington Moore, Social Origins of Dictatorship and Democracy. Lord and Peasant in the Making of the Modern World (Boston: Beacon Press, 1966), pp. 433-52.

7. The Economist, February 2, 1980, pp. 8, 10.

8. Cf. Arturo Valenzuela, Political Brokers in Chile. Local Government in a Centralized Polity (Durham: Duke University Press, 1977), pp. 224-30.

9. This concept was developed by David Easton in "An Approach to the Analysis of Political System," World Politics, Vol. 9, No. 3 (April 1957), pp. 391-93.

10. Cf. Jürgen Habermas, Legitimation Crisis (Boston: Beacon Press, 1975), p. 50.

11. Cf. Seymour Martin Lipset, "Some Social Requisites of Democracy" in Roy C. Macridis and Bernard E. Brown (eds), Comparative Politics. Notes and Readings, 4th ed. (Homewood, Ill.: The Dorsey Press, 1972), pp. 129-137.

12. Alan Wolfe, "Capitalism Shows Its Face," The Nation, November 29, 1975, p. 559. Also, "The Two Faces . . .", p. 651.

13. Jaguaribe, "Dependency and Autonomy . . .", pp. 190-224.

14. Jaguaribe, Economic and Political Development. A Theoretical Approach and a Brazilian Case Study (Cambridge: Harvard University Press, 1968); p. 182 has referred to it as "a model for promoting economic development without changing the existing social order. . . . The adaptation of a fascist model to the condition of dependence on an external metropolitan center converts it into colonial fascism."

15. Cf. "Chile: Autocrítica y Afirmación de la Izquierda," Cuadernos de Marcha (Mexico), No. 6, March-April 1980), pp. 3-104.

16. J. Nef, "Chile: A Post Mortem," New Scholar, Vol. 7, Nos. 1-2, p. 281.

17. Marcio Moreira Alves, "Urban Guerrillas and the Terrorist State" in John Rosenbaum and William D. Tyler (eds.), Contemporary Brazil: Issues in Economic and Political Development (New York: Praeger, 1972), p. 51.

18. The term is used here in Easton's sense as the distribution of scarce resources (or valuables) by acts of "authority." Cf. David Easton, "The Analysis of Political Systems," in Roy C. Macridis and Bernard E. Brown, Comparative Politics. Notes and Readings, 4th ed. (Homewood, Ill.: Dorsey Press, 1972), pp. 73-78.

19. See Fernando Dahase, Mapa de la Extrema Riqueza. Los Grupos Económicos y el Proceso de Concentración de Capitales (Santiago: Aconcagua, 1979), pp. 2-137.

20. This is an elaboration of the argument I discussed in "Importing State Terrorism," The Nation, July 12, 1980, p. 55.

21. For an overview of the Ibañez period (1927-31), cf. Paul W. Drake, Socialism and Populism in Chile 1932-1957 (Urbana: University of Illinois Press, 1928), pp. 58-65.

22. "We refer to the exercise of such 'meta-power' as relational control; that is to control over social relationships and structures, which we distinguish from power within a given structure"; see Tom Baumbartner, Walter Buckley, Tom R. Burns, and Peter Schuster, "Meta-Power and the Structuring of Social Hierarchies," in Tom R. Burns and Walter Buckley (eds.), Power and Control: Social Structures and Their Transformation (Beverly Hills: Sage, 1976), p. 224.

23. Cf. "Democracy Climbs the Andes Again," New York Times, July 19, 1979.

24. Three such broad-ranging publicity campaigns deserve special attention: the U.S. Chamber of Commerce publication marking "the fifth anniversary of a successful return of private

enterprise in Chile": Business Dialogue With Chile (1978); an extended section of The Economist, February 2, 1980; and an Advertising Supplement of the New York Times, February 23, 1980.

25. Cf. Chile News: Economic and Financial Survey, Vol. 17, No. 800, (August 18, 1980).

26. Michel Chossudovsky, "Capital Accumulation and State Violence in the Third World" (Paper presented to the Seventh General Conference of the International Peace Research Association, Oaxtepec, Mexico, December 11-16, 1977), pp. 3-11.

27. Chilean Government Trade and Investment Bureau, The Chilean Economy: A General Survey (New York, c. 1980), p. 6.

28. Instituto de Estudios Generales, A Letter From Chile (Santiago), September 1980, p. 3.

29. See Latin America Regional Report: Southern Cone, December 7, 1979, p. 1; also, "A Quest for Stability," NACLA Report on the Americas, Vol. 12, No. 2 (April-March 1979), pp. 30-35.

30. Cf. James F. Petras's critique of human rights in Latin America, from a leftist viewpoint: "Carter's New Morality and the Logic of Imperialism," LAWG Letter, Vol. 4, No. 3 (October 1977), pp. 3-9.

31. Henry A. Kissinger, quoted in Trialogue, No. 19 (Fall 1979), p. 3.

32. For a noncritical perspective about the Trilateral Commission and its membership, cf. "Trilateral Commission: How Influential," U.S. News and World Report, May 22, 1978, p. 74; also, NACLA, op. cit., pp. 6-7.

33. Jeane Kirkpatrick, in "Human Rights and American Foreign Policy. A Symposium," Commentary, Vol. 72, No. 5 (November 1981), pp. 42-45.

34. Kissinger, in op. cit.

35. President Carter, quoted in NACLA, op. cit., p. 5.

36. Washington Office on Latin America, Latin America Update, Vol. 5, No. 5 (September-October 1980), p. 2.

37. LADOC, Vol. 15, No. 1 (September-October 1980), p. 31.

38. "Red Scare Tactics," The Nation, August 30, 1980, and September 6, 1980, p. 172. Cf. Business Latin America, August 20, 1980, which states that an extreme right-wing group associated with the military "has been linked with terrorist acts, aimed ultimately at destabilizing the Pinochet government in favor of one built on corporatist principles" (p. 272).

39. New York Times, August 5, 1980; also, A Letter From Chile, August 1980, pp. 1-2.

40. New York Times, August 5, 1980.
41. A Letter From Chile, August 1980, p. 2.
42. "Red Scare," loc. cit.
43. Ibid.
44. In 1979, the CNI head of the northern town of Calama (formerly with DINA) robbed a branch of the State Bank, kidnapping two officials. The latter were assassinated and their bodies destroyed to make it appear as if they had run away with the money. The incident has revealed a pattern of gangsterism and unprecedented corruption in the security services. Cf. Hoy, July 8-14, 1981, pp. 11-12. Other references to widespread corruption can be found in Latin America Weekly Report, June 20 and July 25, 1980.
45. New York Times, August 5, 1980.
46. New York Times, August 12, 1980.
47. Business Latin America, August 20, 1980, p. 272.
48. "Plebiscite success strengthens Pinochet's personal position," Latin America Weekly Report, September 19, 1980, p. 6.
49. Business Latin America, July 23, 1980, p. 238.
50. "Plebiscite success," loc. cit.
51. Business Latin America, loc. cit. For an overview of the authoritarian constitution, cf. "Plebiscito: Algunos aspectos fundamentales del proyecto de Constitución Política propuesta por el Gobierno," in Vicaría Pastoral Obrera de Santiago, Dialogando, August 1, 1980.
52. "Plebiscito," op. cit., pp. 1-18.
53. A Letter From Chile, August 1980, p. 3.
54. La Tercera de la Hora, August 17, 1980, p. 13. Interview with Chilean jurist Alejandro Silva Bascuñán. Also, Vicaría Pastoral Obrera de Santiago, "Aportes y Criterios desde una Perspectiva Cristiana," Dialogando, August 15, 1980, p. 9.
55. "Aportes y Criterios," loc. cit.
56. The Economist, February 2, 1980, p. 8.
57. Ibid., p. 10.
58. A Letter From Chile, July 1980, p. 4.
59. Ibid.
60. Latin American Weekly Report, September 19, 1980, p. 2.
61. A Letter From Chile, September 1980, p. 2.
62. Dialogando, No. 39 (October 1980), p. 1.
63. Cf. Jack Anderson, "'Condor': South American Assassins," Washington Post, August 2, August 9, 1979, and Miami Herald, August 3, 1979.
64. See, for instance, U.S. Senate (Staff Report of the Select Committee to Study Governmental Action with respect to

Intelligence Activities), Covert Action in Chile (Washington, D.C.: Government Printing Office, 1975); also, Documentos Secretos de la ITT, 3d ed. (Santiago: Quimantú, 1972), p. 62.

65. Petras, "Carter's 'New Morality,'" pp. 3-9.

66. See Michel Chossudovsky, "La Acumulación de Capital en Chile," Comercio Exterior, Vol. 28, No. 2 (Mexico), February 1978), pp. 156-64. Also, Dahase, Mapa de la Extrema Riqueza, pp. 194-209.

67. Michel Crozier, Samuel Huntington, and Joji Watanuki, The Crisis of Democracy. Report on the Governability of Democracies to the Trilateral Commission (New York University Press, 1975), pp. 1-5, 169.

68. Cf. Jorge Tapia-Videla, "Understanding Organizations and Environments: A Comparative Perspective," Public Administration Review, Vol. 36, No. 6 (November-December 1976), p. 63.

69. This term is used in the sense of a highly pluralistic "brokerage" between society and polity. Cf. Gabriel Almond and James S. Coleman, The Politics of Developing Areas (Princeton: Princeton University Press, 1960), pp. 33-35.

70. For an analysis of "critical awareness" or "conscientisation," see Paulo Freire, Pedagogy of the Oppressed (New York: The Seabury Press, 1968), pp. 157-58.

71. Cf. Gabriel Almond and Sidney Verba, The Civic Culture: Political Attitudes and Democracy in Five Nations (Boston: Little, Brown, 1965), pp. 2-10.

72. Cf. Tapia-Videla, op. cit., pp. 634-635.

73. Cf. Richard Gott, "Repression in Chile," Manchester Guardian (Weekly), February 16, 1974, p. 10.

74. The Economist, loc. cit.

75. Cf. Washington Post, June 13, July 6, 1979, and New York Times, July 4, 1979.

76. Orlando Letelier, "The 'Chicago Boys' in Chile. Economic Freedom's Awful Toll," The Nation, August 29, 1976, pp. 138, 142.

77. Latin America Weekly Report, September 19, 1980, p. 7. Zaldivar was subsequently forbidden reentry into Chile on grounds of "sedition."

78. Ambassador George Landau, quoted in John Dinges and Saul Landau, Assassination on Embassy Row (New York: Pantheon Books, 1980), p. 387.

79. Cf. Thierry Maliniak, "Pinochet's Chile: Stirrings in the Opposition," Manchester Guardian (Weekly), February 5, 1978, p. 13.

ABOUT THE EDITORS

AND CONTRIBUTORS

DAVID H. POLLOCK, originally of Kinistino, Saskatchewan, served in the Royal Canadian Air Force during World War II. He worked at the IBRD (1949-50), the ECLA (1951-63), and UNCTAD (1964-67, as special assistant to the secretary general). From 1968 to 1980, he was director of the UN ECLA Office in Washington. At present, he is the Paterson Professor of International Affairs at the School of International Affairs, Carleton University, Ottawa. He has contributed to many UN reports and has published in Chile, Mexico, the United States, and Canada. He has been a member of UN delegations to numerous international conferences. Among his recent publications are Energy for Development: An International Challenge (coauthored with John Foster, James Howe, and Francisco Parra) (New York: Praeger, 1981); and Latin American Prospects for the 1970s, coedited with A. Ritter (New York: Praeger, 1973).

ARCHIBALD R. M. RITTER, originally of Sudbury and Kingston, Ontario, is currently Associate Professor of Economics and International Affairs, and Associate Director, School of International Affairs, Carleton University, Ottawa. Among his recent publications are The Economic Development of Revolutionary Cuba: Strategy and Performance (New York: Praeger, 1974); and "Stabilizing the International Copper Market: The Viability and Impacts of Alternate Market Management Arrangements" (with H. Labib), Canadian Journal of Development Studies, May 1981.

ALBERT BERRY is Professor of Economics at the University of Toronto. He has previously taught at Yale University and the University of Western Ontario, and also has worked at The Colombian Planning Commission and at the World Bank. Publications have focused on income distribution and on the agricultural sector of developing countries, including Agrarian Structure and Productivity in Developing Countries (with William Cline) and Economic Policy and Income Distribution in Colombia (coedited with Ronald Soligo).

MYRON J. FRANKMAN is a professor in the Department of Economics of McGill University. His research has emphasized problems of employment and urbanization in Latin America, and

exchange-rate policy. Among his publications are "Sectoral
Policy Preferences of the Peruvian Government, 1946-1968,"
Journal of Latin American Studies (1974), and "Urbanization
and Development in Latin America," Cahiers de géographie de
Québec (1971).

ENRIQUE V. IGLESIAS is Executive Secretary of the UN
Economic Commission for Latin America, a post he has held since
1972, first with the rank of Assistant Secretary General and
later as Under Secretary General. Born in 1930, he studied
at universities in Uruguay, the United States, and France, and
has held the Chair of Economic Development at the University
of Montevideo. He has been director of Uruguay's National
Planning Office and president of its Central Bank. He has
held important international positions with the Latin American
Council for Social Sciences (CCACSO), the Inter-American
Development Bank (IDB), the Society for International Development (SID), and the Third World Foundation. He was Secretary
General for the UN Conference on New and Renewable Energy
in Kenya during 1981. He has spoken extensively at international, regional, and national forums, and has published a
number of articles and essays on global and Latin American
development matters.

BASIL A. INCE is the Minister of External Affairs for
Trinidad and Tobago. Previously, he was Director of the
Institute of International Relations, University of the West
Indies, St. Augustine, Trinidad, and a career diplomat. He
has taught at the University of Puerto Rico and the State
University of New York at Binghamton. His major publications
include Decolonization and Conflict in the United Nations:
Guyana's Struggle for Independence; Essays on Race, Economics
and Politics in the Caribbean; and Contemporary International
Relations of the Caribbean. He has also published articles in
several leading journals—among them, the Caribbean Review,
The International Journal, Caribbean Studies, New World
Studies, the South Atlantic Quarterly, the American Political
Science Review, and The Annals.

MARIA HELENA MOREIRA ALVES, of Rio de Janeiro, is
cofounder and Vice President of the Brazilian Institute for
Community Assistance of Rio de Janeiro, an organization which
conducts research and consulting work with grassroots community
associations, trade unions, and the Catholic church. While in
the United States completing a Ph.D. at MIT, she cofounded

the Brazil Labor Information Resource Center, in New York, to provide consulting services for religious organizations and trade unions in the United States and Canada. She is the author of a number of articles on the structures and mechanisms of social control of the Brazilian military state, as well as on the history of the labor movements, the social and political organizations connected to the Catholic church, and the resistance to the policies of the national-security state implanted in Brazil since 1964. She is also preparing a book entitled The State and the Opposition in Military Brazil: The Formation of the National Security State.

JORGE NEF, originally of Chile, is a Professor of Political Science at the University of Guelph, Ontario, and is President of the Canadian Association for Latin American and Caribbean Studies. His research has focused on Chilean politics, state terrorism, and public administration and development. He has published extensively in these areas. Among his publications are "The Politics of Repression: The Social Pathology of the Chilean Military," Latin American Perspectives, 1974; Repression and Liberation in Latin America (editor) (CALACS, 1981); and "Development Theory and Administration: Defense Around an Empty Lot?," Indian Journal of Public Administration (January-March 1981).

LIISA L. NORTH is an Associate Professor of Political Science and Deputy Director of the Center for Research on Latin America and the Caribbean at York University, Toronto. Among her numerous publications are Bitter Grounds: Roots of Revolt in El Salvador (Toronto: Between the Lines, 1981); The Peruvian Revolution and the Officers in Power, 1968-1976 (Montreal: Center for Developing Area Studies, McGill University, 1981) (coauthored with Tanya Korovkin); and Democracy and Development in Latin America (Toronto: CERLAC/LARU, 1980) (coedited with Louis Lefebre).

The late CLAUDIO ORREGO VICUÑA was a professor of sociology at the Catholic University, Santiago. He was elected to the Chilean Chamber of Deputies in March 1973 and served as a Christian Democratic deputy until the military coup d'état. He was President of the Instituto de Estudios Políticos in Santiago. In 1980-81, he was a visiting scholar working on human-rights issues at the Woodrow Wilson International Center for Scholars in Washington, D.C. Among his many publications were the following: Siete Ensayos sobre Arturo Alessandre

Palma (Santiago, 1979); Un Futuro Para Todos: Un Modelo para el Desarrollo de Chile (Santiago, 1979) (coauthor); and El Caso Letelier (Santiago, 1979) (coauthor).

GERT ROSENTHAL, a citizen of Guatemala, is Director of the Mexican Office of the Economic Commission for Latin America.

ALAN B. SIMMONS is a sociologist who has specialized in research on population change in developing countries. He has subsequently done research and taught at York University in Toronto and at the Centro Latinoamericano de Demografia in Santiago. For the past six years, he has been associated with the International Development Research Centre, where he is director of a program on "Population and Development Policies" within the Social Sciences Division. His current research concerns the impact of economic development strategies and of particular agricultural and industrialization policies on labor-force migration and urbanization in both Latin America and West Africa.